VOLUME TWO

Contents

Preface to Fourth Edition

Frank Wood
B.Sc.(Econ.),F.C.A.

FOURTH EDITION

Business Accounting 2

With contributions from
J. Townsley, B.Com.,F.C.A.

© Frank Wood 1993
Fourth edition 1984
Second impression 1985

British Library Cataloguing in Publication Data

Wood, Frank
Business accounting.
2.—4th ed.
1. Accounting

Longman
London and New York

Longman Group Limited

Longman House, Burnt Mill, Harlow
Essex CM20 2JE, England
Associated companies throughout the world

Published in the United States of America
by Longman Inc., New York

First published 1968
Second edition 1973
Third edition 1980
Fourth edition 1984
Second impression 1985

British Library Cataloguing in Publication Data

Wood, Frank
Business accounting.
2. – 4th ed
1. Accounting
I. Title
657   HF5635

ISBN 0-582-41343-5

Printed in Hong Kong
by Sheck Wah Tong Printing Press Ltd

Preface to the Fourth Edition

This is the second volume of the textbook. It completes the coverage for examinations such as the professional foundation examinations: London Chamber of Commerce Intermediate and Higher Stages, Royal Society of Arts Stage II and most of Stage III, and for the General Certificate of Education Advanced Level.

This volume examines all the current Statements of Standard Accounting Practice, in as much detail as is needed at this stage. It also includes the substantial changes in company accounts which started with the introduction of the Companies Act 1981.

Final accounts are shown throughout the book using vertical formats. This accords with modern practice.

I wish to acknowledge the permission to use past examination papers granted by the Institute of Chartered Accountants in England and Wales, the Association of Certified Accountants, the Institute of Cost and Management Accountants, the Chartered Institute of Secretaries and Administrators, the Institute of Bankers, the Royal Society of Arts, the London Chamber of Commerce and Industry, the Association of Business Executives, the Association of Accounting Technicians, the University of London, the Joint Matriculation Board and the Associated Examining Board.

FRANK WOOD
Autumn 1983

1

The Valuation of Stock

To the general public accounting often seems to imply a precision down to the final pence. A firm will usually know the exact amount of debtors or creditors, or the exact amount spent on wages or other expenses, and this gives the appearance of precision in all matters connected with accounting. In fact this is only true of some parts of accounting. A re-examination of the chapter on depreciation in Volume 1 will illustrate a part of accounting dealing with provisions for depreciation which are normally nothing more than sheer guesswork.

Precision is also lacking when stock is valued at the end of each financial year. This does not necessarily mean a lack of precision in actually counting the number of items in stock. In all but the very smallest businesses there will often be errors in checking the quantities in stock. There will be human errors unless everything is double-checked, and the cost of doing this is often not worth while for many items of small value. Then there will be defects in such aids to checking quantities as weighing machines or liquid measures, even though the margin of error may be very small. The real lack of precision exists in giving one indisputable value to the total quantity of stock.

It is possible to state that J. Smith is a debtor for £155 and to be perfectly correct. In this case there is only one correct figure. With stock valuation there is usually a whole spectrum of possible figures. The one chosen will depend on the attitudes and opinions of those whose responsibility it is to value stock.

Up to this point is has been assumed, for the sake of simplicity, that the stock of unsold goods at the end of each financial year is valued at cost. This might appear to be an easy task to be undertaken by the management of the firm. It is, however, far from the truth. Even if 'cost' was the only measure of the value of stock, it will be shown that 'cost' can have many different meanings attached to it.

Assume that a firm has just completed its first financial year and is about to value stock at cost price. It has dealt in only one type of good. A record of the transactions is as follows:

Bought		£	Sold		£
January	10 at £30 each	300	May	8 for £50 each	400
April	10 at £34 each	340	November	24 for £60 each	1,440
October	20 at £40 each	800			
	40	1,440		32	1,840

Still in Stock at 31 December, 8 units.

The total figure of purchases is £1,440 and that of sales is £1,840. The trading account for the first year of trading can now be completed if the closing stock is brought into the calculations. This brings to light the question as to exactly which eight units of stock remain on hand. If each of the units bought had cost exactly the same, then the question would not matter from an accounting point of view. However, the three lots of purchases were bought at different prices. The cost of the goods unsold therefore rests on exactly which goods are taken for this calculation. They are most probably eight of the October purchases, but they could well be eight of the April or January purchases instead, or else be some of each of these purchases. If it is the type of good which is subject to a fairly speedy deterioration because of age, then obviously a great deal of attention will be given to ensure that goods are issued or sold in chronological order. There, are however, many types of goods which do not suffer undue deterioration in the short term, and it will not matter vitally to the firms as to which items are sold first.

Therefore many firms will not know when the units in stock at the end of the financial year were purchased. Even if they could, many firms would not take the trouble of finding this out, nor would they want to incur the cost involved in obtaining the information. The valuation of stock therefore becomes one of an accounting custom rather than one based on any scientific facts. In accounting what matters is not which units were actually sold, but instead rests on the surmise of which units were 'deemed' to have been sold.

Three accounting methods of stating which goods were sold are now listed. It must not be thought that the list is comprehensive.

1. *First In, First Out* (abbreviated as FIFO, this 'shorthand' term often being used).

The first goods received are deemed to be the first to be issued. With this method, using the data already given, the stock figure at 31 December would be calculated as follows:

	Received	Issued	Stock after each transaction	
			£	£
January	10 at £30 each		10 at £30 each	300
			£	£
April	10 at £34 each		10 at £30 each 300	
			10 at £34 each 340	640
May		8 at £30 each	2 at £30 each 60	
			10 at £34 each 340	400
October	20 at £40 each		2 at £30 each 60	
			10 at £34 each 340	
			20 at £40 each 800	1,200
November		2 at £30 each		
		10 at £34 each		
		12 at £40 each		
		——		
		24	8 at £40 each	320
		==		

2. *Last In, First Out* (abbreviated as LIFO)

With this method, as each issue of goods is made they are deemed to be from the last lot of goods received prior to that date, and where the last lot received are insufficient to meet the issue then the balance is deemed to come from the next previous lot received still available. The stock figure at 31 December becomes £240.

	Received	Issued	Stock after each transaction	
			£	£
January	10 at £30 each		10 at £30 each	300
April	10 at £34 each		10 at £30 each 300	
			10 at £34 each 340	640
May		8 at £34 each	10 at £30 each 300	
			2 at £34 each 68	368
October	20 at £40 each		10 at £30 each 300	
			2 at £34 each 68	
			20 at £40 each 800	1,168
November		20 at £40 each		
		2 at £34 each		
		2 at £30 each	8 at £30 each	240
		——		
		24		
		==		

3. *Average Cost*

With each receipt of goods the average cost of goods held in stock is recalculated. Any subsequent issue is then made at that price until a further receipt of goods necessitates the average cost of goods held being recalculated. This shows a stock at 31 December of £296.

	Received	Issued	Average cost per unit of stock held	Number of units in stock	Total value of stock
			£		£
January	10 at £30		30	10	300
April	10 at £34		32	20	640
May		8 at £32	32	12	384
October	20 at £40		37	32	1,184
November		24 at £37	37	8	296

Stock Valuation and the Calculation of Profits

Using each of the three methods already described, the Trading Accounts would appear:

Trading Account for the year ended 31 December 19–

	Methods					
		1		2		3
	£	£	£	£	£	£
Sales		1,840		1,840		1,840
Less Cost of Goods Sold:						
Purchases	1,440		1,440		1,440	
Less Closing Stock	320	1,120	240	1,200	296	1,144
Gross Profit		720		640		696

The amount of profits calculated is therefore always dependent on the basis on which the stock has been valued.

Profits as a Periodic Calculation

While it is true to say that the profits calculated for any year will differ if other bases were used for stock valuation purposes, it must be born in mind that the total profits over the whole life-span of the business will be the same irrespective of which basis is used at the end of each intervening year.

An illustration of this can now be shown. Assume that a business commences without any stock and terminates its activities four years later, the stock then in hand being taken over by the purchaser of the business for £2,000. A record of the sales and purchases, together with two possible stock valuations for each year, are as follows:

	Year 1	Year 2	Year 3	Year 4
	£	£	£	£
Sales (excluding the sale of the final stock)	5,000	7,000	8,000	9,000
Purchases	4,000	5,000	6,200	7,500
Stock valuations:				
Basis (a)		800	1,000	1,500
Basis (b)		500	800	1,100

Trading Account
Stock valuation basis (a)

	Years							
	1		2		3		4	
	£		£		£		£	
Sales		5,000		7,000		8,000		9,000
Less Cost of Goods Sold:								
Opening Stock	–		800		1,000		1,500	
Add Purchases	4,000		5,000		6,200		7,500	
	4,000		5,800		7,200		9,000	
Less Closing Stock	800	3,200	1,000	4,800	1,500	5,700	2,000	7,000
Gross Profit		1,800		2,200		2,300		2,000

Stock valuation basis (a)

	Years							
	1		2		3		4	
	£		£		£		£	
Sales		5,000		7,000		8,000		9,000
Less Cost of Goods Sold:								
Opening Stock	–		500		800		1,100	
Add Purchases	4,000		5,000		6,200		7,500	
	4,000		5,500		7,000		8,600	
Less Closing Stock	500	3,500	800	4,700	1,100	5,900	2,000	6,600
Gross Profit		1,500		2,300		2,100		2,400

Adding the profits together basis (*a*) shows £1,800 + £2,200 + £2,300 + £2,000 = £8,300, while basis (*b*) shows £1,500 + £2,300 + £2,100 + £2,400 = £8,300.

Different Meanings of 'Cost'

Dealing in the first instance with a retailing business, the word 'cost' may well mean just the actual cash paid to the supplier. However, where the retailer has paid separately for carriage inwards on the items bought, then he should undoubtedly treat this as part of the cost. Some firms will in addition add an amount representing the cost of storing the goods prior to resale, other firms will ignore such expenses for stock valuation purposes. Even firms who do bring in an amount for storage expenses will differ in the ways that they calculate it. There is no way that is laid down and adhered to by all firms.

With a manufacturing firm the problem becomes even more complex. It is possible (but see summary of SSAP 9 at the end of the chapter) to value stock of goods manufactured by the firm either at prime cost or at production cost or at some point in between. The difference between the prime cost and production cost is made up of factory indirect expenses. Where these indirect expenses are small relative to the prime cost the difference in the profits calculated may also be small, but the greater the relative indirect expenses then the greater the difference in profit calculations. An example of this can be seen in Exhibits 1.1 and 1.2.

Exhibit 1.1

A firm manufactures its own goods for resale. In its first year of trading it has incurred £10,000 for prime cost of goods completed and £2,000 for factory indirect expenses. There was no work in progress at the end of the year. The number of units made was 1,000 and the number sold was 800 at £20 each.

The directors wish to know what the profit calculations would be (*a*) if prime cost was taken as the stock valuation basis, and (*b*) if production cost was taken.

Trading Account for the year ended . . .

		(*a*)		(*b*)
	£	£		£
Sales		16,000		16,000
Production Cost of Goods b/d from Manufacturing Account	12,000		12,000	
Less Closing Stock (see following calculations)	2,000	10,000	2,400	9,600
Gross Profit		6,000		6,400

$$\text{Closing Stock } (a) \frac{\text{Units in Stock}}{\text{Total Produced}} \times \text{Prime Cost}$$

$$= \frac{200}{1,000} \times £10,000 = £2,000$$

$$(b) \frac{\text{Units in Stock}}{\text{Total Produced}} \times \text{Production Cost}$$

$$= \frac{200}{1,000} \times £12,000 = £2,400$$

Exhibit 1.2

All the facts are the same as in Exhibit 1.1 except that in this case the prime cost is £2,000 and the factory indirect expenses are £10,000.

Trading Account for the year ended . . .

	(a)		(b)	
	£		£	
Sales		16,000		16,000
Production Cost of Goods				
b/d from Manufacturing Account	12,000		12,000	
Less Closing Stock				
(see following calculations)	400	11,600	2,400	9,600
Gross Profit		4,400		6,400

$$\text{Closing Stock } (a) \frac{\text{Units in Stock}}{\text{Total Produced}} \times \text{Prime Cost} = \frac{200}{1,000} \times £2,000 = £400$$

$$(b) \text{ Same as in Exhibit 1.1} = £2,400$$

Reduction to Net Realisable Value

When the cost of the stock, using the applicable method, has been determined, it is necessary to ascertain whether any part of such costs will not be recouped when the goods are sold. To do this the cost is compared with the 'net realisable value', this term meaning the amount that would be received from the sale of stock after deducting all expenditure to be incurred on or before disposal. If the net realisable value is less than the cost, then the stock valuation is reduced to the net realisable value instead of cost.

This is obviously the application of the accounting concept of prudence, already discussed in Chapter 10 in Volume 1. A somewhat exaggerated example will show the necessity for this action. Assume that an art dealer has bought only two paintings during the financial year ended 31 December 19-8. He starts off the year without any stock, and then buys a genuine masterpiece for £6,000, selling this later in the year for £11,500. The other is a fake, but he does not realise this when he buys it for £5,100, only to discover during the year that in fact he had made a terrible mistake and that the net realizable value is £100. The fake remains unsold at the end of the year. The trading accounts, Exhibit 1.3, would appear as (*a*) if stock is valued at cost, and (*b*) if stock is valued at net realisable value.

Exhibit 1.3

Trading Account for the year ended 31 December 19-8

		(a)		(b)
		£		£
Sales		11,500		11,500
Purchases	11,100		11,100	
Closing Stock	5,100	6,000	100	11,000
Gross Profit		5,500		500

Method (*a*) ignores the fact that the dealer had a bad trading year owing to his skill being found wanting in 19-8. If this method were used, then the loss on the fake would reveal itself in the following year's trading account. Method (*b*), however, realises that the loss really occurred at the date of purchase rather than at the date of sale. Following the concept of prudence accounting practice chooses method (*b*).

Stock Groupings and Valuation

It has already been seen that the valuation normally takes the lower or cost or net realisable value. This can be further interpreted in two different ways.

1. The Article Method. The cost and net realisable value are compared for each article and the lower figure taken. These lower figures are then added together to give the total valuation. It must be stressed that an article means a type of good, so that if there are 50 units of an article in stock and that should the lower figure be £5 for one unit of an article, then the stock valuation for this item will be shown as £250.

2. The Category Method. Similar or interchangeable articles are put together into categories. Then the cost and net realisable values for each category are compared, and the lower of these two figures for each category is then taken. For one category it may well be the cost figure, while for another category it will be the net realisable figure. The figures chosen for each category are then added together to give the total valuation.

Exhibit 1.4

From the following data the different stock figures can be calculated

Stock at 31 December 19-8

Article	Different categories	Cost	Net realisable value
		£	£
1	A	10	8
2	A	12	15
3	A	30	40
4	B	18	17
5	B	15	13
6	B	26	21
7	C	41	54
8	C	36	41
9	C	42	31
		230	240

Article Method

Taking the lower figure for each article.

£8 + £12 + £30 + £17 + £13 + £21 + £41 + £36 + £31 = £209

Category Method

	Cost	Net realisable value
Category A	£10 + £12 + £30 = £52	£8 + £15 + £40 = £63
Category B	£18 + £15 + £26 = £59	£17 + £13 + £21 = £51
Category C	£41 + £36 + £42 = £119	£54 + £41 + £31 = £126

The valuation is therefore £52 + £51 + £119 = £222.

SSAP 9 states that the article method should be used, except where this is impractical, and in such a case the category method would be used. The idea of taking the lower of the total of cost or of the total of net realisable value, i.e. the lower of £230 or £240 in Exhibit 1.4, is specifically excluded.

Reduction to Replacement Cost

In other businesses it may well be important to pay attention to the cost at which stock could be replaced, if such a price is less than original cost. This will be particularly applicable where there is uncertainty as to net realisable value; where the selling prices are based on current replacement prices; or where there is a desire to recognise uneconomic buying or production.

The stock may therefore in this case be stated as the lowest of (a) cost, (b) net realisable value, or (c) replacement cost.

Some other Bases in Use

Retail businesses often estimate the cost of stock by calculating it in the first place at selling price, and then deducting the normal margin of gross profit on such stock. Adjustment is made for items which are to be sold at other than normal selling prices.

Where standard costing is in use the figure of standard cost is frequently used.

Factors affecting the Stock Valuation Decision

Obviously the overriding consideration applicable in all circumstances when valuing stock is the need to give a 'true and fair view' of the state of the affairs of the undertaking as on the Balance Sheet date and of the trend of the firm's trading results. There is, however, no precise definition of 'true and fair view'; it obviously rests on the judgement of the persons concerned. It would be necessary to study the behavioural sciences to understand the factors that affect judgement. However, it should be possible to state that the judgement of any two persons will not always be the same in the differing circumstances of various firms.

In fact, the only certain thing about stock valuation is that the concept of consistency should be applied, i.e. that once adopted, the same basis should be used in the annual accounts until some good reason occurs to change it. A reference should then be made in the final accounts as to the effect of the change on the reported profits, if the amount involved is material.

It will perhaps be useful to look at some of the factors which cause a particular basis to be chosen. The list is intended to be indicative rather than comprehensive, and is merely intended as a first brief look at matters which will have to be studied in depth by those intending to make a career in accountancy.

1. Ignorance. The personalities involved may not appreciate the fact that there is more than one possible way of valuing stock.

2. Convenience. The basis chosen may not be the best for the purposes of profit calculation but it may be the easiest to calculate. It must always be borne in mind that the benefits which flow from possessing information should be greater than the costs of obtaining it. The only difficulty with this is actually establishing when the benefits do exceed the cost, but in some circumstances the decision not to adopt a given basis will be obvious.

3. Custom. It may be the particular method used in a certain trade or industry.

4. **Taxation.** The whole idea may be to defer the payment of tax for as long as possible. Because the stock figures affect the calculation of profits on which the tax is based the lowest possible stock figures may be taken to show the lowest profits up to the Balance Sheet date.

5. **The capacity to borrow money or to sell the business at the highest possible price.** The higher the stock value shown, then the higher will be the profits calculated to date, and therefore at first sight the business looks more attractive to a buyer or lender. Either of these considerations may be more important to the proprietors than anything else. It may be thought that businessmen are not so gullible, but all businessmen are not necessarily well acquainted with accounting customs. In fact, many small businesses are bought, or money is lent to them, without the expert advice of someone well versed in accounting.

6. **Remuneration purposes.** Where someone managing a business is paid in whole or in part by reference to the profits earned, then one basis may suit him better than others. He may therefore strive to have that basis used to suit his own ends. The owner, however, may try to follow another course to minimise the remuneration that he will have to pay out.

7. **Lack of information.** If proper stock records have not been kept, then such bases as the average cost method or the LIFO method may not be calculable.

8. **Advice of the Auditors.** Many firms use a particular basis because the auditors advised its use in the first instance. If a different auditor is appointed he may well advise that a different basis be used.

The Conflict of Aims

The list of some of the factors which affect decisions is certainly not exhaustive, but it does illustrate the fact that stock valuation is usually a compromise. There is not usually only one figure which is true and fair, there must be a variety of possibilities. Therefore the desire to borrow money, and in so doing to paint a good picture by being reasonably optimistic in valuing stock, will be tempered by the fact that this may increase the tax bill. Stock valuation is therefore a compromise between the various ends for which it is to be used.

Work in Progress

The valuation of work in progress is subject to all the various criteria and methods used in valuing stock. Probably the cost element is more strongly pronounced than in stock valuation, as it is very often impossible or irrelevant to say what net realisable value or replacement price would be applicable to partly finished goods. Firms in industries such as those which have contracts covering several years have evolved their own methods.

Long term contract work in progress will be dealt with in chapter 21 Contract Accounts.

Goods on Sale or Return

Quite often goods are supplied by a manufacturer (or a wholesaler) to a retailer on the basis of 'sale or return'. This means that should the retailer sell the goods, then he will incur liability for them to the manufacturer. Failing his being able to sell the goods he will then return them to the manufacturer, having incurred no liability for the goods. This is true where part of the goods are sold by the retailer and part are returned, the only goods being payable for to the manufacturer being those which were sold.

There is no one way of accounting for such activities. All that can be said is that the goods are not effectively sold to the retailer until he in turn has sold them to someone else. It is only then that the manufacturer's sales figures should be increased. Such goods still unsold by the retailer at the financial year end are not part of the retailer's stock, they are part of the manufacturer's stock and should be treated as such. Sometimes the manufacturer's sales figures includes goods which are on sale or return, and which the retailer himself has not yet sold. Where this happens adjustments are needed for the Final Accounts.

Exhibit 1.5

A manufacturer's year end is 31 December 19-7. When he sends goods on sale or return to retailers he charges them out as ordinary sales. The following details are relevant to his end of year position:

	£
Stock (at factory) at cost 31 December 19-7	10,400
Sales (including goods on sale or return £15,000 of which £3,000 have not yet been sold by the retailer)	60,000
Debtors at 31 December 19-7 (including goods booked out on sale or return)	8,800

The goods sent on sale or return were at cost price plus 25 per cent for profit (mark-up).

The figures needed for the Final Accounts are:

	£
Sales	60,000
Less Goods on sale or return still unsold	3,000
	57,000
Debtors	8,800
Less Charges for goods on sale or return in respect of goods not sold	3,000
	5,800

Stocks:	£	£
At the factory (at cost)		10,400
Add Goods in customers' hands on sale or return (selling price)	3,000	
Less Profit content (20 per cent of selling price)	600	2,400
		12,800

From the retailer's point of view, goods on sale or return are not purchases until he actually incurs liability for them, i.e. he sells the goods. Neither do they constitute part of his stock, as they belong to the manufacturer.

Stocktaking and the Balance Sheet Date

It is often thought by students that the actual physical counting of stock all takes place after the close of business on the last day of the financial period. This could well be done in some small businesses with only a few items of a limited number of different types of stock. Other businesses will have hundreds, or even thousands, of different types of stock, and each type of stock may consist of thousands of items. Stocktaking in such a case will have to be spread over a period.

At one time it was very rare for the auditors to attend at stocktaking time as observers. The professional accounting bodies now encourage the auditors to be present if at all possible. Some financial year ends are so popular with firms that it would be impossible for a representative of the auditors to be present at all the stocktakings, or even a reasonable number of them, if they were all held at the same time. The practice has started to grow up of the stocktaking being held in large firms at some time before the financial year end, the stock records (not being part of the double entry system of financial accounts) from then to the end of the financial year being relied upon to show the stock at the Balance Sheet date. Naturally this would not be done where it was felt that the stock records could not be relied upon, and various sample checks would be carried out to try to ensure that all was in order. This technique has the advantage, other than that of the auditors attending the stocktaking, of enabling the Balance Sheet to be published at a date earlier than would be normal if all stocktaking was done at the Balance Sheet date.

In many other firms stocktaking takes place after the financial year end, and calculations are needed to work out the stock at the Balance Sheet date. Exhibit 1.6 shows just such a calculation.

Exhibit 1.6

Bloom Ltd has a financial year which ends on 31 December 19-7. The stocktaking is not in fact done until 8 January 19-8. When the items in stock on that date are priced out, it is found that the stock value amounted to £28,850. The following information is available about transactions between 31 December 19-7 and 8 January 19-8:

(i) Purchases since 31 December 19-7 amounted to £2,370 at cost.
(ii) Returns inwards since 31 December 19-7 were £350 at selling price.
(iii) Sales since 31 December 19-7 amounted to £3,800 at selling price.
(iv) The selling price is always made up of cost price + 25 per cent = selling price.

Bloom Ltd
Computation of stock as on 31 December 19-7

			£
Stock (at cost)			28,850
Add Items which were in stock on 31 December 19-7 (at cost)		£	
Sales		3,800	
Less Profit content (20 per cent of selling price)		760	3,040
			31,890
Less Items which were not in stock on 31 December 19-7 (at cost)	£	£	
Returns Inwards	350		
Less Profit content (20 per cent of selling price)	70	280	
Purchases (at cost)		2,370	2,650
Stock in Hand as on 31 December 19-7			29,240

Stock Levels

One of the most common faults found in the running of businesses is that too high a level of stock is maintained. It is not the purpose of this book to deal with this in any detail, but merely to point out the dangers of carrying too much stock.

Generalisation is always dangerous, for the scope and variety of businesses is unlimited. For many firms the danger attached to running out of a particular item of stock can be very high indeed. Imagine a motor car manufacturer who ran out of stock of driving wheels. He would not be able to despatch any cars until new stock of this item was received.

The whole of the various items in stock should be scrutinized. In the case of a motor car manufacturer this consists of several thousand parts which go together in the assembly of a car, whereas for other firms the items will be very few indeed. For each item there should be established:

(a) A maximum stock level beyond which the stock should not be allowed to rise.

(b) A minimum stock level below which it would be highly undesirable for the stock to fall.

Looking at the problem simply, suppose that an item has a minimum stock level of 100 units. The firm uses 50 units per week, and it takes 6 weeks for the supplier to deliver an order. This means that 300 units will be used whilst waiting for the order to be delivered, i.e. 6 weeks × 50 units = 300. The order for 300 units must therefore be placed at the date when stock reaches 400 units, for by the time the delivery takes place 300 units will have been used, and stock will have fallen to 100 units. For each item of stock there should therefore be established:

(c) A re-order stock level. This is the level at which an order should be sent to the supplier, so that stock will be received before the stock in hand of the item falls below the minimum stock level.

Of course, this is looking at the problem very simply indeed. There are many factors to be considered besides those mentioned, such as quantity discounts, the cost of money tied up in stock, warehousing costs and so on. If you proceed further in your studies into a more detailed knowledge of *Business Mathematics* you will find that there are various mathematical techniques to assist in this field.

For a lot of firms in certain industries, it will be found on investigation that the bulk of the stock used consists of a relatively few items. Take a publisher as an instance who has 1,000 different titles which he publishes. Of these titles 50 may be best-sellers accounting for, say, a total of 2 million sales per annum, whilst the other 950 titles may sell only ½ million copies between them. It is obvious therefore that in this firm the highest priority be given to stocking the best-sellers. If a best-seller runs out of stock at a peak time, e.g. before Christmas in the case of novels bought as Christmas presents, the sales lost forever could be considerable. If a low-selling book ran out of stock the loss would normally be relatively small.

A considerable number of firms that have problems of the shortage of finance will find that they can help matters by having a sensible look at the amounts of stock they hold. It would be a very rare firm indeed which, if they had not investigated the matter previously, could not manage to let parts of their stock run down. As this would save spending cash on items not really necessary, this cash could be better utilised elsewhere.

SSAP 9: Stocks and Work-in-Progress[1]

The basic requirements of SSAP 9 have already been given in this chapter, but some over-riding comments and notes are now given.

The LIFO method of stock valuation has been shown in the chapter, but this method provides a rather strange contradiction. SSAP 9 specifically disallowes this method, but the Companies Act 1981, discussed later, accepts the LIFO method.

SSAP 9 also defines 'cost' and certainly in the case of a manufacturing business it will also include overhead expenses, so that prime cost could not be used. The definition is:

Cost is defined in relation to the different categories of stocks and work in progress as being that expenditure which has been incurred in the normal course of business in bringing the product or service to its present location and condition. This expenditure should include, in addition to cost of purchase (as defined later) such costs of conversion (as defined later) as are appropriate to that location and condition.

Cost of purchase comprises purchase price including import duties, transport and handling costs and any other directly attributable costs, less trade discounts, rebates and subsidies.

Cost of conversion comprises:

(a) costs which are specifically attributable to units of production, i.e., direct labour, direct expenses and sub-contracted work;
(b) production overheads (as defined later);
(c) other overheads, if any, attributable in the particular circumstances of the business to bringing the product or service to its present location and condition.

Production overheads: overheads incurred in respect of materials, labour or services for production, based on the normal level of activity, taking one year with another. For this purpose each overhead should be classified according to function (e.g. production selling or administration) so as to ensure the inclusion in cost of conversion of those overheads (including depreciation) which relate to production, notwithstanding that these may accrue wholly or partly on a time basis.

Conclusion to the Chapter

It is not possible in a book of this type to give the arguments for and against the use of different stock bases. Any 'potted' version would probably be more misleading than it would be useful. There is a danger of thinking that the arguments for and against can be summarised in a few words. Many experts have argued on behalf of or

1. See also chapter 25 of this volume.

against the bases described in this chapter, and there is no universal agreement as to which is the best one. Economists and operational research teams are often astounded by the lack of any 'scientific' approach. All that can be said here is that firms would be well advised to rethink their stock valuation procedures in terms of obtaining information from which they can derive the greatest possible benefit, and wherever possible to use different stock figures to serve different purposes.

Exercises

Note: **Questions without the suffix 'A' have answers shown at the back of this book. Questions with the suffix 'A' are set without answers in this book so that teachers/lecturers can set the questions for classwork or homework.**

1.1. The following details are available to you concerning the activity of a manufacturing firm:

		Units
1st year.	Opening Stock	500
	Sales	1,000
	Produced	800
	Closing Stock	300
2nd year.	Opening Stock	300
	Sales	1,000
	Produced	1,400
	Closing Stock	700
3rd year.	Opening Stock	700
	Sales	1,000
	Produced	800
	Closing Stock	500

There was no work in progress at the end of any of these years. For each of the years the prime cost of each unit produced was £1, while the production cost of each units was £2. The selling price of all units was £3 each. You are required to:
(a) Draw up the Trading Account for each year if the stock was valued at prime cost.
(b) Draw up the Trading Account for each year if the stock was valued at production cost.
(c) Which method would you advise if income tax was the main consideration and all profits under £800 per annum were free of tax, while profits above that figure were taxable at the rate of 40 per cent.
(d) What is the main factor contributing to different reported profits under (a) and (b) above.

1.2. B.G.T. Ltd, which manufactures a standard product, classifies its expenses as being fixed, varying in direct proportion to production or varying directly with sales. The company had no finished stocks at 1 January 19-6, and there was no work in progress at either 1 January or 31 December 19-6.

The items relating to production and sales for 19-6 were:

	£
For the production of 120,000 units:	
Raw Materials Consumed	360,000
Direct Wages	570,000
Indirect Wages (fixed)	72,000
Factory Expenses – (fixed)	48,000
(variable)	30,000

	£
Proceeds of sale of 100,000 units	1,200,000
Expenses (not included above) to be charged to	
Profit and Loss Accounts – (fixed)	72,000
(variable)	48,000

You are required to prepare statements showing:

(a) the valuation of the 20,000 units of finished stock at 31 December 19-6
  (i) at factory cost,
  (ii) including only the variable elements in factory cost;
(b) the net profit or loss for the year adopting your valuation of stock under
  (a) (ii) above;
(c) what the net profit or loss would have been if, by spending an extra £5,000 on advertising, the whole of the year's output had been sold at the normal selling price.

1.3. At the end of a company's first financial year on 31 December 19-5, the directors of your firm ask you to ascertain the stock figure. The following information is presented to you.

	Purchases				Items sold		Net realisable value at 31 December 19-5
Item 1	January	500 at	£5	each	July	200	
	September	300 ,,	£6	,,	October	350	£5½ each
Item 2	March	100 ,,	£2	,,	April	50	
	November	200 ,,	£3	,,	December	100	£3⅓ ,,
Item 3	June	600 ,,	£10	,,	July	500	
	September	400 ,,	£12	,,	October	100	£15 ,,
Item 4	April	200 ,,	£16	,,	June	150	
	October	200 ,,	£18	,,	November	50	£14 ,,
Item 5	October	1,000 ,,	£12	,,			
	November	800 ,,	£10	,,	December	1,200	£9 ,,
Item 6	January	200 ,,	£4	,,			
	July	400 ,,	£5	,,	September	500	£7 ,,

You are also told that there are three distinct groups or categories of items, Group A being items 1 and 2, Group B being items 3 and 4, and Group C being items 5 and 6.

You inform the directors that it is possible to arrive at more than one stock figure. The directors thereupon ask you to give them the various figures that are possible using the following bases:

(a) First In, First Out Method;
(b) Last In, First Out Method;
and applying the Category and Article methods to each of these bases.
Show all your workings clearly.

1.4. The annual stocktaking of Ringers Limited did not take place on the company's year end on 30 April 19-0 owing to staff illness.

However, stock was taken at the close of business on 8 May 19-0 and the resultant valuation of £23,850 was used in the preparation of the company's draft accounts for the year ended 30 April 19-0 which showed a gross profit of £158,000, a net profit of £31,640 and net current assets at 30 April 19-0 of £24,600.

Subsequent investigations indicated that during the period from 30 April to 8 May 19-0 sales were £2,900, sales returns £340, purchases £4,200 and purchases returns £500.

In addition it was discovered that:

(a) A quantity of stock bought in 19-0 and included in the stock valuation at 8 May 19-0 at cost of £700 was, in fact, worthless. Instruction have now been given for the destruction of this stock.

(b) Two of the stock sheets prepared on 8 May 19-0 had been overcast by £100 and £40 respectively.

(c) The stock valuation of 8 May 19-0 included the company's office stationery stock of £1,400.
    Note: It can be assumed that the stationery stock did not change between 30 April and 8 May 19-0.

(d) The valuation at 8 May 19-0 had not included goods, which had cost Ringers Limited £400, sent on a sale or return basis to John Winters Limited in February 19-0.

     Half of these goods, in value, were bought by John Winters Limited on 29 April 19-0, but the sale has not been recorded in the company's draft accounts for the year ended 30 April 19-0.

Note: Ringers Limited achieves a uniform rate of gross profit of 20% on all sales revenue.

Required:

(a) A computation of the Ringers Limited's corrected stock valuation at 30 April 19-0.

(b) A computation of Ringers Limited's corrected gross profit and net profit for the year ended 30 April 19-0, and the corrected net current assets at 30 April 19-0.

(Association of Certified Accountants)

1.5. Giotto Ltd. and Cambio Ltd. are two companies which were incorporated on 1st January 19-6 and commenced trading on that date. They continued in business until 31st December 19-9 when they were both taken over by a large public company.

Both companies traded in an identical product and their trading activities, which were identical throughout the four year period, were as follows:

	Units Purchased	Units Sold	Purchase Price (per unit) £	Sales Price (per unit) £
19-6	2,000	1,000	14	20
19-7	3,000	2,000	16	23
19-8	4,000	3,000	18	27
19-9	4,000	7,000	20	30

Giotto Ltd. matches purchases with sales on the basis of first-in first-out (FIFO), Cambio on the basis of last-in first-out (LIFO).

You are required to:

(a) prepare Giotto Ltd.'s trading account for each of the years 19-6 to 19-9 in columnar form.

(b) prepare Cambio Ltd.'s trading account for each of the years 19-6 to 19-9 in columnar form.

(c) calculate the total profits of each company over the four year period.

(d) comment on the results of your calculations under (a) to (c) above.

(*Royal Society of Arts: Stage Two*)

1.6. John Terry, an established trader, decided to add a new article Dib to his product range for a trial period. The selling price of a Dib has been fixed at £15 per unit. The transactions concerning Dibs for the six months from 1 April 19-1 to 30 September 19-1 are as follows:

Purchases

April	400 at £8 each
June	600 at £10 each
August	500 at £12 each

Sales

May	200
July	300
September	100

During September John Terry decided to purchase no more Dibs. On 30 September 19-1 he knows that he can sell 400 Dibs at the full price during October but that the remainder will have to be disposed of at a later date at £5 per unit.

Required:

(a) Calculate the gross profit arising from the sale of Dibs for the six months to 30 September 19-1 showing clearly the value of closing stock using both last in first out (LIFO) and first in first out (FIFO) methods of stock evaluation.

(b) State and explain two accounting concepts that are involved in arriving at a stock valuation.

(c) How does the choice of stock valuation method affect the profit of a business
   (i) in the short run?
   (ii) in the long run?

(*Associated Examining Board G.C.E. 'A' level*)

NOTE: THE FOLLOWING QUESTIONS WITH THE SUFFIX 'A' DO NOT HAVE ANSWERS GIVEN AT THE BACK OF THIS BOOK.

1.7A. You are the owner of a firm which has just completed its first year of trading. Looking at your figures of Sales and Purchases you see the following:

	Purchases				Items sold		Net realisable value at 31 December 19-6
Item A	January	1,000 at	£4 each	March	800		
	October	300 ,,	£5 ,,	November	200	£5.40 each
Item B	February	400 ,,	£7 ,,	May	100		
	November	200 ,,	£8 ,,	December	150	£9 ,,
Item C	April	600 ,,	£9 ,,	June	400	£11 ,,
	December	500 ,,	£10 ,,			
Item D	February	1,000 ,,	£14 ,,	April	700	£12 ,,
	May	600 ,,	£16 ,,			
Item E	January	600 ,,	£17 ,,	March	500		
	August	500 ,,	£18 ,,	October	200	£17.50 ,,
Item F	October	700 ,,	£22 ,,	December	500	£24 ,,

The items fall into three different categories. Items A and B, Items C and D and Items E and F.

Calculate the various figures that are possible using the following bases:

(a) First In, First Out Method;
(b) Last In, First Out Method;

and applying the Category and Article methods to each of these bases.
Show all your workings clearly.

1.8A. You are given the following details of a manufacturing firm:

		Units
1st year	Opening Stock	800
	Sales	4,900
	Produced	5,200
	Closing Stock	1,100
2nd year	Opening Stock	1,100
	Sales	8,000
	Produced	9,200
	Closing Stock	2,300
3rd year	Opening Stock	2,300
	Sales	10,000
	Produced	9,400
	Closing Stock	1,700

There was no work in progress at the end of any of these years. In each year the prime cost per unit produced was £3, whilst the production cost of each unit was £5. The selling price of all units was £6 each. You are required to:

(a) Draw up a Trading Account for each year if the stock was valued at prime cost.
(b) Draw up a Trading Account for each year if the stock was valued at production cost.
(c) Advise as to the method you would think most suitable, assuming that the main factor was to keep the tax bill for these years to a minimum. Assume that there is no tax on the first £3,000 each year, whilst 30 per cent of the excess above that is taken in tax.

1.9A. An evaluation of a physical stock count on 30 April, 19-2 in respect of the financial year ending on that date at Cranfleet Commodities has produced a figure of £187,033.

The firm's book-keeper has approached you, as the accountant, for assistance in dealing with the following matters to enable him to arrive at a final figure of closing stock for inclusion in the annual accounts:

(1) 320 components included at their original cost of £11 each can now be bought in for only £6 each due to over production by the manufacturer. This drop in price is expected to be only temporary and the purchase price is expected to exceed its original figure within 12 months. Cranfleet Commodities intends to continue selling the existing stock at the present price of £15 each.
(2) It has been discovered that certain items which had cost £5,657 have been damaged. It will cost £804 to repair them after which they can be sold for £6,321.
(3) On one stock sheet a sub-total of £9,105 has been carried forward as £1,095.
(4) 480 units which cost £1.50 each have been extended at £15.00 each.
(5) The firm has sent goods with a selling price of £1,500 (being cost plus 25%) to customer on a sale or return basis. At 30 April 19-2, the customer had not signified acceptance, but the goods have not been returned, and consequently had not been included in the physical stock count.
(6) Included in stock were goods bought on credit for £4,679 from Byfleet Enterprises. At 30 April 19-2, Cranfleet Commodities had not paid this account.
(7) Byfleet Enterprises had also sent some free samples (for advertising purposes only). These have been included in stock at their catalogue price of £152.

Required:
Taking account of such of the above facts as are relevant, calculate a closing stock figure for inclusion in the 19-2 annual accounts of Cranfleet Commodities, giving reasons for the action you have taken in each individual case.

(Association of Certified Accountants)

1.10A. Hot Rod Limited sells new and used cars and has a service department. At 31 December 19-0 the stock of used cars was as follows.

	Used Car Number			
	1	2	3	4
	£	£	£	£
Allowed on trade-in	1,700	2,400	1,000	1,400
Over allowance (i)	300	300	200	200
Service Department charges (ii)	60	–	40	160
National Car Dealers' Association estimate of market value (retail):				
at date of trade-in	1,600	2,200	875	1,200
at 31 December 19-0	1,550	2,200	850	1,150
Probable sale price if sold during January 19-1 (iii)	1,600	2,150	825	1,300

Notes:
(i) During 19-0, new cars were being sold at less than manufacturer's list price where no trade-in was involved. All the used cars in stock at Hot Rod Limited on 31 December 19-0 had been acquired as trade-ins for new cars sold. The amounts in this line represent the discount that would have been allowed on the new car sold had that new car been sold for cash with no trade-in.
(ii) The service department makes necessary repairs on used cars and bills the used car department at cost plus a 33⅓% mark up. The amounts in this line represent the bills from the service department.
(iii) With the exception of cars 2 and 4, which are still on hand, the used cars were sold for cash during January 19-1 at the amounts shown in this line.

Discuss the various factors which should be considered in assigning a value to the stock of used cars. Support the discussion by indicating the computations needed to arrive at an acceptable stock value for each car as at 31 December 19-0.

(Joint Matriculation Board G.C.E. 'A' level)

1.11A. R.T.X. Ltd. produces financial reports every three months. The stock was taken on 30th September 19-0 and the final figure was to be incorporated in the financial reports for the three months ending 30th September 19-0. However, the stock controller has lost the stock sheets and by the middle of October 19-0 the quarterly financial reports are urgently required and you are invited to assist. Your investigation reveals the following information:
(i) Stock at 30th June 19-0 was £51,376.
(ii) Goods invoiced to customers in respect of the months July, August and September 19-0 amounted to £64,632, but this amount includes £5,847 which relates to sales despatched to customers in June 19-0.
(iii) Selling prices are determined by a 25 per cent mark-up on cost.
(iv) Goods despatched to customers in September 19-0 amounting to £6,340 at selling price had not yet been invoiced.
(v) Certain items in the stock at 30th June 19-0 valued at £864 were scrapped in August 19-0.
(vi) Your scrutiny of the stock sheets as at 30th June 19-0 reveals the following errors. One sheet had been over-added by £110, and 300 items of a certain stock line costing £14 per item had been extended at £1.40 per item.

(vii) Purchases of goods in respect of the three months ended 30th September 19-0 amounted to £71,326 and had been duly entered in the accounting records. Purchases received in September 19-0 amounting to £4,784 had not yet been invoiced by the supplier.

(viii) Goods returned to suppliers during the quarter amounted to £473, and goods returned by customers in this period amounted to £689 at cost price.

Required:
Compute the appropriate stock value for inclusion in the financial reports for the three months ending 30th September 19-0.

(Institute of Chartered Secretaries and Administrators)

1.12A. Knowles Ltd. is a new company, trading in a single item, which commenced business on 1st January 19-1. The following information is extracted from the books covering the year to 31st December 19-1.

	£
Sales (12,000 units at £15 per unit)	180,000
Advertising expenses	3,000
Insurances paid	2,500
Administration expenses	33,000
Rent and rates	4,000
Purchases	162,000

Purchases have been analysed as follows:

Date of Purchase	Number of items purchased	Purchase price (per unit)
1 January	7,000	10
1 May	4,000	11
1 September	4,000	12
	15,000	

Sales occurred at an even rate during 19-1, i.e. 1,000 units were sold each month.

The insurances paid cover the fifteen months to 31st March 19-2.

All but one of the directors take the view that they should account for purchases on the 'Last-in-first-out' (LIFO) basis. The 'odd one out' says that it would be better to use the 'first-in-first-out' (FIFO) basis as this will result in higher profits.

You are required to:

(a) prepare the trading and profit and loss account for 19-1, accounting for purchases on the LIFO basis.

(b) calculate the effect on reported profit of valuing stocks on the FIFO basis.

(c) calculate the *gross* profit for January 19-2 on (i) the LIFO basis and (ii) the FIFO bais. Asusme that all the items in stock at the end of 19-1 are sold in January 19-2 at an unchanged price of £15 per unit and no new stocks are purchased.

(d) comment on the views expressed by the single director, in the light of the above calculations.

(Royal Society of Arts, Stage II)

2

Bills of Exchange

When goods are supplied to someone on credit, or services performed for him, then that person becomes a debtor. The creditor firm would normally wait for payment by the debtor. Until payment is made the money owing is of no use to the creditor firm as it is not being used in any way. This can be remedied by factoring the debtors, which involves passing the debts over to a finance firm. They will pay an agreed amount for the legal rights to the debts.

Another possibility is that of obtaining a bank overdraft, with the debtors accepted as part of the security on which the overdraft has been granted.

Yet another way that can give the creditor effective use of the money owing to him is for him to draw a bill of exchange on the debtor. This means that a document is drawn up requiring the debtor to pay the amount owing to the creditor, or to anyone nominated by him at any time, on or by a particular date. He sends this document to the debtor who, if he agrees to it, is said to 'accept' it by writing on the document that he will comply with it and appends his signature. The debtor then returns the bill of exchange to the creditor. This document is then legal proof of the debt. The debtor is not then able to contest the validity of the debt but only for any irregularity in the bill of exchange itself. The creditor can now act in one of three ways:

(a) He can negotiate the bill to another person in payment of a debt. That person may also renegotiate it to someone else. The person who possesses the bill at maturity, i.e. the date for payment of the bill, will present it to the debtor for payment.

(b) He may 'discount' it with a bank. 'Discount' here means that the bank will take the bill of exchange and treat it in the same manner as money deposited in the bank account. The bank will then hold the bill until maturity when it will present it to the debtor for payment. The bank will make a charge to the creditor for this service known as a discounting charge.

(*c*) The third way open to the creditor is for him to hold the bill until maturity when he will present it to the debtor for payment. In this case, apart from having a document which is legal proof of the debt and could therefore save legal costs if a dispute arose, no benefit has been gained from having a bill of exchange. However, action (*a*) or (*b*) could have been taken if the need had arisen.

The creditor who draws up the bill of exchange is known as the *Drawer*. The debtor on whom it is drawn is the *Drawee,* when accepted he becomes the *Acceptor,* while the person to whom the bill is to be paid is the *Payee*. In fact it may be recognized that a cheque is a special type of bill of exchange where the drawee is always a bank and in addition is payable on demand. This chapter, however, refers to bills of exchange other than cheques.

To the person who is to receive money on maturity of the bill of exchange the document is known as a 'bill receivable', while to the person who is to pay the sum due on maturity it is known as a 'bill payable'.

Dishonoured Bills

When the debtor fails to make payment on maturity the bill is said to be dishonoured. If the holder is someone other than the drawer then he will have recourse against the person who has negotiated the bill to him, that person will then have recourse against the one who negotiated it to him, and so on until final recourse is had against the drawer of the bill for the amount of money due on the bill. The drawer's right of action is then against the acceptor.

On dishonour a bill is often 'noted'. This means that the bill is handed to a lawyer acting in his capacity as a notary public, who then re-presents the bill to the acceptor. The notary public then records the reasons for it not being discharged. The notary public's fee is known as a 'noting charge'. With a foreign bill, in addition to the bill being noted, it is necessary to 'protest' the bill in order to preserve the holder's rights against the drawer and previous endorsers. 'Protest' is the term which covers the legal formalities needed.

The action to be taken by the drawer depends entirely upon circumstances. Often the lack of funds on the acceptor's part is purely temporary. In this case the drawer will negotiate with the acceptor and agree to draw another bill, or substitute several bills of smaller amounts with different maturity dates, for the amount owing, frequently with an addition for interest to compensate for the extended period of credit. Negotiation is the keynote; it must not be thought that acceptors are always sued when they fail to make payment. They are customers, and where future dealings with them are expected to be profitable harsh measures are certainly to be avoided. Legal action should be the last action to be considered. Any interest charged to the acceptor would be debited to his account and credited to an Interest Receivable Account.

Discounting Charges and Noting Charges

From the acceptor's point of view the discounting of a bill is a matter wholly for the drawer or holder to decide. He, the acceptor, has been allowed a term of credit and will pay the agreed price on the maturity of the bill. Therefore the discounting charge is not one that he should suffer; this should be borne wholly by the person discounting the bill.

On the other hand, the noting charge has been brought about by the acceptors default. It is equitable that his account should be charged with the amount of the expense of noting and protesting.

Retired Bills

Instead of waiting until maturity, bills may be retired, i.e. not allowed to run until maturity. They may be paid off before maturity, in which case a rebate is often allowed because the full term of credit has not been taken; or else renewed by fresh bills being drawn and the old ones cancelled, the new bills often including interest because the term of credit has been extended.

Exhibit 2.1
Drawer's Books

Goods had been sold by D. Jarvis to J. Burgon on 1 January 19-6 for £400. A bill of exchange is drawn by Jarvis and accepted by Burgon on 1 January 19-6, the date of maturity being 31 March 19-6. The following accounts show the entries necessary:

(a) If the bill is held by the drawer until maturity when the drawee makes payment.

J. Burgon

19-6		£	19-6		£
Jan 1	Sales	400	Jan 1	Bill Receivable	400

Bills Receivable

19-6		£	19-6		£
Jan 1	J. Burgon	400	Mar 31	Bank	400

Bank

19-6		£
Mar 31	Bills Receivable	400

(*b*) Where the bill is negotiated to another party by the drawer, in this case to I.D.T. Ltd on 3 January 19-6.

J. Burgon

19-6		£	19-6		£
Jan 1	Sales	400	Jan 1	Bill Receivable	400

Bills Receivable

19-6		£	19-6		£
Jan 1	J. Burgon	400	Jan 3	I.D.T. Ltd	400

(*c*) If the bill is discounted with the bank, in this case on 2 January 19-6, the discounting charges being £6.

J. Burgon

19-6		£	19-6		£
Jan 1	Sales	400	Jan 1	Bill Receivable	400

Bills Receivable

19-6		£	19-6		£
Jan 1	J. Burgon	400	Jan 2	Bank	400

Bank

19-6		£	19-6		£
Jan 2	Bills Receivable	400	Jan 2	Discounting Charges	6

Discounting Charges

19-6		£			
Jan 2	Bank	6			

Acceptor's Books

The instances (*a*), (*b*) and (*c*) in the drawer's books will result in similar entries in the acceptor's books. From the acceptor's point of view two things have happened, (1) The acceptance of the bill, and (2) its discharge by payment. The fact that (*a*), (*b*) and (*c*) would result in different payees is irrelevant as far as the acceptor is concerned.

D. Jarvis

19-6		£	19-6		£
Jan 1	Bills Payable	400	Jan 1	Purchases	400

Bills Payable

19-6		£	19-6		£
Mar 31	Bank	400	Jan 1	D. Jarvis	400

Bank

			19-6		£
			Mar 31	Bill Payable	400

Dishonoured Bills and Accounting Entries

These can be illustrated by reference to Exhibit 2.2.

Exhibit 2.2

On 1 April 19-7 A. Grant sells goods for £600 to K. Lee, a bill with a maturity date of 30 June 19-7 being drawn by Grant and accepted by Lee on 2 April 19-7. On 30 June 19-7 the bill is presented to Lee, but he fails to pay it and it is therefore dishonoured. The bill is noted, the cost of £2 being paid by Grant on 7 July 19-7.

The entries needed will depend on whether or not the bill had been discounted by Grant.

(a) Drawer's Books

(i) *Where the Bill had not been discounted or renegotiated*

K. Lee

19-7		£	19-7		£
Apl 1	Sales	600	Apl 2	Bill Receivable	600
Jun 30	Bill Receivable – dishonoured	600			
July 7	Bank: Noting Charge (A)	2			

Bills Receivable

19-7		£	19-7		£
Apl 2	K. Lee	600	June 30	K. Lee – bill dishonoured	600

Bank

			19-7		£
			July 7	Noting Charges – K. Lee (A)	2

Note:

(A) As the noting charges are directly incurred as the result of Lee's default, then Lee must suffer the cost by his account being debited with that amount.

(ii) Where the Bill had been discounted with a bank

The entries can now be seen as they would have appeared if the bill had been discounted on 5 April 19-7, discounting charges being £9.

K. Lee

19-7		£	19-7		£
Apl 1	Sales	600	Apl 2	Bill Receivable	600
June 30	Bank – bill dis-honoured (C)	600			
July 7	Bank: Noting Charge	2			

Bills Receivable

19-7		£	19-7		£
Apl 2	K. Lee	600	Apl 5	Bank	600

Bank

19-7		£	19-7		£
Apl 5	Bills Receivable	600	Apl 5	Discounting Charges (B)	9
			June 30	K. Lee – bill dis-honoured (C)	600
			July 7	Noting Charges – K. Lee	2

Discounting Charges

19-7		£
Apl 5	Bank (B)	9

Notes:

(B) The discounting charges are wholly an expense of A. Grant. They are therefore charged to an expense account. Contrast this with the treatment of the noting charges.

(C) On maturity the bank will present the bill to Lee. On its dishonour the bank will hand the bill back to Grant, and will cancel out the original amount shown as being deposited in the bank account. This amount is then charged to Lee's personal account to show that he is still in debt.

(b) Acceptor's Books

The entries in the acceptor's books will not be affected by whether or not the drawer had discounted the bill.

A. Grant

19-7		£	19-7		£
Apl 1	Bill Payable	600	Apl 1	Purchases	600
			June 30	Bill Payable – dis-honoured	600
			July 7	Noting Charge (D)	2

Bills Payable

19-7		£	19-7		£
Jun 30	A. Grant – bill dishonoured	600	Apl 1	A. Grant	600

Noting Charges

19-7		£
July 7	A. Grant (D)	2

Note:

(D) The noting charges will have to be reimbursed to A. Grant. To show this fact A. Grant's account is credited while the Noting Charges Account is debited to record the expense.

Bills Receivable as Contingent Liabilities

The fact that bills had been discounted, but had not reached maturity by the Balance Sheet date, could give an entirely false impression of the financial position of the business unless a note to this effect is made on the Balance Sheet. That such a note is necessary can be illustrated by reference to the following Balance Sheets.

Balance Sheet as at 31 December 19-7

		(a)		(b)
	£	£	£	£
Fixed Assets		3,500		3,500
Current Assets:				
Stock	1,000		1,000	
Debtors	1,200		1,200	
Bills Receivable	1,800		–	
Bank	500		2,300	
	4,500		4,500	
Less Current Liabilities	3,000		3,000	
Working Capital		1,500		1,500
		5,000		5,000
		£		£
Financed by:				
Capital		5,000		5,000

Balance Sheet (*a*) shows the position if £1,800 of bills receivable were still in hand. Balance Sheet (*b*) shows the position if the bills had been discounted, ignoring discounting charges. To an outsider, Balance Sheet (*b*) seems to show a much stronger liquid position with £2,300 in the bank. However, should the bills be dishonoured on maturity the bank balance would slump to £500. The appearance of Balance Sheet (*b*) is therefore deceptive unless a note is added, e.g. *Note:* There is a contingent liability of £1,800 on bills discounted at the Balance Sheet date. This note enables the outsider to view the bank balance in its proper perspective of depending on the non-dishonour of the bills discounted.

Exercises

Note: **Questions without the suffix 'A' have answers shown at the back of this book. Questions with the suffix 'A' are set without answers in this book so that teachers/lecturers can set the questions for classwork or homework.**

2.1. N. Gudgeon sells goods to two companies on July 1 19-7.
To R. Johnson Ltd   £2,460
To B. Scarlet & Co. Ltd.   £1,500
He draws bills of exchange on each of them and they are both accepted.
He discounts both of the bills with the bank on July 4 19-7, and suffers discounting charges of £80 on Johnson's bill and £65 on Scarlet's bill. On September 1 19-7 the bills mature and Johnson Ltd. meets its liability. Scarlet's bill is dishonoured and is duly noted on September 4, the noting charge being £6.
Show the above in the necessary accounts:
(*a*) In the books of Gudgeon.
(*b*) In the books of Scarlet Ltd. and of Johnson Ltd.

2.2. P. Cummings buys goods from T. Victor Ltd. on January 21 19-7 for £2,900 and from C. Bellamy & Co. for £4,160. Bills are drawn on him and he accepts them.

T. Victor Ltd. Discount their bill with their bank on January 29, the discounting charge being £110.

C. Bellamy & Co. simply keep their bill waiting for maturity.

On maturity of the bills on April 21 19-7, Cummings duly meets (pays) Bellamy's bill. He is unable to pay Victor's bill and it is accordingly dishonoured. Victor duly has it noted on April 28 19-7 the noting charge being £10.

Show the entries necessary in:
(a) The books of P. Cummings.
(b) The books of T. Victor Ltd.
(c) The books of C. Bellamy & Co.

2.3. K.C. owed T.M. £960. K.C. accepted a Bill of Exchange at three months date for this amount T.M. discounted for £948.

Before the due date of the bill T.M. was informed that K.C. was unable to meet the bill and was offering a composition of 37½ per cent of each £ to his creditors. This offer was accepted and cash equivalent to the composition was received.

Show the ledger entries to record the above in T.M.'s ledger.

2.4. Draw up a Sales Ledger Control Account for the month of August 19-6 from the following:

19-6	£
Aug 1 Balances (Dr)	12,370
Balances (Cr)	105
Totals for the month:	
Sales Journal	16,904
Returns Inwards Journal	407
Cheques Received from customers	15,970
Bills receivable accepted	1,230
Cash received from customers	306
Bad Debts written off	129
Cash discounts allowed	604
Bill receivable dishonoured	177
Aug 31 Balances (Cr)	88
Balances (Dr)	?

2.5. A Purchases Ledger Control Account should be drawn up for February 19-7 from the following:

19-7		£
Feb 1	Balances (Dr)	33
	Balances (Cr)	8,570
	Totals for the month:	
	Purchases Journal	11,375
	Returns Outwards Journal	568
	Bills Payable accepted by us	1,860
	Cheques paid to suppliers	9,464
	Cash paid to suppliers	177
	We were unable to meet a bill payable on maturity and it was therefore dishonoured	800
	We agreed to suffer noting charge on dishonoured bill	20
Feb 28	Balances (Dr)	47
	Balances (Cr)	?

2.6A. Indicate by Journal entries how the following would appear in the ledger accounts of (a) Noone, (b) Iddon.

19-8

Jan 1 Iddon sells goods £420 to Noone, and Noone sends to Iddon a three months' acceptance for this amount.

,, 1 Iddon discounts the acceptance with the Slough Discount Co. Ltd, receiving its cheque for £412.

Feb 29 One third of Noone's stock, valued at £3,600, is destroyed by fire. Noone claims on the underwriters at Lloyds with whom he is insured.

Apr 1 The underwriters admit the claim for £3,000 only as the total stock was only insured for £9,000.

,, 4 In view of Noone's difficulties Iddon meets the acceptance due today by giving his cheque for £420 to the Slough Discount Co. Ltd.; he draws on Noone a further bill for one month for £430 (to include £10 interest) which Noone accepts.

,, 9 Noone receives cheque from the underwriters in settlement of the admitted claim.

May 7 Noone's bank honours the acceptance presented by Iddon as due today.

2.7A. Enter the following in the appropriate ledger accounts of R. Smith:

19-0

Jan 5 R. Smith sold goods to P. Thomas, £320, and Thomas accepted Smith's bill for three months for this amount.

,, 6 R. Smith discounted Thomas's bill at the London Discount Co. for £304, and pays this amount into his account at the bank.

Apr 8 The London Discount Co. notified Smith that Thomas's bill had been dishonoured. Smith at once set cheque to the London Discount Co. for the full amount of the bill plus £3 charges.

,, 14 Smith agreed that Thomas's bankers should accept a further bill for one month for the total amount owing plus £10 interest, and received the new acceptance.

May 18 Smith's bank informed him the new bill had been paid.

2.8A. On 1 June 19-2, X purchased goods from Y for £860 and sold goods to Z for £570.

On the same date, X drew a bill (No. 1) at three months on Z for £400 and Z accepted it.

On 12 June 19-2, Z drew a bill (No. 2) at three months on Q for £150 which Q accepted.

On 14 June, Z endorsed bill No. 2 over to X and, on 16 June, X endorsed this bill over to Y.

On 20 June, X accepted a bill (No. 3) at three months for £720 drawn by Y in full settlement of his account, including interest. On 23 June, Y discounted bill No. 3 at his bank.

On 17 September, Y informed X that Q's acceptance had been dishonoured and X sent a cheque for £150 to Y. The other bills were paid on the due dates.

On 20 September, X received a cheque from Z for half the amount due from him.

Show the entries to record these transactions in the ledger and cash book of X.

2.9A. Balances and transactions affecting a company's control accounts for the months of May 19-2 are listed below.

	£
Balances at 1 May 19-2:	
Sales ledger	9,123 (debit)
	211 (credit)
Purchases ledger	4,490 (credit)
	88 (debit)
Transactions during May 19-2:	
Purchases on credit	18,135
Allowances from suppliers	629
Receipts from customers by cheque	27,370
Sales on credit	36,755
Discounts received	1,105
Payments to creditors by cheque	15,413
Contra settlements	3,046
Allowances to customers	1,720
Bills of exchange receivable	6,506
Customers' cheques dishonoured	489
Cash receipts from credit customers	4,201
Refunds to customers for overpayment of accounts	53
Discounts allowed	732
Balances at 31 May 19-2:	
Sales ledger	136 (credit)
Purchases ledger	67 (debit)

Required:

(a) Explain the purposes for which Control Accounts are prepared.

(b) Post the Sales Ledger and Purchases Ledger control accounts for the month of May 19-2 and derive the respective debit and credit closing balances on 31 May 19-2.

(Association of Certified Accountants)

3

Joint Venture Accounts

Sometimes it is to the mutual advantage of two or more persons or firms to tackle a particular business venture together instead of engaging in it separately. These are known as joint ventures. Early versions of Joint Venture Accounts being kept were by the Venetian merchants trading in the Mediterranean in the fifteenth century. One merchant might provide the ship, another the goods and another the capital. Any profits or losses would then be split in an agreed ratio. Present-day versions are to be found where a produce merchant provides the capital, the transport to market and the selling skills, while the farmer actually grows the produce. The profits are then shared between them. Joint ventures may seem to be exactly the same as partnerships. In fact a joint venture is a form of partnership, but it is limited to a particular transaction. There may be several joint ventures as between the same parties, but each one is a separate venture, and the agreements may be different for each one, e.g. in respect of the sharing of profits and losses.

Some joint ventures may be of such magnitude that a bank account is opened especially for the venture and separate books kept. The calculation of the profits and the eventual withdrawal of their money by the parties involved is quite a straightforward matter. However, it is usually found that each party will record in his own books only those transactions with which he has been concerned. No one party to the venture will therefore have a full record of all the transactions. An example of this is now given:

Exhibit 3.1

Black, of London, Johnson, of Manchester, and Graham of Glasgow, enter into a joint venture. Black and Johnson are both to supply some of the materials, whilst only Johnson and Graham will sell the finished goods. Profits are to be shared, Black 3: Johnson 2: Graham 1:

Details of the transactions are:

	£
Black supplied materials costing	450
Johnson supplied materials costing	300
Black paid wages	180
Black paid storage expenses	40
Johnson paid for carriage	90
Graham paid selling expenses	120
Johnson received cash from sales	800
Graham received cash from sales	1,100

Each party has entered in his own books the transactions which have been his concern. He will have opened a 'Joint Venture (with the names of the other two parties) Account'. Payments will have been credited to his Cash Book and debited to the Joint Venture Account. Goods supplied will be credited to his Purchases Account and debited to the Joint Venture Account. This Joint Venture Account will appear as follows:

Black's Books (in London)
Joint Venture with Johnson and Graham

	£		
Purchases: Materials	450		
Cash: Wages	180		
Cash: Storage expenses	40		

Johnson's Books (in Manchester)
Joint Venture wth Black and Graham

	£		£
Purchases: Materials	300	Cash: Sales	800
Cash: Carriage	90		

Graham's Books (in Glasgow)
Joint Venture with Black and Johnson

	£		£
Cash: Selling Expenses	120	Cash: Sales	1,100

Now, as things stand, each party knows only the details concerning the transactions he has recorded in his own books. Each one is unaware of (i) the amount of his share of the profit, and (ii) how much he will have to pay to, or receive from, the other parties in final settlement of the joint venture. The only way that this can be settled is for each person to take a copy of his own Joint Venture Account and to send it to the other parties. Each one will then have the account in his own books and one copy of each of the accounts in the other person's books. As this consists of all records of transactions from the start to the completion of the venture, then the profit or loss is now capable of being calculated by each party to the venture. Each person will therefore draw up a Profit and Loss Account for the venture. This will be called a Joint Venture Memorandum Account. It is a memorandum account because the account itself is not going to be incorporated into each person's double entry recording. All that will be required is an entry in each set of books to record their shares of the profits or losses.

Black, Johnson and Graham
Memorandum Joint Venture Account

	£		£
Materials	750	Sales	1,900
Wages	180		
Storage expenses	40		
Carriage	90		
Selling expenses	120		
Net Profit:			
Black (one-half)	360		
Johnson (one-third)	240		
Graham (one-sixth)	120		
	720		
	1,900		1,900

Now that each person's share of the profit is known an entry can be made. The share of the net profit on the venture will need to be credited to that person's Profit and Loss Account. The debit is to the source of the profit, the Joint Venture Account. After the entries have been made the balance on the Joint Venture Account can be carried down. If the balance carried down is a credit one then the person has received more from the joint venture than he is entitled to keep, and he will have to pay this amount to the person(s) who has received less than his entitlement, this being shown by a debit balance.

The Joint Venture Accounts now completed can be shown.

Black's Books (in London)
Joint Venture with Johnson and Graham

	£		£
Purchases: Materials	450	Balance c/d	1,030
Cash: Wages	180		
Cash: Storage expenses	40		
Share of profit transferred			
to Profit and Loss Account	360		
	1,030		1,030

	£		£
Balance b/d	1,030	Cash received in settlement:	
		From Johnson	170
		From Graham	860
	1,030		1,030

Johnson's Books (in Manchester)
Joint Venture with Black and Graham

	£		£
Purchases: Materials	300	Cash: Sales	800
Cash: Carriage	90		
Share of Profit transferred			
to Profit and Loss Account	240		
Balance c/d	170		
	800		800
Cash in settlement to Black	170	Balance b/d	170

Graham's Books (in Glasgow)
Joint Venture with Black and Johnson

	£		£
Cash: Selling expenses	120	Cash: Sales	1,100
Share of profit transferred			
to Profit and Loss Account	120		
Balance c/d	860		
	1,100		1,100
Cash in settlement to Black	860	Balance b/d	860

Exercises

Note: **Questions numbered without the suffix 'A' have answers at the back of the book.**

3.1. Ollier and Avon enter a joint venture, to share profits or losses equally, resulting from dealings in second-hand cars. Both parties take an active part in the business, each recording his own transactions. They have no joint banking account or separate set of books.

19-3
Jan 1 Ollier buys three cars for £900.
,, 31 Ollier pays for repairs and respraying of vehicles £60.
Mar 1 Avon pays garage rental £20 and advertising expenses £10.
Apr 12 Avon pays for licence and insurance renewal of vehicles, £36.
Aug 10 Avon buys a vehicle in excellent condition for £100.
,, 31 Ollier sells the four vehicles, to various clients, the sales being completed on this date, totalling £1,600.
    Show the relative accounts in the books of both partners.

3.2. Plant, Hoe & Reap entered into a joint venture for dealing in carrots. The transactions connected with this venture were:

19-1

Jan   8 Plant rented land cost £156

,,   10 Hoe supplied seeds cost £48

,,   17 Plant employed labour for planting £105

,,   19 Hoe charged motor expenses £17

,,   30 Plant employed labour for fertilizing £36

Feb 28 Plant paid the following expenses: Sundries £10, Labour £18, fertilizer a/c £29

Mar 17 Reap employed labour for lifting carrots £73

,,   30 Sale expenses London paid by Reap £39

,,   31 Reap received cash from sale proceeds gross £987.

    You are required to show the joint venture accounts in the books of Plant, Hoe & Reap. Also show in full the method of arriving at the profit on the venture which is to be apportioned: Plant seven-twelfths; Hoe three-twelfths; Reap two-twelfths.

    Any outstanding balances between the parties are settled by cheque on 30 April.

3.3A. Wild, Wood and Bine enter into a joint venture for dealing in antique brass figures. The following transactions took place:

19-4

Mar   1 Wild rented a shop, paying 3 months' rent £150

,,   2 Wood bought a motor van for £2,700

,,   4 Wood bought antiques for £650

,,   15 Bine received cash from sale proceeds of antiques £3,790

,,   28 Wild bought antiques for £1,200

Apr 11 Motor Van broke down. Bine agreed to use his own van for the job, until cessation of the joint venture, at an agreed charge of £400

,,   13 Motor van bought on May 2 was sold for £2,100. Proceeds were kept by Wild.

,,   15 Sales of antiques, cash being kept by Wood £780.

,,   18 Lighting bills paid for shop by Bine £120.

,,   30 Bine bought antiques for £440.

May 4 General expenses of shop paid for £800, Bine and Wild paying half each

,,   19 Antiques sold by Bine £990, proceeds being kept by him.

,,   31 Joint venture ended. The antiques still in stock were taken over at an agreed valuation of £2,100 by Wood.

    You are required to show the joint venture accounts in the books of each of the three parties. Show in full the workings needed to arrive at the profit on the venture. The profit or loss was to be split: Wood one-half; Wild one-third; Bine one-sixth. Any oustanding balances between the parties were settled on 31 May 19-4.

4

Consignment Accounts

A consignment of goods is the sending of them by the owner (the consignor) to his agent (the consignee) who agrees to collect, store and sell them on behalf of the owner. When the two parties are both trading in the same country it is not difficult for sales of goods consigned to an agent to be recorded in the owner's books, in the same manner as sales of goods stored in his own premises. When the owner is in this country and the agent is overseas, modern methods of communication enable the consignor to similarly record sales made on his behalf by the agent, which is, perhaps, the reason why consignment accounts are not met as frequently today. However, in the days before telecommunications and air travel it was usually too difficult for sales by the agent to be entered in the consignor's books, using separate accounts for the overseas customers, so the practice grew of allowing the agent to collect the money from the overseas customers supplied by him, deduct his expenses and commission, and remit the balance to the consignor.

Consignor's Records

The difficulty of recording individual overseas sales led to an interesting development in profit measurement long before today's advanced techniques. By drawing up consignment accounts it was possible to measure the profit or loss on each consignment thus allowing the consignor to compare the performance of different agents and to separate such profits or losses from those of his main business.

A consignment account is, in effect, a combined Trading and Profit and Loss Account related solely to the consignment. On the debit side is entered the cost of the goods, transport costs, agent's disbursements such as import duties, dock charges, warehouse rent and distribution expenses, and agent's commission, while on the credit side is entered the proceeds of sales. The difference between the two sides represents the profit or loss. If the agent completes the sales before the end of the consignor's financial year, the accounting work is simple. An example to illustrate the entries in the consignor's books can now be seen.

Exhibit 4.1

Robson, of London, whose financial year ends on 31 December, consigned goods to Boateng, his Agent in Ghana, on 16 January 19-8. Robson had purchased the goods for £500 and paid £50 on 28 February for carriage and freight to Ghana. Boateng paid £25 import duty and £30 distribution expenses. He sold the goods for £750, deducted his disbursements and his commission which was at the rate of 6 per cent of the sales, and, on 20 April 19-8, remitted the balance to Robson. Of course, Boateng's transactions were in cedis but all items were converted into £ sterling for inclusion in Robson's books.

While the student at this stage will readily follow the Consignment Account, he must not consider it in isolation. If he does not understand the other parts of the double entry he will share the unnecessary difficulty regularly experienced by students.

The first occurrence to be recorded is the separation of the £500 cost of the goods from Robson's other purchases. Even if they were bought specially for the consignment it is desirable that they should first be entered in the Purchases Account. If the goods were those normally traded in and were simply diverted to the consignment they would already be included in the purchases total, or, if they were in stock when the last Trading Account was drawn up, they would be included in the balance on Stock Account. In either event the £500 would be included eventually somewhere on the debit of the Trading Account which must therefore be credited to show the transfer of the goods from the principal trading activity. The entry on the credit side of the Trading Account would read 'Goods sent on Consignment' and the corresponding debit would be on the Consignment Account − if it were not for a practical difficulty. At the time when the Consignment Account is being entered, the Trading Account will not be set up; also there might be several consignments in the financial period for which the Trading Account will be prepared. Therefore there is need for an intermediate account to 'hold' the credit destined for the Trading Account and to permit the accumulation of a total for all consignments so that the Trading Account can be relieved of unnecessary detail. This intermediate account is called simply, 'Goods Sent on Consignments Account'. At the end of the financial year it is closed by a transfer to the Trading Account. The first entry, letter A, in Robson's books for his consignment to Ghana is therefore

Debit − Consignment to Boateng, Accra, Ghana
Credit − Goods sent on Consignments

Note that Boateng, the agent, has not been debited − the goods are still the property of Robson, and Boateng has so far incurred no financial obligation to him.

Expenses incurred by the consignor for carriage and freight, letter B, are debited to the Consignment Account and credited to the Cash Book bank columns, unless they are not paid separately, in which case the credit will be on the account of the carrier.

Robson makes no further entries until he receives a report from his agent. This is usually called an 'Account Sales' and it is shown in traditional form in Exhibit 4.2. Robson received it on 23 April and made the recording entries necessary to incorporate its contents into his books.

The sales are entered, letter C, by crediting the Consignment Account (instead of the main Trading Account) and by debiting the agent (who stands in place of the separate overseas customers).

Expenses incurred on Robson's behalf and paid by Boateng, letter D, are entered by a debit on the Consignment Account (instead of the main Profit and Loss Account) and a credit on the agent's account.

The commission due to the agent, normally by way of a percentage on sales, letter E, is debited to the Consignment Account and credited to Boateng.

The account of the agent is closed by recording, letter F, his payment of the balance due which is usually by bank transfer or bill of exchange. The bank column of the Cash Book is debited and the agent's account is credited.

Referring to the Consignment Account, it is noted that the credit side exceeds the debit by £100 which is the measure of the profit. A transfer to Profit and Loss Account would close it but, because the firm does not wish to wait until the Profit and Loss Account is prepared at the end of the accounting period, another intermediate account is needed to 'hold' the amount in the meantime. This account will also serve the purpose of combining the profits and losses of all consignments in the accounting period. To close the Consignment Account, letter G, it is debited with the £100 and 'Profit and Loss on Consignments' is credited.

Exhibit 4.1

Consignment to Boateng, Accra, Ghana

		£			£
Jan 16 (A)	Goods sent on consignments	500	Apl 23 (C) Boateng: Sales		750
Feb 28 (B)	Bank: carriage and freight	50			
Apl 23 (D)	Boateng:				
	Import duty	25			
	Distribution	30			
(E)	Commission	45			
(G)	Profit and loss on consignment	100			
		750			750

Goods sent on Consignments

	£				£
Dec 31 Trading Account	...	Apl 23 (A)	Consignment to Boateng		500

Boateng, Accra, Ghana

		£				£
Apl 23 (G)	Consignment: sales	750	Apl 23	Consignment:		
				(D)	Import duty	25
					Distribution	30
				(E)	Commission	45
				(F)	Bank	650
		750				750

Profit and Loss on Consignments

	£				£
Dec 31 Profit and loss	...	Apl 23 (G)	Consignment to Boateng		100

Exhibit 4.2

Account Sales
(Converted into £)

Boateng,
Accra,
Ghana.

Consignment of electrical goods ex M.V. Enterprise sold on behalf of Robson, London, England.

	£	£
Sales per attached schedule (not reproduced)		750
Payments:		
Import duty	25	
Distribution expenses	30	
Commission: 6 per cent of £750	45	
		100
Balance due for which sight draft enclosed		650

Accra, 2 April 19-8.   (signed) Boateng.

Consignor's Accounting Year and Incomplete Consignments

When the consignor's accounting year comes to a close and there is an incomplete consignment, the agent will be required to submit an interim report or 'Account Sales'. Two related problems arise:

1. How is the unsold stock to be valued?
2. What is the profit earned up to date?

It should be appreciated that these two are so connected that the calculation of one of them will produce the answer to the other.

Unsold stock is valued at cost unless net realizable value or replacement prices, as appropriate, is lower. Cost includes all expenditure incurred in bringing the goods to a saleable condition and location and so an appropriate part of carriage, freight, insurance and import duty can properly be included in the valuation. On the Consignment Account the stock so valued is credited above, and debited below, the line. The difference between the two sides above the line is the measure of profit earned up to date and the balance below the line is the asset, or part of it, shown in the Balance Sheet as stock on consignments. Instead of including part of the carriage, etc., in the stock figure, some might prefer to carry it forward as a prepayment but this method is not recommended. For it to be followed to its logical conclusion, any carriage inwards paid on ordinary trading stock would also need to be shown as a prepayment and this would be absurd. Care must be taken to distinguish between expenditure which can be regarded as part of the cost of unsold stock and that which refers only to goods which have been sold, e.g. selling expenses and commission.

Before working through another example which will demonstrate the points discussed, there are two terms to be explained which often feature in consignments.

The first is *del credere commission*. This is an Italian term, based on creed or faith, which refers to additional commission paid to an agent who guarantees the debts incurred by customers supplied by him. To the consignor it is a form of credit insurance.

Second is *pro forma*. In the home trade this refers to an invoice sent to a customer who is required to pay for goods before they are delivered to him. It is used when the supplier does not know the credit-worthiness of the customer. When used in the context of consignments, the term means either a value to be used for overseas customs purposes or a minimum selling price. In either case the figure is not brought into the accounts although a student might have to calculate the cost of the goods from the *pro forma* figure. For instance, a problem might use the phrase, 'invoiced *pro forma* at £1,000 being cost plus 25 per cent'. The student is properly expected to be able to calculate the cost figure of £800.

Exhibit 4.3

On 19 August 19-8 Campbell, a merchant in Glasgow, sent a consignment of 50 cases of goods to Katta, his agent in Freetown, Sierra Leone. On 26 August Campbell received Katta's acceptance of a six months' bill of exchange for £2,000 drawn by Campbell and immediately discounted it for £1,950. The goods had cost Campbell £40 per case and carriage, freight and insurance paid by him on 30 September amounted to £50. During the voyage two cases on the consignment were completely destroyed by fire and on 31 October Campbell received the appropriate compensation from the insurance company.

Campbell's accounting year ended on 31 December 19-8 and Katta sent him an interim Account Sales made up to that date. It disclosed that 28 cases had been sold for £60 each and landing charges and import duty, £192, and distribution expenses, £20, had been paid. Commission at 5 per cent on sales plus 2½ per cent *del credere* was charged.

On 15 March 19-9, Campbell received the final Account Sales showing that the remainder of the consignment had been sold for £62 per case, distribution charges, £32, had been paid, and commission was deducted. A bill of exchange was enclosed for the balance due to Campbell.

The accounts are shown in Exhibit 4.3 and the accounts sales in 4.4. Explanations are limited to those entries which are additional to those in the previous example.

The bill of exchange was drawn by the consignor by way of security and he had the choice of holding it until maturity or discounting it. That he chose the latter in order to have use of the money is not directly concerned with the consignment, and so the discount charges are best debited in the general Profit and Loss Account because the main business activities benefited.

An insurance claim will normally cover the full cost of the goods up to time of loss, but not the expected profit. In our example, the cost per case is £41 made up of original cost £40 and carriage, etc., £1.

In valuing the stock unsold at 31 December, the original cost and carriage etc., have been apportioned over 50 cases, whereas the landing charges, etc., have been related to the 48 cases landed. The distribution expenses are regarded as selling expenses.

While noting that the £274 profit up to 31 December is the balance of the Consignment Account after carrying down the value of unsold stock, it should be realized that the profit can be checked as follows:

	£	£
Sales	28 at 60	1,680
Cost per case:		
Original	40	
Carriage, etc.	1	
Landing charges, etc.	4	
	£	
	28 at 45	1,260
Distribution expenses		20
Commission		126
		1,406
Profit		274

This, of course, demonstrates the relationship between stock valuation and profit mentioned at the beginning of this section.

Exhibit 4.3

Bills Receivable

Aug 26	£ 2,000	Aug 26 Bank	£ 1,950
		Discount charges	50
	2,000		2,000

Consignment to Katta, Freetown, Sierra Leone

	Cases	£		Cases	£
Aug 19 Goods sent on			Oct 31 Bank: insurance		
consignments	50	2,000	claim	2	82
Sep 30 Bank: Carriage			Dec 31 Katta: Sales	28	1,680
freight and In-			Stock c/d	20	
surance		50	20/50 × 2,050	820	
Dec 31 Katta:			20/48 × 192	80	
Landing charges					900
and duty		192			
Distribution		20			
Commission		126			
P. & L. on con-					
signments		274			
	50	2,662		50	2,662
Jan 1 Stock b/d	20	900	Mar 15 Katta: Sales	20	1,240
Mar 15 Katta:					
Distribution		32			
Commission		93			
P. & L. on con-					
signments		215			
	20	1,240		20	1,240

Katta, Freetown, Sierra Leone

	£		£
Dec 31 Consignment: Sales	1,680	Aug 26 Bill Receivable	2,000
Balance c/d	658	Dec 31 Consignment:	
		Landing charges	
		and duty	192
		Distribution	20
		Commission	126
	2,338		2,338
Mar 15 Consignment: Sales	1,240	Jan 1 Balance b/d	658
		Mar 15 Consignment:	
		Distribution	32
		Commission	93
		Bank	457
	1,240		1,240

Exhibit 4.4

Interim Account Sales

Katta, Freetown, Sierra Leone.
Consignment of goods sold on behalf of Campbell, Glasgow.

		£	£	£
Sales	28 cases at £60 each			1,680
Payments: Landing charges and import duty at £4				
per case			192	
Distribution expenses			20	
Commission at 5 per cent		84		
at 2½ per cent *del credere*		42		
			126	
				338
				1,342
Acceptance				2,000
Balance in my favour, carried forward				658
Freetown, Sierra Leone, 31 December 19-8			(signed) Katta	

Extract from the Final Account Sales

		£	£	£
Sales	20 cases at £62			1,240
Payments: Distribution expenses			32	
Commission at 5 per cent		62		
at 2½ per cent *del credere*		31		
			93	
				125
				1,115
Balance in my favour, brought forward				658
Sight draft herewith				457

Freetown, Sierra Leone, 15 March 19-9

Consignee's Records

In considering the consignee's records of a consignment the reader should again refer to Chapter 10 of Volume I where basic concepts are described. The first two, money measurement and business entity, are especially relevant in helping to decide which aspects of the consignment should be entered.

When the agent receives the goods he is under an obligation to sell them on behalf of the owner but that obligation cannot really be measured in monetary terms. Although the original cost might be known to the agent, it does not concern him and it should not be entered in his accounts. He will, of course, need to keep a stock record of quantities held but this will be quite separate from the double entry accounts, as it is for any trader. The reader will have seen earlier that because purchases and sales of goods are entered at different price levels the Purchase and Sales Accounts do not provide a record of stock held.

The consignee's transactions usually commence when he takes possession (but not ownership) of the goods. He will probably pay landing charges and customs duties on behalf of the owner, and he will expect to be reimbursed eventually by subtracting such amounts from those received from the sales of goods. The entries are simply: debit the personal account of the consignor; credit the Bank Account. A Balance Sheet of the agent drawn up just after such a payment would include as a current asset the amount due from the consignor but would not include the stock of goods held on his behalf.

As the sales are made the debits will be either on the Cash or Bank Account, if they are cash sales; or on the personal accounts of the customers, if they are credit sales. The credits will be on the personal account of the consignor and not on the Sales Account (if any). The reader might object here and suggest that it is being inconsistent in refusing to enter the receipt of the goods, on the grounds that they are not the property of the consignee, while advocating entering the sales of them. It is submitted that each sale directly affects the agent in so far as he is obliged to account to the owner for that particular amount of money. The possibility of a bad debt not covered by *del credere commission* does not alter this for the agent is still required to take all reasonable steps to obtain payment. If the agent also sells his own goods it is clearly necessary for him to carefully distinguish between sales of them and sales of goods sent to him on consignment.

Commission earned by the consignee is debited to the consignor's Personal Account and credited to a commission account for subsequent transfer to the agent's own Profit and Loss Account.

By way of illustration, the accounts of Katta, the consignee in the second example in the previous section, are shown in Exhibit 4.5. Additional information is introduced in order to show a more complete picture. Assume that Katta sold 15 cases on credit and 2 for cash during October, 7 cases on credit in November, and 4 cases on credit in December. The landing charges and import duty were paid on 31 August and the distribution expenses on 29 December. During 19-9, 20 cases were sold on credit in February and the distribution expenses were paid on 10 March.

Exhibit 4.5

(Books of Katta)
Campbell, Glasgow, U.K.

	£		£
Aug 26 Bill Payable	2,000	Oct 31 Debtors	900
,, 31 Bank: Landing		Bank	120
charges and im-		Nov 30 Debtors	420
port duty	192	Dec 31 Debtors	240
Dec 29 Bank: Distribution		Balance c/d	658
charges	20		
,, 31 Commission	126		
	2,338		2,338
Jan 1 Balance b/d	658	Feb 28 Debtors	1,240
Feb 28 Commission	93		
Mar 10 Bank: Distribution			
charges	32		
,, 15 Bill payable	457		
	1,240		1,240

Commission

	£		£
Dec 31 P. & L. a/c	. . .	Dec 31 Campbell	126

For simplicity, the financial year of Katta has been taken as the same as Campbell's. The coincidence will not often occur in practice and the student should realize that the entries for commission can be made on a monthly basis so that the amount earned in the consignee's year can be properly included.

Exercises

Note: **Questions numbered without the suffix 'A' have answers at the back of the book.**

4.1. On 8 February 19-5 P.J., a London trader, consigned 120 cases of goods to M.B., an agent in New Zealand.

The cost of the goods was £25 a case. P.J. paid carriage to the port £147 and insurance £93.

On 31 March 19-5 P.J. received an Account Sales from M.B., showing that 100 cases had been sold for £3,500 and M.B. had paid freight, at the rate of £2 a case, and port charges amounting to £186. M.B. was entitled to a commission of 5 per cent on sales. A sight draft for the net amount due was enclosed with the Account Sales.

You are required to show the accounts for the above transactions in the ledger of P.J. and to show the transfer to Profit and Loss Account at 31 March 19-5.

(Chartered Institute of Secretaries and Administrators)

4.2. On 15 November 19-5, Hughes consigned 300 cases of wooden items to Galvez of Madrid. On 31 December 19-5, Galvez forwarded an account sales, with a draft for the balance, showing the following transactions:
1. 250 cases sold at £20 each and 50 at £18 each.
2. Port and duty charges £720.
3. Storage and carriage charges £410.
4. Commission on sales 5% + 1% *del credere.*

You are required to:
(a) prepare the Account Sales, and
(b) show the Consignment Inward Account in the books of Galvez.
    Ignore interest.

4.3A. Stone consigned goods to Rock on 1 January 19-6, their value being £12,000, and it was agreed that Rock should receive a commission of 5 per cent on gross sales. Expenses incurred by Stone for freight and insurance amount to £720. Stone's financial year ended on 31 March 19-6, and an Account Sales made up to that date was received from Rock. This showed that 70 per cent of the goods had been sold for £10,600 but that up to 31 March 19-6, only £8,600 had been received by Rock in respect of these sales. Expenses in connection with the goods consigned were shown as being £350, and it was also shown that £245 had been incurred in connection with the goods sold. With the Account Sales, Rock sent a sight draft for the balance shown to be due, and Stone incurred bank charges of £12 on 10 April 19-6, in cashing same.

Stone received a further Account Sales from Rock made up to 30 June 19-6, and this showed that the remainder of the goods had been sold for £4,800 and that £200 had been incurred by way of selling expenses. It also showed that all cash due had been received with the exception of a debt for £120 which had proved to be bad. A sight draft for the balance due was sent with the Account Sales and the bank charged Stone £9 on 1 July 19-6, for cashing same. You are required to write up the necessary accounts in Stone's books to record these transactions.

(Institute of Chartered Accountants)

5

Partnership Dissolution

Technically a partnership is dissolved whenever a new partner is admitted or a partner leaves the partnership firm; in addition there may be other reasons why the partnership can no longer be carried on, such as a court order insisting that the partnership be dissolved. Someone may cease to be a partner because of death, retirement, bankruptcy, insanity, etc. In their accepted sense, 'dissolution accounts' mean that the debts of the partnership are discharged and the assets distributed in accordance with the partnership deed or the provisions of the Partnership Act 1890. This is also the sense in which the term is used in examinations. However, the full dissolution of a partnership very rarely takes place just because of a change in partners. A full dissolution would in fact normally only take place when some disagreement between the partners that could not be settled amicably had occurred, or where the court had ordered it.

Upon a full dissolution of the partnership then, unless the partners otherwise agree, the amounts obtained from the realization of the assets plus any amounts paid in by partners to clear off debit balances on Capital or Current Accounts shall be disbursed in the following order:

1. In paying the debts and liabilities of the firm to persons who are not partners. It would in fact be an illegal act to pay any monies due to a partner before the creditors were paid, unless it was obvious that the creditors would be paid in full.

2. In paying to each partner the amount due to him in respect of advances as distinguished from capital. If the amount available is sufficient to pay (1) but not (2), then the amounts payable will be in proportion to the amount owing. For example, if there was only £3,000 left after (1) had been paid, and the advances to be repaid were £4,000 from A and £1,000 from B, then A would receive

$$\frac{£4,000}{£4,000 + £1,000} \times £3,000 = £2,400, \text{ and B would receive}$$

$$\frac{£1,000}{£4,000 + £1,000} \times £3,000 = £600.$$

3. To pay to each partner the amount finally due to him according to his Capital and Current Accounts. Any profit on realization will, subject to any agreement to the contrary, be credited to the partners' Capital Accounts in their profit- and loss-sharing ratios, while any loss will be debited in the same proportions. If a partner's final net balance on his Capital and Current Accounts is a debit balance, then he will be required to pay that amount into the partnership bank account. Should the partner not be able to meet all, or part, of such a deficiency, then the rule in *Garner* v. *Murray* will apply (see page 58) unless otherwise agreed. It should be noted that the Garner v Murray rule does not apply in Scotland.

When the business is being realized it is not necessary for all of the assets to be sold to outside parties. Very often one of more of the partners may take over some of the assets. The amount at which such assets will pass to him will be agreed to by all the partners. It is not necessary that he actually pays in an amount for them; it would be more normal for them to be charged to his Capital Account and so reduce the amount finally due to him.

The account opened to record the dissolution is the Realization Account. This is the account in which the profit or loss on realization is calculated, so that transfers can be made of the profits or losses to increase or reduce the amounts repayable to the partners, or by them, in respect of their Capital Accounts. To do this, the book values of the assets (with the exception of the cash and bank balances as these already represent 'realized' assets) are transferred to the debit of the Realization Account, while the amounts realized for them are credited to that account. As the Realization Account is nothing more than a Profit and Loss Account for a special purpose, an excess of credits over debits indicates a profit on realization, the converse represents a loss. Any costs of realizing the assets will also have been debited to the Realization Account. The profit or loss on realization will be divided between the partners in the profit- and loss-sharing ratio and will be transferred to their Capital Accounts.

It is a common failing of students to transfer the liabilities to the Realization Account. However, as realization for this purpose means 'sold' it will be obvious that liabilities are not realized, they are discharged, and it would therefore be an error of principle to show them in the Realization Account. As a matter of convenience it is often found that discounts on creditors, being a gain, are shown on the credit side of the Realization Account. They could instead be divided in the profit- and loss-sharing ratios and credited to the partners' Capital Accounts.

A fully worked example is shown in Exhibit 5.1. While every account is shown here, it would not be normal in examinations to show every account, the accounts normally shown in examinations have an (S) after the title of the account. This is because these accounts alone will demonstrate that the candidate understands the principles concerned. To show all the other accounts would only be time-consuming and would not really demonstrate the possession of any further knowledge. Of course, in real firms every account is shown.

Exhibit 5.1

On 31 December 19-8, P, Q and R decided to dissolve partnership. They had always shared profits in the ratio of P 3:Q 2:R 1.

Their goodwill was sold for £3,000, the machinery for £1,800 and the stock for £1,900. There were three motor-cars, all taken over by the partners at agreed values, P taking one for £800, Q one for £1,000 and R one for £500. The premises were taken over by R at an agreed value of £5,500. The amounts collected from debtors amounted to £2,700 after bad debts and discounts had been deducted. The creditors were discharged for £1,600, the difference being due to discounts received. The costs of dissolution amounted to £1,000.

Their last Balance Sheet is summarized as:

Balance Sheet as at 31 December 19-8

	£	£	£
Fixed Assets			
Premises			5,000
Machinery			3,000
Motor Vehicles			2,500
			10,500
Current Assets			
Stock		1,800	
Debtors	3,000		
Less Provisions for bad debts	200	2,800	
Bank		1,400	
		6,000	
Less Current Liabilities			
Creditors		1,700	4,300
			14,800
Capitals: P		6,000	
Q		5,000	
R		3,000	14,000
Current Accounts: P		200	
Q		100	
R		500	800
			14,800

The accounts recording the dissolution are now shown. A description of each entry follows the accounts. The letters (A) to (K) against each entry indicates the relevant description.

Premises

	£			£
Balance b/fwd	5,000	Realization	(B)	5,000

Machinery

	£			£
Balance b/fwd	3,000	Realization	(B)	3,000

Motor Vehicles

	£			£
Balance b/fwd	2,500	Realization	(B)	2,500

Stock

	£			£
Balance b/fwd	1,800	Realization	(B)	1,800

Debtors

	£			£
Balance b/fwd	3,000	Provisions for bad debts	(A)	200
		Realization	(B)	2,800

Realization (S)

		£			£
Assets to be realized:			Bank: Assets sold		
Premises	(B)	5,000	Goodwill	(C)	3,000
Machinery	(B)	3,000	Machinery	(C)	1,800
Motor Vehicles	(B)	2,500	Stock	(C)	1,900
Stock	(B)	1,800	Debtors	(C)	2,700
Debtors	(B)	2,800	Taken over by partners:		
Bank: Costs	(G)	1,000	P: Motor-car	(D)	800
Profit on realization:	(H)		Q: Motor-car	(D)	1,000
	£		R: Motor-car	(D)	500
P	600		R: Premises	(D)	5,500
Q	400		Creditors:		
R	200	1,200	Discounts	(F)	100
		17,300			17,300

Creditors

		£		£
Bank	(E)	1,600	Balance b/fwd	1,700
Realization (Discounts)	(F)	100		
		1,700		1,700

Bank (S)

		£			£
Balance b/fwd		1,400	Creditors	(E)	1,600
Realization: Assets sold			Realization: Costs	(G)	1,000
Goodwill	(C)	3,000	P: Capital	(K)	6,000
Machinery	(C)	1,800	Q: Capital	(K)	4,500
Stock	(C)	1,900			
Debtors	(C)	2,700			
R: Capital	(J)	2,300			
		13,100			13,100

P Capital (S)

		£			£
Realization: Motor-car	(D)	800	Balance b/fwd		6,000
Bank	(K)	6,000	Current Account transferred	(I)	200
			Realization: Share of profit	(H)	600
		6,800			6,800

Provision for Bad Debts

		£			£
Debtors	(A)	200	Balance b/fwd		200

P Current Account

		£		£
P: Capital	(I)	200	Balance b/fwd	200

Q Current Account

		£		£
Q: Capital	(I)	100	Balance b/fwd	100

Q Capital (S)

		£			£
Realization: Motor-car	(D)	1,000	Balance b/fwd		5,000
Bank	(K)	4,500	Current Account transferred	(I)	100
			Realization: Share of profit	(H)	400
		5,500			5,500

R Capital (S)

		£			£
Realization: Motor-car	(D)	500	Balance b/fwd		3,000
Realization: Premises	(D)	5,500	Current Account transferred	(I)	500
			Realization: Share of profit	(H)	200
			Bank	(J)	2,300
		6,000			6,000

R Current Account

		£		£
R: Capital	(I)	500	Balance b/fwd	500

Description of transactions:

(A) The provision accounts are transferred to the relevant asset accounts, so that the net balance on the asset accounts may be transferred to the Realization Account. Dr Provision Accounts, Cr Asset Accounts.

(B) The net book values of the assets are transferred to the Realization Account. Dr Realization Account, Cr Asset Accounts.

(C) Assets sold. Dr Bank Account, Cr Realization Account.

(D) Assets taken over by partners. Dr Partners' Capital Accounts, Cr Realization Account.

(E) Liabilities discharged. Cr Bank Account, Dr Liability Accounts.

(F) Discounts on creditors. Dr Creditors' Account, Cr Realization Account.

(G) Costs of dissolution. Cr Bank Account, Dr Realization Account.

(H) Profit or Loss split in profit/loss-sharing ratio (subject to contrary agreement). Profit – Dr Realization Account, Cr Partners' Capital Accounts. The converse if a loss.

(I) Transfer the balances on the partners' Current Accounts to their Capital Accounts.

(J) Any partner with a Capital Account in deficit, i.e. debits exceed credits, must now pay in the amount needed to cancel his indebtedness to the partnership firm. Dr Bank Account, Cr Capital Account.

(K) The credit balances on the partners' Capital Accounts can now be paid to them. Cr Bank Account, Dr Partners' Capital Accounts.

The payments made under (K) should complete the elimination of all the balances in the partnership books. It should be checked that the balance in hand at the bank, after all other payments and receipts have been made, should exactly equal the amounts to be repaid to the partners. If it does not, then an error has been made. This fact often bewilders students meeting it for the first time. The fact that it should be true is a further reiteration of the accounting equation. The steps in a partnership dissolution may be shown thus for a firm where A takes three-quarters of the profit and B takes one-quarter.

(a)   Capital   + Liabilities   = Assets
       A £3,000 + B £2,000   + Creditors £1,000   = £6,000
(b) Liabilities discharged
                   Capital = Assets
       A £3,000 + B £2,000   = (£6,000 − £1,000)   = £5,000
(c) Assets sold at a loss of £1,200
                   Capital = Assets
       A (£3,000 − ¾ loss £900) £2,100 + B (£2,000 − ¼ loss £300) £1,700
                             = (£5,000 − £1,200) £3,800 Bank

The final bank balance of £3,800 therefore exactly equals the totals of the balances on the partners' Capital Accounts. The equality of Capital + Liabilities = Assets must always hold true, and after the liabilities have been discharged, then it becomes Capital = Assets. The assets are all converted into a final bank balance, any loss on sale having been deducted not only on the assets side but also from the Capital Accounts. The final asset, i.e. the bank balance, will therefore always equal the final balances on the Capital Accounts.

The Rule in Garner v. Murray (does not apply in Scotland)

It sometimes happens that a partner's Capital Account finishes up with a debit balance. Normally the partner will pay in an amount to clear his indebtedness to the firm. However, sometimes he will be unable to pay all, or part, of such a balance. In the case of *Garner v. Murray* in 1904 (a case in England) the court ruled that, subject to any agreement to the contrary, such a deficiency was to be shared by the other partners *not* in their profit- and loss-sharing ratios but in the ratio of their 'last agreed capitals'. By 'their last agreed capitals' is meant the credit balances on their Capital Accounts in the normal Balance Sheet drawn up at the end of their last accounting period. It must be borne in mind that the balances on their Capital Accounts after the assets have been realized may be far different from those on the last Balance Sheet. Where a partnership deed is drawn up it is commonly found that agreement is made to use normal profit- and loss-sharing ratios instead, thus rendering the *Garner v. Murray* rule inoperative. The Garner v Murray rule does not apply to partnerships in Scotland.

Exhibit 5.2

After completing the realization of all the assets, in respect of which a loss of £4,200 was incurred, but before making the final payments to the partners, the Balance Sheet appears:

Balance Sheet

	£	£
Cash at bank		6,400
		6,400
Capitals: R	5,800	
S	1,400	
T	400	
	7,600	
less Q (debit balance)	1,200	6,400
		6,400

According to the last Balance Sheet drawn up before the dissolution, the partners' Capital Account credit balances were: Q £600; R £7,000; S £2,000; T £1,000; while the profits and losses were shared Q 3:R 2:S 1:T 1.

Q is unable to meet any part of his deficiency. Each of the other partners therefore suffer the deficiency as follows:

$$\frac{\text{Own capital per Balance Sheet before dissolution}}{\text{Total of all solvent partners' capitals per same Balance Sheet}} \times \text{Deficiency}$$

This can now be calculated.

$$R \quad \frac{£7,000}{£7,000 + £2,000 + £1,000} \times £1,200 = \quad £840$$

$$S \quad \frac{£2,000}{£7,000 + £2,000 + £1,000} \times £1,200 = \quad £240$$

$$T \quad \frac{£1,000}{£7,000 + £2,000 + £1,000} \times £1,200 = \quad £120$$

$$£1,200$$

When these amounts have been charged to the Capital Accounts, then the balances remaining on them will equal the amount of the bank balance. Payments may therefore be made to clear their Capital Accounts.

	Credit balance B/fwd		Share of deficiency now debited		Final credit balances
	£		£		£
R	5,800	−	840	=	4,960
S	1,400	−	240	=	1,160
T	400	−	120	=	280
Equals the bank balance					6,400

The rule has often been criticized, many parties maintaining that it would be more equitable if the normal profit- and loss-sharing ratios were used. The basic idea behind the rule is that an agreement to share profits and losses refers to those accruing from trading operations, the fact that a partner may not honour his obligations concerning capital is a risk which attaches to capital only. However, in a case such as that shown in Exhibit 5.2 it is possible, if fluctuating Capital Accounts had been used, that both R, S and T could each have started with £1,000 capital each some years ago. R allows a much greater part of his profits to remain in the business than the other partners. It would seem a strange way of rewarding him for the financing benefits which have flowed from R's behaviour tó make him suffer a more than proportionate share of Q's deficiency. The rule would act as a deterrent to a partner wishing to leave undrawn profits in the firm. The use of separate agreements to ignore the rule and of Current Accounts which are ignored for this purpose, have been the ways used by the accounting profession to circumvent the *Garner v. Murray* decision.

Piecemeal Realization of Assets

Frequently the assets may take a long time to realize. The partners will naturally want payments made to them on account as cash is received. They will not want to wait for payments until the dissolution is completed just for the convenience of the accountant. There is, however, a danger that if too much is paid to a partner, and he is unable to repay it, then the person handling the dissolution could be placed in a very invidious position.

Therefore the concept of prudence is brought into play. The view taken is to treat each receipt of sale money as being the last money receivable. Any loss then calculated is shared between the partners in their profit- and loss-sharing ratio. Should any partner's Capital Account then show a debit balance it is assumed that he will be unable to meet such a deficit, and this will be shared (subject to any contrary agreement) between the other partners using the *Garner v. Murray* rule. After payment of the liabilities and the costs of dissolution the remainder of the cash is then paid to the partners.

In this manner, even if no further money was received, or should a partner become insolvent, the division of the available cash would be strictly in accordance with the legal requirements. Exhibit 5.3 shows such a series of calculations.

Exhibit 5.3

The following is the summarized Balance Sheet of H, I, J and K as at 31 December 19-5. The partners had shared profits in the ratios H 6:I 4:J 1:K 1.

Balance Sheet as at 31 December 19-5

		£
Assets		8,400
		8,400
Capitals:		
H		600
I		3,000
J		2,000
K		1,000
Creditors		1,800
		8,400

On 1 March 19-6 some of the assets were sold for cash £5,000. Out of this the creditors £1,800 and the cost of dissolution £200 are paid, leaving £3,000 distributable to the partners.

On 1 July 19-6 some more assets are sold for £2,100. As all of the liabilities and the costs of dissolution have already been paid, then the whole of the £2,100 is available for distribution between the partners.

On 1 October 19-6 the final sale of the assets realized £1,200.

First Distribution: 1 March 19-6

	H £	I £	J £	K £
Capital balances before dissolution	600	3,000	2,000	1,000
Loss if no further assets realized – Assets £8,400 – Sale£5,000 = £3,400 + Costs £200 = £3,600 loss				
Loss shared in profit/loss ratios	1,800	1,200	300	300
	1,200 Dr	1,800 Cr	1,700 Cr	700 Cr

H's deficiency shared in *Garner v. Murray* ratios	³⁄₆ 600	²⁄₆ 400	¹⁄₆ 200
Cash paid to partners (£3,000)	1,200	1,300	500

Second Distribution: 1 July 19-6

	H £	I £	J £	K £
Capital balances before dissolution	600	3,000	2,000	1,000
Loss if no further assets realized – Assets £8,400 – Sales (£5,000 + £2,100) = £1,300 + costs £200 = £1,500 loss.				
Loss shared in profit/loss ratios	750	500	125	125
	150 Dr	2,500 Cr	1,875 Cr	875 Cr

H's deficiency shared in *Garner v. Murray* ratios		75	50	25
		2,425	1,825	850
Less first distribution already paid		1,200	1,300	500
Cash now paid to partners (£2,100)		1,225	525	350

Third and Final Distribution: 1 October
19-6

Capital balances before dissolution	600	3,000	2,000	1,000
Loss finally ascertained –				
Assets £8,400 – Sales (£5,000 + £2,100 + £1,200) = £100 + costs £200 = £300 loss.				
Loss shared in profit/loss ratios	150	100	25	25
	450 Cr	2,900 Cr	1,975 Cr	975 Cr
(No deficiency now exists on any Capital Account)				
Less first and second distributions	–	2,425	1,825	850
Cash now paid to partners (£1,200)	450	475	150	125

In any subsequent distribution following that in which all the partners have shared, i.e. no partner could then have had a deficiency left on his Capital Account, all receipts of cash are divided between the partners in their profit- and loss-sharing ratios. Following the above method would give the same answer for these subsequent distributions but obviously an immediate division in the profit- and loss-sharing ratios would be quicker. The reader is invited to try it to satisfy himself that it would work out at the same answer.

Exercises

Note: **Questions numbered without the suffix 'A' have answers at the back of the book.**

5.1. Moore and Stephens, who share profits and losses equally, decide to dissolve their partnership as at 31 March 19-1.

Their balance sheet on that date was as follows:

	£		£
Capital Account: Moore	2,000	Buildings	800
Stephens	1,500	Tools and fixtures	850
		Debtors	2,800
	3,500	Cash	1,800
Sundry creditors	2,750		
	6,250		6,250

The debtors realized £2,700, the buildings £400 and the tools and fixtures £950. The expenses of dissolution were £100 and discounts totalling £200 were received from creditors.

Prepare the accounts necessary to show the results of the realization and of the disposal of the cash.

5.2A.   *Balance Sheet of D, E and F*
as at 31 March 19-0

	£		£
		Capitals: *D*	16,000
Premises	24,000	*E*	8,000
Furniture, etc.	2,624	*F*	8,000
Stock	6,400		
Debtors	1,696		32,000
		Creditors	2,200
		Bank overdraft	520
	34,720		34,720

D, E and *F* share profits and losses in proportion to their Capitals.

The partnership is being dissolved as on 31 March 19-0.

E is continuing in business on his own account and it is agreed he shall take over the stock at a valuation of £7,200, the furniture for £2,200, and the Debtors at £1,640.

E also take over the premises. These are re-valued at £42,000. *E* secures a mortgage of £32,000 and a cheque for this amount is paid into the partnership banking account. By agreement the balance which *E* owes to the partnership is to be treated as a loan from *D* for the time being, settlement (with agreed interest) to be made within a year.

The creditors of the partnership are paid in full.

Show the entries in the ledger of the partnership to give effect to the foregoing.

5.3. Feet and Yard were in partnership sharing profits and losses: Feet three-fifths, Yard two-fifths. The following was the summarized Balance Sheet of the partnership as on 31 December 19-4:

	£	£		£	£
Capital Accounts:			Buildings, plant,		
Feet	7,516		machinery and		
Yard	4,408		equipment		8,400
		11,924	Investments		3,200
Loan: Feet	3,000		Current assets:		
Interest accrued	80		Stock	4,000	
		3,080	Debtors	3,500	
Creditors		2,500			7,500
Bank overdraft		1,596			
		19,100			19,100

1.   Feet and Yard, wishing to dissolve partnership, accepted the offer of Measures Ltd to purchase the business. The company agreed:

(i)   to take over the stock and buildings, plant, machinery, and equipment, with the exception of two motor cars whose book values were £800 and £400 respectively, and

(ii) that the consideration, £20,000, was to be satisfied by a cash payment of £11,000 and the balance by the transfer to the partners of 21,000 ordinary shares of 50p each.

2. Feet took over the first-mentioned motor-car at a valuation of £850 and Yard the other at a valuation of £350.

3. Feet's loan, together with the interest accrued thereon, was transferred to his Capital Account.

4. Cash realized on the sale of investments amounted to £2,800. The debtors realized £3,300 and the creditors were settled for £2,400.

5. Costs incurred were £150.

6. The partners agreed to divide the ordinary shares in proportion to the balances on their capital accounts after realization, settling their final balances by cash.

You are required to prepare:

(a) the Realization Account,

(b) the Bank Account, and

(c) Partners' Capital Accounts showing the final settlement between them.

(*Institute of Chartered Accountants*)

5.4. X, Y and Z have been in partnership for several years, sharing profits and losses in the ratio of 3:2:1. Their last balance sheet which was prepared on 31 October 19-1 is as follows:

Balance Sheet of X, Y and Z
as at 31 October 19-1

	£			£
Capital X	4,000	*Fixed Assets*		
Y	4,000	at cost	20,000	
Z	2,000	*less* depreciation	6,000	
	10,000			14,000
		Current Assets		
		Stock	5,000	
Current liabilities		Debtors	21,000	
Bank	13,000			26,000
Creditors	17,000			
	30,000			
	£40,000			£40,000

Despite making good profits during recent years they had become increasingly dependent on one credit customer Smithson and in order to retain his custom they had gradually increased his credit limit until he owed the partnership £18,000. It has now been discovered that Smithson is insolvent and that he is unlikely to repay any of the money owed by him to the partnership. Reluctantly X, Y and Z have agreed to dissolve the partnership on the following terms:

(i) The stock is to be sold to Nelson Ltd. for £4,000.

(ii) The fixed assets will be sold for £8,000 except for certain items with a book value of £5,000 which will be taken over by X at an agreed valuation of £7,000.

(iii) The debtors, except for Smithson, are expected to pay their accounts in full.

(iv) The costs of dissolution will be £800 and discounts received from creditors will be £500.

Z is unable to meet his liability to the partnership out of his personal funds.

Required

(a) The realisation account.

(b) The capital accounts of the partners recording the dissolution of the partnership. (*Associated Examining Board – GCE 'A' level*)

5.5A. Jerome, Harris and George were in partnership, sharing profits and losses equally. They decided to dissolve the partnership on 29 February 19-0, when the balance sheet of the partnership was as follows.

Balance Sheet

Capital Accounts		£	Fixed Assets		£
Jerome		3,000	Goodwill		10,000
Harris		2,000	Premises		10,000
George		1,000	Plant		3,000
		6,000			23,000
Current Accounts			Current Assets		
Jerome	4,000		Stock	5,000	
Harris	3,000		Debtors	1,000	
George	1,000		Bank	1,000	
		8,000			7,000
		14,000			
Creditors		16,000			
		30,000			30,000

Note: there is no partnership agreement.

The following additional information is available.

(i) Jerome has decided to continue in business and agrees to take over the premises and plant at an agreed valuation of £12,000 and the stock at £4,000.

(ii) Debtors and creditors were realised and paid, respectively, at their book values.

(iii) George has been declared a bankrupt.

(a) Prepare the ledger accounts to record the dissolution of the partnership.

(b) Discuss the decision in *Garner v Murray*.

(Joint Matriculation Board – 'A' level)

5.6A. The following trial balance has been extracted from the books of Gain and Main as at 31 March 19-2; Gain and Main are in partnership sharing profits and losses in the ratio 3 to 2:

	£	£
Capital Accounts:		
Gain		10,000
Main		5,000
Cash at Bank	1,550	
Creditors		500
Current Accounts:		
Gain		1,000
Main	2,000	
Debtors	2,000	
Depreciation: Fixtured and Fittings		1,000
Motor Vehicles		1,300
Fixtures and Fittings	2,000	
Land and Buildings	30,000	
Motor Vehicles	4,500	
Net Profit (for the year to 31 March 19-2)		26,250
Stock, at cost	3,000	
	£45,050	£45,050

In appropriating the net profit for the year, it has been agreed that Main should be entitled to a salary of £9,750. Each partner is also entitled to interest on his opening capital account balance at the rate of 10% per annum.

Gain and Main have decided to convert the partnership into a limited company, Plain Limited, as from 1 April 19-2. The company is to take over all the assets and liabilities of the partnership, except that Gain is to retain for his personal use one of the motor vehicles at an agreed transfer price of £1,000.

The purchase consideration will consist of 40,000 ordinary shares of £1 each in Plain Limited, to be divided between the partners in profit sharing ratio. Any balance on the partners current accounts is to be settled in cash.

You are required to:

Prepare the main ledger accounts of the partnership in order to close off the books as at 31 March 19-2.

(*Association of Accounting Technicians*)

5.7A. A, B and C are partners sharing profits and losses in the ratio of 2:2:1. The balance sheet of the partnership as at 30th September 19-7 was as follows:

	£		£	£
Freehold premises	18,000	Capital Accounts		
Equipment and machinery	12,000	A	22,000	
Motor cars	3,000	B	18,000	
Inventory	11,000	C	10,000	
Debtors	14,000			50,000
Bank	9,000	Loan Account – A		7,000
		Creditors		10,000
	£67,000			£67,000

The partners agreed to dispose of the business to C.N.O. Limited with effect from 1st October 19-7 under the following conditions and terms:

(i)   C.N.O. Limited will acquire the goodwill, all fixed assets and the inventory for the purchase consideration of £58,000. This consideration will include a payment of £10,000 in cash and the issue of 12,000 10 per cent Preference Shares of £1 each at par, and the balance by the issue of £1 Ordinary Shares at £1.25 per share.

(ii) The partnership business will settle amounts owing to creditors.

(iii) C.N.O. Limited will collect the debts on behalf of the vendors.

Purchase consideration payments and allotments of shares were made on 1st October 19-7.

The partnership creditors were paid off by 31st October 19-7 after the taking of cash discounts of £190.

C.N.O. Limited collected and paid over all partnership debts by 30th November 19-7 except for bad debts amounting to £800. Discounts allowed to debtors amounted to £400.

Required:

(*a*) Journal entries (including those relating to cash) necessary to close the books of the partnership, and

(*b*) Set out the basis on which the shares in C.N.O. Limited are allotted to the partners.

Ignore Interest.

(*Chartered Institute of Secretaries and Administrators*)

6

Branch Accounts

From an accounting point of view, a firm which has branches is either one which keeps all the financial accounts at the head office, or it is one where each branch maintains its own full accounting system.

1. Where the Head Office Maintains all the Accounts

The purpose behind the accounts is not merely to record transactions so that changes in assets, liabilities or capital can be calculated but also attempts wherever possible to keep a check by remote control as to whether or not the firm is being defrauded of goods or cash. For a firm with branches this is obviously of utmost importance. The managers who run the businesses are thus handling considerable amounts of money and goods, and the actual feeling of not being able to be seen continually by the head office staff may well induce the manager or his staff, into feeling that they could misappropriate large sums of cash or goods without being found out.

The solution of the problem will differ between firms. One firm with several branches which only sold expensive luxury cars could keep control easily, because the number of cars bought and sold would be relatively few, and the location of each car could be traced with very little effort. The opposite of this would be a grocery firm with hundreds of branches selling numerous different lines of goods. To keep a check on each carton of salt or bag of flour is clearly uneconomic even if it could be done, and not many customers would be happy to wait at the cashier's desk while all the reference numbers on the goods sold were recorded.

The accounting solution to this is extremely simple in its basic form. This is to translate all the transactions at the branch into selling prices. Taking a small branch as an example, and given various pieces of information, it is possible to calculate the closing stock, if wastages, breakages and pilfering by customers are ignored.

	£
Stock on hand at 1 January – at selling price	500
January – Goods sent to the Branch by the Head Office – at selling price	4,000
January – Sales by the Branch – obviously at selling price	3,800

The calculation of the closing stock becomes:

	£
Opening Stock 1 January (selling price)	500
Add Goods sent to the Branch (selling price)	4,000
Goods which the Branch had available for sale (selling price)	4,500
Less Goods Sold (selling price)	3,800
Closing Stock at 31 January should therefore be (selling price)	700

An allowance will be made for wastages, breakages and pilferages, this being based on experience. For instance, it may be normal to allow a figure of 1 per cent of goods sent to the branch to cover those items, therefore an actual stock at selling price of £700 less £40 (1 per cent of £4,000) = £660 would be tolerated. An actual stock of less than £660 would call for investigation. The allowance may well differ as between branches, for instance in Uptown the pilferage rate may be very small whereas in Lowtown there may be a high incidence of pilferages. An oil firm with branches (e.g. petrol stations) situated in many countries will obviously allow more for evaporation of petrol in hot climates than it will in cold climates. Experience and common sense are the only guides.

If a manager, or one of his staff is suspected of fraud, then the policy of the firm will dictate the action to be taken. It may involve the transfer of the manager to another branch to see whether or not the deficiencies cease at the old branch and restart at his new branch. A branch which only transfers managers when they are suspected of fraud will, of course, merely put the man on his guard. Some firms therefore transfer managers fairly frequently, but accounting needs should always be the servant of the firm and not the master.

It may well have occurred to the reader that the manager could say that the stock was a certain figure even though it was not true. For instance, a manager who has stolen £1,000 in goods or cash may try to cover this up by overstating his stock by £1,000. To counteract this many firms will carry out spot inspections of stock. This means that representatives of the firm may call at the branch without notifying the manager in advance and conduct a stocktaking. They they will compare the actual stock with the stock calculated as follows – all items being shown at selling price –

1. Stock per the branch manager at the date of the last stocktaking by the branch.
2. Add goods received by branch since the date of (1).
3. Less sales since the date of (1).

4. Less allowances for wastages, etc.
5. The stock should be equal to $(1+2)-(3+4)$.

The knowledge that such spot checks are carried out will act as a deterrent to showing false stock figures.

The head office will normally insist that all branches will bank its full cash takings each day. The money will be paid into a local bank, and special paying-in slips will be used so that the amount deposited will be transferred through the banking system into the firm's main bank account at the head office's bank. Each entry will be coded so that the head office will be able to tell quickly if a branch is not banking its takings. Cash payments made by the branch will be kept on a basis similar to the petty cash imprest system, with the head office reimbursing the amount spent at regular intervals.

(a) The Double Column System

At regular intervals, obviously at least once a year, but usually more frequently, the head office may draft a Trading and Profit and Loss Account for each branch. The Trading Account can be shown with two columns, one in which goods sent to the branch or in stock are shown at cost price, i.e. the normal basis for any business. This column is therefore part of a normal Trading Account for the branch. The other column will show all Trading Account items at selling price. This is the column where deficiencies in trading can be compared with the normal deficiency allowed for wastages, pilferages, etc.. It is not a part of the double entry recording; it is a memorandum column for control purposes only.

Exhibit 6.1

This is drafted up from the following details for a firm which sells goods at a uniform mark-up of 33⅓ per cent profit on cost price:

	£
Stock 1 Jan 19-8 (at cost)	1,200
Goods sent to the Branch during the year (at cost)	6,000
Sales (selling price)	7,428
Stock 31 Dec 19-8 (at cost)	1,500
Allowances for wastage, etc., 1 per cent of Sales	
Expenses	1,000

As the actual deficiency of £172 exceeds the amount to be tolerated, i.e. 1 per cent of £7,428 = £74 approximately, this means that an investigation will be made.

This method is suitable where all the sales are for cash, there being no sales on credit.

Branch Trading and Profit and Loss Account for the year ended 31.12.19-8

	At selling price			At selling price	
	£	£		£	£
Stock 1 Jan 19-8	1,600	1,200	Sales	7,428	7,428
Goods from Head			Deficiency		
Office	8,000	6,000	(difference)		172
	9,600	7,200			
Less Stock 31 Dec 19-8	2,000	1,500			
	7,600	5,700			
Gross Profit c/d		1,728			
	7,600	7,428		7,600	7,428
Expenses		1,000	Gross Profit b/d		1,728
Net Profit		728			
		1,728			1,728

(b) The Stock and Debtors System

Where a branch also sells goods on credit terms then further refinements are necessary to ensure that the control element applies also to debtors. This system can either be operated on the basis that the control element is built in as part of the double entry effected, or else as memoranda columns so far as the stock is concerned. The method using memoranda columns would certainly appear to have all the benefits of simplicity and ease of operation, and is the one to be preferred in practice. The fully integrated method does, however, seem to be preferred by examiners, perhaps this is because this method is indicative of the way that will be illustrated of calculating gross profits using profit margins only.

Using the following basic data, Exhibit 6.2 shows the records where the memoranda method is used, while Exhibit 6.3 shows the records where the fully integrated method is in use.

Data: A branch sells all its goods at a uniform mark-up of 50 per cent profit on cost price. Credit customers are to pay their accounts direct to the head office.

		£
First day of the period –		
Stock (at cost)	A	2,000
Debtors	B	400
During the period –		
Goods sent to the Branch (at cost)	C	7,000
Sales – Cash	D	6,000
Sales – Credit	E	4,800
Cash remitted by Debtors to Head Office	F	4,500
At the close of the last day of the period –		
Stock (at cost)	G	1,800
Debtors	H	700

The letters A to H beside the figures have been inserted in order that the entries in Exhibit 6.3 can be more easily understood. The entries for each of the above items will have the relevant letter shown beside it.

Exhibit 6.2

Memoranda Columns in Use
Branch Stock

	Selling price memo. only			Selling price memo. only	
	£	£		£	£
Stock b/fwd	3,000	2,000	Sales: Cash	6,000	6,000
Goods Sent	10,500	7,000	Credit	4,800	4,800
Gross Profit to			Stock c/d	2,700	1,800
Profit and Loss		3,600			
	13,500	12,600		13,500	12,600
Stock b/d	2,700	1,800			

Branch Debtors

	£		£
Balances b/fwd	400	Cash	4,500
Branch Stock	4,800	Balance c/d	700
	5,200		5,200
Balance b/d	700		

Goods Sent to Branches

	£		£
Transfer to Head Office		Branch Stock	7,000
Trading Account	7,000		

Cash Book

	£
Branch Stock – Cash Sales	6,000
Branch Debtors	4,500

The branch Stock Account is thus in effect a Trading Account, and is identical to the type used in the Double Column System. In addition, however, a Branch Debtors Account is in use.

The balance of the Goods Sent to Branches Account is shown as being transferred to the Head Office Trading Account. This figure is deducted from the purchases in the Head Office Trading Account, in order that goods bought for the branch can be disregarded when the gross profit earned by the head office is being calculated.

The fully integrated system introduces the idea that the gross profit earned by a firm can be calculated by reference to profit margins only. A simple example illustrates this point. Assume that a self-employed travelling salesman sells all his goods at cost price plus 25 per cent for profit. At the start of a week he has £4 stock at cost, he buys goods costing £40, he sells goods for £45 (selling price) and he has goods left in stock at the end of the week which had cost him £8. A normal Trading Account based on this data is shown below.

Trading Account for the week ended . . .

	£	£
Sales		45
Less Cost of Goods Sold:		
Opening Stock	4	
Add Purchases	40	
	44	
Less Closing Stock	8	36
Gross Profit		9

This could, however, also be shown as:

	£
Profit made when opening stock is sold	1
Profit made when purchases are sold	10
Profit made when all goods are sold	11
But he still has left unsold goods (cost £8) on which the profit still has to be realised	2
Therefore profit realised	9

This could be expressed in account form as:

Salesman's Adjustment Account

	£		£
Gross Profit	9	Unrealised Profit b/fwd	1
Unrealised Profit c/d	2	Goods Bought	10
	11		11

The fully integrated system uses a form of adjustment account. Goods sent to the branch are shown at cost price in an account for that purpose, while the Branch Stock Account is shown at selling price. To show one entry at selling price and the other at cost would mean that debit amounts would not equal credit amounts, thus violating double entry principles. To rectify this a Branch Adjustment Account is opened and the profit loading on the goods is recorded to preserve the equality of amounts of debit and credit entries. The Branch Stock Account by being entirely concerned with selling prices acts as a control upon stock deficiencies, while the Branch Adjustment Account shows the amount of gross profit earned during the period. In the example seen worked out in Exhibit 6.3 a stock deficiency does not exist. The action required when such a deficiency arises is demonstrated later in this chapter.

Exhibit 6.3

Branch Stock (Selling Price)

		£			£
Balance b/fwd	A	3,000	Sales: Cash	D	6,000
Goods sent to Branch	C	10,500	Credit	E	4,800
			Balance c/d	G	2,700
		13,500			13,500
Balance b/d	G	2,700			

Branch Debtors (Selling Price)

		£			£
Balances b/fwd	B	400	Cash	F	4,500
Branch Stock	E	4,800	Balances c/d	H	700
		5,200			5,200
Balances b/d	H	700			

Goods Sent to Branches (Cost Price)

	£			£
Transfer to Head Office Trading Account	7,000	Branch Stock	C	7,000

Branch Adjustment (Profit Loading)

	£			£
Gross Profit to Profit		Unrealised Profit		
and Loss	3,600	b/fwd	A	1,000
Unrealised Profit c/d	G 900	Branch Stock –		
		goods sent	C	3,500
	4,500			4,500
		Unrealised Profit b/d	G	900

The opening and closing stocks are shown in the Branch Stock Account at selling price. However, the Balance Sheet should show the stock at cost price (if for simplicity the fact that the net realisable value etc., may be lower than cost can be ignored). The previous Balance Sheet should therefore have shown stock at cost £2,000. This is achieved by having a compensating £1,000 credit balance brought forward in the Branch Adjustment Account, so that the debit balance of £3,000 in the Branch Stock Account, when it comes to being shown in the Balance Sheet, has the £1,000 credit balance deducted to show a net figure of £2,000. Similarly, at the close of the period the balance sheet will show stock at £1,800 (Branch Stock debit balance £2,700 less Branch Adjustment credit balance £900).

The Fully Integrated System – Further Considerations

(*a*) *Returns*. Goods may be returned –

(i) From the branch stock to the head office.
(ii) From the branch debtors to the branch stock.
(iii) From the branch debtors to the head office.

To show the entries needed look at a firm which sells goods at cost plus 25 per cent profit, and according to the categories stated the following goods were returned, all prices shown being selling prices: (i) £45, (ii) £75, (iii) £15. The entries needed are:

Branch Stock (Selling Price)

		£				£
Returns from Debtors	(ii)	75	Returned to Head Office	(i)		45

Branch Adjustment (Profit Loading)

		£
Returns from Branch	(i)	9
Returns from Debtors	(iii)	3

Goods Sent to Branches (Cost Price)

		£
Returns from Branch	(i)	36
Returns from Debtors	(iii)	12

Branch Debtors (Selling Price)

		£
Returns to Branch	(ii)	75
Returns to Head Office	(iii)	15

Entries (ii) both being in accounts shown at selling price were two in number, i.e. £75 Dr and £75 Cr Entries (i) and (iii) each needed entries in three accounts, (i) being £45 Cr and £9 Dr and £36 Dr, (iii) being £15 Cr and £12 Dr and £3 Dr.

(b) Different Physical and Book Stock Figures

It has been assumed so far that the stock figures according to the accounts have been exactly the same as the actual stocks on hand. This will rarely be true, as there are almost bound to be errors made in selling prices, giving wrong change in cash sales, breakages, wastages, pilferages, or it could perhaps be that   ds have been sold at a different profit mark-up from that which is normal in the business.

The stock to be carried forward in the Branch Stock Account is, however, the selling price of the actual stock on hand. The difference between the actual stock and the unadjusted balance on the stock account will normally be a deficiency of stock. The converse would only apply where goods had been sold at higher than normal profit mark-up. A deficiency of stock is entered by crediting the difference to the Branch Stock Account and debiting a similar amount to the Branch Adjustment Account. The converse applies to an excess of stock.

To understand why this should be so, a firm's accounts can be seen where a deficiency of stock exists.

Exhibit 6.4

A firm with one branch has a uniform mark-up of 50 per cent. The following details are known:

	£
Opening Stock − at selling price	1,800
Goods sent to the Branch − at selling price	6,000
Sales by the Branch − at selling price	6,300
Closing Stock − per actual stocktaking − at selling price	1,350

Branch Stock (Selling Price)

	£		£
Balance b/fwd	1,800	Sales	6,300
Goods sent to Branch	6,000	Deficiency (difference	
		between the two sides	
		of the account)	150
		Balance c/d	1,350
	7,800		7,800
Balance b/d	1,350		

Branch Adjustment (Profit Loading)

	£		£
Branch Stock (deficiency)	150	Unrealised Profit in	
		Opening Stock b/fwd	600
Gross Profit to Profit and		Goods sent to Branch	2,000
Loss	2,000		
Unrealised Profit in Closing			
Stock c/d	450		
	2,600		2,600
		Unrealised Profit in Stock	
		b/d	450

Suppose an ordinary Trading Account had been drafted, it would have appeared:

Trading Account for the Period . . .

	£	
Sales		6,300
Less Cost of Goods Sold:		
Opening Stock	1,200	
Add Goods from Head Office	4,000	
	5,200	
Less Closing Stock	900	4,300
Gross Profit		2,000

Thus the profit calculated by the normal method and the Branch Adjustment method remains the same. The fact that the Adjustment Account is charged with the full selling price of the stock deficiency is because the gross profit part of the deficiency, £50, had already been taken into account in the £2,000 credited to the Adjustment Account, as it has not been realised it must be cancelled. In addition, the cost of the stock deficiency, £100, is a charge when calculating the gross profit, e.g. goods breakages mean less gross profit.

Missing Figures

It is the common practice of many examiners to omit certain figures when giving details for questions using the Stock and Debtors system. The student is entitled in such a case to assume that where one figure is missing in an account, then that figure may be taken to be the difference between the totals of the two sides.

2. *Where Each Branch Maintains Full Accounting Records*

This would very rarely be found in a firm with many branches, it is more common in a firm with just one or two or a few branches, and is particularly relevant where the branch is large enough to warrant a separate accounting staff being employed.

A branch cannot operate on its own without resources, and it is the firm that provides these in the first instance. The firm will want to know how much money it has invested in each branch, and from this arises the concept of Branch and Head Office Current Accounts. The relationship between the branch and the head office is seen as that of a debtor/creditor identity. The current accounts are medias where the branch is shown as a debtor in the head office records, while the head office is shown as a creditor in the branch records. This is purely for expediency, because as the branch and the head office both belong to the same firm it is apparent that a firm cannot owe money to itself.

The current accounts are used for those transactions that are concerned with supplying resources to the branch or in retrieving resources. For such transactions full double entry records are needed both in the branch records and also in the head office records, i.e. each item will be recorded twice in each set of records. Some transactions will, however, concern the branch only, and these will merely need two entries in the branch records and none in the head office records. Exhibit 6.5 shows several transactions and the records needed.

Exhibit 6.5

A firm with its head office in London opened a branch in Manchester. The following transactions took place in the first month:

A   Opened a bank account at Manchester by transferring £1,000 from the London bank account.

B   Bought premises in Manchester, paying by cheque drawn on the London bank account, £5,000.

C   Manchester bought a motor van, paying by cheque £600 from its own bank account.

D   Manchester bought fixtures on credit from A. B. Equipment Ltd, £900.

E   London supplied a machine valued at £250 from its own machinery.

F   Manchester bought goods from suppliers, paying by cheque on its own account, £270.

G   Manchester's cash sales banked immediately in its own bank account, £3,000.
H   Goods invoiced at cost to Manchester during the month by London (no cash or cheques being paid specifically for these goods by Manchester), £2,800.
I   A cheque is paid to London by Manchester as general return of funds, £1,800.
J   Goods returned to London by Manchester – at cost price, £100.

The exact dates have been deliberately omitted. It will be seen later that complications arise because of differences in the times of transactions. Each transaction has been identified by a capital letter. The relevant letter will be shown against each entry in the accounts.

Head Office Records (in London)
Manchester Branch Current Account

		£			£
Bank	A	1,000	Bank	I	1,800
Bank – Premises	B	5,000	Returns from Branch	J	100
Machinery	E	250			
Goods sent to Branch	H	2,800			

Bank

		£			£
Manchester Branch	I	1,800	Manchester Branch	A	1,000
			Manchester Premises	B	5,000

Machinery

					£
			Manchester Branch	E	250

Goods Sent to Branch

		£			£
Returns from Branch	J	100	Manchester Branch	H	2,800

Branch Records (in Manchester)
Head Office Current Account

		£			£
Returns	J	100	Bank	A	1,000
Bank	I	1,800	Premises	B	5,000
			Machinery	E	250
			Goods from Head Office	H	2,800

Bank

		£			£
Head Office	A	1,000	Motor Van	C	600
Cash Sales	G	3,000	Purchases	F	270
			Head Office	I	1,800

Premises

		£
Head Office	B	5,000

Motor Van

		£
Bank	C	600

Fixtures

		£
A.B. Equipment Ltd.	D	900

A.B. Equipment Ltd.

		£
Fixtures	D	900

Machinery

		£
Head Office	E	250

Purchases

		£
Bank	F	270

Sales

		£
Bank	G	3,000

Goods from Head Office

		£			£
Head Office	H	2,800	Head Office – returns	J	100

It can be seen that items, C, D, F and G are entered only in the Manchester records. This is because these items are purely internal transactions and are not concerned with resources flowing between London and Manchester.

Profit or Loss and Current Accounts

The profit earned by the branch (or loss incurred by it) does not belong to the branch. It belongs to the firm and must therefore be shown as such. The head office represents the central authority of the firm and profit of the branch should be credited to the Head Office Current Account, any loss being debited.

The branch will therefore draw up its own Trading and Profit and Loss Account. After agreement with the head office the net profit will then be transferred to the credit of the Head Office Current Account. The head office in its own records will then debit the Branch Current Account and credit its own Profit and Loss Account. Taking the net profit earned in Exhibit 6.5 as £700, the two sets of books would appear thus:

Head Office Records (in London)
London Profit and Loss Account

	£
Net Profit earned by the Manchester Branch	700

Manchester Branch Current Account

	£		£
Bank	1,000	Bank	1,800
Bank: Premises	5,000	Returns from Branch	100
Machinery	250		
Goods sent to Branch	2,800		
Net profit to main Profit and Loss Account	700	Balance c/d	7,850
	9,750		9,750
Balance b/d	7,850		

Branch Records (in Manchester)
Manchester Profit and Loss Account

	£
Net Profit carried to the Head Office Current Account	700

Head Office Current Account

	£		£
Returns to Head Office	100	Bank	1,000
Bank	1,800	Premises	5,000
		Machinery	250
		Goods from Head Office	2,800
Balance c/d	7,850	Profit and Loss Account	700
	9,750		9,750
		Balance b/d	7,850

The Combined Balance Sheet

After the Trading and Profit and Loss Accounts have been drawn up a Balance Sheet is required for the whole firm. The branch will send its trial balance to the head office which will add the assets in its own trial balance to those in the branch trial balance to give the total for each type of asset to be shown in the Balance Sheet, and a similar procedure will be carried out for the liabilities.

In the trial balances the Head Office Current Accounts will be a debit balance while the Branch Current Accounts will be a credit balance, e.g. the two figures of £7,850 in the London and Manchester books. These therefore cancel out and are not shown in the combined Balance Sheet. This is in order, as the two balances do not in fact represent assets or liabilities, but are merely a measure of the resources at the branch.

Items in Transit

It was stated earlier that the timing of transactions raised complications. Obviously a cheque sent by a Manchester branch one day would probably arrive in London the next day, while goods sent from London to Manchester, or returned from Manchester to London, could well take longer than that. Both the head office and the branch will have entered the transactions at the dates of remittance or receipt, and as the remittance from one place will occur on one day and the receipt occur at the other place on another day, then where items are in transit at the end of a financial period each set of records will not contain identical figures. This will mean that the balances on the current accounts will not be equal to one another.

It is, however, necessary to have identical amounts of balances on the current accounts so that they will cancel out when the combined Balance Sheet is prepared. As the two sets of records contain some figures which are different from each other they must somehow be reconciled so that the balances carried down are the same. Which set of figures are to be altered? The answer is one of expediency. It would be normal to find the most experienced accountants at the head office, and therefore the amendments should all be made in the head office books, instead of leaving it to junior accountants at the branches who would be more likely to make mistakes. Also if there are several branches the problems of communicating specific instructions to several accountants some distance away make it easier for all amendments to be made at the head office.

Exhibit 6.6 is for a second month of the business shown in Exhibit 6.5. However, whereas there were no items in transit at the end of the first month, this does not hold true at the conclusion of the second month.

Exhibit 6.6

Head Office Records (showing current accounts only)

	£
Goods sent to Branch	3,700
Cheques received from Branch	2,950
Returns received from Branch	440

Branch Records

	£
Goods received from Head Office	3,500
Cheques sent to Head Office	3,030
Returns sent to Head Office	500

It may be assumed that the net profit as shown by the Profit and Loss Account of the branch is £800.

Branch Records (in Manchester)
Head Office Current Account

	£		£
Bank	3,030	Balance b/fwd	7,850
Returns to Head Office	500	Goods from Head Office	3,500
Balance c/d	8,620	Net Profit	800
	12,150		12,150
		Balance b/d	8,620

Head Office Records (in London)
Manchester Branch Current Account

	£			£
Balance b/fwd	7,850	Bank	B	2,950
Goods sent to Branch	A 3,700	Returns received	C	440
Net Profit	800			

At this point the following items are observed to be in transit at the end of the period (these should be confirmed to ensure that they are not merely errors in accounting records):

1. Goods sent to the branch amounting to £200 (£3,700 − £3,500).
2. Cheques sent by the branch amounting to £80 (£3,030 − £2,950).
3. Returns from the branch amounting to £60 (£500 − £440).

(A) needs amending to £3,500. This is done by crediting the account with £200.

(B) needs amending to £3,030. This is done by crediting the account with £80.

(C) needs amending to £500. This is done by crediting the account with £60.

As these are items in transit they need to be taken to the period in which they arrive, i.e. the next month. This is effected by carrying them down as balances into the next period. The Branch Current Account will now be completed.

It may appear at first sight to be rather strange that all the items in transit are shown as debit balances. However, it must be appreciated that goods (including returns) and money in transit are assets of the firm at the end of a financial period. That they are in transit is merely stipulating that the assets are neither at the head office nor at the branch but are somewhere else. Assets are always shown as debit balances and there is no reason why it should be different just because they have not reached their destination on a certain date.

Manchester Branch Current Account

	£		£
Balance b/fwd	7,850	Bank	2,950
Goods sent to Branch	3,700	Returns Received	440
Net Profit	800	Goods in Transit c/d	200
		Cheques in Transit c/d	80
		Returns in Transit c/d	60
		Balance c/d	8,620
	12,350		12,350
Balance b/d	8,620		
Goods in Transit b/d	200		
Cheques in Transit b/d	80		
Returns in Transit b/d	60		

All of these four balances are shown in the trial balance. When the combined Balance Sheet is being prepared the balance of the two current accounts, i.e. in this case £8,620, will cancel out as it is a debit balance in one trial balance and a credit balance in the other. The goods in transit £200 and the returns in transit £60, both being goods, are added to the stock in the Balance Sheet. This is because stock is made up of the following items:

At the end of the second month:

	£
Stock at London	
Add Stock at Manchester	
Add Stocks in Transit (£200 + £60)	260
Total Stock	

Similarly, the balance for cheques or remittances in transit is added to the bank balances at London and Manchester.

	£
Bank Balance at London	
Add Bank Balance in Manchester	
Add Remittances in Transit	80

This is rather like a man who has £14 in one pocket and £3 in another. He takes a £5 note from the pocket containing the larger amount and is transferring it to his other pocket when someone asks him to stay perfectly still and calculate the total cash in his possession. He therefore has:

	£
Pocket 1	9
Pocket 2	3
Cash in Transit	5
Total Cash	17

Exhibit 6.7

Trial Balances as at 29 February 19-8

	Lodon Head Office		Manchester Branch	
	Dr	Cr	Dr	Cr
	£	£	£	£
Premises	10,000		5,000	
Machinery	2,000		400	
Fixtures	3,100		1,400	
Motor Vans	1,500		900	
Closing Stock	3,800		700	
Debtors	1,100		800	
Bank	12,200		600	
Head Office Current Account				8,620
Branch Current Account	8,620			
Goods in Transit	200			
Cheques in Transit	80			
Returns in Transit	60			
Creditors		1,300		1,180
Capital Account as at 1 Jan 19-8		37,860		
Net Profit for the two months (Branch £1,500 + Head Office £2,000)		3,500		
	42,660	42,660	9,800	9,800

Using the figures already given in Exhibit 6.6, but adding some further information, trial balances for London Head Office and the

Manchester Branch are now shown in Exhibit 6.7 after the Profit and Loss accounts have been drawn up for the second month.

The combined Balance Sheet can now be drawn up.

Balance Sheet as at 29 February 19-8

	£	£
Fixed Assets		
Premises		15,000
Machinery		2,400
Fixtures		4,500
Motor Vans		2,400
		24,300
Current Assets		
Stocks	4,760	
Debtors	1,900	
Bank	12,880	
	19,540	
Less Current Liabilities		
Creditors	2,480	
Working Capital		17,060
		41,360
Capital		
Balance at 1 January 19-8		37,860
Add Net Profit:		
London		2,000
Manchester		1,500
		41,360

Notes:

	£		£
Stocks: London	3,800	Bank: London	12,200
Manchester	700	London	600
In Transit		In Transit	80
(£200 + £60)	260		
	4,760		12,880

Foreign Branch Accounts

The treatment of the accounts of foreign branches is subject to only one exception from that of branches in your own county. This is concerned with the fact that when the trial balance is drawn up by the branch then this will be stated in a foreign currency. To amalgamate these figures with your own country's figures will mean that the foreign branch figures will have to be translated into your currency.

There are rules for general guidance as to how this can be done. SSAP 20: Foreign Currency Translation: gives rules for organisations to follow. These are the ones which will be shown.

The amount of a particular currency which one can obtain for another currency is known as the exchange rate. Taking an imaginary country with a currency called chips, there might be a general agreement that the exchange rate should stay about 5 chips to equal £1. At certain times the exchange rate will exactly equal that figure, but due to all sorts of economic reasons it may well be 5.02 chips to £1 on one day and 4.97 chips to £1 several days later. In addition, some years ago there may have been an act of devaluation by one of the countries involved; the exchange rate could well have then been 3 chips to £1. To understand more about exchange rates and devaluation the reader of this book would be well advised to read a relevant economics textbook.

It is clear, however, that all items in the trial balance should not be converted to your currency on the basis of the exchange rate ruling at the date of the trial balance. The rules in SSAP 20 have been devised in an attempt to bring about conversion into your currency so as not to distort reported trading results.

Now for the rules:

1. (a) Fixed assets at the exchange rate ruling when the assets were bought. If fixed assets have been bought on different dates, then different rates will have to be used for each separate purchase.

   (b) Depreciation on the fixed assets at the same rate as the fixed assets concerned.

2. Current assets and current liabilities – at the rate ruling at the date of the trial balance.

3. Opening stock in the Trading Account – at the rate ruling at the previous Balance Sheet date.

4. Goods sent by the head office to the branch, or returns from the branch – at the actual figures shown in the Goods sent to Branches Account in the head office books.

5. Trading and Profit and Loss Account items, other than depreciation, opening and closing stocks, or goods sent to or returned by the branch – at the average rate for the period covered by the accounts.

6. The Head Office Current Account – at the same figures as shown in the Branch Current Account in the head office books.

When the conversion of the figures into your currency is completed, the totals of the debit and credit sides of your currency trial balance will not normally be equal to one another. This is due to different exchange rates being taken for conversion purposes. A balancing figure will therefore be needed to bring about the equality of the totals. For this purpose a Difference on Exchange Account will be opened and a debit entry made therein if the lesser total is on the debit side of the credit side. When the head office redrafts the Profit and Loss Account any debit balance on the Difference on Exchange Account should be transferred to it as an expense. A credit balance on the Difference on Exchange Account should be transferred to the credit of the Profit and Loss Account as a gain.

In consolidated accounts, Chapter 27 onwards, special rules are applied for foreign exchange conversion. This will be dealt with in the relevant chapters.

Exhibit 6.8

An example of the conversion of a trial balance into British currency is now shown. The branch is in Flavia, and the unit of currency is the Flavian dollar. The exchange rates needed are:

(a) On 1 January 19-3, 10 dollars = £1
(b) On 1 January 19-5, 11 dollars = £1
(c) On 1 January 19-8, 17 dollars = £1
(d) On 31 December 19-8, 15 dollars = £1
(e) If no further information were given the average rate for 19-8 would have to be taken as (c) + (d) ÷ 2, i.e. 16 dollars = £1. This is not an advisable procedure in practice, the fact that the average has been calculated from only two readings could mean that the average calculated might be far different from a more accurate one calculated from a larger number of readings.

Trial Balance as on 31 December 19-8

	Dr (dol.)	Cr (dol.)	Exchange rates	Dr £	Cr £
Fixed Assets:					
Bought 1 Jan 19-3	10,000		10 = £1	1,000	
Bought 1 Jan 19-5	8,800		11 = £1	800	
Stock 1 Jan 19-8	6,800		17 = £1	400	
Expense Accounts	8,000		16 = £1	500	
Sales		32,000	16 = £1		2,000
Goods from Head Office	21,900		£ per account in Head Office books	1,490	
Head Office Current Account		43,000	£ per account in Head Office books		3,380
Debtors	9,000		15 = £1	600	
Creditors		4,500	15 = £1		300
Bank	15,000		15 = £1	1,000	
	79,500	79,500		5,790	5,680
Difference on Exchange Account					110
				5,790	5,790

The stock at 31 December 19-8 is 12,000 dollars. When the Trading Account is drawn up this will be converted at 15 dollars = £1, i.e. £800.

88

Exercises

Note: **Questions numbered without the suffix 'A' have answers at the back of the book.**

6.1. Octopus Ltd, whose head office is at Cardiff, operates a branch at Swansea. All goods are purchased by head office and invoiced to and sold by the branch at cost plus 33⅓ per cent.

Other than a sales ledger kept at Swansea, all transactions are recorded in the books at Cardiff.

The following particulars are given of the transactions at the branch during the year ended 28 February 19-7:

	£
Stock on Hand, 1 March 19-6, at invoice price	4,400
Debtors on 1 March 19-6	3,946
Stock on Hand, 28 February 19-7, at invoice price	3,948
Goods sent from Cardiff during the year at invoice price	24,800
Credit Sales	21,000
Cash Sales	2,400
Returns to Head Office at invoice price	1,000
Invoice value of goods stolen	600
Bad Debts written off	148
Cash from Debtors	22,400
Normal loss at invoice price due to wastage	100
Cash Discount allowed to Debtors	428

You are required to write up the Branch Stock Account and Branch Total Debtors Account for the year ended 28 February 19-7, as they would appear in the head office books.

(Institute of Chartered Accountants)

6.2. A Co Ltd has a branch in Everton at which a full set of books are kept. At the end of the year the following is a summary of the transactions between the branch and the head office as recorded in the latter's books:

	£
Balance due from Branch 1 January	20,160
Cash received from Branch	30,000
Goods supplied to Branch	23,160
Goods returned by Branch	400
Expenses paid on behalf of Branch	6,000

At 30 June the branch Profit and Loss Account showed a net profit of £3,500.

(a) Show the above items as they would appear in the ledger of the head office.

(b) How can any resulting balance from these figures be proved, and what does it indicate?

6.3. Stone and Millington are in partnership as retailers of books. Stone manages the head office where new books are sold and Millington manages a branch that sells second-hand books. All books are purchased by the head office and second-hand books are invoiced to the branch at cost plus 25%. The partnership agreement allows for interest on capital accounts at 10% per annum and each partner receives a commission of 15% of the net profits of his shop. This remaining profits or losses are shared equally.

The trial balances as at 31 December 19-1 were as follows.

	Head Office		Branch	
	£	£	£	£
Capital accounts		11,000		11,000
Drawings	8,000		8,000	
Fixtures – net book value	10,000		12,000	
Stock at cost 31 December 19-0	4,000			
Stock at invoiced value 31 December 19-0			6,000	
Sales		60,000		40,000
Purchases	50,000			
Goods sent to branch at invoiced value		20,000	18,000	
Branch and head office current account	3,000			1,000
Salaries	3,500		2,500	
Rent	7,500		4,500	
Administration	6,000		–	
Provision for unrealised profit		1,200		
Creditors		800		1,000
Bank	1,000		2,000	
	93,000	93,000	53,000	53,000

The following additional information is available.

(i) Stock at 31 December 19-1 (excluding goods in transit) amounted to: head office (cost) £5,000 and branch (invoiced value) £7,000.

(ii) The fixtures and fittings for both the head office and the branch are to be depreciated at 20% per annum on the reducing balance method.

(iii) On 31 December 19-1 the head office sent to the branch books at invoiced value of £2,000 which were not recorded in the books of the branch until 3 January 19-2.

Any adjustments necessary are to be made in the head office books.

Prepare trading, profit and loss accounts, in columnar format, for the head office, branch and combined head office and branch for the year ended 31 December 19-1 and the appropriation account for that year. Prepare the balance sheet as at 31 December 19-1.

(Joint Matriculation Board 'A' level)

6.4. Packer and Stringer were in partnership as retail traders sharing profits and losses: Packer three-quarters, Stringer one-quarter. The partners were credited annually with interest at the rate of 6 per cent per annum on their fixed capitals; no interest was charged on their drawings.

Stringer was responsible for the buying department of the business. Packer managed the head office and Paper was employed as the branch manager. Packer and Paper were each entitled to a commission of 10 per cent of the net profits (after charging such commission) of the shop managed by him.

All goods were purchased by head office and goods sent to the branch were invoiced at cost.

The following was the trial balance as on 31 December 19-4:

	Head office books		Branch books	
	Dr	Cr	Dr	Cr
	£	£	£	£
Drawings Accounts and Fixed Capital Accounts:				
Packer	2,500	14,000		
Stringer	1,200	4,000		
Furniture and Fittings, at cost	1,500		1,100	
Furniture and Fittings, provision for depreciation as on 31 December 19-3		500		350
Stock on 31 December 19-3	13,000		4,400	
Purchases	37,000			
Goods sent to Branches		18,000	17,200	
Sales		39,000		26,000
Provision for doubtful debts		600		200
Branch and Head Office Current Accounts	6,800			3,600
Salaries and Wages	4,500		3,200	
Paper, on account of commission			240	
Carriage and Travelling Expenses	2,200		960	
Admininstrative Expenses	2,400			
Trade and General Expenses	3,200		1,800	
Sundry Debtors	7,000		3,000	
Sundry Creditors		5,800		400
Bank Balances	600			1,350
	81,900	81,900	31,900	31,900

You are given the following additional information:
(i) Stocks on 31 December 19-4, amounted to: head office £14,440, branch £6,570.
(ii) Administrative expenses are to be apportioned between head office and the branch in proportion to sales.
(iii) Depreciation is to be provided on furniture and fittings at 10 per cent of cost.
(iv) The provision for doubtful debts is to be increased by £50 in respect of head office debtors and decreased by £20 in the case of those of the branch.

(v) On 31 December 19-4 cash amounting to £2,400, in transit from the branch to head office, has been recorded in the branch books but not in those of head office, and on that date goods invoiced at £800, in transit from head office to the branch, had been recorded in the head office books but not in the branch books.

Any adjustments necessary are to be made in the head office books.
You are required to:

(a) prepare Trading and Profit and Loss Accounts and the Appropriation Account for the year ended 31 December 19-4, showing the net profit of the head office and branch respectively.

(b) prepare the Balance Sheet as on that date, and

(c) show the closing entries in the Branch Current Accounts giving the make-up of the closing balance.

Income tax is to be ignored.

(*Institute of Chartered Accountants*)

6.5A. Norsea Ltd has a head office in Hull, and operates a branch in Grimsby.

All purchases are made by the head office and goods for the branch are invoiced at selling price, being cost price plus 50 per cent.

On 30 April 19-8 stock of goods at the branch, at selling price, amounted to £4,020 and debtors £1,652.

During the year ended 30 April 19-9 the following transactions took place at the branch:

	£
Cash sales	25,200
Credit sales	18,000
Cash discounts allowed to debtors	452
Cash received from debtors	17,156
Debts written off as bad	149
Goods received by the branch at selling price	45,000
Goods returned to head office at selling price	420

On 30 April 19-9 stock of goods at the branch, at selling price, amounted to £5,250.

You are required to write up the ledger accounts in the head office books to record the above transactions, and compute the branch gross profit for the year ended 30 April 19-9.

(*Institute of Chartered Accountants*)

6.6A. Stainless Ltd operates from a head office in London and a branch at Leeds where separate books are kept. The company makes up its accounts to 31 December in each year.

Goods sent to the branch by head office are charged at cost plus 10 per cent. Other than the sales to branch, head office sales are made at a uniform gross profit of 25 per cent on selling price. Leeds sales are all made at a uniform gross profit to the branch of 20 per cent on selling price.

You are given the following relevant information regarding the year ended 31 December 19-7:

1. Expenses paid during the year:

	London	Leeds
Wages	6,415	2,418
Selling expenses	4,220	1,610
Overhead expenses	2,991	2,021

2. Overhead expenses accrued:

31 December 19-6	249	156
31 December 19-7	416	82

3. Purchases at head office totalled £97,680, and sales, included £44,000 invoiced to Leeds branch, were £119,000.

4. In addition to goods received from head office the Leeds branch had purchased goods from outside suppliers amounting to £9,200. On 31 December 19-7, there were goods in transit from head office at an invoice price of £3,400 which were not received by the branch until 3 January 19-8.

5. Sales at Leeds were £60,000 and discounts allowed to customers during the year amounted to £910.

6. The stocks on hand on 31 December 19-6 had been £17,250 at London and £7,500 at Leeds, being cost to the branch. The stock at Leeds included stock invoiced by head office at £5,600. On 31 December 19-7, the stock at Leeds contained stock invoiced by head office amounting to £7,700.

You are required to prepare, in columnar form, the head office, branch and combined Trading and Profit and Loss Accounts for the year ended 31 December 19-7.

(Institute of Chartered Accountants)

6.7A. L. R., a trader, commenced business on 1 January 19-9, with a head office and one branch.

All goods were purchased by the head office and goods sent to the branch were invoiced at a fixed selling price of 25 per cent above cost. All sales, both by the head office and the branch, were made at the fixed selling price.

The following trial balance was extracted from the books at the head office at 31 December 19-9.

	£	£
Capital		52,000
Drawings	1,740	
Purchases	123,380	
Sales		83,550
Goods sent to branch (at selling price)		56,250
Branch current account	24,550	
Fixed assets	33,000	
Debtors and creditors	7,980	11,060
General expenses	8,470	
Balance at bank	3,740	
	202,860	202,860

No entries had been made in the head office books for cash in transit from the branch to head office at 31 December 19-9, £1,000.

When the balances shown below were extracted from the branch books at 31 December 19-9, no entries had been made in the books of the branch for goods in transit on that date from head office to branch, £920 (selling price).

In addition to the balances which can be deduced from the information given above, the following balances appeared in the branch books on 31 December 19-9:

	£
Fixed assets	6,000
General expenses	6,070
Debtors	7,040
Creditors (excluding head office)	1,630
Sales	51,700
Balance at Bank	1,520

When stock was taken on 31 December 19-9, it was found that there was no shortage at the head office, but at the branch there were shortages amounting to £300, at selling price.

You are required to prepare trading and profit and loss accounts (i) for head office, and (ii) for the breach, as they would have appeared if goods sent to the branch had been invoiced at cost, and a balance sheet of the whole business as on 31 December 19-9.

Head Office and branch stocks are to be valued at cost.

Ignore depreciation of fixed assets.

(*Chartered Institute of Secretaries and Administrators*)

6.8. EG Company Limited, a manufacturing business, exports some of its products through an overseas branch whose currency is 'florins', which carries out the final assembly operations before selling the goods.

The trial balances of the head office and branch at 30 June 19-8 were:

	Head office		Branch	
	£	£	*'Fl.'*	*'Fl.'*
Freehold buildings at cost	14,000		63,000	
Debtors/creditors	8,900	9,500	36,000	1,560
Sales		104,000		432,000
Authorised and issued capital		40,000		
Components sent to branch		35,000		
Head office/branch accounts	60,100			504,260
Branch cost of sales			360,000	
Depreciation provision, machinery		1,500		56,700
Head office cost of sales (including goods to branch)	59,000			
Administration costs	15,200		18,000	
Stock at 30 June 19-8	28,900		11,520	
Profit and loss account		2,000		
Machinery at cost	6,000		126,000	
Remittances		28,000	272,000	
Balance at bank	4,600		79,200	
Selling and distribution costs	23,300		28,800	
	220,000	220,000	994,520	994,520

The following adjustments are to be made:

1. The cost of sales figures include a depreciation charge of 10 per cent per annum on cost for machinery.

2. A provision of £300 for unrealised profit in branch stock is to be made.

3. On 26 June 19-8 the branch remitted 16,000 'Fl.'; these were received by the head office on 4 July and realised £1,990.

4. During May a branch customer in error paid the head office for goods supplied. The amount due was 320 'Fl.' which realised £36. It has been correctly dealt with by head office but not yet entered in the branch books.

5. A provision has to be made for a commission of 5 per cent of the net profit of the branch after charging such commission, which is due to the branch manager.

The rates of exchange were:

At 1 July 19-7	10 'Fl.'	= £1
At 30 June 19-8	8 'Fl.'	= £1
Average for the year	9 'Fl.'	= £1
On purchase of buildings and machinery	7 'Fl.'	= £1

You are required to prepare, for internal use:

(a) detailed operating accounts for the year ended 30 June 19-8;
(b) combined head office and branch balance sheet as at 30 June 19-8;
(c) the branch account in the head office books, in both sterling and currency, the opening balance on 1 July 19-7 being £25,136 (189,260 'Fl.').

Taxation is to be ignored.

(Institute of Cost and Management Accountants)

6.9A. O.T.L. Ltd commenced business on 1 January 19-0. The head office is in London and there is a branch in Highland. The currency unit of Highland is the crown.

The following are the trial balances of the head office and the Highland branch as at 31 December 19-0:

	Head office		Highland branch	
	£	£	crowns	crowns
Branch account	65,280			
Balances at bank	10,560		66,000	
Creditors		21,120		92,400
Debtors	18,480		158,400	
Fixed assets (purchased 1 January 19-0)	39,600		145,200	
Head office account				316,800
Profit and loss account (net profit for the year)		52,800		79,200
Issued share capital		86,400		
Stocks	26,400		118,800	
	160,320	160,320	488,400	488,400

The trial balance of the head office was prepared before any entries had been made in respect of any profits or losses of the branch.

Remittance from head office to branch and from branch to head office were recorded in the books at the actual amounts paid and received.

The rates of exchange were:

On 1 January 19-0   5 crowns = £1
Average rate for year 19-0   4.4 crowns = £1
On 31 December 19-0   4 crowns = £1

Required:
1. The trial balance of the Highland branch as at 31 December 19-0, in sterling.
2. The closing entries, as at 31 December 19-0, in the branch account in the books of the head office.
3. A summary of the balance sheet of O.T.L. Ltd as at 31 December 19-0.

Ignore depreciation of fixed assets.

Ignore taxation.

(Chartered Institute of Secretaries and Administrators)

7

Further Methods of Providing for Depreciation

In Chapters 19 and 20 of Volume 1 the Straight-line and Reducing Balance methods of making provisions for depreciation were discussed in detail. This chapter is concerned with some further methods of making provisions for depreciation. It must not be thought that this chapter will complete an examination of all the different methods in use. It is quite possible to devise one's own method of providing for depreciation. If it stands up to the test of common sense and does not distort the reported trading results of the firm, then the specially devised method will often be more applicable than those commonly used. There is therefore no limit to the number of different depreciation provision methods.

This chapter deals in some detail with the Revaluation method, the Depreciation Sinking Fund method, and the Endowment Policy method. Some other methods are discussed in outline only. There is no information easily available of the number of firms using particular depreciation methods. It would, however, seem likely that the Revaluation method is widely used for certain kinds of assets, while the Depreciation Sinking Fund method and the Endowment Policy method are not now used to any great extent, at least in the private sector of industry.

1. The Revaluation Method

There are some fixed assets for which it is inappropriate, or not worth while, to calculate depreciation provisions in a formal way, whereby each asset has to be identifiable and accurate records kept of its location and adjusting entries made when the asset is put out of use by the firm. Examples of these assets are loose tools such as spanners, screwdrivers, small drills, etc., in an engineering works, or barrels, bottles and crates in a brewery. A fixed asset such as a spanner or a barrel may be capable of a long life but its use may well be short-lived.

Some will be lost, others stolen, some broken or damaged through ill-use, and all of these facts will not be reported to management. Even if an accounting system could be devised to throw up such wastage of assets the operation of the system could well, except in a few instances, cost more than the savings to be gained from it. A spanner costing less than £1 and which is used infrequently, could well last for seven years. If the Straight Line or Reducing Balance methods were in use, then theoretically a calculation would have to be made of the over-depreciation of under-depreciation provided on the asset when it is put out of use, and an adjusting entry made to correct the accounts. With such an asset it is clearly not worth while to make accounting entries in such a fashion. In addition some firms may well make their own tools, etc., and it might be difficult and costly to keep elaborate records for each small tool made.

To provide a solution at a reasonable cost the Revaluation method of calculating depreciation provisions is used. The method used is simply that the assets are valued at the start of the period, the additions increase the value and then the assets are revalued at the end of the period. The amount of the decrease in value shows the amount by which the asset is deemed to have depreciated. This is now illustrated in Exhibit 7.1 by reference to a firm which uses metal crates.

Exhibit 7.1

The firm starts in business on 1 January 19-6.

	£
In its first year it buys crates costing	800
Their estimated value at 31 December 19-6	540
Crates bought in the year ended 31 December 19-7	320
Estimated value of all crates in hand on 31 December 19-7	530
Crates bought in the year ended 31 December 19-8	590
Estimated value of all crates in hand on 31 December 19-8	700

Crates

19-6		£	19-6		£
Dec 31 Cash (during the year)		800	Dec 31 Profit and Loss		260
			,, 31 Stock c/d		540
		800			800

19-7		£	19-7		£
Jan 1 Stock b/d		540	Dec 31 Profit and Loss		330
Dec 31 Cash (during the year)		320	,, 31 Stock c/d		530
		860			860

Crates

19-8		£	19-8		£
Jan 1	Stock b/d	530	Dec 31	Profit and Loss	420
Dec 31	Cash (during the year)	590	,, 31	Stock c/d	700
		1,120			1,120
19-9					
Jan 1	Stock b/d	700			

Profit and Loss Account for the year ended 31 December

		£
19-6	Use of crates	260
19-7	Use of crates	330
19-8	Use of crates	420

The balance of the Crates Account at the end of each year is shown as a fixed asset in the Balance Sheet.

In an engineering firm the cost of wages and materials used in making loose tools may or may not be known. If it is known the cost should be charged to the Loose Tools Account. If not known, the Loose Tools Account cannot be charged with the cost of such additions, and may well appear to reveal an appreciation in the value of tools rather than depreciation. The appreciation would be transferred to the credit of the Manufacturing Account (or shown as a deduction on the debit side). The different treatment makes no difference to the calculated profit as can now be shown in Exhibit 7.2.

Exhibit 7.2

	£
At 1 January 19-7 loose tools valued at	800
During the year the cost of all raw materials used in the factory amounted to	10,000
The cost of all wages in the factory was	20,000
At 31 December 19-7 the loose tools are valued at	1,000

However, in the Loose Tools Account and Manufacturing Account shown as (A) it is known that materials £300 and wages £400 have been used in making loose tools, while in the accounts lettered (B) this information is not known.

Loose Tools (A)

19-7		£	19-7		£
Jan 1	Stock b/d	800	Dec 31	Manufacturing	
Dec 31	Transfer from wages	400		Account	500
,, 31	Transfer from		,, 31	Stock c/d	1,000
	Materials	300			
		1,500			1,500
19-8					
Jan 1	Stock b/d	1,000			

Manufacturing Account (A) for the year ended 31 December 19-7

	£		
Materials (i.e. *less* transfer £300)	9,700		
Wages (i.e. *less* transfer £400)	19,600		
Use of Loose Tools	500		

The total effective debits are therefore £19,600 + £9,700 + £500 = £29,800

Loose Tools (B)

19-7		£	19-7		£
Jan 1	Stock b/d	800	Dec 31	Stock c/d	1,000
Dec 31	Manufacturing Account	200			
		1,000			1,000
19-8					
Jan 1	Stock b/d	1,000			

Manufacturing Account (B) for the year ended 31 December 19-7

	£		£
Materials	10,000	Increase in the value of	
Wages	20,000	loose tools	200

The total of effective debits is £10,000 + £20,000 − £200 = £29,800.

In both cases (A) and (B) the Balance Sheet on 31 December 19-7, will show a fixed asset of Loose Tools £1,000.

Some firms show the stock of such assets in the same way as the stock of goods or raw materials. Given the information in Exhibit 7.2 it would appear as Manufacturing Account (C) which now follows.

Manufacturing Account (C) for the year ended 31 December 19-7

	£
Materials	10,000
Wages	20,000
Add Stock of Loose Tools on 1 January 19-7	800
	30,800
Less Stock of Loose Tools on 31 December 19-7	1,000
	29,800

Here again the total effective debits amount to £29,800.

Manufacturing Account (A) gives the most useful information as it shows the cost of using tools during 19-7. In the other Manufacturing Accounts all that is known is that the estimated value of loose tools has risen by £200. This by itself is a relatively meaningless piece of information. Suppose that it was possible to hire loose tools instead of owning them, and that this could be done at a cost of £300 per year. Manufacturing Account (A) would show that tool hire would be the cheaper method, assuming that the experience in 19-7 was typical. The other Manufacturing Accounts would not reveal this figure for comparison. However, like most accounting statements it is only one measure to be taken into account when making a business decision. Other factors may well be: (a) What will the reactions of the firm's own toolmakers and of their trade unions? (b) Could our own tools cost less if our methods were changed? (c) How long will it take to renew any tool when required? (d) What provisions are made for normal replacements? (e) Would it make the firm too dependent on the firm of tool hirers?

The 'value' to be carried forward is in fact the reappraised figure of the costs which should be carried forward to the following period. The 'value' is thus the 'unapportioned cost value'. Expediency and custom will play a large part in any such valuation. It would be quite ludicrous for a firm with several thousand barrels of the same size to have any sort of scientific appraisal of every barrel at the end of each financial period with the object of placing a valuation on it. It would more likely be found that the number of barrels would be counted in some way and then multiplied by an amount which the management considered reflected the average value of all the barrels.

The cattle belonging to a farmer is one of his fixed assets. Like all other fixed assets depreciation should be provided for, but during the early life of an animal it will probably be appreciating in value only to depreciate later. The task of calculating the cost of an animal becomes almost impossible if it has been born on the farm, reared on the farm by grazing on the pasture land and from other foodstuffs, some grown by the farmer and others bought by him. Expediency therefore takes over and the Revaluation method is used, the livestock being brought into account in the same way as stocks of goods. The cost factor being such an elusive one for many animals has led to the general practice being observed of valuing livestock at the price that the animals would fetch if sold at market. This therefore is an exception to the general rules regarding fixed assets being shown at cost price.

2. The Depreciation Sinking Fund Method

None of the methods dealt with have set out specifically to arrange for funds to be available for the replacement of an asset at the end of its estimated useful life with a firm. The objective of these methods has been the apportioning of the cost of an asset over various accounting periods.

The method now being considered is an attempt to achieve both of these objectives. This is probably an outdated concept except under special circumstances. There is a need not just to budget for the replacement of fixed assets when necessary but also for additions of fixed assets and for achieving a desired level of bank funds and of working capital. This comes within the wider scope of budgetary control.

The method involves the investment of cash outside the business. The aim is to make the regular investment of money which, together with the accumulated interest or dividends, is sufficient to finance the replacement of the asset when it is put out of use by the firm. The exact achievement of the aim is not an easy one because of one or more of the following reasons:

(a) When the time arrives for the replacement of the asset, even if the type of asset has not changed, prices may well have risen. A more unlikely assumption in recent years is that the price may have fallen.

(b) The asset may have become obsolete and will be replaced by something quite unlike it in construction or cost.

(c) The asset may have a longer or a shorter life than expected.

(d) Changes in the taxation system may affect the dividends or interest received and the amount received on sales of the investment.

(e) The market value of the investment may rise or fall, so that the realised value may differ considerably from that expected when the original scheme was drafted.

The example used in Exhibit 7.3 is an ideal one in that it conforms exactly to the original plan, none of the points (a) to (e) will apply.

Before calculations become too involved a simple proposition can be examined. As each period's interest (or dividend) is received, then that amount is immediately reinvested. Apart from the reinvestment of interest the other money taken for investment is to be an equal amount each period. This being so, if the money is to be invested at 5 per cent per annum, and the cost of the asset is £500 to be replaced in five years' time, then how much should be taken for investment each year? If £100 was taken each year for five years, then this would amount to more than £500 because of the interest and of the interest on the reinvested interest. Most readers will recognise this as money being invested as compound interest. Therefore something less than £100 per annum is needed. The exact amount can be calculated by the use of the compound interest formula. Chapter 24 illustrates how the amount needed can be calculated. As these calculations are left until later in the book, a summarised set of tables is now shown to help the student at this stage.

Annual Sinking Fund Instalments to Provide £1

Years	3%	3½%	4%	4½%	5%
3	0·323530	0·321933	0·320348	0·318773	0·317208
4	0·239028	0·237251	0·235490	0·233744	0·232012
5	0·188354	0·186481	0·184627	0·182792	0·180975
6	0·154597	0·152668	0·150761	0·148878	0·147017
7	0·130506	0·128544	0·126609	0·124701	0·122819
8	0·112456	0·110476	0·108527	0·106609	0·104721
9	0·098433	0·096446	0·094493	0·092574	0·090690
10	0·087230	0·085241	0·083291	0·081378	0·079504

The table gives the amount required to provide £1 at the end of the relevant number of years. To provide £1,000 multiply by 1,000, to provide for £4,986 multiply by 4,986.

Exhibit 7.3

A five-year lease is bought on 1 January 19-1 for £10,000. An option is obtained whereby the lease can be renewed on 1 January 19-6 for five years under identical terms. The firm therefore decides to set aside an equal annual amount which, together with interest reinvested immediately, will provide £10,000 on 31 December 19-5. According to the table £0·180975 invested annually will provide £1 in five years' time. Therefore £0·180975 × 10,000 will be needed annually = £1,809·75. This is the amount charged as depreciation in the Profit and Loss Account for each year and credited to the Depreciation Fund Account. An identical amount is then invested, the credit entry being in the Cash Book while the debit entry is in the Depreciation Fund Investment Account.

Depreciation Fund

	£			£
		19-1		
		Dec 31 Profit and Loss		1,809·75
		19-2		
		Dec 31 Cash: Interest		
19-2			(5% of £1,809·75)	90·49
Dec 31 Balance c/d	3,709·99	,,	31 Profit and Loss	1,809·75
	3,709·99			3,709·99
		19-3		
		Jan	1 Balance b/d	3,709·99
		Dec 31 Cash: Interest		
19-3			(5% of £3,709·99)	185·49
Dec 31 Balance c/d	5,705·23	,,	31 Profit and Loss	1,809·75
	5,705·23			5,705·23

		19-4	
		Jan 1 Balance b/d	5,705·23
19-4		Dec 31 Cash: Interest	
Dec 31 Balance c/d	7,800·24	(5% of £5,705·23)	285.26
		,, 31 Profit and Loss	1,809·75
	7,800·24		7,800·24
		19-5	
		Jan 1 Balance b/d	7,800·24
		Dec 31 Cash: Interest	
19-5		(5% of £7,800·24)	390·01
Dec 31 Lease now written		,, 31 Profit and Loss	1,809·75
off	10,000·00		
	10,000·00		10,000·00

Depreciation Fund Investment

19-1	£		£
Dec 31 Cash	1,809·75		
19-2			
Dec 31 Cash (see note A)	1,900·24		
19-3			
Dec 31 Cash (see note B)	1,995·24		
19-4		19-5	
Dec 31 Cash (see note C)	2,095·01	Dec 31 Cash: Sale of	
		Investment	7,800·24
	7,800·24		7,800·24

Notes
Cash invested

	A	B	C
	£	£	£
The yearly instalment	1,809·75	1,809·75	1,809·75
Add Interest received reinvested immediately	90·49	185·49	285·26
	1,900·24	1,995·24	2,095·01

Lease

19-1		£	19-5		£
Jan 1 Cash		10,000	Dec 31 Depreciation Fund		
			– expired lease		
			written off		10,000

New Lease

19-6		£
Jan 1 Cash		10,000

The instalment for 19-5 is not in fact invested, nor is the interest received on 31 December 19-5 reinvested. The money to renew the lease is required on 1 January 19-6, and there is not much point (even if it was possible, which would very rarely hold true) in investing money one day only to withdraw it the day afterwards. The amount required to renew the lease is £10,000 and is available from the following sources:

	£
Dec 31 19-5 Sale of investment	7,800·24
,, 31 19-5 Interest received but not reinvested	390·01
,, 31 19-5 The fifth year's instalment not invested	1,809·75
	10,000·00

On reflection the reader may well question the validity of this method of providing for depreciation. The asset in Exhibit 7.3 cost £10,000 and was valueless at the end of five years. Therefore the depreciation amounted to £10,000, yet in the Profit and Loss Account there has been charged £1,809·75 for each of five years = £9,048·75. The fact is that only the net depreciation provision has been charged, after allowing for interest received on the investment. It would be normal for investment income to be shown as a credit in the Profit and Loss Account, yet this method credits the Depreciation Fund Account instead. What has appeared as:

Profit and Loss Account for the Five Years to 31 December 19-5

	£
Depreciation (5 × £1,809·75)	9,048·75

is in effect the following:

Profit and Loss Account for the Five Years to 31 December 19-5

	£		£
Depreciation (5 × £1,809·75)	9,048·75	Interest on Investments not entered in Profit and	
Depreciation not entered in Profit and Loss Account since it is cancelled out by Interest on Investments also entered	951·25	Loss Account which cancels out part of depreciation provisions	951·25

3. The Depreciation Sinking Fund with Endowment Policy

The main difference between this and the method described already is that instead of buying securities a form of endowment policy is taken out to mature at the end of the asset's expected useful life. The insurance company will quote the amount of premium required. Another difference is that with the other Depreciation Fund method the money is invested at the end of each period, whereas the premium is payable on the endowment policy on the first day of each period.

Exhibit 7.4

A five-year lease is bought for £500 on 1 January 19-1. An endowment policy is taken out for £500 to mature on 31 December 19-5, the annual premium being £90. The lease is renewed for £500 on 1 January 19-6.

Depreciation Fund

19-5	£	19-1	£
Dec 31 Lease written off	500	Dec 31 Profit and Loss	90
		19-2	
		Dec 31 Profit and Loss	90
		19-3	
		Dec 31 Profit and Loss	90
		19-4	
		Dec 31 Profit and Loss	90
		19-5	
		Dec 31 Profit and Loss	90
		,, 31 Endowment Policy	
		– interest factor	
		transferred	50
	500		500

Endowment Policy

19-1			£	19-5	£
Jan	1	Cash	90	Dec 31 Cash (policy	
19-2				matures)	500
Jan	1	Cash	90		
19-3					
Jan	1	Cash	90		
19-4					
Jan	1	Cash	90		
19-5					
Jan	1	Cash	90		
Dec	31	Interest factor –			
		transferred to			
		Depreciation Fund	50		
			500		500

Lease

19-1		£	19-5		£
Jan 1 Cash		500	Dec 31 Depreciation Fund: lease written off		500

New Lease

19-6		£
Jan 1 Cash		500

4. Other Methods

(a) Depletion Unit Method

With fixed assets such as mines or quarries the depreciation is often based on the quantity of raw materials extracted compared with the estimated total quantity available. For instance, if a firm bought for £5,000 a small mine which had an expected capacity of 1,000 tons of ore, then for each ton extracted during an accounting period the firm would provide for depreciation of the asset by £5 (expected average depreciation cost per ton).

(b) Machine Hour Method

With a machine the depreciation provision may be based on the number of hours that the machine was operated during the period compared with the total expected running hours during the machine's life with the firm. A firm which bought a machine costing £2,000 having an expected running life of 1,000 hours, and no scrap value, could provide for depreciation of the machine at the rate of £2 for every hour it was operated during a particular accounting period.

(c) Sum of the years' digits

This method is popular in the U.S.A. but not common in Britain. It provides for higher depreciation to be charged early in the life of an asset with lower depreciation in later years.

Give an asset costing £3,000 which will be in use for 5 years, the calculations will be:

From purchase the asset will last for	5 years
From the second year the asset will last for	4 years
From the third year the asset will last for	3 years
From the fourth year the asset will last for	2 years
From the fifth year the asset will last for	1 year
Sum of these digits	15

	£
1st year of 5/15ths of £3,000 is charged =	1,000
2nd year of 4/15ths of £3,000 is charged =	800
3rd year of 3/15ths of £3,000 is charged =	600
4th year of 2/15ths of £3,000 is charged =	400
5th year of 1/15th of £3,000 is charged =	200
	3,000

SSAP 12 Accounting for depreciation

This was issued in December 1977 and revised in November 1981. The contents of chapters 19 and 20 in volume 1 and chapter 7 in volume 2 have complied with the SSAP. There are however a few points which need stressing:

(i) A change from one method of providing depreciation to another is permissible only on the grounds that the new method will give a fairer presentation of the results and of the financial position. In these circumstances the unamortised cost should be written off over the remaining useful life commencing with the period in which the change is made.

(ii) Where assets are revalued and effect is given to the revaluation in the financial statements, the charge for depreciation thereafter should be based on the revalued amount and, in the year of change, there should be disclosed by way of note to the financial statemnents the subdivision of the charge between that applicable to original cost (or valuation if previously revalued) and that applicable to the change in value on the current revaluation, if material.

(iii) It is not appropriate to omit charging depreciation of a fixed asset on the grounds that its market value is greater than its net book value. If account is taken of such increased value by writing up the net book value of a fixed asset then, as indicated above, an increased charge for depreciation will become necessary.

(iv) Freehold land, unless subject to depletion by, for example, the extraction of minerals or to reduction in value due to other circumstances, will not normally require a provision for depreciation. However, the value of freehold land may be adversely affected by considerations such as the desirability of its location either socially or in relation to available sources of materials, labour or sales and in these circumstances it should be written down.

(v) Buildings have a limited life which may be materially affected by technological and environmental changes and they should be depreciated having regard to the same criteria as in the case of other fixed assets.

(vi) As in the case of other assets an increase in the value of land or buildings does not remove the necessity for charging depreciation on the buildings.

SSAP 4 Accounting for Government Grants

Many different types of grants are, or have been obtainable from government departments. Where these relate to revenue expenditure, e.g. subsidies on wages, they should be credited to revenue in the period when the revenue is incurred.

Where there are grants relating to capital expenditure, then SSAP 4 states that they should be credited to revenue *over the expected useful life of the asset.* This may be achieved by:

(*a*) Crediting the fixed asset account by the amount of the grant, depreciation then being on the net figure. This method will accordingly spread the benefit of the grant over the life of the asset, as each year's depreciation figure will be correspondingly reduced.

(*b*) Treating the amount of the grant as a deferred credit, a portion of which is credited to the profit and loss account annually, over the life of the asset, thus reducing the cost of depreciation. If this method is chosen, the amount of the deferred credit should, if material, be shown separately. It should not be shown as part of shareholders' funds.

It will be appreciated that the net effect of both methods (*a*) and (*b*) will be the same as far as the profit and loss accounts are concerned.

Exercises

Note: **Questions numbered without the suffix 'A' have answers at the back of the book.**

7.1. On 1 January 19-6 Prefab Ltd acquired for £3,000 the lease of some factory premises of which five years were unexpired. The amortise this lease over the five years and to provide for renewal it was decided to set up a sinking fund by taking annual instalments out of profits and investing cash of the same amount at 5 per cent compound interest.

Taking 0·180975 as the annual instalment required to produce £1 in five years, write up the sinking fund account and the investment account for the whole period, showing the closing entries.

(*Association of Certified Accountants*)

7.2. A firm both buys loose tools and also makes some itself. The following data is available concerning the years ended 31 December 19-4, 19-5, and 19-6.

19-4		£
Jan 1	Stock of Loose Tools	1,250
	During the year:	
	Bought loose tools from suppliers	2,000
	Made own loose tools: the cost of wages of employees being £275 and the materials cost £169	
Dec 31	Loose Tools valued at	2,700

19-5		
	During the year:	
	Loose tools bought from suppliers	1,450
	Made own loose tools: the cost of wages of employees being £495 and the materials cost £390	
Dec 31	Loose Tools valued at	3,340

19-6		
	During the year:	
	Loose tools bought from suppliers	1,890
	Made own loose tools: the cost of wages of employees being £145 and the materials cost £290. Received refund from a supplier for faulty tools returned to him	88
Dec 31	Loose Tools valued at	3,680

You are to draw up the Loose Tools Account for the three years, showing the amount transferred as an expense in each year to the Manufacturing Account.

7.3A. On 1 January 19-2 Booker Ltd acquired the lease of its factory premises for five years for £8,000. It was decided to amortise this over five years by the use of a sinking fund. Annual instalments were to be taken out of profits and invested in securities of 5 per cent, compounded annually.

£0·180975 is the amount required, invested at 5 per cent compounded, to produce £1 after five years.

Write up the sinking fund account and the investment account for the whole period, showing the closing entries.

7.4A. A firm both buys tools and make them for itself. The following information is available to you for the year ended 31 December 19-5, 19-6 and 19-7.

19-5		£
Jan 1	Stock of Tools	3,890
	Bought during the year 19-5	1,570
	Own Tools made: Cost of wages	705
	Cost of materials	500
Dec 31	Tools valued at	5,020
19-6		
	During the year:	
	Bought during 19-6	1,990
	Own Tools made: Cost of wages	908
	Cost of materials	486
Dec 31	Tools valued at	4,950
19-7		
	During the year:	
	Bought during 19-7	3,665
	Own Tools made: Cost of wages	1,290
	Cost of materials	880
Dec 31	Tools valued at	6,868

Write up the Tools Account for the three years, showing the figure transferred each year to the Manufacturing Account.

7.5. The net profits of the Cool Clear Co. for the years ending 31 March 19-0, 19-1 and 19-2 were £55,736; £59,408; and £60,011 respectively. The profit had been determined after calculating depreciation on machinery, and fixtures and fittings by the straight line method.

All the assets in question were acquired one year earlier on 1 April 19-9 for £241,024 (machinery) and £48,202 (Fixtures and Fittings), and it was estimated that the machinery had a working life of 14 years, and a scrap value of £18,830. The fixtures and fittings on the other hand were estimated to have a working life of 10 years and scrap value of £7,532.

The firm's management now favour the use of the reducing balance method of depreciation as being more appropriate for the firm, and the managing director is anxious to have the last three years' profits recalculated using this method.

You are required to
1. recalculate to the nearest £1, the profits for 19-0, 19-1 and 19-2 using the following reducing balance rates of depreciation:
   Machinery 25 per cent per annum and
   Fixtures and Fittings 12½ per cent per annum.
2. Show the assets in the balance sheet as at 31 March 19-2.

(*Association of Business Executives*)

8

Container Accounts

A container is anything in which goods are contained. This may consist of a packet containing cigarettes, a large wooden crate containing tractor parts, or a liquid gas cylinder. Some will be returnable by the purchaser after use, an obvious example being the gas cylinder, while others such as the cigarette packet will be disposed of at will by the customer. The returnable containers will often be subject to a deposit being charged to the customer, a refund being allowed when the container is returned in good condition to the supplier.

In suppliers' books it is therefore convenient to divide containers into those which are (1) not chargeable to the customers, and (2) where a deposit charge is made to the customer.

1. Containers not Charged to Customers

Many containers will be treated as manufacturing expenses, e.g. cigarette packets, flour bags or tin cans containing foods. Theoretically they are a distribution expense if the contents and the containers are regarded as being two distinct items, and as such would be chargeable to the Profit and Loss Account, but really the containers for such items are an integral part of the goods sold and are therefore chargeable to the Manufacturing Account. On the other hand, returnable cylinders in which goods are delivered would be chargeable to the Profit and Loss Account.

There will normally be a stock of containers in hand at the end of each accounting period. Exhibit 8.1 shows an account for cartons in which salt is packed for sale.

Exhibit 8.1

	£
Stock of containers 1 January 19-6	100
Containers bought in the year ended 31 December 19-6	2,800
Stock of containers 31 December 19-6	300

Containers

19-6		£	19-6		£
Jan 1 Stock b/d		100	Dec 31 Manufacturing		
Dec 31 Cash (during the				Account	2,600
	year)	2,800	,, 31 Stock c/d		300
		2,900			2,900
19-7					
Jan 1 Stock b/d		300			

For returnable containers on which deposits are not charged the question of whether or not accurate statistical records would be kept would depend on the nature and value of containers.

2. Containers on which Deposits are Charged to Customers

There are containers which many purchasers would not return if they were not charged with a deposit refunded only on return. These are obviously containers which require more than a marginal effort to return, or those which could be put to alternative uses. The deposit chargeable must therefore be sufficient to discourage the purchaser from keeping the containers after use, but should not be so great as to deter him from buying the goods in the first place. In some instances a time limit is fixed within which the container is to be returned to obtain a cancellation of the deposit charged. Common sense must however prevail, as it would be unwise to refuse refunds of deposits in circumstances which could bring about a worsening in the firm's relationship with customers it wished to retain.

Accounting must therefore fulfil two needs, (a) it must enable some form of check on the stock of containers, and (b) it must reveal the amount of deposit returnable to customers. This can be satisfied, for (a) a Containers Stock Account can be kept, and for (b) a Containers Suspense Account may be opened.

Chapter 7 has already illustrated the need for the depreciation of containers to be provided normally by the Revaluation method. The Container Stock Account will therefore provide for the depreciation element by the process of revaluing the containers at the end of each accounting period. Each container account may also include, in addition to the £ columns, further columns for quantities and for the monetary rates at which the transactions are carried out.

Exhibit 8.2

A new firm, I.V.Y. and Co, sells its goods in crates on which a deposit is chargeable to the customer, a credit being allowed on their return within three months.

During the year ended 31 December 19-5:
(A) 50 crates were bought for £3 each.
(B) 180 crates were sent to customers, these being charged to their accounts at £4 deposit each. You may well wonder how 180 crates can be sent out when only 50 have been bought by I.V.Y. and Co. The fact is that the figure of 180 consists of recounting the same crates, as they are sent out and returned several times each year. However, during the year 180 debits of £4 each have been made in customers' accounts.
(C) 150 crates were returned by customers, credits being entered in their accounts for £4 each.
(D) 10 crates were kept by customers beyond the three months' limit, and they therefore forfeited their right to return them to obtain a refund of the deposit.
(E) 2 crates were damaged and were sold for £1 each.

On 31 December 19-5 the following facts are relevant:
(F) There were 20 returnable crates with customers.
(G) There were 18 crates at I.V.Y.'s warehouse.

The stock of crates at 31 December 19-5 are to be valued at £2 each to provide for depreciation through usage.

The identifying letters (A) to (G) are shown against the recorded transactions in the accounts that now follow.

Containers Stock

	Rate	Quan-tity			Rate	Quan-tity	
	£		£		£		£
19-5				19-5			
Dec 31 Cash (during the year) (A)	3	50	150	Dec 31 Containers Suspense: kept by customers (D)	4	10	40
				,, 31 Cash: damaged crates (E)	1	2	2
				,, 31 Profit and Loss: Cost of container usage			32
				,, 31 Stock: c/d In Warehouse (G)	2	18	36
				At Customers (F)	2	20	40
		50	150			50	150
19-6							
Jan 1 Stock b/d							
In Warehouse (G)	2	18	36				
At Customers (F)	2	20	40				

Containers Suspense

	Rate	Quan-tity	£		Rate	Quan-tity	£
19-5				19-5			
Dec 31 Sales Ledger: crates credited to customers' accounts on return (C)	4	150	600	Dec 31 Sales Ledger: crates charged to customers' accounts (B)	4	180	720
,, 31 Containers Stock: kept by customers (D)	4	10	40				
,, 31 Deposits on crates returnable c/d (F)	4	20	80				
		180	720			180	720
				19-6			
				Jan 1 Deposits on crates returnable b/d (F)	4	20	80

The Balance Sheet will show the balances in the following manner:

I.V.Y. & Co

Balance Sheet as at 31 December 19-5

	£
Current Assets	
Crates – at valuation	76
Current Liabilities	
Containers Suspense – deposits returnable	80

Sometimes containers are charged out to customers at an initial price greater than that allowed on their return. The difference therefore represents a hiring charge. If the same data is taken as in Exhibit 8.2 but instead of £4 being allowed on return this had been restricted to £3 instead, then the accounts would have appeared as follows:

Containers Stock

	Rate	Quan-tity	£	£		Rate	Quan-tity	£	£
19-5					19-5				
Dec 31 Cash (during the year)	3	50		150	Dec 31 Containers Suspense: kept by customers	3	10		30
,, 31 Profit and Loss: Profit on container usage				138	,, 31 Cash: damaged crates	1	2		2
					,, 31 Containers Suspense: Hiring charge				180
					,, 31 Stock: c/d				
					In Warehouse	2	18		36
					At Customers	2	20		40
		50		288			50		288
19-6									
Jan 1 Stock b/d									
In Warehouse	2	18		36					
At Customers	2	20		40					

Containers Suspense

	Rate	Quan-tity	£	£		Rate	Quan-tity	£	£
19-5					19-5				
Dec 31 Sales Ledger: crates credited to customers' accounts on return		150		450	Dec 31 Sales Ledger: crates charged to customers' accounts	4	180		720
,, 31 Containers Stock: kept by customers	3	10		30					
,, 31 Containers Stock: Hiring charge				180					
,, 31 Deposits on crates returnable	3	20		60					
		180		720			180		720
					19-6				
					Jan 1 Deposits on crates returnable b/d	3	20		60

The Balance Sheet would have appeared in the following manner:

I.V.Y. & Co
Balance Sheet as at 31 December 19-5

	£
Current Assets	
Crates – at valuation	76
Current Liabilities	
Containers Suspense – deposits returnable	60

Exercises

Note: **Questions numbered without the suffix 'A' have answers at the back of the book.**

8.1. D. Clark's manufactures are sold in boxes which are returnable. They are charged out to customers at £8 each and credit of £6 is given for each box returned within two months. For the purpose of the annual accounts, the value of boxes in the factory and those in customers' hands, which had been invoiced within two months, was taken as being £1.50 each. The quantities of these on 31 January 19-3 were 600 and 4,000 respectively.

The following were the transactions as regards boxes during the year ended 31 January 19-3:

Purchases – 5,000 at £2 each.
Invoiced to customers – 17,000.
Returned by customers – 14,000.
450 could no longer be used and were sold, realising £100.

The number of boxes invoiced after 30 November 19-3 and still in customers' hands on 31 January 19-4 was 6,200.

Write up the accounts in the books of D. Clark to record these transactions and to show the profit on boxes and the quantities involved.

8.2. A company makes a charge to its customers for cases in which the product is delivered. If they are returned in good condition within two months a refund is made.

At the start of the year there were 9,600 cases in stock at the company's warehouse and 6,100 in the hands of customers supplied within the previous two months. The company bought 18,000 new cases during the year and following a dispute with a supplier returned 4,000 new cases for which a credit note of £11,610 was received. At 31 December 19-6 there were still in the hands of customers 4,800 supplied during the previous two months.

During the year 19-6, 47,600 cases were sent to customers and 43,100 returned by them. The company scrapped 3,500 damaged cases and sold the timber for £55. A physical check of cases in stock in 31 December 19-6 revealed an unaccounted deficit of 420 cases.

New cases cost £3 each
Charged out to customers at £5 each
Credited on return at £4 each
Valued for stocktaking at £2 each

Show the accounts in the books for 19-6 to record the above, and the balances of cases, in quantities and values at 31 December 19-6.

You are entitled to deduce the following missing information from the details above:

(*a*) The number of cases kept by customers over the two-month limit for returning them.

(*b*) The number of cases in the warehouse on 31 December 19-6.

8.3A. K.R.R. Ltd sells goods in containers which are charged to customers at £2.00 each. Customers are credited with £1.25 for each container returned within four months.

On 31 December 19-7, there were 1,580 containers on the company's premises and 5,520 containers, the time limit for the return of which had not expired, were held by customers.

During 19-8:

(i) K.R.R. Ltd purchased 8,700 containers for £1 each.

(ii) 26,460 containers were charged to customers.

(iii) 23,720 containers were returned by customers and credited to them.

On 31 December 19-8, customers held 6,000 containers, the time limit for the return of which had not expired.

For purposes of the annual accounts of K.R.R. Ltd, all stocks of containers on the company's premises and returnable containers in the possession of customers are valued, at £1 each.

You are required to show the container stock account and the container trading account for the year 19-8. These accounts should be provided with additional memorandum columns in which quantities are to be shown.

(*Chartered Institute of Secretaries and Administrators*)

8.4A. The G Company supplies gas in expensive containers which are returnable after use. These containers cost £20 each and are charged out to customers on sale or return within six months at £26 each. Provided they are returned within the six months period they are credited at £23 each. As each container is returned it is inspected and overhauled at a cost of £2.

At the end of the year the company values all returnable containers in customers hands and containers held in stock at £16 each.

You are advised that:

	At the beginning of the year	At the end of the year
Containers held by the company	2,760	3,144
Returnable containers held by customers	4,790	2,910

During the year 3,100 new containers were purchased, 20,620 were invoiced to customers and 17,960 were returned. On inspection 260 required additional repairs costing £325 and 56 had to be sold as scrap for £60.

From the information given above prepare:

(*a*) returnable containers suspense account;

(*b*) an account showing the profit or loss on dealings in containers.

(*Institute of Cost and Management Accountants*)

9

Royalty Accounts

In some classes of business the owner of some form of privilege or monopoly can allow other firms to utilise this right, the owner being remunerated by reference to the extent which it has been used. The name given to payments for certain of these rights is 'royalty'. Instances of payments of royalties are as follows:

(a) For the extraction of minerals from the ground.
(b) The publisher of a book remunerating the author.
(c) For the use of a patent.

Where the remuneration is simply a case of a fixed amount per unit of use the accounting necessary is quite straightforward. The payer of the royalty will simply charge it as an expense in a Royalty Account.

Complications start to appear when a certain minimum amount is payable per annum even though the actual use of the right may result in a lesser figure for royalties. Such agreements are commonly found in the case of mining and quarrying. These agreements are understandable because of the desire of the owner to be certain of a minimum income. Without a minimum amount the lack of activity on the part of the user would result in a small income for the owner. Carried to extremes no activity would result in no income. On the other hand, the user would probably feel aggrieved if he not only had to pay the minimum amount in a period of low activity but also have to pay the full amount in a period of high activity. The part of the minimum amount not represented by use of the right, in the case of a mine, is known as 'short workings'. It is very often found that royalty agreements provide for such short workings to be carried forward to reduce royalties payable in future years where the activity results in the royalties being in excess of the minimum agreed amount. A limit is usually set upon the number of years for which such short workings can be carried forward for this purpose. Once the final date has been reached, such short workings are then irrecoupable. Exhibit 9.1 illustrates such a case.

Exhibit 9.1

The lessee of a mine is to pay £1 for each ton of ore extracted. The minimum rent is to be £400 per annum. Any payments for short workings are recoupable only in the two years following that in which they occurred. The following table shows the effect of extraction figures contained in column (a). As the minimum rent is £400, then obviously column (b) must never show a figure of less than £400.

Year	(a) Tons extracted	(b) Payable	(c) Short workings carried forward	(d) Short workings recouped	(e) Short workings now irrecoupable
		£	£	£	£
1	420	420			
2	310	400	90		
3	560	470		90	
4	280	400	120		
5	440	400	80	40	
6	450	400		50	30
7	780	780			

Notes:

Column (c) shows the value of the short working at the end of each year which can still be set off against future royalties. £120 is carried forward at the end of year 4, of this £40 is set off against the royalties for year 5, leaving £80 carried forward at the end of year 5.

Column (e). The £120 short workings originating in year 4 are partly recouped by £40 in year 5 and £50 in year 6. The remaining £30 can no longer be recouped as the time limit of two years following the year of origin comes into play. The £30 cannot therefore be carried forward to year 7, so that it is in year 6 that it is shown as being irrecoupable.

The short workings carried forward can in fact be likened to the prepayment of an expense. The minimum amount exceeds the actual royalties, therefore the excess is in effect a prepayment of royalties.

All of the accounting calculations have now been made, the only action necessary is that the table is to be translated into double entry terms. This now follows. It is assumed that the financial year is the same as the calendar year and that the landlord is paid on the last day of each year.

Royalties

	£		£
Year 1		Year 1	
Dec 31 Landlord	420	Dec 31 Operating Account (A)	420
Year 2		Year 2	
Dec 31 Landlord	310	Dec 31 Operating	310

Royalties

	£		£
Year 3		Year 3	
Dec 31 Landlord	560	Dec 31 Operating	560
Year 4		Year 4	
Dec 31 Landlord	280	Dec 31 Operating	280
Year 5		Year 5	
Dec 31 Landlord	440	Dec 31 Operating	440
Year 6		Year 6	
Dec 31 Landlord	450	Dec 31 Operating	450
Year 7		Year 7	
Dec 31 Landlord	780	Dec 31 Operating	780

Short Workings

	£		£
Year 2		Year 3	
Dec 31 Landlord	90	Dec 31 Landlord (recouped amount)	90
Year 4		Year 5	
Dec 31 Landlord	120	Dec 31 Landlord (recouped amount)	40
		Year 5	
		Dec 31 Balance c/d	80
	120		120
Year 6		Year 6	
Jan 1 Balance b/d	80	Dec 31 Landlord (recouped amount)	50
		,, 31 Profit and Loss — amount now irrecoupable	30
	80		80

Landlord

	£		£
Year 1		Year 1	
Dec 31 Cash	420	Dec 31 Royalties	420

	Landlord			
		£		£

Year 2			Year 2	
Dec 31 Cash		400	Dec 31 Royalties	310
			,, 31 Short Workings	90
		400		400

Year 3			Year 3	
Dec 31 Short Workings – recouped		90	Dec 31 Royalties	560
,, 31 Cash		470		
		560		560

Year 4			Year 4	
Dec 31 Cash		400	Dec 31 Royalties	280
			,, 31 Short Workings	120
		400		400

Year 5			Year 5	
Dec 31 Short Workings – recouped		40	Dec 31 Royalties	440
,, 31 Cash		400		
		440		440

Year 6			Year 6	
Dec 31 Short Workings – recouped		50	Dec 31 Royalties	450
,, 31 Cash		400		
		450		450

Year 7			Year 7	
Dec 31 Cash		780	Dec 31 Royalties	780

Operating Account for the year(s) ended 31 December . . . (extracts)

	£
Year 1 Royalties	420
Year 2 ,,	310
Year 3 ,,	560
Year 4 ,,	280
Year 5 ,,	440
Year 6 ,,	450
Year 7 ,,	780

Profit and Loss Account for the year(s) ended 31 December . . . (extracts)

		£
Year 6	Irrecoupable Short Workings Written off (B)	30

Balance Sheet(s) as at 31 December (extracts)
Current Assets

		£
Year 2	Short Workings Recoupable	90
Year 4	Short Workings Recoupable	120
Year 5	Short Workings Recoupable	80

Notes:

(A) The term Operating Account is used. This could instead be called a Working Account or a similar name could be used; in the case of a manufacturer it would be Manufacturing Account. Where royalties are paid per unit of use they can be seen to be an example of what in costing would be called a direct expense.

(B) The irrecoupable short workings can hardly be charged to an Operating Account, as they are an expense connected with non-operation.

It must not be thought that the method described is the only one by which the double entry can be carried out. Obviously the various methods finish up with the same answers eventually, it is merely the ways by which these answers are worked out that are different.

Sub-Leases

Quite often a concern obtains a lease of a mine, quarry, land etc., and is given the right to sub-let part of the asset to someone else, ie. a sub-lessee. Just as it may have to pay a minimum rent to the owner of the asset, with a right to a carry foward of short workings, then so may the lessee make similar sorts of agreements with the sub-lessees.

The entries in the lessee's books are the reverse of those used for royalties payable. Usually separate accounts for royalties payable and royalties receivable are opened. If the royalties payable and receivable are at the same rate, the royalties receivable will be transferred to the royalties payable account at each year end, so that the *net* royalties will be charged as a expense in the Operating Account. If the royalties charged to the sub-lessee are at a higher rate, the excess must be transferred to the credit of the Profit and Loss Account.

To help avoid confusion, the short workings of the sub-lessee are entered in a 'Short Workings Allowable' account', whilst the short-workings to be recovered from the landlord are entered in a 'Short Workings Recoverable' account.

Exercises

Note: **Questions numbered without the suffix 'A' have answers at the back of the book.**

9.1. Smoker, who had patented a tobacco filter, granted to Piper & Co a licence for seven years to manufacture and sell the filter on the following terms:
(i) Piper & Co to pay a royalty of £1 for every 100 filters sold with a minimum payment of £1,000 per annum. Calculations to be made annually as on 31 December, and payment on 31 January.
(ii) If, for any year, the royalties calculated on filters sold amount to less than £1,000, Piper & Co may set off the deficiency against royalties payable in excess of that sum in the next two years.

The number of filters sold were:
   Year to 31 December
   19-1   60,000
   19-2   80,000
   19-3   120,000
   19-4   140,000

You are required to show the ledger accounts recording the above transactions in respect of royalties in the books of Piper & Co, which are closed annually on 31 December.

(Institute of Chartered Accountants)

9.2. T.T. owned the patent rights for a bottle opener. On 1 April 19-2 he granted O.B. & Co. Ltd. a licence for ten years to manufacture and sell the bottle opener on the following terms:
(i) O.B. & Co. Ltd were to pay T.T. a royalty of 50p for each opener sold.
(ii) The minimum royalty for each of the first three covered by the licence was to be £500.
(iii) If royalties on openers sold amounted to less than £500 O.B. & Co Ltd were entitled to deduct the deficiency from royalties in excess of that sum payable in respect of each of the first three years of the agreement.
(iv) After the first three years royalties were to be payable on the actual number of bottle openers sold each year.
(v) Accounts were to be settled to 31 March in each year.

The numbers of bottle openers sold in the first four years were as follows:

   Year ended 31 March
   19-3   860
   19-4   980
   19-5   1,090
   19-6   1,050

Show the accounts relating to the above transactions in the books of O.B. & Co Ltd for the first four years of the agreement.

9.3. Shipton, who had patented an automatic door closer, granted Doors Ltd a licence for ten years to manufacture and sell the door closer on the following terms:

(i) Doors Ltd to pay a royalty of £1 for every closer sold with a minimum payment of £500 per annum. Calculations to be made annually as on 31 December and payment to be made on 31 January.

(ii) If, for any year, the royalties calculated on closers sold amount to less than £500, Doors Ltd may set off the deficiency against royalties payable in excess of that sum in the next two years.

With effect from the end of the second year the agreement was varied and a minimum annual payment of £400 was substituted for £500, the other terms of the annual agreement remaining unchanged.

The numbers of the closers sold were:

Year ended 31 December
19-2	200
19-3	400
19-4	600
19-5	500

You are required to show the ledger accounts recording the above transactions in respect of royalties in the books of Doors Ltd which are closed annually on 31 December.

(Institute of Chartered Accountants)

9.4A. Laurie Ltd (sand and gravel merchants) entered into an agreement to purchase from Sands Ltd over a period of five years such quantities of sand as they might require from time to time and which they were to extract from a sand pit belonging to Sands Ltd. on the following terms:

1. Laurie Ltd to pay a royalty of 10p per ton for all material extracted with a minimum rent of £2,000 per annum.

2. If, for any of the first three years, the royalties on sand extracted fall short of the minimum rent, the short fall is to be set off against any royalties payable in excess of the rent for those three years.

3. The following quantities were extracted:

	Tons
First year	4,000
Second year	16,000
Third year	28,000

Prepare the ledger accounts recording these transactions in the books of Laurie Ltd, assuming that the payments due for any year were made during the following year.

Income Tax is to be ignored.

(Association of Certified Accountants)

10

Hire Purchase and Payments by Instalments

When goods are bought under a hire purchase agreement, the legal title to the goods does not pass to the purchaser until every instalment has been paid and a small amount, usually included in the last payment, is paid which legally exercises an option to buy the goods. Thus to buy on hire purchase is legally to hire the goods until a certain time, when an option can be exercised to take over the legal title to the goods. Normally the hire purchaser is not compelled to complete the transaction. If he so wishes he may return the goods and not pay any further instalments. He will, however, forfeit the right to have any of his previous instalments repaid to him. On default the seller can reclaim the goods, subject to certain provisions of the Hire Purchase Acts.

In contrast to this are credit sales payable by instalments, in which the absolute ownership passes immediately to the purchaser. The seller cannot reclaim the goods, but can sue for the unpaid instalments. There is also a class of sale known as a 'conditional sale agreement', which legally has some of the characteristics of both hire purchase and credit sale transactions.

A book on Hire Purchase Law should be studied for the precise legal position of the three types of sales payable for by instalments. From the accounting point of view the three types have a great deal in common. The total amount payable for the asset is made up of (*a*) the cash price, this being the amount that would have been payable if payment had been made immediately on acquisition instead of being paid for by instalments, and (*b*) the interest element. A firm would not normally sell goods for exactly the same price to customer (i) who is being given two years to pay for the goods by regular instalments, than they would to customer (ii) who is to pay immediately for the goods. Therefore customer (i) will have to pay something extra to compensate the selling firm for extra administration expenses, the risk element of default by the purchaser, and the loss of working capital for a period of time. The rate of interest should therefore be fixed so that it is adequate to cover these items.

Exhibit 10.1

A car which had a cash sale price of £500 might have a hire purchase price of £600 calculated as follows:

	£
Cash Price	500
Add Hire Purchase Interest – 10 per cent of £500 for two years	100
Hire Purchase Price	600

Payable by 24 monthly instalments of £25 each.

Substitute the words 'credit sale' or 'conditional sale' for the words 'hire purchase' and the facts apply to these other two cases.

Of course, requirements concerning deposits and lengths of repayment allowed change with various governmental attempts to control the economy. If a deposit of £100 had been required, the agreement for the car may have been as follows:

Exhibit 10.2

	£
Cash Price	500
Add Hire Purchase Interest – 10 per cent of £400 for two years	80
Hire Purchase Price	580

Deposit of £100 paid, therefore the interest is only calculated on the actual amount owing, i.e. £500 – £100 = £400. Payment is completed by 24 monthly instalments of £20 each.

From this point in the chapter the items dealt with will be goods bought and sold on hire purchase. The accounting treatment of credit sale and conditional sale items can well be exactly the same as for hire purchase items. Therefore in each of the examples the substitution of 'credit sale' or 'conditional sale' would convert the method from being one used only for hire purchase.

Hire Purchaser's Books

Because of the restriction on the resale of goods bought on hire purchase the goods normally bought by a firm are in the nature of fixed assets. There are those who maintain that as the legal title to the goods does not pass until the final payment has been made, then it is wrong to bring the full cash price into the books until this has been done. This would seem to be an extreme view in most cases, and one which should normally be avoided. The vast majority of firms enter into hire purchase agreements with the intention of honouring them.

Hire purchase is nothing more than the means of financing the purchase of a fixed asset. To capitalise only the proportion of the cash price actually paid is a case of the concept of prudence being carried to extremes. It is also misleading to anyone who is interested in the analysis of the Balance Sheet, as the fixed assets which have been used to win the profits are not fully represented. This method will not therefore be used in this book.

The main problem is that of splitting the amount actually paid between that which refers to hire purchase interest and that which refers to a reduction in the amount of the cash price still owing. Hire purchase interest is normally the cost of borrowing money which is used to buy a fixed asset. Like the cost of borrowing money generally, such as bank overdraft interest or loan interest, it is revenue expenditure and should therefore be charged to the Profit and Loss Account. The cash price is the actual cost of the asset itself; the fact that the asset is bought on hire purchase has no relevance as far as the asset itself is concerned. The extra money paid for hire purchase is due, not to the asset itself but because the firm did not possess the amount of liquid resources available at the time of purchase to pay for the asset immediately. The cash price is therefore capital expenditure and will have to be shown accordingly in the Balance Sheet. If the hire purchase agreement was begun and terminated in the same accounting period, then the apportioning of the amount actually paid between hire purchase interest and the cash price would be a simple matter. If a car was bought for a total hire purchase price of £96, being cash price £90 and hire purchase interest £6, and this was paid by six monthly instalments of £16 each, then the Cash Book would show credits of £96 in all and the debits would be £90 in the Motor Car Account and £6 in the Hire Purchase Interest Account. Either an intermediate account called a Hire Purchase Account could be used to which the £96 would be debited, and the £90 and the £6 then transferred to the relevant accounts, or else with every credit of £16 in the Cash Book the debits could be made of £1 in the Hire Purchase Interest Account and of £15 in the Motor Car Account. The full cash price of £90 would still show in the Balance Sheet, because the purchase is completed before the year end.

On the other hand where the agreement is not started and completed within the accounting period, then the separation of the interest from the proportion of the cash price paid is not a simple matter. The aim is to show the full cash price of the asset in the Balance Sheet. If not fully paid for, then the amount owing will have to also be shown in the Balance Sheet as being owed. This is similar to any asset bought which has not been paid for at the Balance Sheet date. However, the liability to be shown is not the amount of the hire purchase price that is to be paid, but is instead confined to the part of the cash price which still has to be paid. The hire purchase interest which has to be paid in the future is not a liability of the firm at that point in time. Interest is essentially based on the time factor and is only charged in the Profit and Loss Account when it accrues. Therefore future hire purchase interest will only be chargeable as an expense during the years when it accrues, and is not chargeable in this year's Profit and Loss Account. This is rather like saying that if premises were bought they would be shown as an asset in the Balance Sheet, and that if they were only partly paid for, then the liability would also be shown in the Balance Sheet, but revenue expenditure such as rates will only appear in the accounts, and therefore in the Balance Sheet as a liability as it falls due.

How accurately this can be done depends on whether or not the 'true' running rate of interest is known. In Exhibit 10.3 below the rate of interest is stated to be 10 per cent per annum. This interest is only payable on the amounts actually owing from time to time, i.e. the interest is calculated on the reducing balance owed. On the other hand, if the interest is calculated as a percentage rate of the original amount owing, then this is not a 'true' running rate of interest. An example of this is in Exhibit 10.1 where a car is bought for £500 and the interest chargeable is said to be 10 per cent. The 10 per cent for two years was calculated by reference to the £500, the original amount owing. However, after each instalment has been paid the amount of the £500 still owing will fall. The 'true' running rate of interest refers to the interest rate per annum which would have to be applied to each reducing balance so as to bring the amount owing down to zero after the payment of the last instalment.

The method of calculating the 'true' rate of interest is covered in chapter 24. That chapter also contains a method, known as the 'Rule of 78', which can be used by firms which want to keep their mathematical computations at a low level.

In considering financing operations one must consider like with like. It is no use comparing the nominal rate of interest offered by one organization against the 'true' rate offered by another. Comparison can only be achieved by data calculated on the same basis, and therefore the two rates should be expressed as 'true' rates. An example of this is the bank overdraft on which interest is expressed in 'true' interest terms, while a personal bank loan is in 'nominal' rate terms. Hire purchase interest rates, especially in the retail field, are usually expressed in nominal rate terms.

The necessary accounts needed can now be considered.

Exhibit 10.4
1. True Rate of Interest Known. Equal Instalments

A machine is bought for £3,618 hire purchase price from Suppliers Ltd on 1 January 19-3, being paid for by three instalments of £1,206 on 31 December of 19-3, 19-4 and 19-5. The cash price is £3,000. The true rate of interest is 10 per cent. (For convenience all figure are rounded off, fractions of pounds are not shown.)

Machinery

19-3			£
Jan 1 Suppliers Ltd	(A)	3,000	

Suppliers Ltd

19-3			£	19-3			£
Dec 31	Bank	(B)	1,206	Jan 1	Machinery	(A)	3,000
,, 31	Balance c/d	(D)	2,094	Dec 31	H.P. Interest	(C)	300
			3,300				3,300
19-4				19-4			
Dec 31	Bank	(B)	1,206	Jan 1	Balance b/d	(D)	2,094
,, 31	Balance c/d	(D)	1,097	Dec 31	H.P. Interest	(C)	209
			2,303				2,303
19-5				19-5			
Dec 31	Bank	(B)	1,206	Jan 1	Balance b/d	(D)	1,097
				Dec 31	H.P. Interest	(C)	109
			1,206				1,206

Hire Purchase Interest

19-3			£	19-3			£
Dec 31	Suppliers Ltd	(C)	300	Dec 31	Profit and Loss	(E)	300
19-4				19-4			
Dec 31	Suppliers Ltd	(C)	209	Dec 31	Profit and Loss	(E)	209
19-5				19-5			
Dec 31	Suppliers Ltd	(C)	109	Dec 31	Profit and Loss	(E)	109

Provision for Depreciation: Machinery

				19-3			£
				Dec 31	Profit and Loss	(F)	600
				19-4			
				Dec 31	Profit and Loss	(F)	600
				19-5			
				Dec 31	Profit and Loss	(F)	600

Balance Sheets as at 31 December

		£	£
19-3	Machinery (at cost)	3,000	
	Less Depreciation	600	2,400
	Owing on Hire Purchase Agreement		2,094
19-4	Machinery (at cost)	3,000	
	Less Depreciation to date	1,200	1,800
	Owing on Hire Purchase Agreement		1,097
19-5	Machinery (at cost)	3,000	
	Less Depreciation to date	1,800	1,200

Description of entries:

(A) When the asset is acquired the cash price is debited to the asset account and the credit is in the supplier's account.

(B) The instalments paid are credited to the Bank Account and debited to the supplier's account.

(C) The interest is credited to the supplier's account for each period as it accrues, and debited to the expense account, later to be transferred to the Profit and Loss Account for the period (E).

(D) The balance carried down each year is the amount of the cash price still owing.

(F) Depreciation provisions are calculated on the full cash price, as the depreciation of an asset is in no way affected by whether or not is has been fully paid for.

The Balance Sheet consists of balance (A) the cash price, less balance (F) the amount of cash price apportioned as depreciation. Balance (D) the amount of the cash price still owing at each Balance Sheet date is shown as a liability.

2. True Rate of Interest Known. Unequal Instalments

Sometimes the cash price portion is repaid by equal instalments, while the interest portion is paid as it accrues. As the interest falls due, the proportion of the cash price owing on which the interest is based is being reduced each year, thus it will be obvious that the total repayments will be different for each accounting period.

Assuming that the same details applied as in (1), but that £1,000 was to be paid off the cash price each year, plus the whole of the interest as it accrued, then Suppliers Ltd Account would appear as follows:

Exhibit 10.5

Suppliers Ltd

19-3		£	19-3		£
Dec 31	Bank	1,300	Jan 1	Machinery	3,000
,, 31	Balance c/d	2,000	Dec 31	H.P. Interest (10 per cent of £3,000)	300
		3,300			3,300
19-4			19-4		
Dec 31	Bank	1,200	Jan 1	Balance b/d	2,000
,, 31	Balance c/d	1,000	Dec 31	H.P. Interest (10 per cent of £2,000)	200
		2,200			2,200
19-5			19-5		
Dec 31	Bank	1,100	Jan 1	Balance b/d	1,000
			Dec 31	H.P. Interest (10 per cent of £1,000)	100
		1,100			1,100

All the ways in which the debit and credit entries were made in (1) will be repeated in this case. The only difference will be that the figures will be governed by the transfers now to be effected from Suppliers Ltd Account.

The Seller's Books

There are a considerable number of ways of drawing up the final accounts of a business which sells goods on hire purchase and of calculating the amounts to be shown therein. The methods chosen should be suitable for the particular firm and needs obviously vary. There is a vast gulf between the old-established firm which sells quality goods to well-known reputable customers, and the back-street firm which sells cheap, easily breakable goods, to anyone without enquiring very deeply as to the customer's creditworthiness.

It can, however, be stipulated that the interest earned from hire purchase sales is earned because money is owed to the firm for a period of time. The interest that should be credited to the Trading Account is therefore the amount which has accrued during the period covered by the account.

On the other hand the profit made on the goods sold is usually either:

(*a*) Treated as being profit of the firm entirely in the period in which it was first sold to the purchaser, i.e. when the agreement was entered into and the goods delivered to him.

(*b*) A proportion of the profits is brought into the Trading Account, this being in the ratio which the cash actually received during the period bears to the total cash receivable.

It is inappropriate in a book at this level to go into intricate details of the methods used in practice by firms. With firms that have many hire purchase transactions the methods of apportioning interest and profit are often ones of expediency, exact accuracy often being too costly to achieve. Therefore in an examination the examiner's instructions should always be carried out, he may be envisaging such a situation. The fact that the examinee may disagree with the method used is irrelevant for this purpose.

Exhibit 10.6 shows the accounts needed by a firm with two departments, one department uses method (*a*), while the other department uses method (*b*).

Exhibit 10.6

A. Phelps started business on 1 January 19-5. He sold cash registers of a uniform type which cost him £90 each, for a cash price of £120, and also on hire purchase terms for £140, being payable by a deposit of £20 followed by three instalments of £40 each on the first, second and third anniversaries of the date of the contract. The total price of £140 included compound interest at 10 per cent on the reducing balance owed (calculated after each year's payment) of the normal cash price. It is assumed that the sales were evenly spread over the year.

He also sold calculators of a uniform type on hire purchase only. These required an initial deposit of £6 followed by 12 quarterly instalments of £2 each over a period of three years. The cost of calculators was £18 each.

The following trial balance was extracted as on 31 December 19-5:

	£	£
Capital: Cash Introduced		50,000
Fixed Assets	10,000	
Hire Purchase Sales – Cash Registers (200 at £140 each)		28,000
Cash Sales – Cash Registers (50 at £120 each)		6,000
Cash collected from hire purchasers of calculators (1,000 calculators sold)		9,600
Debtors	24,000	
Purchases – Cash Registers (350 at £90)	31,500	
Purchases – Calculators (1,200 at £18)	21,600	
Bank	8,900	
Creditors		6,400
Salaries and General Expenses	4,000	
	100,000	100,000

It was decided to take credit, in the annual accounts, for the normal gross profit (excluding interest) on cash registers sold to customers and to apportion the interest on a time basis.

In view of the large number of transactions in calculators, and the difficulty of apportioning the interest, it was decided to adopt for this section of the business the alternative method of taking credit for the profit, including interest, on calculators only in proportion to the cash collected.

Stocks were valued at cost, being cash registers (100) £9,000, and calculators (200) £3,600.

The following accounts demonstrate the methods used. The letters (A) to (H) refer to the narratives which follow the accounts and are needed to explain those items that are not self-evident.

Cash Registers Trading Account for the year ended
31 December 19-5

		£	£
Cash Sales			6,000
Hire Purchase Sales – at Cash Prices	(A)		24,000
Hire Purchase Interest	(C)		1,000
			31,000
Less Cost of Goods Sold:			
Purchases		31,500	
Less Closing Stock		9,000	22,500
Gross Profit c/d			8,500

Cash Registers – Interest Suspense

		£				£
Trading Account – 10% per annum on £20,000 for six months	(C)	1,000	Hire Purchase Sales – Interest included in Hire Purchase Price		(B)	4,000
Interest not yet earned c/d	(D)	3,000				
		4,000				4,000

Cash Registers – Hire Purchase Sales

		£		£
Interest Suspense – 200 × £20	(B)	4,000	Debtors	28,000
Trading Account – Cash Price of Sales	(A)	24,000		
		28,000		28,000

(A) As the interest factor of profit is being calculated separately the cash price of goods sold on hire purchase is transferred so that the goods factor of profit can be dealt with.

(B) The whole interest factor is transferred to the suspense account.

(C) The apportionment of the interest earned in this period is now calculated. For simplicity it has been stated that the sales were spread evenly throughout the year. This means that the average time that money was owing was six months. The interest of 10 per cent per annum is based on the part of the cash price owing. As only the deposits of £20 were paid in this year the balance of £100 of the cash price was therefore owing for each machine, i.e. 200 machines = £20,000. As this money had been owed for six months on average, then the interest is £20,000 for six months at the rate of 10 per cent per annum = £1,000. This now needs transferring to the Trading Account as it constitutes part of this year's profit.

Of course, if the sales have not been spread evenly over the year, then the interest earned would have been different. If most of the sales had taken place at the start of the year the average time that each £100 was owing would be greater than six months, if most of the sales had taken place at the end of the year, then each £100 would have been owing for an average time of less than six months. It all depends on the facts. Calculations must therefore be based on the facts in each firm.

(D) When the goods have been sold on hire purchase the total hire purchase price has been debited to each customer's account. However, of the £4,000 total hire purchase interest, £3,000 still has to be earned and is accordingly carried forward to the next accounting period. As the figure of debtors includes this amount, then the debtors need to be shown net in the Balance Sheet after the deduction of the unearned interest.

(E) As the interest factor and the profit on goods factor are not being separated for profit calculations, there is no need to show them separately.

(F) The provision for unrealised profit is debited to the Trading Account, and will be credited to a Provision for Unrealised Profit Account. At the end of each accounting period the provision will need adjusting, sometimes it will have to be increased, this will be done by debiting the Trading Account and crediting the Provision Account. At other times the provision will need reducing, this will necessitate the debiting of the Provision Account and the crediting of the Trading Account. It will now be seen to work in a similar manner to a Bad Debts Provision Account, the main difference being that provision for unrealised profits affects the Trading Account while provision for bad debts affects the Profit and Loss Account instead. Also, like the bad debts example, the balance of the Provision for Unrealised Profit Account is deducted from the instalments owing in the Balance Sheet.

The provision is calculated thus:

$$\frac{\text{Cash yet to be collected}}{\text{Total Cash collectable from the Sales}} \times \text{Total Gross Profit (incl. interest)}$$

$$= \frac{20,400}{30,000}(G) \times £12,000(H) = £8,160$$

Calculators Trading Account for the year ended 31 December 19-5

Sales at Hire Purchase Price	(E)		30,000
Purchases		21,600	
Less Closing Stock		3,600	
Cost of Goods Sold		18,000	
Provision for Unrealised Profit	(F)	8,160	26,160
Gross Profit c/d			3,840

(G) The £20,400 is found by taking the total cash collectable from the sales less the amount already collected: i.e. £30 × 1,000 = £30,000 *less* £9,600 (see trial balance) = Cash yet to be collected £20,400.

(H) This figure is found by taking the profit for each calculator (including interest) and multiplying by the number of units sold. Hire purchase price £30 *less* cost £18 = £12 profit (including interest) per unit. 1,000 units sold, therefore £12 × 1,000 = £12,000 total profit.

Profit and Loss Account for the year ended 31 December 19-5

	£
Gross Profit b/d	
On Cash Registers	8,500
On Calculators	3,840
	12,340
Less Salaries and General Expenses	4,000
Net Profit	8,340

Balance Sheet as at 31 December 19-5

	£	£	£
Fixed Assets			10,000
Current Assets			
Stocks		12,600	
Hire Purchase Instalments not yet due			
Cash Registers	24,000		
Less Provisions for Interest not due	3,000	21,000	
Calculators	20,400		
Less Provision for Unrealised Profit	8,160	12,240	
Bank		8,900	
		54,740	
Less Current Liabilities			
Creditors		6,400	48,340
			58,340
Financed by:			
Capital			
Cash Introduced		50,000	
Add Net Profit		8,340	58,340
			58,340

Repossessions

If in the accounts shown, some of the people buying calculators had defaulted on their payments and the goods had been repossessed, then this would need special accounting treatment. The sums paid by the customers would have been forfeited by them. On the other hand, the repossessed items taken back into stock are not new and will therefore have to be revalued accordingly.

The Calculator Trading Account can now be reconstructed if, in addition to the transactions already described, a further 10 calculators on which a total of £8 each had been paid were repossessed, (i.e. 1,010 sold originally, 10 of these being repossessed later). On 31 December 19-5 they were not valued at cost, i.e. £18 each, but were valued as being worth £13 each.

Calculator Trading Account for the year ended 31 December 19-5

	£	£
Sales at Hire Purchase Price		30,000
Instalments Received on Repossessions		80
		30,080
Less Cost of Goods Sold:		
Purchases	21,600	
Less Stock (I)	3,550	
	18,050	
Provision for Unrealised Profit	8,160	26,210
Gross Profit		3,870

(I) The final stock is now made up of:

	£
Unsold Items – 190 × £18	3,420
Items Repossessed – 10 × £13	130
	3,550

The gross profit is now £3,870. This can be explained as follows:

		£	£
(i)	Original profit		3,840
	Additional transactions –		
	Received instalments 10 × £8	80	
	Loss of value – cost *less* new value £18 – £13 = £5 × 10	50	
	Therefore additional profit		30
	Revised Profit		3,870

Company Accounts

A change introduced by the 1981 Companies Act is that an amount owing on a hire-purchase contract cannot now be deducted from the value of the asset in the balance sheet.

Accounting for Leases

In October 1981 Exposure Draft 29 was issued by the Accounting Standards Committee. It is almost certain to become an accounting standard. The background was stated in the following terms.

Leasing and hire purchase contracts are means by which companies finance the right to use or the purchase of fixed assets. In the UK there is normally no provision in a lease contract for legal title to the leased asset to pass to the lessee during the term of a lease. In contrast under a hire purchase contract the hirer may acquire legal title by exercising an option to purchase the asset upon fulfilment of certain conditions (normally the payment of an agreed number of instalments). Current tax legislation provides for capital allowances to be claimed by the lessor under a lease contract and by the hirer under a hire purchase contract.

Lessors fall into three broad categories. They may be companies, including banks and finance houses, which provide finance under lease contracts to enable a single customer to acquire the use of an asset for the greater part of its useful life; they may operate a business which involves the renting out of assets for varying periods of time probably to more than one customer; or they may be manufacturer or dealer lessors who use leasing as a means of marketing their products, which may involve leasing a product to one customer or to several customers. As a lessor and lessee are both parties to the same transaction it is appropriate that the same definitions should be used and the accounting treatment recommended should ideally be complementary. However, this will not mean that the recorded balances in both financial statements will be the same, because the pattern of cash flows and the taxation consequences will be different.

Leases can appropriately be classified into finance leases and operating leases. The distinction between a finance lease and an operating lease will usually be evident from the substance of the contract between the lessor and the lessee. A finance lease usually involves repayment to a lessor by a lessee of the full cost of the asset together with a return on the finance provided by the lessor. As such, a lease of this type is normally non-cancellable or cancellable only under certain conditions, and the lessee enjoys substantially all the risks and rewards associated with the ownership of an asset, other than the legal title.

An operating lease involves the lessee paying a rental for the hire of an asset for a period of time which is normally substantially less than its useful economic life. The lessor retains the risks and rewards of ownership of an asset in an operating lease and normally assumes responsibility for repairs, maintenance and insurance.

Briefly, this standard requires that a finance lease should be accounted for by the lessee as if it were the purchase of the property rights in an asset with simultaneous recognition of the obligation to make future payments, in the same way that a hire purchase is normally accounted for. Under an operating lease, only the rental will be taken into account by a lessee. The standard recognises that the substance of a transaction rather than its legal form should govern the accounting treatment.

Exercises

10.1. An engineering concern purchased machines on the H.P. system over a period of three years paying £846 down on 1 January 19-3, and further annual payments of £2,000 due on 31 December 19-3, 19-4 and 19-5.

The cash price of the machine was £6,000, the vendor company charging interest at 8 per cent per annum on outstanding balances.

Show the appropriate ledger accounts in the hire purchaser's books for the three years and how the items would appear in the balance sheet at 31 December 19-3; depreciation at 10 per cent per annum on the written down value is to be charged and interest calculated to the nearest £.

10.2. On 1 January 19-3 J. Donkins bought a machine (cash price £2,092) from C.D. & Co Ltd on the following hire purchase terms. Donkins was to make an immediate payment of £600 and three annual payments of £600 on 31 December in each year. The rate of interest chargeable is 10 per cent per annum.

Donkins depreciates this machinery by 10 per cent on the diminishing balance each year.

(a) Make the entries relating to this machine in Donkin's ledger for the year 19-3, 19-4 and 19-5. (All calculations are to be made to the nearest £.)

(b) Show how the item machinery would appear in the Balance Sheet as at 31 December 19-3.

10.3A. Bulwell Aggregates Ltd. wish to expand their transport fleet and have purchased three heavy lorries with a list price of £18,000 each. Robert Bulwell has negotiated hire purchase finance to fund this expansion, and the company has entered into a hire purchase agreement with Granby Garages PLC on the 1 January 19-1. The agreement states that Bulwell Aggregates will pay a deposit of £9,000 on 1 January 19-1, and two annual instalments of £24,000 on 31 December 19-1, 19-2, and a final instalment of £20,391 on 31 December 19-3.

Interest is to be calculated at 25% on the balance outstanding on 1 January each year and paid on 31 December each year.

The depreciation policy of Bulwell Aggregates Ltd. is to write off the vehicles over a four year period using the straight line method and assuming a scrap value of £1,333 for each vehicle at the end of its useful life.

The cost of the vehicles to Granby Garages is £14,400 each.

Required:

(a) Account for the above transactions in the books of Bulwell Aggregates Ltd., showing the entries in the Profit and Loss Account and Balance Sheet for the years 19-1, 19-2, 19-3 and 19-4.

(b) Account for the above transactions in the books of Granby Garages PLC, showing the entries in the Hire Purchase Trading Account for the years 19-1, 19-2, 19-3. This is the only hire purchase transaction undertaken by this company.

Calculations to the nearest £.

(Association of Accounting Technicians)

10.4A. J. York was acquiring two cars under hire purchase agreements, details of which are as follows:

Registration Number	JY 1	JY 2
Date of purchase	31 May 19-6	31 October 19-6
Cash price	£18,000	£24,000
Deposit	£3,120	£4,800
Interest (deemed to accrue evenly over the period of the agreement)	£1,920	£2,400

Both agreements provided for payment to be made in twenty-four monthly instalments commencing on the last day of the month following purchase.

On 1 September 19-7, vehicle JY1 became a total loss. In full settlement on 20 September 19-7:

(i) an insurance company paid £12,500 under a comprehensive policy, and
(ii) the hire purchase company accepted £6,000 for the termination of the agreement.

The firm prepared accounts annually to 31 December and provided depreciation on a straight line basis at a rate of 20 per cent per annum for motor vehicles, apportioned as from the date of purchase and up to the date of disposal.

All instalments were paid on the due dates.

The balance on the Hire Purchase Company Account in respect of vehicle JY1 is to be written off.

You are required to record these transactions in the following accounts, carrying down the balances as on 31 December 19-6, and 31 December 19-7:

(a) Motor Vehicles,
(b) Depreciation, and
(c) Hire Purchase Company,
(d) Assets Disposal.

10.5. On 30 September 19-7, B. Wright, who prepares final accounts annually to 30 September, bought a motor lorry on hire purchase from the Vehicles and Finance Co Ltd. The cash price of the lorry was £3,081. Under the terms of the hire purchase agreement, Wright paid a deposit of £1,000 on 30 September 19-7, and two instalments of £1,199 on 30 September, 19-8 and 19-9. The hire vendor charged interest at 10 per cent per annum on the balance outstanding on 1 October each year. All payments were made on the due dates.

Wright maintained the motor lorry account at cost and accumulated the annual provision for depreciation, at 25 per cent on the diminishing balance method, in a separate account.

You are required to:

(i) prepare the following accounts as they would appear in the ledger of B. Wright for the period of the contract:

(a) Vehicles and Finance Co Ltd.
(b) Motor Lorry on hire purchase.
(c) Provision for depreciation of motor lorry.
(d) Hire purchase interest payable.

(ii) show how the above matters would appear in the balance sheet of B. Wright at 30 September 19-8.

The Vehicles and Finance Co Ltd prepares final accounts annually to 30 September, on which date it charges B. Wright with the interest due.

Make calculations to the nearest £.

140

10.6. S. Craven started business on 1 October 19-5 selling machines of one standard type on hire purchase terms. During the year to 30 September 19-6 he purchased machines at a uniform price of £60 and sold 1,900 machines at a total price under hire purchase agreements of £100 per machine, payable by an initial deposit of £30 and 10 quarterly instalments of £7.

The following trial balance was extracted from Craven's books as at 30 September 19-6.

	£	£
Capital		76,000
Drawings	4,000	
Fixed Assets	10,000	
Purchases	120,000	
Cash collected from Customers		83,600
Rent, Rates and Insurance	4,500	
Wages	8,600	
General Expenses	10,270	
Balance at Bank	10,630	
Sundry Trade Creditors		8,400
	168,000	168,000

The personal accounts of customers are memorandum records (i.e. they are not part of the double entry system).

Craven prepares his annual accounts on the basis of taking credit for profit (including interest) in proportion to cash collected from customers.

Prepare Craven's Hire Purchase Trading Account and a Profit and Loss Account for the year ended 30 September 19-6 and a Balance Sheet as at that date.

Ignore depreciation of fixed assets.

10.7A. R.J. commenced business on 1 January 19-8. He sells refrigerators, all of one standard type, on hire-purchase terms. The total amount, including interest, payable for each refrigerator, is £300. Customers are required to pay an initial deposit of £60, followed by eight quarterly instalments of £30 each. The cost of each refrigerator to R.J. is £200.

The following trial balance was extracted from R.J.'s books as on 31 December 19-8.

Trial Balance

	£	£
Capital		100,000
Fixed assets	10,000	
Drawings	4,000	
Bank overdraft		19,600
Creditors		16,600
Purchases	180,000	
Cash collected from customers		76,500
Bank interest	400	
Wages and salaries	12,800	
General expenses	5,500	
	£212,700	£212,700

850 machines were sold on hire-purchase terms during 19-8.

The annual accounts are prepared on the basis of taking credit for profit (including interest) in proportion to the cash collected from customers.

You are required to prepare the hire purchase trading account, and the profit and loss account for the year 19-8 and balance sheet as on 31 December 19-8.

Ignore depreciation of fixed assets.

Show your calculations.

(*Chartered Institute of Secretaries and Administrators*)

10.8A. On 1 January 19-6, F Limited commenced business selling goods on hire-purchase. Under the terms of the agreements, an initial deposit of 20 per cent is payable on delivery, followed by four equal quarterly instalments, the first being due three months after the date of sale.

During the year sales were made as follows:

H.P.
Cost price sales price

	£	£
10 January	150	225
8 March	350	525
12 May	90	135
6 July	200	300
20 September	70	105
15 October	190	285
21 November	160	240

The goods sold in July were returned in September and eventually sold in November for £187 cash. All other instalments are paid on the due dates.

It may be assumed that:

(a) gross profit and interest are credited to profit and loss account in the proportion that deposits and instalments received bear to hire purchase price, or

(b) the cost is deemed to be paid in full before any credit is taken for gross profit and interest.

You are to prepare for the first year of trading, a hire-purchase trading account compiled firstly on assumption (a) and secondly on assumption (b) and give the relevant balance sheet entries under each assumption.

Workings should be clearly shown.

(*Institute of Cost and Management Accountants*)

11

Limited Companies: General Background

A very brief introduction was made to the accounts of limited companies in Chapter 41 of Volume 1. It was intended to show some of the basic outlines of the Final Accounts of limited companies to those people who would be finishing their studies of accounting with the completion of Volume 1. This volume now carries the study of limited companies accounting to a more advanced stage.

The Acts of Parliament now governing limited companies are five in number, the Companies Acts of 1948, of 1967, of 1976, of 1980 and finally, of 1981. These Acts, when cited, should be shown as the 'Companies Acts 1948 to 1981'. As each of the last four Acts has amended and added to the previous ones, it can in practice lead to the Acts being difficult to comprehend. Eventually the Acts will be consolidated into one Companies Act, but this is still some time away. As this volume is concerned with basic principles the complications are better left until the reader has reached a more advanced stage in his studies.

The Companies Acts 1948 to 1981 are the descendants of modern limited liability company legislation which can be traced back to the passing of the Companies Act 1862. This act was a triumph for the development of the limited liability principle which had been severely restricted since the so-called 'Bubble Act' of 1720, this latter act being the remedy for a multitude of spectacular frauds perpetuated behind the cloak of limited liability. Not until 1862 was general prejudice overcome, and the way paved for the general use of the limited liability principle which is now commonplace. Company law therefore consists of the Companies Acts 1948 to 1981, together with a considerable body of case law which has been built up over the years. It must be borne in mind that there are still a number of Chartered Companies in existence which were incorporated by Royal Charter, such as the Hudson's Bay Company, or else which were formed by special Acts of Parliament, such as the Mersey Docks and Harbour Board.

The 1981 Companies Act has, as its prime purpose, the harmonisation of company law in the European Economic Community (EEC). The Act also brings in a completely new development in the United Kingdom. Before this act companies *had* to disclose certain information. The way that the accounts were drawn up, so long as the necessary information was shown, was completely at the discretion of the company itself. The 1981 Act however sets out detailed rules on the format of the accounts and these will be considered later in this book.

The 1981 Companies Act does not apply to banks, insurance companies and shipping companies. They therefore may continue to produce accounts as before. Banks and Insurance companies will be the subject of separate future EEC directives.

The Companies Acts also cover companies with unlimited liability. These are now very rarely met in practice. Also covered are companies limited by guarantee, which may or may not have a share capital, but the Companies Act 1980 forbade the future formation of such companies. Both of these types of limited company are relatively unimportant, and therefore any future reference to a 'limited company' or merely a 'company' will be concerned with limited liability companies of the normal type.

Until the act of 1980 you could not tell from the title of a company whether it was a private company or a public company. With the passing of the Act of 1980, however, public companies were required to end their names with the words 'public limited company'. Such a public limited company would have to have a minimum issued share capital of £50,000. Instead of using the words 'public limited company' in full, the abbreviation 'plc', or in capitals PLC, may be used. If the registered office is in Wales the Welsh equivalent is permitted, this is 'cwmni cyfyngedig cyhoeddus'.

A private company, on the other hand, does not have to state that it is a private company. This means that should the words 'public limited company', or the abbreviation, or the Welsh equivalent, not be shown, then the company is a private limited company.

Another change which may be noted is that the minimum number of persons who may form a public company is now two, instead of seven the number which used to prevail before the 1980 Act.

The outstanding feature of a limited company is that, no matter how many individuals have bought shares in it, yet it is treated in its dealings with the outside world as if it were a person in its own right, it is said to be a separate 'legal entity'. Just as the law can create this separate legal person, then so also can it eliminate it, but its existence can only be terminated by using the proper legal procedures. Thus the identity of the shareholders in a large concern may be changing daily as shares are bought and sold by different people. On the other hand, a small private company may have the same shareholders from when it is incorporated (the day it legally came into being), until the date when liquidation is completed (the cessation of a company, often known also as 'winding up' or being 'wound up'). A prime example of its identity as a separate legal entity is that it may sue its own shareholders, or in turn be sued by them.

The legal formalities by which the company comes into existence can be gleaned from any textbook on Company Law. It is not the purpose of this book to discuss Company Law in any great detail, this is far better left to a later stage of one's studies. As companies must, however, comply with the law, the essential Company Law concerning accounting matters will be dealt with in this book as far as is necessary. This is not a book in which company accounts should be discussed in great detail.

What is important is that the basic principles connected with company accounts can be seen in operation. In order that the student may not be unduly confused, points which very rarely occur, or on which the legal arguments are extremely involved and may not yet have been finally settled, will be left out completely or merely mentioned in passing. This means that some generalisations will bear closer scrutiny when accounting studies reach a more advanced stage.

Each company is governed by two documents, known as the Memorandum of Association and the Articles of Association, generally referred to as the 'memorandum' and the 'articles'. The memorandum consists of five clauses, which contain the following details:

(1) The name of the company.

(2) The part of the United Kingdom where the registered office will be situated.

(3) The objects of the company.

(4) A statement (if a limited liability company) that the liability of its members is limited.

(5) Details of the share capital which the company is authorised to issue.

(6) A public limited company will also have a clause stating that the company is a public limited company.

The memorandum is said to be the document which discloses the conditions which govern the company's relationship with the outside world.

The principle of limited liability underlying clause 4 has been of the utmost importance in industry and commerce. It is inconceivable that large business units, such as Imperial Chemical Industries Ltd or Great Universal Stores Ltd, could have existed except for a very few instances. The investor in a limited company, who therefore buys shares in it, is a shareholder, the most he can lose is the money he has paid for the shares, or where he has only partly paid for them, then he is also liable for the unpaid part in addition. With public companies, where their shares are dealt in on a Stock Exchange, he can easily sell them whenever he so wishes. The sale of a share in a private company is not so easily effected.

Classes of Shares

The main classes of shares are Ordinary shares and Preference shares. Unless clearly stated in the memorandum or articles of association Preference shares are assumed to be of the cumulative variety already described in Chapter 41 of volume one.

There are also a variety of other shares. The rights attaching to these shares are purely dependent on the skill and ingenuity of the draftsman of the memorandum and articles of association. An entirely new type of share may be created provided it does not contravene the law.

The shares which carry the right to the whole of the profits remaining after the Preference shares (and any other fixed dividend shares) have been paid a dividend are often known as the equity share capital or as 'equities'.

Until the Companies Act 1981 the only type of share which could be bought back from the shareholders by the company itself were redeemable preference shares. This has now changed completely, and it will be considered in detail in chapter 13.

Dividends

In volume 1, chapter 41, the calculation of dividends from profits available for distribution was shown. Until the 1980 Act there never had been a definition of 'distributable profits', and students had to learn a considerable number of law cases which had bearing on the meaning of distributable profits.

The 1980 Act stated that companies must not make a distribution except out of profits available for the purpose. As the definition of profits involves an understanding of factors to be examined in later chapters, this will not be considered in detail until chapter 19.

Table A

Besides the Memorandum of Association every company must also have Articles of Association. Just as the memorandum governs the company's dealings with the outside world, the articles govern the relationships which exist between the members and the company, between one member and the other members, and other necessary regulations. The Companies Act 1948, in the first schedule attached to it, has a model set of articles known as Table A. A company may, if it so wishes, have its articles exactly the same as Table A, commonly known as 'adopting Table A', or else adopt part of it and have some sections altered. The adoption of the major part of Table A is normal for most private companies. In accounting textbooks, unless stated to the contrary, the accounting examples shown are usually on the basis that Table A has been adopted.

Table A lays down regulations concerning the powers of the directors of the company. On the other hand, the company may draft its own regulations for the powers of directors. Any such regulations are of the utmost importance when it is realised that the legal owners of the business, the shareholders, have entrusted the running of the company to the directors. The shareholders' own rights are largely limited to attending Annual General Meetings and having voting rights thereat, although some shares do not carry voting rights. The Companies Acts make the keeping of proper sets of accounting records and the preparation of Final Accounts compulsory for every company. In addition the accounts must be audited, this being quite different from a partnership or a sole trader's business where an audit is not compulsory at all.

Companies having limited liability, whether they are private or public companies, have to send a copy of their Final Accounts, drawn up in a prescribed manner, to the Registrar of Companies. Chapter 18 is concerned with stating the accounting requirements of the Companies Acts.

The shares of most of the public companies are dealt in on one or other of the recognised Stock Exchanges. The shares of private companies cannot be bought and sold on any Stock Exchange, as this would contravene the requirements for the company being recognised as a 'private' company. The sale and purchase of shares on the Stock Exchanges have no effect on the accounting entries made in the company's books. The only entry made in the company's books when a shareholder sells all, or some, of his shares to someone else, is to record the change of identity of the shareholders. The price at which shares were sold on the Stock Exchange does not enter into the company's books. While no accounting entries are necessary, probably apart from a small charge being made to the shareholder to compensate the company for administrative expenses in recording the change of identity caused by the share transfer and the completion of certain legal documents by the company, the price of the shares on the Stock Exchange has repercussions on the financial policy of the company. If some new shares are to be issued, the fact at what price they are to be issued will be largely dependent on the Stock Exchange valuation. If another firm is to be taken over by the company, part of the purchase price being by the means of shares in the company, then the Stock Exchange value will also affect the value placed upon the shares being given. A takeover bid from another firm may well be caused because the Stock Exchange value of the shares has made a takeover seem worthwhile. It must be recognised that the Stock Exchanges are the 'second-hand market' for a company's shares. The company does not actually sell (normally called 'issue') its shares by using the Stock Exchange as a selling place. The company issues new shares directly to the people who make application to it for the shares at the time when the company has shares available for issue. The company does not sell to, or buy from, the Stock Exchanges. This means that the shares of a public company sold and bought on Stock Exchanges are passing from one shareholder to another person who will then become a shareholder. Apart from the effect upon the financial policies of the firm the double entry accounts of the company are not affected.

Chapter 17 contains the details whereby the shares of a company may be made into 'stock'. Thus 500 Ordinary Shares of £1 each may be made into £500 Stock. The dividends paid on the shares or the stock would be the same, and the voting powers would also be the same. Apart from administrative convenience there is really no difference between shares and stock.

12

The Issue of Shares and Debentures

The Issue of Shares

In the case of public companies a new issue of shares can be very costly indeed, and the number of shares issued must be sufficient to make the cost worthwhile. However, for simplicity, so that the principles are not obscured by the difficulties of grappling with large amounts, the numbers of shares shown as issued in the illustrations that follow will be quite small.

Shares can be issued being payable for (a) immediately on application, or (b) by instalments. The first instances will be of shares being paid for immediately. Issues of shares may take place on the following terms connected with the price of the shares:

(i)   Shares issued at par. This would mean that a share of £1 nominal value would be issued for £1 each.

(ii) Shares issued at a premium. In this case a share of £1 nominal value would be issued for more than £1 each, say for £3 each.

(iii) Until the change per the Companies Act 1980, shares could be issued at a discount. This is now expressly forbidden. Shares each of £5 nominal value might have been issued for £3 each.

This will all seem rather strange at first. How can a £1 share, which states that value on the face of it, be issued for £3 each, and who would be foolish enough to buy it? On the other hand, surely there would have been a queue of people waiting to buy a £5 share for £3 each. The reasons for this apparently strange state of affairs stems from the Companies Act requirement that the Share Capital Accounts always show shares at their nominal value, irrespective of how much the shares are worth or how much they are issued for. To illustrate this, the progress of two firms can be looked at, firm A and firm B. Both firms started in business on 1 January .19-1 and issued 1,000 ordinary shares each of £4 nominal value at par. Ignoring any issue expenses, the Balance Sheets on that date would appear:

Firms A Ltd and B Ltd

Balance Sheet as at 1 January 19-1

	£
Bank	4,000
Capital	4,000

Five years later, on 31 December 19-5, the Balance Sheets show that the companies have fared quite differently. It is to be assumed here, for purposes of illustration, that the Balance Sheet values and any other interpretation of values happen to be identical.

£4,000 capital is needed by A Ltd, and this is to be met by issuing more ordinary shares. Suppose that another 1,000 ordinary shares of £4 nominal value each are issued at par. Column (*a*) shows the Balance Sheet before the issue, and column (*b*) shows the Balance Sheet after the issue has taken place.

A Ltd Balance Sheets (Solution 1) as at 31 December 19-5

	(*a*) £	(*b*) £
Fixed Current Assets (other than bank)	9,000	9,000
Bank	1,000	5,000
	10,000	14,000
Financed by:		
Ordinary Share Capital	4,000	8,000
Profit and Loss	6,000	6,000
	10,000	14,000

Now the effect of what has happened can be appreciated. Before the new issue there were 1,000 shares. As there were £10,000 of assets and no liabilities, then each share was worth £10. After the issue there are 2,000 shares and £14,000 of assets, so that now each share is worth £7. This would be extremely disconcerting to the original shareholders who see the value of each of their shares fall immediately by £3. On the other hand, the new shareholder who has just bought shares for £4 each sees them rise immediately to be worth £7 each. Only in one specific case would this be just, and that is where each original shareholder buys an equivalent number of new shares. Otherwise this obviously cannot be the correct solution. What is required is a price which is equitable as far as the interests of the old shareholders are concerned, and yet will attract sufficient applications to provide the capital required. As in this case the Balance Sheet value and the real value are the same, the answer is that each old share was worth £10 and therefore each new share should be issued for £10 each. The Balance Sheets will now appear:

A Ltd Balance Sheets (Solution 2) as at 31 December 19-5

	(a)	(b)
	£	£
Fixed and Current Assets (other than bank)	9,000	9,000
Bank	1,000	11,000
	10,000	20,000
Financed by:		
Ordinary Share Capital (at normal value)	4,000	8,000
Share Premium (see note below)		6,000
Profit and Loss	6,000	6,000
	10,000	20,000

Thus in (a) above 1,000 shares own between them £10,000 of assets = £10 each, while in (b) 2,000 shares are shown as owning £20,000 of assets = £10 each. Both the old and new shareholders are therefore satisfied with the bargain that has been made.

Note: The Share Premium shown on the Capital side of the Balance Sheet is needed, ignoring for a moment the legal requirements to be complied with in company Balance Sheets, simply because the Balance Sheet would not balance without it. If shares are stated at nominal value, but issued at another price, the actual amount received increases the bank balance, but the Share Capital shown is increased by a different figure. The Share Premium therefore represents the excess of the cash received over the nominal value of the shares issued.

The other, B Ltd, has not fared so well. it has, in fact, lost money. The accumulated losses are reflected in a debit balance on the Profit and Loss Appropriation Account as shown in the following Balance Sheet (c). It can be seen that there are £3,000 of assets to represent the shareholders, stake in the firm of 1,000 shares, i.e. each share is worth £3 each. If more capital was needed 1,000 more shares could be issued. From the action taken in the previous case it will not be obvious that each new share of £4 nominal value will be issued for its real value of £3 each. The Balance Sheets will appear:

B Ltd Balance Sheets (correct solution) as at 31 December 19-5

	(c)	(d)
	£	£
Fixed and Current Assets (other than bank)	2,000	2,000
Bank	1,000	4,000
Discounts on Shares (see note below)		1,000
Profit and Loss − Debit balance	1,000	1,000
	4,000	8,000
Ordinary Share Capital	4,000	8,000

Once again, as the share capital is shown at nominal value, but the shares issued at a different figure, the difference being Discounts on Shares must be shown in order that the Balance Sheet may balance. It is, of course, not actually an asset, it is merely a balancing figure needed because the entries already made for an increase in the Ordinary Share Capital and the increase in the bank balance have been at different figures. The figure for Discounts on Shares therefore rectifies the double entry 'error'.

Although shares cannot now be issued at a discount, there will still be items in company balance sheets for discounts in shares issued before 1980. Although not listed as an item in the balance sheet formats per the 1981 Companies Act, a separate heading will have to be inserted to accommodate the item.

For the purpose of making the foregoing explanations easier it was assumed that Balance Sheet values and other values were the same. This is very rarely true for all the assets, and in fact there is more than one other 'value'. A Balance Sheet is a historical view of the past based on records made according to the firm's interpretation and use of accounting concepts and conventions. When shares are being issued it is not the historical view of the past that is important, but the view of the future. Therefore the actual premiums and discounts on shares being issued is not merely a matter of Balance Sheet values, but on the issuing company's view of the future and its estimate of how the investing public will react to the price at which the shares are being offered.

It is to be noted that there are no restrictions on issuing shares at par or at a premium.

The actual double entry accounts can now be seen.

1. Shares Payable in Full on Application

The issue of shares in illustrations (i), (ii) and (iii) which follow are based on the Balance Sheets that have just been considered.

(i) Shares issued at par.
1,000 ordinary shares with a nominal value of £4 each are to be issued. Applications, together with the necessary money, are received for exactly 1,000 shares. The shares are then allotted to the applicants.

Bank

		£
Ordinary Share Applicants	(A)	4,000

Ordinary Share Applicants

		£			£
Ordinary Share Capital	(B)	4,000	Bank	(A)	4,000

152

Ordinary Share Capital

			£
	Ordinary Share Applicants	(B)	4,000

It may appear that the Ordinary Share Applicants Account is unnecessary, and that the only entries needed are a debit in the Bank Account and a credit in the Ordinary Share Capital Account. However, applicants do not always become shareholders; this is shown later. The applicant must make an offer for the shares being issued, accompanied by the necessary money, this is the application. After the applications have been vetted the allotments of shares are made by the company. This represents the acceptance of the offer by the company and it is at this point that the applicant becomes a shareholder. Therefore (A) represents the offer by the applicant, while (B) is the acceptance by the company. No entry must therefore be made in the Share Capital Account until (B) happens, for it is not until that point that the share capital is in fact in existence. The Share Applicants Account is therefore an intermediary account pending allotments being made.

(ii) Shares issued at a premium
1,000 Ordinary Shares with a nominal value of £4 each are to be issued for £10 each (see A Ltd previously). Thus a premium of £6 per share has been charged. Applications and the money are received for exactly 1,000 shares.

Bank

	£
Balance b/fwd	1,000
Ordinary Share Applicants	10,000

Ordinary Share Applicants

		£		£
Ordinary Share Capital	(A)	4,000	Bank	10,000
Share Premium	(B)	6,000		
		10,000		10,000

Share Premium

			£
	Ordinary Share Applicants	(B)	6,000

Ordinary Share Capital (A Ltd)

	£
Balance b/fwd	4,000
Ordinary Share	
Applicants (A)	4,000

Note: (A) is shown as £4,000 because the share capital is shown at nominal value and not as total issued value. (B) The £6,000 share premiums must therefore be credited to a Share Premium Account to preserve double entry balancing.

(iii) Shares issued at a discount (prior to 1980)

1,000 Ordinary Shares with a nominal value of £4 each are to be issued for £3 each (see B Ltd previously). Thus a discount of £1 per share is being allowed. Applications and the money are received for exactly 1,000 shares.

Bank

	£
Balance b/fwd	1,000
Ordinary Share Applicants	3,000

Ordinary Share Applicants

	£		£
Ordinary Share Capital	4,000	Bank	3,000
		Discounts on Shares	1,000
	4,000		4,000

Ordinary Share Capital

	£
Balance b/fwd	4,000
Ordinary Share Capital	4,000

Discounts on Shares

	£
Ordinary Share Applications	1,000

(iv) Oversubscription and undersubscription for shares.

When a public company invites investors to apply for its shares it is obviously very rare indeed if in fact that applications for shares equal exactly the number of shares to be issued. Where more shares are applied for than are available for issue, then the issue is said to be 'oversubscribed'. Where fewer shares are applied for than are available for issue, then the issue has been 'undersubscribed'.

With a brand-new company a minimum amount is fixed as being necessary to carry on any further with the running of the company. If the applications are less than the minimum stated, then the application monies must be returned to the senders. This does not apply to an established company. If therefore 1,000 shares of £1 each are available for issue, but only 875 shares are applied for, then only 875 will be issued, assuming that this is above the fixed minimum figure. The accounting entries will be in respect of 875 shares, no entries being needed for the 125 shares not applied for, as this part does not represent a transaction.

The opposite of this is where the shares are oversubscribed. In this case some sort of rationing is applied so that the issue is restricted to the shares available for issue. The process of selecting who will get how many shares depends on the policy of the firm. Some firms favour large shareholders because this leads to lower administrative costs. Why the costs will be lower will be obvious if the cost of calling a meeting of two companies each with 20,000 shares is considered. H Ltd has 20 shareholders with an average holding of 1,000 shares each. J Ltd has 1,000 shareholders with an average holding of 20 shares each. They all have to be notified by post and given various documents including a set of the final accounts. The cost of printing and sending these is less for H Ltd with 20 shareholders than for J Ltd with 1,000 shareholders. This is only one example of the costs involved, but it will also apply with equal force to many items connected with the shares. Conversely, the directors may prefer to have more shareholders with smaller holdings, one reason being that it decreases the amount of voting power in any one individual's hands. The actual process of rationing the shares is then a simple matter once a policy has been agreed. It may consist of scaling down applications, of drawing lots or some other chance selection, but it will eventually bring the number of shares to be issued down to the number of shares available. Excess application monies will then be refunded by the company.

An issue of shares where 1,000 ordinary shares of £1 nominal value each are to be issued at par payable in full, but 1,550 shares are applied for, will appear as follows:

Bank

	£		£
Ordinary Share Applicants	1,550	Ordinary Share Applicants (refunds)	550

Ordinary Share Applicants

	£		£
Bank	550	Bank	1,550
Ordinary Share Capital	1,000		
	1,550		1,550

	£
Ordinary Share Applicants	1,000

Issue of Shares payable by Instalments

The shares considered so far have all be issued as paid in full on application. Conversely, many issues are made which require payment by instalments. These are probably more common with public companies than with private companies.

The various stages, after the initial invitation has been made to the public to buy shares by means of advertisements (if it is a public company), etc., are as follows:

(A) Applications are received together with the application monies.

(B) The applications are vetted and the shares allotted, letters of allotment being sent out.

(C) The excess application monies from wholly unsuccessful, or where the application monies received exceed both the application and allotment monies required, and partly unsuccessful applicants, are returned to them. Usually, if a person has been partly unsuccessful, his excess application monies are held by the company and will reduce the amount needed to be paid by him on allotment.

(D) Allotment monies are received.

(E) The next instalment, known as the first call, is requested.

(F) The monies are received from the first call.

(G) The next instalment, known as the second call, is requested.

(H) The monies are received from the second call.

This carries on until the full number of calls have been made, although there is not usually a large number of calls to be made in an issue.

The reasons for the payments by instalments becomes obvious if it is realised that a company will not necessarily require the immediate use of all the money to be raised by the issue. Suppose a new company is to be formed, it is to buy land, erect a factory, equip it with machinery and then go into production. This might take two years altogether. If the total sum needed was £1,000,000, the allocation of this money could be:

Ordinary Share Capital

	£
Cost of land, payable within 1 month	200,000
Cost of buildings, payable in 1 year's time	300,000
Cost of machinery, payable in 18 months' time	200,000
Working capital required in 2 years' time	300,000
	1,000,000

The issue may therefore well be on the following terms:

	Per cent
Application money per share, payable immediately	10
Allotment money per share, payable within 1 month	10
First call, money payable in 12 months' time	30
Second call, money payable in 18 months' time	20
Third call, money payable in 24 months' time	30
	100

The entries made in the Share Capital Account should equal the amount of money requested to that point in time. However, instead of one Share Applicants Account, this is usually split into several accounts to represent the different instalments. For this purpose application and allotment are usually joined together in one account, the Application and Allotment Account, as this cuts out the need for transfers where excess application monies are held over and set off against allotment monies needed. When allotment is made, and not until then, an entry of £200,000 (10 per cent + 10 per cent) would be made in the Share Capital Account. On the first call an entry of £300,000 would be made in the Share Capital Account, likewise £200,000 on the second call and £300,000 on the third call. The Share Capital Account will therefore contain not the monies received, but the amount of money requested. Exhibit 12.1 now shows an instance of a share issue.

Exhibit 12.1

A company is issuing 1,000 7 per cent Preference Shares of £1 each, payable 10 per cent on application, 20 per cent on allotment, 40 per cent on the first call and 30 per cent on the second call. Applications are received for 1,550 shares. A refund of the money is made in respect of 50 shares, while for the remaining 1,500 applied for, an allotment is to be made on the basis of 2 shares for every 3 applied for (assume that this will not involve any fractions of shares). The excess application monies are set off against the allotment monies asked for. The remaining requested instalments are all paid in full. The letters by the side of each entry refer to the various stages outlined on page 155.

Bank

		£			£
Application and Allotment:			Application and		
Application monies	(A)	155	Allotment refund	(C)	5
Allotment monies					
(£1,000 × 20% *less*					
excess application					
monies £50)	(B)	150			
First call	(F)	400			
Second call	(H)	300			

Application and Allotment

		£			£
Bank – refund of			Bank	(A)	155
application monies	(C)	5	Bank	(B)	150
Preference Share Capital	(B)	300			
		305			305

First Call

		£			£
Preference Share Capital	(E)	400	Bank	(F)	400

Second Call

		£			£
Preference Share Capital	(G)	300	Bank	(H)	300

7 per cent Preference Share Capital

	£			£
		Application and		
		Allotment	(B)	300
		First Call	(E)	400
Balance c/d	1,000	Second Call	(G)	300
	1,000			1,000
		Balance b/d		1,000

If more than one type of share is being issued at the same time, e.g. preference shares and ordinary shares, then separate Share Capital Accounts and separate Application and Allotment Accounts and Call Accounts should be opened.

Forfeited Shares

Sometimes, although it is probably fairly rare in recent times, a shareholder fails to pay the calls requested from him. The Articles of Association of the company will probably provide that the shareholder will have his shares forfeited, provided that certain safeguards for his protection are fully observed. In this case the shares will be cancelled, and the instalments already paid by the shareholder will be lost to him.

After the forfeiture, the company may reissue the shares, unless there is a provision in the Articles of Association to prevent it. There are certain conditions as to the prices at which the shares can be reissued. These are that the amount received on reissue plus the amount received from the original shareholder should at least equal (*a*) the called-up value where the shares are not fully called up, or (*b*) the nominal value where the full amount has been called up. Any premium previously paid is disregarded in determining the minimum reissue price.

Exhibit 12.2

Take the same information as that contained in Exhibit 12.1, but instead of all the calls being paid, Allen, the holder of 100 shares, fails to pay the first and second calls. He had already paid the application and allotment monies on the required dates. The directors conform to the provisions of the Articles of Association and (A) Allen is forced to suffer the forfeiture of his shares. (B) The amount still outstanding from Allen will be written off. (C) The directors then reissue the shares at 75 per cent of nominal value to J. Dougan. (D) Dougan pays for the shares.

First Call

	£			£
Preference Share Capital	400	Bank		360
		Forfeited Shares	(B)	40
	400			400

Second Call

	£			£
Preference Share Capital	300	Bank		270
		Forfeited Shares	(B)	30
	300			300

7 per cent Preference Share Capital

		£			£
Forfeited Shares	(A)	100	Application and Allotment		300
Balance c/d		900	First Call		400
			Second Call		300
		1,000			1,000
			Balance b/d		900
Balance c/d		1,000	J. Dougan	(C)	100
		1,000			1,000
			Balance b/d		1,000

		£			£
First Call	(B)	40	Preference Share Capital	(A)	100
Second Call	(B)	30			
Balance c/d		30			
		100			100
J. Dougan (see following note)		25	Balance b/d		30
Balance c/d		5			
		30			30

Bank

	£
First Call (£900 × 40%)	360
Second Call (£900 × 30%)	270
J. Dougan (D)	75

J. Dougan

		£			£
Preference Share Capital		100	Bank	(D)	75
			Forfeited Shares (discount on reissue) see following note		25
		100			100

The transfer of £25 from Forfeited Shares Account to J. Dougan's Account is needed because the reissue was entered in Preference Share Capital Account and Dougan's Account at nominal value, i.e. following standard practice of a Share Capital Account being concerned with nominal values, but Dougan was not to pay the full nominal price. Therefore the transfer of £25 is needed to close his account.

The balance of £5 on the Forfeited Shares Account can be seen to be: Cash Received from original shareholder on application and allotment £30 + from Dougan £75 = £105. This is £5 over the nominal value so that the £5 appears as a credit balance. This is usually stated to be either transferred to a Profit on Reissue of Forfeited Shares Account, but it really cannot be thought that this is followed in practice for small amounts. More normally it would be transferred to the credit of a Share Premium Account.

Calls in Advance and in Arrear and the Balance Sheet

At the Balance Sheet date some shareholders will not have paid all the calls made, these are collectively known as calls in arrear. On the other hand, some shareholders may have paid amounts in respect of calls not made by the Balance Sheet date. These are calls in advance.

Calls in arrear, i.e. 'Called up share capital not paid' is to be shown in the balance sheet in one of the positions shown in the format per the 1981 Companies Act, see chapter 19. there is no specified place for calls in advance, so this will be inserted in the balance sheet as an extra heading.

Rights Issues

The costs of making a new issue of shares can be quite high. A way to reduce the costs of raising new long-term capital in the form of issuing shares may be by way of a rights issue. To do this the company circularises the existing shareholders, and informs them of the new issue to be made and the number of shares which each one of them is entitled to buy of the new issue. In most cases the shareholder is allowed to renounce his rights to the new shares in favour of someone else. The issue is usually pitched at a price which will make the rights capable of being sold, i.e. if the existing shareholder does not want the shares he can renounce them to A who will give him £x for the right to apply for the shares in his place, a right that A could not otherwise obtain. If any shareholder does not either buy the shares or transfer his rights, then the directors will usually have the power to dispose of such shares not taken up by issuing them in some other way.

Debentures

A debenture is a bond, acknowledging a loan to a company, usually under the company's seal, which bears a fixed rate of interest. Unlike shares, which normally depend on profits out of which to appropriate dividends, debenture interest is payable whether profits are made or not.

A debenture may be redeemable, i.e. repayable at or by a specified date. Conversely they may be irredeemable, redemption only taking place when the company is eventually liquidated, or in a case such as when the debenture interest is not paid within a given time limit.

People lending money to companies in the form of debentures will obviously be interested in how safe their investment will be. Some debentures are given the legal right that on certain happenings the debenture holders will be able to take control of specific assets, or of the whole of the assets. They can then sell the assets and recoup the amount due under their debentures, or deal with the assets in ways specified in the deed under which the debentures were issued. Such debentures are known as being secured against the assets, the term 'mortgage' debenture often being used. Other debentures have no prior right to control the assets under any circumstances. These are known as 'simple' or 'naked' debentures.

The Issue of Debentures

The entries for the issue of debentures are similar to those for shares. It would, however, certainly not be the normal modern practice to issue debentures at a premium. If the word 'debentures' appears instead of 'share capital', the the entries in the accounts would be identical.

Shares of no Par Value

It can be seen that the idea of a fixed par value for a share can be very misleading. For anyone who has not studied accounting, it may well come as a shock to them to find that a share with a par value of £1 might in fact be issued for £5. If the share is dealt in on the Stock Exchange he might find a £1 share selling at £10 or even £20, or equally well may sell for only 10p.

Another disadvantage of a par value is that it can give people entirely the wrong impression of the activities of a business. If a par value is kept to, and the dividend based on that, then with a certain degree of inflation the dividend figure can look excessive. Many trade union leaders would howl with disapproval if a dividend of 100 per cent was declared by a company. But is this so excessive? Exhibit 12.3 gives a rather different picture.

Exhibit 12.3

Allen buys a share 40 years ago for £1. He is satisfied with a return of 5 per cent on his money. With a 5 per cent dividend he could buy a certain amount of goods which will be called x. Forty years later to buy that amount of goods, x, he would need (say) 20 times as much money. Previously £5 would have bought x, now it would take £100. To keep his dividend at the same level of purchasing power he would need a dividend now of 100 per cent, as compared with the 5 per cent he was receiving 40 years ago.

In the United States of America, Canada and Belgium as well as other countries, no par value is attached to shares being issued. A share is issued at whatever price is suitable at the time, and the money received is credited to a Share Capital Account.

162

Exercises

12.1. A limited company has a nominal capital of £120,000 divided into 120,000 Ordinary Shares of £1 each. The whole of the capital was issued at par on the following terms:

	Per share
Payable on Application	£0.125
Payable on Allotment	£0.25
First Call	£0.25
Second Call	£0.375

Applications were received for 160,000 shares and it was decided to allot the shares on the basis of three for every four for which applications had been made. The balance of application monies were applied to the allotment, no cash being refunded. The balance of allotment monies were paid by the members.

The calls were made and paid in full by the members, with the exception of a member who failed to pay the first and second calls on the 800 shares allotted to him. A resolution was passed by the directors to forfeit the shares. The forfeited shares were later issued to D. Reagan at £0.90 each.

Show the ledger accounts recording all the above transactions, and the relevant extracts from a Balance Sheet after all the transactions had been completed.

12.2. Badger Ltd has an authorised capital of £100,000 divided into 20,000 ordinary shares of £5 each. The whole of the shares were issued at par, payments being made as follows:

	£
Payable on Application	0.5
Payable on Allotment	1.5
First Call	2.0
Second Call	1.0

Applications were received for 32,600 shares. It was decided to refund application monies on 2,600 shares and to allot the shares on the basis of two for every three applied for. The excess application monies sent by the successful applicants is not to be refunded but is to be held and so reduce the amount payable on allotment.

The calls were made and paid in full with the exception of one member holding 100 shares who paid neither the first nor the second call and another member who did not pay the second call on 20 shares. After requisite action by the directors the shares were forfeited. They were later reissued to B. Mills at a price of £4 per share.

You are to draft the ledger accounts to record the transactions.

12.3A. The authorised and issued share capital of Cosy Fires Ltd was £75,000 divided into 75,000 ordinary shares of £1 each, fully paid. On 2 January 19-7, the authorised capital was increased by a further 85,000 ordinary shares of £1 each to £160,000. On the same date 40,000 ordinary shares of £1 each were offered to the public at £1.25 per share payable as to £0.60 on application (including the premium), £0.35 on allotment and £0.30 on 6 April 19-7.

The lists were closed on 10 January 19-7, and by that date applications for 65,000 shares had been received. Applications for 5,000 shares received no allotment and the cash paid in respect of such shares was returned. All shares were then allocated to the remaining applicants pro rata to their original applications, the balance of the monies received on application being applied to the amounts due on allotment.

The balance due on allotment were received on 31 January 19-7, with the exception of one allottee of 500 shares and these were declared forfeited on 4 April 19-7. These shares were re-issued as fully paid on 2 May 19-7, at £1.10 per share. The call due on 6 April 19-7 was duly paid by the other shareholders.

You are required:
1. To record the above-mentioned transactions in the appropriate ledger accounts, and
2. To show how the balances on such accounts should appear in the company's Balance Sheet as on 31 May 19-7.

(Association of Certified Accountants)

12.4A. Applications were invited by the directors of Grobigg Ltd for 150,000 of its £1 ordinary shares at £1.15 per share payable as follows:

	Per share
On application on 1 April 19-8	£0.75
On allotment on 30 April 19-8	
(including the premium of £0.15 per share)	£0.20
On first and final call on 31 May 19-8	£0.20

Applications were received for 180,000 shares and it was decided to deal with these as follows:
1. To refuse allotment to applicants for 8,000 shares.
2. To give full allotment to applicants for 22,000 shares.
3. To allot the remainder of the available shares pro rata among the other applicants.
4. To utilise the surplus received on applications in part payment of amounts due on allotment.

An applicant, to whom 400 shares had been allotted, failed to pay the amount due on the first and final call and his shares were declared forfeit on 31 July 19-8. These shares were re-issued on 3 September 19-8 as fully paid at £0.90 per share.

Show how the transactions would be recorded in the company's books.

(Association of Certified Accountants)

13

Companies Purchasing and Redeeming Own Shares and Debentures

Purchasing and Redeeming Own Shares

To a student the words 'purchasing' and 'redeeming' may appear to be exactly the same as far as this chapter is concerned. To all intents and purposes it is the same, for it involves an outflow of cash by the company to get back its own shares and then cancel them. However, from a rather more legal and precise point of view, 'redeeming' means the buying back of shares which were originally issued as being 'redeemable' in that the company stated when they were issued that they would be, or could be, redeemed (i.e. bought back by the company). The terms of the 'redemption' (buying back) would be stated at the time when the shares were issued. However, when shares are issued and are not stated to be 'redeemable' then, when they are bought back by the company it is then said to be the 'purchase' of its shares by the company.

Until the Companies Act 1981 a company in the United Kingdom could not in normal circumstances 'purchase' its own shares. In addition 'redemption' was limited to one type of share, these were 'redeemable preference shares'. This had not been the case in the United States and Europe for many years where companies had, with certain restrictions, been allowed to buy back their own shares. The basic reason why this was not allowed in the U.K. was the fear that the interests of creditors could be adversely affected if the company used its available cash to buy its own shares, thus leaving less to satisfy the claims of the creditors. The possibilities of abuse with preference shares was considered to be less than with ordinary shares, thus the ability to be able to have redeemable preference shares.

Now, under the Companies Act 1981, a company may, if it is authorised to do so by its articles of association:

(a) Issue redeemable shares of any class (preference, ordinary etc). Redeemable shares include those that are to be redeemed on a particular date as well as those that are merely liable to be redeemed at the discretion of the shareholder or of the company. (Section 45).

There is an important proviso that a company can only issue redeemable shares if it has in issue shares that are *not* redeemable. Without this restriction a company could issue only redeemable shares, then later redeem all of its shares, and thus finish up without any shareholders.

(b) 'Purchase' its own shares (i.e. shares that were not issued as being redeemable shares). Again there is a proviso that the company must, *after* the purchase, have other shares in issue at least some of which are not redeemable. This again is to stop the company redeeming its whole share capital and thus ceasing to have members. The company must have, after the purchase, at least two members.

Advantages of Purchase and Redemption of Shares

Certainly there are quite a few possible advantages of a company being able to buy back its own shares. These are strongest in the case of private companies. For public companies the main advantage is that those with surplus cash resources could find it useful to be able to return some of this surplus cash back to its shareholders by buying back some of its own shares, rather than have pressure put on them to use such cash in uneconomic ways.

For private companies the main possible advantages would appear to be overcoming snags which occur when a shareholder cannot sell his shares on the 'open market', i.e. a stock exchange. This means that:

(i)   It will help shareholders who have difficulties in selling their shares to another individual to be able to realise their value when needed, for any reason.

(ii) People will be more willing to buy shares from private companies. The fear of not being able to dispose of them, previously led to finance being relatively difficult for private companies to obtain from people outside the original main proprietors of the company.

(iii) In many 'family' companies cash is needed to pay for taxes on the death of the shareholder.

(iv) Shareholders with grievances against the company can be bought out, thus contributing to the more efficient management of the company.

(v)   Family owned companies will be helped in their desire to keep control of the company when a family shareholder with a large number of shares dies or retires.

(vi) Similar to public companies, as described above, the company could return unwanted cash resources back to its shareholders.

(vii) For both private companies, and for public companies whose shares are not listed on a stock exchange, it may help boost share schemes for employees, as the employees would know that they could fairly easily dispose of the shares instead of being stuck with them.

Accounting Entries

The accounting entries for either 'purchase' or 'redemption' of shares are exactly the same, except that the word 'Redeemable' will appear as the first word in the title of the accounts for shares that are redeemable. The figures to be entered will naturally be affected by the *terms* under which shares are redeemed or purchased, but the actual type of *location* of the debits and credits to be made will be the same.

The reader will more easily understand the rather complicated entries needed if he understands the reasoning behind the Companies Act 1981. The protection of the creditor was uppermost in the minds of Parliament. The general idea is that 'capital' should not be returned to the shareholders, except under certain circumstances. If 'capital' is returned to the shareholders, thus reducing the cash and bank balances, then the creditors could lose out badly if there was not then sufficient cash/bank balances to be able to pay their claims. Thus the shareholders, seeing that things were not progressing too well in the company, could get their money out possibly at the expense of the creditors.

There are dividends which can quite legitimately be paid to the shareholders out of distributable profits, but the idea is to stop the shareholders withdrawing their 'capital'. Included under the general heading of 'capital' for this purpose are those particular reserves which cannot be used up for the payment of cash dividends. There are special exceptions to this, namely the 'reduction' of capital by public companies (see chapter 17) and the special powers of a private company to purchase or redeem its own shares out of capital (see later this chapter), but apart from these special cases the company law regulations are intended to ensure that 'capital' figures do not fall when shares are redeemed or purchased. This general purpose is behind the accounting entries which are now to be examined.

It is important to note that in *all* cases shares can only be redeemed or purchased when they are fully paid.

The safeguards for the protection of 'capital' contained in the Companies Act, Sections 45 and 46, may be summarised as follows:

(a) In respect of the *nominal* value of shares redeemed or purchased there must be either:

(i) A new issue of shares to provide the funds for redemption or purchase

or

(ii) Sufficient distributable profits must be available (i.e. a large enough credit balance on the Appropriation Account) which could be diverted from being used up as dividends to being treated as used up for the purpose of redeeming or purchasing the shares. Therefore, when shares are redeemed or purchased *other* than by out of the proceeds of a new issue, then, and only then, the amount of distributable profits treated as being used up by the nominal value or shares redeemed or purchased is debited to the Appropriation Account and credited to a Capital Redemption Reserve. (Before the Companies Act 1981 this was called a Capital Redemption Reserve Fund. The use of the word 'Fund' has now been dropped). Thus the old Share Capital will equal the total of the new Share Capital *plus* the Capital Redemption Reserve. The Capital Redemption Reserve is a 'non-distributable' reserve. This means that it cannot be transferred back to the credit of the Appropriation Account, and so increase the profits available for distribution as *cash* dividends. The process of diverting profits from being usable for dividends means that the non-payment of the dividends leaves more cash in the firm against which creditors could claim if necessary.

In all the examples which follow, the shares being redeemed/purchased could either be redeemable shares or those not specifically stated to be redeemable. Obviously, in a real company, the titles of the accounts would state which shares were redeemable.

To get the reader used to journal entries, and then seeing the effect on the face of the balance sheet, journal style entries will be shown first, followed by the balances for the balance sheet.

Exhibit 13.1

£2,000 Preference Shares are redeemed/purchased at par, a new issue of £2,000 Ordinary Shares at par being made for the purpose.

		Dr £	Cr £
(A1)	Bank	2,000	
(A2)	Ordinary Share Applicants		2,000
	Cash received from applicants		
(B1)	Ordinary Share Applicants	2,000	
(B2)	Ordinary Share Capital		2,000
	Ordinary Shares allotted		
(C1)	Preference Share Capital	2,000	
(C2)	Preference Share Purchase*		2,000
	Shares to be redeemed/purchased		
(D1)	Preference Share Purchase*	2,000	
(D2)	Bank		2,000
	Payment made to redeem/purchase shares		

*Note: In all the examples which follow, the shares being purchased/redeemed are preference shares. In fact they could be any type of share, ordinary, preference, preferred ordinary etc.. Secondly, the shares to be redeemed/purchased are transferred to a Preference Share Purchase account.

In fact if they were being redeemed it would be a Preference Share Redemption Account. It will make it easier to follow if the answers are standardised.

	Balances Before £		Effect Dr £		Cr £	Balances After £
Net Assets (except bank)	7,500					7,500
Bank	2,500	(A1)	2,000	(D2)	2,000	2,500
	10,000					10,000
Ordinary Share Capital	5,000			(B2)	2,000	7,000
Ordinary Share Applicants	–	(B1)	2,000	(A2)	2,000	–
Preference Share Capital	2,000	(C1)	2,000			
Preference Share Purchase	–	(D1)	2,000	(C2)	2,000	
	7,000*					7,000*
Profit & Loss	3,000					3,000
	10,000					10,000

*Notice: total 'capitals' remain the same.

Exhibit 13.2

£2,000 Preference Shares are redeemed/purchased at par, with *no* new issue of shares to provide funds for the purpose. Therefore an amount equal to the nominal value of the shares redeemed *must* be transferred from the Profit & Loss Appropriation Account to the credit of a Capital Redemption Reserve. (Until 1981 the title of this account was the Capital Redemption Reserve Fund. The use of the word 'Fund' here has now ceased).

		Dr £	Cr £
(A1)	Preference Share Capital	2,000	
(A2)	Preference Share Purchase		2,000
	Shares to be redeemed/purchased		
(B1)	Preference Share Purchase	2,000	
(B2)	Bank		2,000
	Cash paid as purchase/redemption		
(C1)	Profit & Loss Appropriation	2,000	
(C2)	Capital Redemption Reserve		2,000
	Transfer per Companies Act 1981, Section 45		

	Balances Before £		Effect Dr £		Cr £	Balances After £
Net Assets (except bank)	7,500					7,500
Bank	2,500			(B2)	2,000	500
	10,000					8,000
Ordinary Share Capital	5,000					5,000
Preference Share Capital	2,000	(A1)	2,000			–
Preference Share Purchase	–	(B1)	2,000	(A2)	2,000	–
Capital Redemption Reserve	–			(C2)	2,000	2,000
	7,000*					7,000*
Profit & Loss	3,000	(C1)	2,000			1,000
	10,000					8,000

*Notice: total 'capitals' (share capital + non-distributable reserves) remain the same at £7,000.

Exhibit 13.3

£2,000 Preference Shares redeemed/purchased at par, being £1,200 from issue of Ordinary Shares at par and partly by using Appropriation Account balance.

		Dr £	Cr £
(A1)	Bank	1,200	
(A2)	Ordinary Share Applicants		1,200
	Cash received from applicants		
(B1)	Ordinary Share Applicants	1,200	
(B2)	Ordinary Share Capital		1,200
	Ordinary Shares allotted		
(C1)	Profit & Loss Appropriation	800	
(C2)	Capital Redemption Reserve		800
	Part of redemption/purchase not covered by new issue, to comply with Sec. 45, Companies Act 1981		
(D1)	Preference Share Capital	2,000	
(D2)	Preference Share Purchase		2,000
	Shares being redeemed/purchased		
(E1)	Preference Share Purchase	2,000	
(E2)	Bank		2,000
	Payment made for redemption/purchase		

	Balances Before £		Effect Dr £		Cr £	Balances After £
Net Assets (except bank)	7,500					7,500
Bank	2,500	(A1)	1,200	(E2)	2,000	1,700
	10,000					9,200
Ordinary Share Capital	5,000			(B2)	1,200	6,200
Ordinary Share Applicants	–	(B1)	1,200	(A2)	1,200	–
Preference Share Capital	2,000	(D1)	2,000			–
Preference Share Purchase	–	(E1)	2,000	(D2)	2,000	–
Capital Redemption Reserve	–			(C2)	800	800
	7,000*					7,000*
Profit & Loss	3,000	(C1)	800			2,200
	10,000					9,200

*Notice: total 'capitals' remain the same.

(b) The next requirement under Section 45, Companies Act 1981, when shares are being redeemed/purchased at a premium, but they were *not* originally issued at a premium, then an amount equal to the premium *must* be transferred from the Appropriation Account to the credit of the Share Purchase/Redemption Account. This again is to divert profits away from being distributable to being part of 'capital'.

Exhibit 13.4

£2,000 Preference Shares which were originally issued at par are redeemed/purchased at a premium of 20 per cent. There is no new issue of shares for the purpose. In this example the Ordinary Shares had been originally issued at a premium, thus the reason for the Share Premium Account being in existence. However it is *not* the Ordinary Shares which are being redeemed and therefore the Share Premium *cannot* be used for the premium on redemption/purchase of the preference shares.

	Dr £	Cr £
(A1) Preference Share Capital	2,000	
(A2)　Preference Share Purchase		2,000
Shares being redeemed/purchased		
(B1) Profit & Loss Appropriation	400	
(B2)　Preference Share Purchase		400
Premium on purchase/redemption of shares *not* previously issued at premium		
(C1) Profit & Loss Appropriation	2,000	
(C2)　Capital Redemption Reserve		2,000
Transfer because shares redeemed/purchased out of distributable profits		
(D1) Preference Share Purchase	2,400	
(D2)　Bank		2,400
Payment on purchase/redemption		

	Balances Before £		Effect Dr £		Effect Cr £	Balances After £
Net Assets (except bank)	7,500					7,500
Bank	2,500			(D2)	2,400	100
	10,000					7,600
Ordinary Share Capital	4,500					4,500
Ordinary Share Capital	2,000	(A1)	2,000			–
Preference Share Purchase	–	(D1)	2,400	(A2)	2,000	–
				(B2)	400	
Capital Redemption Reserve	–			(C2)	2,000	2,000
Share Premium	500					500
	7,000*					7,000*
		(C1)	2,000			
Profit & Loss	3,000	(B1)	400			600
	10,000					7,600

*Notice: Total 'Capitals' remain the same.

(c) Under Section 45, para 6, Companies Act 1981. When shares are being redeemed or purchased at a premium,

and

they were originally issued at a premium,

and

a new issue of shares is being made for the purpose, then the Share Premium Account *can* have an amount calculated as followed transferred to the credit of the Share Purchase/Redemption Account. This is shown as (E).

Share Premium Account

			£
	Balance before new issue	(A)	xxx
Add	Premium on new issue	(B)	xxx
	Balance after new issue	(C)	xxx
	Amount that *may* be transferred	(E)	
	is lesser of:		
	Premiums that were received when it		
	first issued the shares now being		
	redeemed/purchased (D)		xxx
	or		
	Balance after new issue (C) above		xxx
	Transfer to Share Purchase/Redemption	(E)	xxx
	New Balance for Balance Sheet (could be nil)		xxx

Where the amount being deducted (E) is *less* than the premium paid on the *current* redemption or purchase, then an amount equivalent to the difference must be transferred from the debit of the Appropriation Account to the credit of the Share Purchase/Redemption Account. (An instance of this is shown in Exhibit 13.5). This again diverts profits away from being distributable.

Exhibit 13.5

£2,000 Preference Shares originally issued at premium of 20 per cent now being purchased/redeemed at a premium of 25 per cent. The position can be shown in three different companies if for the purpose of purchase/redemption:

Company 1 issues 2,400 Ordinary £1 shares at par

Company 2 issues 2,000 Ordinary £1 share at 20 per cent premium

Company 3 issues 1,600 Ordinary £1 shares at 50 per cent premium.

172

Share Premium Account

		Company 1 £	Company 2 £	Company 3 £
Balance before new issue	(A)	150*¹	400	400
Premium on new issue			400	800 (B)
Balance after new issue	(C)	150	800	1,200
Amount transferable to Share Purchase/Redemption is therefore lower of (C) or original premium on issue (£400)		150*²	400*²	400*²
New balance for balance sheet		–	400	800

*¹ In Company 1 it is assumed that of the original £400 premium the sum of £250 had been used up to issue bonus shares (see Chapter 16 later).
*² As these figures are less than the premium of £500 *now* being paid, the differences (Company 1 £350: Companies 2 and 3 £100 each) must be transferred from the debit of the Appropriation Account to the credit of the Preference Share/Purchase Redemption Account.

Journal Entries:

	Company 1 Dr £	Company 1 Cr £	Company 2 Dr £	Company 2 Cr £	Company 3 Dr £	Company 3 Cr £
(A1) Bank	2,400		2,400		2,400	
(A2) Ordinary Share Applicants		2,400		2,400		2,400
Cash Received from Applicants						
(B1) Ordinary Share Applicants	2,400		2,400		2,400	
(B2) Ordinary Share Capital		2,400		2,000		1,600
(B3) Share Premium		–		400		800
Ordinary Shares Allotted						
(C1) Preference Share Capital	2,000		2,000		2,000	
(C2) Preference Share Purchase		2,000		2,000		2,000
Shares being redeemed/purchased						
(D1) Share Premium Account	150		400		400	
(D2) Preference Share Purchase		150		400		400
Amount of Share Premium Account used for redemption/purchase						
(E1) Profit & Loss Appropriation	350		100		100	
(E2) Preference Share Purchase		350		100		100
Excess of premium payable over amount of share premium account usable for the purpose						
(F1) Preference Share Purchase	2,500		2,500		2,500	
(F2) Bank		2,500		2,500		2,500
Amount paid on redemption/purchase						

Exhibit 13.6

The following balance sheet for the three companies of Exhibit 13.5 are given *before* the purchase/redemption. The balance sheets are then shown *after* purchase/redemption.

Balance Sheets (*before* redemption/purchase)

	Company 1 £	Company 2 £	Company 3 £
Net Assets (except bank)	7,500	7,500	7,5000
Bank	2,500	2,500	2,500
	10,000	10,000	10,000
Ordinary Share Capital	4,850	4,600	4,600
Preference Share Capital	2,000	2,000	2,000
Share Premium	150	400	400
	7,000	7,000	7,000
Profit & Loss Account	3,000	3,000	3,000
	10,000	10,000	10,000

Balance Sheets (*after* redemption/purchase)

	Company 1 £	Company 2 £	Company 3 £
Net Assets (except bank)	7,500	7,500	7,500
Bank	2,400	2,400	2,400
	9,900	9,900	9,900
Ordinary Share Capital	7,250	6,600	6,200
Share Premium	–	400	800
	7,250	7,000	7,000
Profit & Loss Account	2,650	2,900	2,900
	9,900	9,900	9,900

Private Companies: Redemption or Purchase of Shares out of Capital

The Companies Act 1981, section 54, introduced a *new* power for a *private* company to redeem/purchase its own shares where *either* it has insufficient distributable profits for the purpose *or* it cannot raise the amount required by a new issue. Previously it would have had to apply to the court for 'capital reduction' as per chapter 17. The 1981 legislation makes it far easier to achieve the same objectives, both in terms of time and expense.

A book on Company Law should be read for the detail of the various matters which must be dealt with. A *very brief* outline may be given as follows:

(a) The Company must be authorised to do so by its articles of association.

(b)   Directors, to certify that, after the 'permissible capital payment', the company will be able to carry on as a going concern during the next twelve months, and be able to pay its debts immediately after the payment and also during the next twelve months.

(c)   Auditors to make a satisfactory report.

(d)   Permissible capital payment is the amount by which the price of redemption or purchase exceeds aggregate of (i) company's distributable profits and (ii) proceeds of any new issue. This means that a private company should use its available profits and any share proceeds before making a payment out of capital.

Permissible Capital Payments

(a)   Where the 'permissible capital payment' is *less* than the nominal value of shares redeemed/purchased, the amount of the difference *shall* be transferred to the Capital Redemption Reserve from the Appropriation Account (or undistributed profits). Section 54, para (4), Companies Act 1981.

(b)   Where the 'permissible capital payment' is *greater* than the nominal value of Shares redeemed/purchased, *any* non-distributable reserves (e.g. share premium account, capital redemption reserve, revaluation reserve etc) or fully paid share capital can be reduced by the excess, Section 54, para (5), Companies Act 1981.

    This can best be illustrated by taking two companies R & S with similar account balances *before* the purchase/redemption, but redeeming on different terms:

Exhibit 13.7

Company R	Before £		Dr £		Cr £	After £
Net Assets (except Bank)	2,500					2,500
Bank	7,500			(B2)	4,000	3,500
	10,000					6,000
Ordinary Shares	1,000					1,000
Preference Shares	4,000	(A1)	4,000			–
Non-Distributable Reserves	2,000					2,000
Capital Redemption Reserve				(C2)	3,000	3,000
Preference Share Purchase	–	(B1)	4,000	(A2)	4,000	
	7,000					
Profit & Loss	3,000	(C1)	3,000			
	10,000					6,000

Preference Shares redeemed at par £4,000. No new issue.

Therefore pay	£4,000
Less Profit and Loss Account	£3,000
Permissible capital payment	£1,000
Nominal amount shares redeemed/purchased	£4,000
Less Permissible capital payment	£1,000
Deficiency to transfer to Capital Redemption Reserve (C1 & C2)	£3,000

(A1) and (A2) represents transfer of shares redeemed/purchased
(B1) and (B2) represents payment to shareholders.

Company S	Before £	Dr £		Cr £		After £
Net Assets (except bank)	2,500					2,500
Bank	7,500			(D2)	7,200	300
	10,000					2,800
Ordinary Share Capital	1,000					1,000
Preference Shares	4,000	(A1)	4,000			–
Non-Distributable Reserves	2,000	(C1)	200			1,800
Capital Redemption Reserve						–
Preference Share Purchase		(D1)	7,200	(A2)	4,000	
				(B2)	3,000	
				(C2)	200	
	7,000					2,800
Profit & Loss	3,000	(B1)	3,000			–
	10,000					2,800

Preference Shares redeemed/purchased at premium 80%. No new issue.

Therefore pay	£7,200
Less Profit & Loss Account	£3,000
Permissible capital payment	£4,200
Permissible capital payment	£4,200
Less Nominal amount redeemed/purchased	£4,000
Excess from *any* of non-distributable reserves (or capital) (C1 & C2)	£200

(A1) & (A2) represents shares redeemed/purchased
(B1) & (B2) is transfer to redemption/purchase account of part of source of funds
(D1) & (D2) is payment to shareholders.

Cancellation of Shares Purchased/Redeemed

All shares purchased/redeemed must be cancelled immediately. They cannot be kept in hand by the company and traded in like any other commodity.

Redemption of Debentures

Unless they are stated to be irredeemable, debentures are redeemed according to the terms of the issue. The necessary funds to finance the redemption may be from:

(*a*) An issue of shares or debentures for the purpose.

(b) The liquid resources of the company.

Resembling the redemption of redeemable preference shares, when the redemption is financed as in (a), no transfer of profits from the Profit and Loss Appropriation Account to a Reserve Account is needed. However, when financed as in (b) it is good accounting practice, although not legally necessary, to divert profits from being used as dividends by transferring an amount equal to the nominal value redeemed from the debit of the Profit and Loss Appropriation Account to the credit of a Reserve Account.

Redemption may be effected:

1. By annual drawings out of profits.

2. By purchase in the open market when the price is favourable, i.e. less than the price which will have to be paid if the company waited until the last date by which redemption has to be carried out.

3. In a lump sum to be provided by the accumulation of a sinking fund.

These can now be examined in more detail.

1. Regular Annual Drawings out of Profits

(i) When redeemed at a premium.

In this case the source of the bank funds with which the premium is paid should be taken to be (a) Share Premium Account, or if this does not exist, or the premium is in excess of the balance on the account, then any part not covered by a Share Premium Account is deemed to come from (b) The Profit and Loss Appropriation Account. Exhibit 13.8 shows the effect of a Balance Sheet where there is no Share Premium Account, while Exhibit 13.9 illustrates the case when a Share Premium Account is in existence.

Exhibit 13.8

Starting with the Before Balance Sheet, £400 of the debentures are redeemed at a premium of 20 per cent.

Balance Sheets

	Before	+ or −	After
	£	£	£
Other Assets	12,900		12,900
Bank	3,400	− 480(A)	2,920
	16,300		15,820
Share Capital	10,000		10,000
Debenture Redemption Reserve	−	+ 400(B)	400
Debentures	2,000	− 400(A)	1,600
Profit and Loss	4,300	− 400(B)	
		− 80(A)	3,820
	16,300		15,820

Exhibit 13.9

Starting with the Before Balance Sheet, £400 of the debentures are redeemed at a premium of 20 per cent.

| | Balance Sheets | | |
	Before	+ or −	After
	£	£	£
Other Assets	13,500		13,500
Bank	3,400	− 480(A)	2,920
	16,900		16,420
Share Capital	10,000		10,000
Share Premium	600	− 80(A)	520
Debenture Redemption Reserve	−	+ 400(B)	400
Debentures	2,000	− 400(A)	1,600
Profit and Loss	4,300	− 400(B)	3,900
	16,900		16,420

In both Exhibits 13.8 and 13.9 the Debenture Redemption Reserve Account is built up each year by the nominal value of the debentures redeemed each year. When the whole issue of debentures has been redeemed, then the balance on the Debenture Redemption Reserve Account should be transferred to the credit of a General Reserve Account. It is, after all, an accumulation of undistributed profits.

(ii) Redeemed – originally issued at a discount.

The discount originally given was in fact to attract investors to buy the debentures, and is therefore as much a cost of borrowing as is debenture interest. The discount therefore needs to be written off during the life of the debentures. It might be more rational to write it off to the Profit and Loss Account, but in fact accounting custom, as permitted by law, would first of all write if off against any Share Premium Account or, secondly, against the Profit and Loss Appropriation Account.

The amounts written over the life of the debentures.

(a) Equal annual amounts over the life of the debentures.

(b) In proportion to the debenture debt outstanding at the start of each year. Exhibit 13.10 shows such a situation.

Exhibit 13.10

£30,000 debentures are issued at a discount of 5 per cent. They are repayable at par over five years at the rate of £6,000 per annum.

Year	Outstanding at start of each year	Proportion written off		Amount
	£			£
1	30,000	$\frac{30}{90} \times £1,500$	=	500
2	24,000	$\frac{24}{90} \times £1,500$	=	400
3	18,000	$\frac{18}{90} \times £1,500$	=	300
4	12,000	$\frac{12}{90} \times £1,500$	=	200
5	6,000	$\frac{6}{90} \times £1,500$	=	100
	90,000			1,500

2. Redeemed by Purchase in the Open Market

A sum equal to the cash actually paid on redemption should be transferred from the debit of the Profit and Loss Appropriation Account to the credit of the Debenture Redemption Reserve Account. The sum actually paid will of course have been credited to the Cash Book and debited to the Debentures Account.

Any discount (or profit) on purchase will be transferred to a Reserve Account. Any premium (or loss) on purchase will be deemed to come out of such a Reserve Account, or if no such account exists or it is insufficient, then it will be deemed to come out of the Share Premium Account. Failing the existence of these accounts any loss must come out of the Profit and Loss Appropriation Account. It may seem that purchase would not be opportune if the debentures had to be redeemed at a premium. However, it would still be opportune if the premium paid was not as high as the premium to be paid if the final date for redemption was awaited.

3. By Means of a Sinking Fund

First of all the Sinking Fund and the Sinking Fund Investment Account are built up as with the Depreciation Sinking Fund method.
Final entries are:

Debit Bank Account ⎫ With the sale of the
Credit Sinking Fund Investment Account ⎬ investments

Debit Debentures Account ⎫ With the cheques paid on
Credit Bank Account ⎬ redemption of the debentures

At this point the account now open is the Sinking Fund Account with a credit balance. This credit balance is now transferred to the credit of a General Reserve Account. Compare this with the similar stage of the Depreciation Sinking Fund, which then had a credit balance on the Sinking Fund Account and a debit balance on the Old Asset Account. The Sinking Fund Account balance was then transferred to extinguish the Old Asset Account balance. Therefore the redemption of a liability by this method leaves eventually a higher credit balance in the General Reserve Account, while the replacement of an asset leaves no balances, if the Bank Account is ignored.

Sometimes debentures bought in the open market are not cancelled, but are kept 'alive' and are treated as investments of the sinking fund. The annual appropriation of profits is credited to the Sinking Fund Account, while the amount expended on the purchase of the debentures is debited to the Sinking Fund Investment Account. Interest on such debentures is debited to the Profit and Loss Account and credited to the Sinking Fund Account, thus the interest, as far as the Sinking Fund Account is concerned, is treated in the same fashion as if it was cash actually received by the firm from an outside investment. The sum then expended on investments will then be equal to the annual appropriation + the interest on investments actually received + the interest on debentures kept in hand.

Exercises

13.1. Given the same commencing balance sheet, now shown, Exercises 13.1(i) to 13.1(v) inclusive are based on it.

R.S.V. Ltd.
Balance Sheet

	£
Net Assets (except bank)	20,000
Bank	13,000
	33,000
Preference Share Capital	5,000
Ordinary Share Capital	15,000
Share Premium	2,000
	22,000
Profit and Loss	11,000
	33,000

Note that each of questions 13.1(i) to (v) are independent of each other. They are not cumulative.

13.1(i) R.S.V. Ltd., per 13.1, redeems £5,000 Preference Shares at par, a new issue of £5,000 Ordinary Shares at par being made for the purpose. Show the balance sheet after completion of these transactions. Workings are to be shown as journal entries.

13.1(ii) R.S.V. Ltd., per 13.1, redeems £5,000 Preference Shares at par, with no new issue of shares to provide funds. Show the balance sheet after completing the transaction. Workings: show journal entries.

13.1(iii) R.S.V. Ltd., per 13.1, redeems £5,000 Preference Shares at par. To help finance this an issue of £1,500 Ordinary Shares at par is effected. Show the balance sheet after these transactions have been completed, also show the necessary journal entries.

13.1(iv) R.S.V. Ltd., per 13.1, redeems £5,000 Preference Shares at a premium of 25 per cent. There is no new issue of shares for the purpose. In this question the Share Premium Account is taken as being from the issue of Ordinary Shares some years ago. Show the balance sheet after these transactions have been completed, and the supporting journal entries.

13.1(v) R.S.V. Ltd., per 13.1, redeems £5,000 Preference Shares at a premium of 40 per cent. There is an issue of £7,000 Ordinary Shares at par for the purpose. The Preference Shares had originally been issued at a premium of 30 per cent. Show the balance sheet after these transactions have been completed, also supporting journal entries.

13.2A. Questions 13.2A(i) to 13.2(v) are based on the same commencing balance sheet, as follows:

B.A.R. Ltd.
Balance Sheet

	£
Net Assets (except bank)	31,000
Bank	16,000
	47,000
Preference Share Capital	8,000
Ordinary Share Capital	20,000
Share Premium	4,000
	32,000
Profit and Loss	15,000
	47,000

Note that questions 13.2A(i) to (v) are independent of each other. They are not cumulative.

13.2A(i) B.A.R. Ltd., per 13.2A, purchases £10,000 of its own Ordinary Share Capital at par. To help finance this £7,000 Preference Shares are issued at par. Show the necessary journal entries and the balance sheet after the transactions have been completed.

13.2A(ii) B.A.R. Ltd., per 13.2A, purchases £12,000 of its own Ordinary Shares at a premium of 20 per cent. No new issue of shares is made for the purpose. It is assumed that the Share Premium account is in respect of the issue of Preference Shares some years before. Show the balance sheet after the transactions have been completed, also the supporting journal entries.

13.2A(iii) B.A.R. Ltd., per 13.2A, purchases all the Preference Share Capital at par. These shares were not originally Redeemable Preference Shares. There is no new issue of shares to provide funds. Show the requisite journal entries, and the closing balance sheet when the transaction has been completed.

13.2A(iv) B.A.R. Ltd., per 13.2A, purchases £12,000 of its own Ordinary Shares at par, a new issue of £12,000 Preference Shares at par being made for the purpose. Show the journal entries needed and the balance sheet after completing these transactions.

13.2A(v) B.A.R. Ltd., per 13.2A, purchases £6,000 Ordinary Shares at a premium of 50 per cent, they had originally been issued at a premium of 20 per cent. There is an issue of £10,000 Preference Shares at par for the purpose. Show the amended balance sheet, together with journal entries.

13.3 A company's balance sheet appears as follows:

	£
Net Assets (except Bank)	12,500
Bank	13,000
	25,500
Preference Share Capital	5,000
Ordinary Share Capital	10,000
Non-Distributable Reserves	6,000
	21,000
Profit and Loss	4,500
	25,500

(i) If £6,000 of the ordinary shares were purchased at par, there being no new issue of shares for the purpose, show the journal entries to record the transactions and the amended balance sheet.

(ii) If, instead of (i), £6,000 ordinary shares were purchased at a premium of 100 per cent, there being no new issue of shares for the purpose, show the journal entries to record the transactions and the amended balance sheet.

14

Limited Companies Taking Over Other Businesses

Limited companies will often take over other businesses which are in existence as going concerns. The purchase considerations may either be in cash, by giving the company's shares to the owners, by giving the company's debentures, or by any combination of these three factors.

It must not be thought that because the assets bought are shown in the selling firm's books at one value that the purchasing company must record the assets taken over in its own books at the same value. The values shown in the purchasing company's books are those values at which the company is buying the assets, such values being frequently quite different than those shown in the selling firm's books. As an instance of this, the selling firm may have bought premises many years ago for £1,000 but they may now be worth £5,000. The company buying the premises will obviously have to pay £5,000 and it is therefore this value that is recorded in the buying company's books. Alternatively, the value at which it is recorded in the buying company's books may be less than that shown in the selling firm's books. Where the total purchase consideration exceeds the total value of the identifiable assets then such excess is the goodwill, and will need entering in a Goodwill Account in the purchasing company's books. Should the total purchase consideration be less than the values of the identifiable assets, then the difference would be entered in a Capital Reserve Account.

Before the accounting entries necessary to record the purchase of a going business are looked at, it must be pointed out that such recording of the transactions is the simple end of the whole affair. The negotiations that take place before agreement is reached, and the various strategies undertaken by the various parties is a study in itself. The accounting entries are in effect the 'tip of the iceberg', i.e. that part of the whole affair which is seen by the eventual reader of the accounts.

Taking over a Sole Trader's Business

It is easier to start with the takeover of the simplest sort of business unit, that of a sole trader. Some of the Balance Sheets shown will be deliberately simplified so that the principles involved are not hidden behind a mass of complicated calculations.

Exhibit 14.1

Earl Ltd is to buy the business of M. Kearney. The purchase consideration is to be £6,000 cash, the company placing the following values on the assets taken over – Machinery £3,000, Stock £1,000. The goodwill must therefore be £2,000, because the total price of £6,000 exceeds the values of Machinery £3,000 and Stock £1,000 by the sum of £2,000. The company's Balance Sheets will be shown before and after the takeover, it being assumed that the transactions are all concluded immediately.

M. Kearney
Balance Sheet

	£
Machinery	1,700
Stock	1,300
	3,000
Capital	3,000

Earl Ltd
Balance Sheet(s)

	Before	+ or −	After
	£	£	£
Goodwill		+2,000	2,000
Machinery	11,000	+3,000	14,000
Stock	5,000	+1,000	6,000
Bank	9,000	−6,000	3,000
	25,000		25,000
Share Capital	20,000		20,000
Profit and Loss	5,000		5,000
	25,000		25,000

Exhibit 14.2

Suppose the purchase had been made instead by issuing 7,000 shares of £1 each at par to Kearney. The goodwill would then be £7,000 – assets taken over £4,000 = £3,000. The Balance Sheets of Earl Ltd would be:

Earl Ltd
Balance Sheets

	Before	+ or −	After
	£	£	£
Goodwill		+3,000	3,000
Machinery	11,000	+3,000	14,000
Stock	5,000	+1,000	6,000
Bank	9,000		9,000
	25,000		32,000
Share Capital	20,000	+7,000	27,000
Profit and Loss	5,000		5,000
	25,000		32,000

Exhibit 14.3

If the purchase had been made by issuing 5,000 shares of £1 each at a premium of 50 per cent, then the total consideration would have been worth £7,500, which, if the assets of £4,000 are deducted leaves goodwill of £3,500. The Balance Sheets would then be:

Earl Ltd
Balance Sheet(s)

	Before	+ or −	After
	£	£	£
Goodwill		+3,500	3,500
Machinery	11,000	+3,000	14,000
Stocks	5,000	+1,000	6,000
Bank	9,000		9,000
	25,000		32,500
Share Capital	20,000	+5,000	25,000
Share Premium		+2,500	2,500
Profit and Loss	5,000		5,000
	25,000		32,500

Exhibit 14.4

Now if the purchase had been made by the issue of 1,000 shares of £1 each at a premium of 40 per cent, £3,000 worth of 7 per cent debentures at par and £4,000 in cash, then the total purchase consideration would be shares valued at £1,400, debentures valued at £3,000 and cash £4,000, making in all £8,400. The assets are valued at £4,000, the goodwill must be £4,400. The Balance Sheets would appear:

Earl Ltd.
Balance Sheet(s)

	Before £	+ or − £	After £
Goodwill		+ 4,400	4,400
Machinery	11,000	+ 3,000	14,000
Stocks	5,000	+ 1,000	6,000
Bank	9,000	− 4,000	5,000
	25,000		29,400
Share Capital	20,000	+ 1,000	21,000
Share Premium		+ 400	400
Profit and Loss	5,000		5,000
Debentures		+ 3,000	3,000
	25,000		29,400

In each of Exhibits 14.1 to 14.4 it has been assumed that all transactions were started and completed within a few moments. The fact is that an intermediary account would be created but then closed almost immediately when the purchase consideration was handed over. Taking Exhibit 14.3 as an example, there will be a credit in the Share Capital Account and in the Share Premium Account, and debits in the Goodwill, Machinery and Stock Accounts. Nevertheless, shares cannot be issued to goodwill, machinery or stocks. They have in fact, been issued to M. Kearney. This means that there should have been an account for M. Kearney, but that the balance on it was cancelled on the passing of the purchase consideration. The actual accounts for Exhibit 14.3 were as follows in the books of Earl Ltd:

Share Premium

		£
	M. Kearney	2,500

Share Capital

	£		£
Balance c/d	25,000	Balance b/fwd	20,000
		M. Kearney	5,000
	25,000		25,000
		Balance b/d	25,000

Profit and Loss

		£
	Balance b/fwd	5,000

Goodwill

	£		
M. Kearney	3,500		

Machinery

	£		£
Balance b/fwd	11,000		
M. Kearney	3,000	Balance c/d	14,000
	14,000		14,000
Balance b/d	14,000		

Stock

	£		£
Balance b/d	5,000		
M. Kearney	1,000	Balance c/d	6,000
	6,000		6,000
Balance c/d	6,000		

(In actual fact the £1,000 would probably be entered in the Purchases Account. It does, however, obviously increase the actual amount of stock.)

Bank

	£		
Balance b/fwd	9,000		

M. Kearney

	£		£
Consideration Passing:		Assets Taken Over	
Share Capital	5,000	Goodwill	3,500
Share Premium	2,500	Machinery	3,000
		Stock	1,000
	7,500		7,500

Some accountants would have preferred to use a Business Purchase Account instead of a personal account such as that of M. Kearney.

Sometimes the company taking over the business of a sole trader not only pays a certain amount for the assets but also assumes responsibility for paying the creditors in addition. Take the case of a sole trader with assets valued at Premises £5,000 and Stock £4,000. To gain control of these assets the company is to pay the sole trader £11,000 in cash, and in addition the company will pay off creditors £1,000. This means that the goodwill is £3,000, calculated as follows:

		£
Paid by the company to gain control of the sole trader's assets:		
Cash to the Sole Trader		11,000
Cash to the Sole Trader's Creditors		1,000
		12,000
The Company receives Assets	£	
Premises	5,000	
Stock	4,000	
		9,000
Excess paid for Goodwill		3,000

Partnership Business taken over by a Limited Company

The entries are the same as for those of taking over a sole trader's business, with the exception that there will be a personal account for each partner. There are, however, difficulties about the distribution of shares as between the partners when the balances on their Capital Accounts are not in the same ratio with one another as their profit-sharing ratios. This is, however, better left to a more advanced stage of studies in accounting.

The partnership will, of course, show a Realization Account in its own books. The total purchase consideration will be credited to the Realization Account and debited to the company's personal account. The discharge of the purchase consideration will close the partnership books.

The Takeover of a Limited Company by another Limited Company

One company make take over another company by one of two methods:
1. By buying all the assets of the other company, the purchase consideration being by cash, shares or debentures. The selling company may afterwards be wound up, the liquidators either distributing the purchasing company's shares and debentures between the shareholders of the selling company, or else the shares and debentures of the buying company may be sold and the cash distributed instead.
2. By giving its own shares and debentures in exchange for the shares and debentures of the selling company's share and debenture holders. Exhibit 14.5 is an illustration of each of these methods.

Exhibit 14.5

The following are the Balance Sheets of three companies as on the same date.

| | | *Balance Sheets* | |
	R Ltd	*S Ltd*	*T Ltd*
	£	£	£
Buildings	13,000	–	1,000
Machinery	4,000	2,000	1,000
Stock	3,000	1,000	2,000
Debtors	2,000	1,000	3,000
Bank	1,000	2,000	3,000
	23,000	6,000	10,000
Share Capital (£1 shares)	18,000	3,000	5,000
Profit and Loss	2,000	1,000	4,000
Current Liabilities	3,000	2,000	1,000
	23,000	6,000	10,000

R takes over S by exchanging with the shareholders of S two shares in R at a premium of 10 per cent for every share they hold in S.

R takes over T by buying all the assets of T, the purchase consideration being 12,000 £1 shares in R at a premium of 10 per cent, and R will pay off T's creditors. R values T's assets at Buildings £2,000, Machinery £600, Stock £1,400, Debtors £2,500, and the Bank is £3,000, a total of £9,500.

R's deal with the shareholders of S means that R now has complete control of S Ltd, so that S Ltd becomes what is known as a subsidiary company of R Ltd, and will be shown as an investment in R's Balance Sheet.

On the other hand, the deal with T has resulted in the ownership of the assets resting with R. These must therefore be added to R's assets in its own Balance Sheet. As R has given 12,000 £1 shares at a premium of 10 per cent plus taking over the responsibility for creditors £1,000, the total purchase consideration for the assets taken over is £12,000 + £1,200 (10 per cent of £12,000) + £1,000 = £14,200. Identifiable assets as already stated are valued at £9,500, therefore the goodwill is £14,200 − £9,500 = £4,700.

The distinction between the acquisition of the two going concerns can be seen to be a rather fine one. With S the shares are taken over, the possession of these in turn giving rise to the ownership of the assets. In the books of R this is regarded as an investment. With T the actual assets and liabilities are taken over so that the assets now directly belong to R. In the books of R this is therefore regarded as the acquisition of additional assets and liabilities and not as an investment (using the meaning of 'investment' which is used in the Balance Sheets of companies). The Balance Sheet of R Ltd therefore becomes:

R Ltd

Balance Sheet

	Before	+ or −		After
	£		£	£
Goodwill		+ (T)	4,700	4,700
Buildings	13,000	+ (T)	2,000	15,000
Machinery	4,000	+ (T)	600	4,600
Investment in S at cost		+	6,600	6,600
Stock	3,000	+ (T)	1,400	4,400
Debtors	2,000	+ (T)	2,500	4,500
Bank	1,000	+ (T)	3,000	4,000
	23,000			43,800
Share Capital	18,000	+ (S)	6,000	
		+ (T)	12,000 =	36,000
Share Premium		+ (S)	600	
		+ (T)	1,200 =	1,800
Profit and Loss	2,000			2,000
Current Liabilities	3,000	+ (T)	1,000	4,000
	23,000			43,800

No entry is necessary in the books of S Ltd, as it is merely the identity of the shareholders that has changed. This would be duly recorded in the register of members, but this is not really an integral part of the double entry accounting system.

If, however, T Ltd is now liquidated, then a Realization Account must be drawn up and the distribution of the shares (or cash if the shares are sold) to the shareholders of T Ltd must be shown. Such accounts would appear as follows:

Books of T Ltd

Realization

	£		£
Book Values of Assets		R Ltd: Total Purchase	
Disposed Of:		Consideration	14,200
Buildings	1,000		
Machinery	1,000		
Stock	2,000		
Debtors	3,000		
Bank	3,000		
Profit on Realization			
transferred to Sundry			
Shareholders	4,200		
	14,200		14,200

Share Capital

	£		£
Sundry Shareholders	5,000	Balance b/fwd	5,000

Profit and Loss

	£		£
Sundry Shareholders	4,000	Balance b/fwd	4,000

Creditors

	£		£
R Ltd – taken over	1,000	Balance b/fwd	1,000

R Ltd

	£		£
Realization:		Creditors	1,000
Total Consideration	14,200	Sundry Shareholders:	
		12,000 £1 shares	
		received at premium	
		of 10 per cent	13,200
	14,200		14,200

Sundry Shareholders

	£		£
R Ltd; 12,000 £1 shares		Share Capital	5,000
at premium of 10 per cent	13,200	Profit and Loss	4,000
		Profit on Realization	4,200
	13,200		13,200

It can be seen that the items possessed by the sundry shareholders have been transferred to an account in their name. These are (i) the share capital which obviously belongs to them, (ii) the credit balance on the Profit and Loss Account built up by withholding cash dividends from the shareholders, and (iii) the profit on realization which they, as owners of the business, are entitled to take. As there were 5,000 shares in T Ltd, and 12,000 shares have been given by R Ltd, then each holder of 5 shares in T Ltd will now be given 12 shares in R Ltd to complete the liquidation of the company.

The Exchange of Debentures

Sometimes the debentures in the company taking over are to be given in exchange for the debentures of the company being taken over. This may be straightforward on the basis of £100 debentures in company A in exchange for £100 debentures in company B. However, the problem often arises where the exchange is in terms of one of both sets of debentures being at a discount or at a premium. The need for such an exchange may be two-fold:

(a) To persuade the debenture holders in company B to give up their debentures some form of inducement may be needed, such as letting them have A's debentures at a discount even though they may well be worth the par value.

(b) There may be a difference in the debenture interest rates. For instance, a person with a £100 7 per cent debenture would not normally gladly part with it in exchange for a £100 6 per cent debenture in another company. The first debenture gives him £7 a year interest, the second one only £6 a year. Thus the debenture in the second company may be issued at a discount to redeem the debenture in the first company at a premium. As the amount of interest is only one factor, there are also others such as the certainty of the debenture holder regaining his money if the firm had to close down, the precise terms of the exchange cannot be based merely on arithmetical calculations of interest rates, but it is one of the measures taken when negotiating the exchange of debentures.

Exhibit 14.6

(i) D Ltd is to give the necessary debentures at a discount of 10 per cent necessary to redeem £9,000 debentures in J Ltd at a premium of 5 per cent. The problem here is to find exactly what amount of debentures must be given by D Ltd.

Answer: Total nominal value of debentures in J Ltd to be redeemed (exchanged) $\times$ $\dfrac{\text{Redeemable value of each £100 debenture of J Ltd}}{\text{Issue value of each £100 debenture of D Ltd}}$

$=$ Total nominal value of D Ltd to be issued

$= £9,000 \times \frac{105}{90} = £10,500$

Thus, to satisfy the agreement, debentures of D Ltd of a total nominal value of £10,500 are issued at a discount of 10 per cent to the debenture holdings of J Ltd.

(ii) H Ltd is to give the necessary debentures at par to redeem £5,000 debentures in M Ltd at a premium of 4 per cent.

£5,000 $\times \frac{104}{100} =$ Debentures of £5,200 nominal value are given by H Ltd at par

Profit (or Loss) prior to Incorporation

Quite frequently companies take over businesses from a date which is actually before the company was itself incorporated. It could be that two persons enter into business and start trading with the intention of running the business as a limited company. However, it takes more than a few days to attend to all the necessary formalities before the company can be incorporated. Obviously it depends on the speed with which the formation is pushed through and the solution of any snags which crop up. When the company is in fact incorporated it may enter into a contract whereby it adopts all the transactions retrospectively to the date that the firm, i.e. with two persons it was a partnership, had started trading. This means that the company accepts all the benefits and disadvantages which have flowed from the transactions which have occurred. The example used was that of a brand-new business; it could well have been an old-established business that was taken over from a date previous to incorporation.

Legally a company cannot earn profits before it comes into existence, i.e. is incorporated, and therefore to decide what action will have to be taken such profits will first of all have to be calculated. Any such profits are of a capital nature and must be transferred to a Capital Reserve Account, normally titled Pre-Incorporation Profit Account or Profit Prior to Incorporation Account. That this should be so is apparent if it is realized that though the actual date from which the transactions have been adopted falls before the date of incorporation, yet the price at which the business is being taken over is influenced by the values of the assets, etc., at the date when the company actually takes over, i.e. the date of incorporation. Suppose that Doolin and Kershaw start a business on 1 January 19-5 with £1,000 capital, and very shortly afterwards Davie and Parker become interested as well, and the four of them start to form a company in which they will all become directors, Davie and Parker to start active work when the company is incorporated. The company is incorporated on 1 May 19-5 and the original owners of the business, Doolin and Kershaw, are to be given shares in the new company to compensate them for handing over the business. If they know, not necessarily with precision, that the original £1,000 assets will have grown to net assets of £6,000, then they most certainly would not part with the business to the company for £1,000. Ignoring goodwill they would want £6,000 of shares. Conversely, if the net assets will shrink to £400, then would Davie and Parker be happy to see £1,000 of shares handed over? This means that the price at which the business is taken over is dependent on the expected value at the date of the company incorporation, and not at the value at the date on which the company is supposed to take over. Taking the case of the increase in net assets to £6,000 the £5,000 difference is made up of profits. If these profits could be distributed as dividends, then in effect the capital payment of £6,000 in shares is being part used up for dividend purposes. This is in direct contradiction to the normal accounting practice of retaining capital intact (the accountant's meaning of 'capital' and not the meaning given to 'capital' by the economist). The £5,000 profits must therefore be regarded as not being available for dividends. They are thus a capital reserve.

Although the profit cannot be regarded as free for use as dividends, any such loss can be taken to restrict the dividends which could be paid out of the profits made after incorporation. This is the concept of prudence once again coming into play, and if the price paid on take-over was misjudged and a high figure was paid, only to find out later that a loss had been made, then the restriction of dividends leads to the capital lost being replaced by assets held back within the firm. Alternatively the amount of the pre-incorporation loss could be charged to a Goodwill Account, as this is also another way of stating that a higher price has been paid for the assets of the firm than is represented by the value of the tangible assets taken over.

It is possible for the profits up to the date of incorporation to be calculated quite separately from those after incorporation. However, the cost of stocktaking, etc., may be felt to be not worth while merely to produce accounts when in fact the accounts could be left until the normal financial year end. This is invariably the case in examination questions. Therefore when the accounts for the full financial year are being made up, they will consist of profits before and after incorporation. The accounts must therefore be split to throw up the two sets of profit (or loss), so that distinction can be made between those profits usable, and those not usable, for dividend purposes. There is no hard-and-fast rule as to how this shall be done. Known facts must prevail, and where an arbitrary apportionment must be made it should meet the test of common sense in the particular case. Exhibit 14.7 shows an attempt to calculate such profits.

Exhibit 14.7

Slack and King, partners in a firm, are to have their business taken over as from 1 January 19-4 by Monk Ltd which is incorporated on 1 April 19-4. It was agreed that all profits made from 1 January 19-4 should belong to the company, and that the vendors be entitled to interest on the purchase price from 1 January to date of payment. The purchase price was paid on 30 April 19-4, including £1,600 interest. A Profit and Loss Account is drawn up for the year ended 31 December 19-4. This is shown as column (X). This is then split into, before incorporation, shown as column (Y), after incorporation, being column (Z). The methods used to apportion the particular items are shown after the Profit and Loss Account, the letters (A) to (I) against the items being the references to the notes. These particular methods must definitely not be used in all cases for similar expenses, they are only an indication of different methods of apportionment. The facts and the peculiarities of each firm must be taken into account, and no method should be slavishly followed. Assume for this example that all calendar months are of equal length.

Monk Ltd
Profit and Loss Account for the year ended 31 December 19-4

		(X) Before		(Y) Before		(Z) After	
		£	£	£	£	£	£
Gross Profit	(A)		38,000		8,000		30,000
Less:							
Partnership Salaries	(B)	1,000		1,000			
Employees Remuneration	(C)	12,000		3,000		9,000	
General Expenses	(C)	800		200		600	
Commission on Sales	(D)	1,700		200		1,500	
Distribution Expenses	(E)	1,900		400		1,500	
Bad Debts	(F)	100		20		80	
Bank Overdraft Interest	(G)	200				200	
Directors' Remuneration	(H)	5,000				5,000	
Directors' Expenses	(H)	400				400	
Debenture Interest	(H)	500				500	
Depreciation	(C)	1,000		250		750	
Interest paid to Vendors	(I)	1,600		1,200		400	
			26,200		6,270		19,930
Net Profit			11,800				
Transferred to Capital Reserves					1,730		
Carried down to the Appropriation Account							10,070

Notes:

(A) For the three months to 31 March Sales amounted to £40,000, and for the remaining nine months they were £150,000. Gross profit is at a uniform rate of 20 per cent of selling price throughout the year. Therefore the gross profit is apportioned (Y) 20 per cent of £40,000 = £8,000, and (Z) 20 per cent of £150,000 = £30,000.

(B) The partnership salaries of the vendors, Slack and King, obviously belong to (Y), because that is the period of the partnership.

(C) These expenses, in this particular case, have accrued evenly throughout the year and are therefore split on the time basis of Y three twelfths, Z nine-twelfths.

(D) Commission to the salesmen was paid at the rate of $\frac{1}{2}$ per cent on sales up to 31 March, and 1 per cent thereafter. The commission figure is split:

(Y) $\frac{1}{2}$ per cent of £40,000	=	200
(Z) 1 per cent of £150,000	=	1,500
		1,700

(E) In this particular case (but not always true in every case) the distribution expenses have varied directly with the value of sales. They are therefore split:

$$\text{(Y)} \frac{\text{Y Sales}}{\text{Total Sales}} \times \text{Expenses} = \frac{40,000}{190,000} \times £1,900 = \tfrac{4}{19} \times £1,900 = £400$$

$$\text{(Z)} \frac{\text{Z Sales}}{\text{Total Sales}} \times \text{Expenses} = \frac{150,000}{190,000} \times £1,900 = \tfrac{15}{19} \times £1,900 = £1,500$$

(F) The bad debts were two in number:
(i) In respect of a sale in January, the debtor dying penniless in March, £20.
(ii) In respect of a sale in June, the debtor being declared bankrupt in December, £80.

(G) The bank account was never overdrawn until June, so that the interest charged must be for period (Z).

(H) Only in companies are such expenses as Directors' Salaries, Directors' Expenses and Debenture Interest to be found. These must naturally be shown in period (Z).

(I) The interest paid to the vendors was due to the fact that the company was receiving all the benefits from 1 January but did not in fact pay any cash for the business until 30 April. This is therefore in effect loan interest which should be spread over the period it was borrowed, i.e. three months to (Y) and 1 months to (Z).

Exercises

14.1. Checkers Ltd was incorporated on 1 April 19-5 and took over the business of Black and White, partners, as from 1 January 19-5. It was agreed that all profits made from 1 January should belong to the company and that the vendors should be entitled to interest on the purchase price from 1 January to date of payment. The purchase price was paid on 31 May 19-5 including £1,650 interest.

The following is the Profit and Loss Account for the year to 31 December 19-5:

	£		£
Salaries of Vendors	1,695	Gross Profit	28,000
Wages and General Expenses	8,640		
Rent and Rates	860		
Distribution Expenses	1,680		
Commission on Sales	700		
Bad Debts	314		
Interest paid to Vendors	1,650		
Directors' Remuneration	4,000		
Directors' Expenses	515		
Depreciation:	£		
Motors	1,900		
Machinery	575		
	2,475		
Bank Interest	168		
Net Profit	5,303		
	28,000		28,000

You are given the following information:
1. Sales amounted to £20,000 for the three months to 31 March 19-5 and £50,000 for the nine months to 31 December 19-5. Gross Profit is at a uniform rate of 40 per cent of selling price throughout the year, and commission at a rate of 1 per cent is paid on all sales.
2. Salaries of £1,695 were paid to the vendors for their assistance in running the business up to 31 March 19-5.
3. The Bad Debts written off are:
(a) A debt of £104 taken over from the vendors.
(b) A debt of £210 in respect of goods sold in August 19-5.
4. On 1 January 19-5 motors were bought for £7,000 and machinery for £5,000. On 1 March 19-5 another motor van was bought for £3,000, and on 1 October 19-5 another machine was added for £3,000. Depreciation has been written off motors at 20 per cent per annum, and machinery 10 per cent per annum.
5. Wages and general expenses and rent and rates accrued at an even rate throughout the year.
6. The bank granted an overdraft in June 19-5.
Assuming all calendar months are of equal length.
(a) Set out the Profit and Loss Account in columnar form, so as to distinguish between the period prior to the company's incorporation and the period after incorporation
(b) To state how you would deal with the profit prior to incorporation.
(c) To state how you would deal with the results prior to incorporation if they turned out to be a net loss.

14.2. On 31 December 19-6 Breeze Ltd acquired all the assets, except the investments, of Blow Ltd.

The following are the summaries of the Profit and Loss Accounts of Blow Ltd for the years 19-4, 19-5 and 19-6:

	19-4	19-5	19-6		19-4	19-5	19-6
	£	£	£		£	£	£
Motor Expenses	1,860	1,980	2,100	Trading Profits	22,050	25,780	25,590
Depreciation of Plant &				Investment Income	290	340	480
Machinery	4,000	3,200	2,560	Rents Received	940	420	–
Bank Overdraft Interest	180	590	740	Profit on Sale of Property		4,800	
Wrapping Expenses	840	960	1,020				
Preliminary Expenses							
written off	–	690	–				
Net Profit	16,400	23,920	19,650				
	23,280	31,340	26,070		23,280	31,340	26,070

The purchase price is to be the amount on which an estimated maintainable profit would represent a return of 25 per cent per annum.

The maintainable profit is to be taken as the average of the profits of the three years 19-4, 19-5 and 19-6, after making any necessary adjustments.

You are given the following information:

(i) The cost of the plant and machinery was £20,000. It is agreed that depreciation should have been written off at the rate of 12½ per cent per annum using the straight line method.

(ii) A form of new plastic wrapping material introduced on to the market means that wrapping expenses will be halved in future.

(iii) By a form of long-term rental of motor vehicles, it is estimated that motor expenses will be cut by one-third in future.

(iv) Stock treated as valueless at 31 December 19-3 was sold for £1,900 in 19-5.

(v) The working capital of the new company is such that an overdraft is not contemplated.

(vi) Management remuneration has been inadequate and will have to be increased by £1,500 a year in future.

You are required to set out your calculation of the purchase price. All workings must be shown. In fact, your managing director, who is a non-accountant, should be able to decipher how the price was calculated.

14.3. CJK Ltd was incorporated on 15 December 19-9 with an authorised capital of 200,000 ordinary shares of £0.20 each to acquire as at 31 December 19-9 the businesses of C K, a sole trader, and RP Ltd, a company.

From the following information you are required to prepare:

(a) the realization and capital accounts in the books of CK and RP Ltd showing the winding up of these two concerns;

(b) the journal entries to open the books of CJK Ltd, including cash transactions and the raising of finance;

(c) the balance sheet of CJK Ltd after the transactions have been completed.

The balance sheet of CK as at 31 December 19-9 is as follows:

Balance Sheet

	£
Freehold premises	8,000
Plant	4,000
Stock	2,000
Debtors	5,000
Cash	200
	19,200
Capital	16,000
Creditors	3,200
	19,200

The assets (excluding cash) and the liabilities were taken over at the following values: freehold premises £10,000, plant £3,500, stock £2,000, debtors £5,000 less a bad debts provision of £300, goodwill £7,000, creditors £3,200 less a discount provision of £150. The purchase consideration, based on these values, was settled by the issue of shares at par.

The balance sheet of RP Ltd as at 31 December 19-9 is as follows:

Balance Sheet

	£
Freehold premises	4,500
Plant	2,000
Stock	1,600
Debtors	3,400
	11,500
Share capital: 10,000 shares at £0.40 each	4,000
Revenue surplus	2,500
Creditors	1,500
Bank overdraft	3,500
	11,500

The assets and liabilities were taken over at book value with the exception of the freehold premises which were revalued at £5,500. The purchase consideration was a cash payment of £1 and three shares in CJK Ltd at par in exchange for every two shares in RP Ltd.

Additional working capital and the funds required to complete the purchase of RP Ltd were provided by the issue for cash of:
(i) 10,000 shares at a premium of £0.30 per share;
(ii) £8,000 7 per cent Debenture Stock at 98.

The expenses of incorporating CJK Ltd were paid, amounting to £1,200.

(Institute of Cost and Management Accountants)

14.4A. *Tables Ltd*

	£
Net assets (Assets minus liabilities)	67,000
	67,000
Issued share capital: 5 per cent Preference Shares of £1 each	9,000
Ordinary Shares of £1 each	30,000
Revenue reserves	28,000
	67,000

Chairs Ltd

	£
Net assets (Assets minus liabilities)	57,000
	57,000
Issued share capital:	
7½ per cent Preference Shares of £1 each	10,000
Ordinary Shares of £1 each	40,000
Revenue reserves	7,000
	57,000

The above are the summarized balance sheets of Tables Ltd and Chairs Ltd at 31 December 19-6:

The dividends proposed on the ordinary share capital of the companies in 19-6 were £6,000 for Tables Ltd and £4,000 for Chairs Ltd. These amounts, together with proposed dividends for the year on the preference shares, were included among liabilities in the balance sheets of the companies at 31 December 19-6.

On 1 January 19-7, the two companies amalgamated to form a new company, Furniture Ltd, which took over the net assets of Tables Ltd and Chairs Ltd at that date.

Shares were issued by Furniture Ltd to the former shareholders of Tables Ltd and Chairs Ltd as consideration for the surrender of their interests in those companies.

The shares were allocated on the following basis:

1. The ordinary and preference dividends payable by Furniture Ltd for 19-7 are intended to be the same as the total amount of dividends payable by Tables Ltd and Chairs Ltd for 19-6, and shares in Furniture Ltd were allocated to ensure that former shareholders in both Tables Ltd and Chairs Ltd receive the same amounts of dividends from Furniture Ltd for 19-7 as they received for 19-6.

2. The former preference shareholders of Tables Ltd and Chairs Ltd were issued with 6 per cent preference shares of £1 each, at par, in Furniture Ltd.

3. The former ordinary shareholders of Tables Ltd and Chairs Ltd were issued with ordinary shares of £1 each, at par, in Furniture Ltd. It is intended that the *rate* of dividend on the ordinary share capital of Furniture Ltd shall be 8 per cent in 19-7.

The net assets of the amalgamated companies are to be valued in the accounts of Furniture Ltd at an amount equal to that company's total share capital.

Prepare the balance sheet of Furniture Ltd at 1 January 19-7, after these transactions have taken place. Divide the share capital section of the balance sheet between shares issued to former shareholders of Tables Ltd and shares issued to former shareholders of Chairs Ltd.

(Institute of Bankers)

14.5A. The Balance Sheet of Hubble Ltd as at 31 May 19-0 is shown below.

Hubble Ltd

	£	£
Fixed Assets:		
Freehold Premises at Cost		375,000
Plant and Machinery at Cost		
Less Depreciation £48,765		101,235
Motor Vehicles at Cost		
Less Depreciation £1,695		6,775
		483,010
Current Assets:		
Stock in Trade	102,550	
Debtors	96,340	
Cash in Hand	105	
		198,995
		682,005
Authorized Share Capital:		
650,000 Ordinary Shares of £1 each		650,000
Issued Share Capital:		
400,000 Ordinary Shares of £1 each Fully Paid		400,000
Profit and Loss Account		180,630
		580,630
Current Liabilities:		
Trade Creditors	63,200	
Bank Overdraft	38,175	
		101,375
		682,005

Hubble Ltd agreed to purchase at this date the Freehold Premises, Plant and Machinery and Stock of A. Bubble at agreed valuations of £100,000, £10,000 and £55,000, respectively. The purchase price was to be fully settled by the issue to Bubble of 120,000 Ordinary Shares of £1 each in Hubble Ltd, and a cash payment to Bubble of £25,000. Bubble was to collect his debts and to pay his creditors.

Hubble Ltd sold one of its own premises prior to taking over Bubble for £75,000 (cost £55,000) and revalued the remainder at £400,000 (excluding those acquired from Bubble).

You are required to:
(a) Show the journal entries, including cash items, in the books of Hubble Ltd to give effect to the above transactions, and
(b) Show the Balance Sheet of Hubble Ltd after completing them.

(Association of Certified Accountants)

14.6A. From the following information you are required to:

(*a*) prepare a statement apportioning the unappropriated profit between the pre-incorporation and post-incorporation period, showing the basis of apportionment;

(*b*) show the share capital and profits on the balance sheet of the company as at 31 March 19-0.

VU Limited was incorporated on 1 July 19-9 with an authorized share capital of 60,000 ordinary shares of £1 each, to take over the business of L and Sons as from 1 April 19-9.

The purchase consideration was agreed at £50,000 for the net tangible assets taken over, plus a further £6,000 for goodwill.

Payment was satisfied by the issue of £30,000 8 per cent Debentures and 26,000 ordinary shares both at par, on 1 August 19-9. Interest at 10 per cent per annum on the purchase consideration was paid up to this date.

The company raised a further £20,000 on 1 August 19-9 by the issue of ordinary shares at a premium of £0.25 per share.

The abridged profit and loss account for the year to 31 March 19-0 was as follows:

	£	£
Sales:		
1 April 19-9 to 30 June 19-9	30,000	
1 July 19-9 to 31 March 19-0	95,000	
		125,000
Cost of Sales for the Year	80,000	
Depreciation	2,220	
Directors' Fees	500	
Administration Salaries and Expenses	8,840	
Sales Commission	4,375	
Goodwill Written Off	1,000	
Interest on Purchase Consideration, Gross	1,867	
Distribution Costs (60 per cent variable)	6,250	
Preliminary Expenses written off	1,650	
Debenture Interest, Gross	1,600	
Proposed Dividend on Ordinary Shares	7,560	
		115,862
Unappropriated Profit carried forward		9,138

The company sells one product only, of which the unit selling price has remained constant during the year, but due to improved buying the unit cost of sales was reduced by 10 per cent in the post-incorporation period as compared with the pre-incorporation period.

Taxation is to be ignored.

(*Institute of Cost and Management Accountants*)

14.7A. Rowlock Ltd was incorporated on 1 October 19-8 to acquire Rowlock's mail order business, with effect from 1 June 19-8.

The purchase consideration was agreed at £35,000 to be satisfied by the issue on 1 December 19-8 to Rowlock or his nominee of:
20,000 Ordinary Shares of £1 each, fully paid, and £15,000 7 per cent Debentures.

The entries relating to the transfer were not made in the books which were carried on without a break until 31 May 19-9.

On 31 May 19-9 the trial balance extracted from the books is:

	£	£
Sales		52,185
Purchases	38,829	
Wrapping	840	
Postage	441	
Warehouse Rent and Rates	921	
Packing Expenses	1,890	
Office Expenses	627	
Stock on 31 May 19-8	5,261	
Director's Salary	1,000	
Debenture Interest (gross)	525	
Fixed Assets	25,000	
Current Assets (other than stock)	9,745	
Current Liabilities		4,162
Formation Expenses	218	
Capital Account – Wysocka, 31 May 19-8		29,450
Drawings Account – Wysocka	500	
	85,797	85,797

You also ascertain the following:
1. Stock on 31 May 19-9 amounted to £4,946.
2. The average monthly sales for June, July and August were one-half of those for the remaining months of the year. The gross profit margin was constant throughout the year.
3. Wrapping, postage and packing expenses varied in direct proportion to sales, whilst office expenses were constant each month.
4. Formation expenses are to be written off.

You are required to prepare the Trading and Profit and Loss Account for the year ended 31 May 19-9 apportioned between the periods before and after incorporation, and Balance Sheet as on that date.

(Institute of Cost and Management Accountants)

15

Taxation in Accounts

This chapter is concerned with the entries made in the accounts of firms in respect of taxation. It is not concerned with the actual calculations of the taxes. Taxation legislation is now extremely complex and contains many exceptions to the general rules applicable to companies. It is impossible in a book at this level to delve into too many of the complications, and it should therefore be appreciated that, as far as companies are concerned though the facts in this chapter apply to the great majority of limited companies, there are in fact some other complications in a small minority of cases.

Taxation can be split between:

1. Direct taxes, payable to the Inland Revenue, this being the government department responsible for the calculation and collection of the taxes. For a company these taxes are corporation tax and income tax.

SSAP 8 deals with the treatment of taxation in accounts, this SSAP will be adhered to in this chapter.

2. Value Added Tax, abbreviated as VAT. This has been dealt with in Volume 1.

1. Limited Companies + Corporation Tax and Income Tax

The tax which limited companies suffer is known as Corporation Tax. It is legally appropriation of profits, it is not an expense, and it should therefore be shown in the Profit and Loss Appropriation Account. Two law cases, many years ago, did in fact settle any arguments as to whether it was an expense or appropriation, both cases being decided in favour of the view that it was an appropriation of profits.

When a company make profits, then such profits are assessable to corporation tax. It does not mean that corporation tax is payable on the net profits as shown in the accounts. What it does mean is that the corporation tax is assessable on the profit calculated after certain adjustments have been made to the net profit shown according to the Profit and Loss Account. There adjustments are not made in the actual accounts, they are made in calculations performed quite separately from the drafting of Finance Accounts. Suppose that K Ltd. has the following Profit and Loss Account:

K Ltd Profit and Loss Account for the year ended 31 March 19-8

	£	£
Gross Profit		100,000
Less: General Expenses	30,000	
Depreciation of Machinery	20,000	
		50,000
Net Profit		50,000

The depreciation provision for machinery is the accounting figure used for the financial accounts. It is not usually the same figure as that allowed by the Inland Revenue for the depreciation of the machinery. The allowances made for depreciation by the Inland Revenue are known as 'capital allowances'. These are calculated on rules which usually vary at one point or another from the methods applied by the company in determining depreciation provisions. A detailed study of a textbook on taxation would be necessary to see exactly how capital allowances are calculated. In some fairly rare cases, hardly ever found in large or medium-sized concerns but probably more common in very small firms, the capital allowances are calculated and the financial provision for depreciation is taken at the same figure. In the case of K Ltd assume that the capital allowances amount to £27,000, and that the rate of corporation tax is 50 per cent on assessable profits. The calculation of the corporation tax liability would be:

	£
Net Profit per the Financial Accounts	50,000
Add Depreciation provision not allowed as a deduction for corporation tax purposes	20,000
	70,000
Less Capital Allowances	27,000
Adjusted Profits assessable to corporation tax	43,000

As the corporation tax is assumed to be at the rate of 50 per cent of assessable profits, the corporation tax liability will be £43,000 × 50 per cent = £21,500. Sometimes the adjusted profits are greater than the net profits shown in the financial accounts, but may equally well be less. This illustrates the fact that it is relatively rare for the external observer to be able to calculate the corporation tax payable merely by knowing the net profit made by the company. In fact, there are also other items than depreciation provisions that need adjusting to find the correct assessable profits for corporation tax purposes. All that is needed here is the understanding that profit per the Profit and Loss Account is normally different from assessable profit for corporation tax calculations.

The rate of corporation tax is fixed by the Chancellor of the Exchequer in his budget, normally presented to Parliament in April of each year. There have been budgets in other months of the year, but it is normal practice for the April budget to fix corporation tax rates. This rate is to be applied to the assessable profits of companies earned during the twelve months to 31 March before the budget. If the Chancellor announced in April 19-8 that the rate was to be 50 per cent, then this refers to each company's adjusted profits for the government financial year 1 April 19-7 to 31 March 19-8, Likewise, if in April 19-4 the corporation tax rate was announced as 45 per cent, this would refer to profits from 1 April 19-3 to 31 March 19-4. A company whose financial year end is not 31 March will therefore span two governmental financial years.

Example

Company T Ltd. Adjusted profits for the year ended 31 December 19-7. £160,000.
Rate of corporation tax for the governmental financial year ended 31 March 19-7, 50 per cent.
Rate of corporation tax for the governmental financial year ended 31 March 19-8, 52½ per cent.

	£
Three months profit from 1 January 19-8 to 31 March 19-7, $\frac{3}{12} \times £160,000 = £40,000$ at 50 per cent	20,000
Nine months profit from 1 April 19-7 to 31 December 19-7, $\frac{9}{12} \times £160,00 = £120,000$ at 52½ per cent	63,000
	83,000

Corporation Tax — When Payable

1. Mainstream Corporation Tax

This depends on when the company first started trading.

(a) Companies trading before 1 April 1965
Mainstream corporation tax is payable annually on 1 January. To find when it has to be paid on the adjusted profits for a firm's financial

year, the simple, but rather peculiar, way of doing it is to find the next 6 April following the firm's financial year end and then the 1 January following that particular 6 April is the date on which the tax is due.

Example

(i) Firm's year ended 31 March 19-3. Mainstream corporation tax payable 1 January 19-4.

(ii) Firm's year ended 30 April 19-3. Mainstream corporation tax payable 1 January 19-5.

(iii) Firm's year ended 30 June 19-6. Mainstream corporation tax payable 1 January 19-8.

(iv) Firm's year ended 31 December 19-7. Mainstream corporation tax payable 1 January 19-9.

It might appear that a mistake has been made by the author. (i) shows a gap of nine months between the end of the firm's financial year end and the date for payment of corporation tax, (ii) shows twenty months, (iii) reveals eighteen months, and (iv) is twelve months. The reasons for this rather strange timing for tax payments cannot be fully appreciated unless a full study of taxation is undertaken. The reasons are bound up with the tax laws which were in existence before corporation tax was first introduced.

(b) Companies starting trading from 1 April 1965 onwards
Mainstream corporation tax is due for payment nine months after the company's financial year end.

Every company is not so prompt as to have its accounts submitted to the Inland Revenue, and to have its corporation tax liability agreed before the due date for the payment of the tax arrives. In both cases (*a*) and (*b*) the tax is due for payment one month after the making of the assessment (the bill for the corporation tax), if such an assessment is made later than the due date mentioned in (*a*) and (*b*).

For the rest of this chapter, unless mentioned otherwise, corporation tax will be assumed to be at the rate of 50 per cent for the purposes of illustration. In fact companies with relatively small profits can pay at a lower rate than companies with larger profits.

2. Advance Corporation Tax

When a dividend is paid by the company, a sum equal to a fraction of that figure must be paid to the Inland Revenue by the company. The fraction to be found will depend on the standard rate of income tax in operation at the time.
The fraction will be found thus:

$$\frac{\text{Standard rate of income tax}}{100 - \text{standard rate}}$$

Therefore, if the standard rate of income tax is 33 per cent, the fraction will be $\dfrac{33}{100-33} = \dfrac{33}{67}$. For the sake of simplicity in working, the standard rate of income tax will always be assumed for this purpose to be 30 per cent, so that the fraction will be $\dfrac{30}{100-30} = \dfrac{3}{7}$. This will make the arithmetic rather easier to attempt. This is *not* deducted from the dividend, the dividend is paid in full, it is merely that this advance payment is *equal* to $\frac{3}{7}$ of the dividend paid, and is payable to the Inland Revenue within 3 months of the payment of the dividend to the shareholder.

An illustration will now be used to summarise the payment situation.

Exhibit 15.1

In the year to 31 March 19-5 a company has adjusted profits of £100,000 on which it must suffer corporation tax at the rate of 50 per cent. It pays a dividend of £42,000 in that year.

		£
Advance Corporation Tax payable:		
£42,000 × $\frac{3}{7}$		18,000
Corporation Tax liability:		
£100,000 × 50 per cent	50,000	
Less Advance Corporation Tax	18,000	
Mainstream Corporation Tax payable at the due date		32,000
Total Corporation Tax paid		50,000

There is however one restriction on the amount of advance corporation tax payment that can be set off against the mainstream corporation tax payment. The mainstream corporation tax payament must equal at least 20 per cent of the taxable profits, and consequently the amount of advance corporation tax which can be set off against that year's corporation tax is restricted accordingly. This is shown in Exhibit 15.2.

Exhibit 15.2

	£	£	£
Taxable Profits	50,000		
Dividend Paid	49,000		
Advance Corporation Tax £49,000 × $\frac{3}{7}$			21,000
Corporation Tax Liability £50,000 × 50 per cent		25,000	
Less Advance Corporation Tax (restricted)(A)		15,000	
Mainstream Corporation Tax payable at the due date			10,000
Total Corporation Tax Paid			31,000

Although normally £21,000 would be deducted it would mean that the mainstream corporation tax would have been £4,000 (i.e. £25,000 – £21,000). The figure of £4,000 would be less than 20 per cent of the taxable profits, and this just would not be allowed. As £10,000 is 20 per cent of the taxable profits of £50,000 the figure allowed as an advance payment per (A) is the amount needed so that the Corporation Tax liability less (A) equals £10,000. The amount of restricted advance corporation tax which would be allowed is therefore £15,000. The surplus advance corporation tax paid, i.e. £21,000 – £15,000 = £6,000 can be set off against the corporation tax for the past two periods or carried forward and set off against future corporation tax liability.

Income Tax

As already stated, companies do not pay income tax, instead they suffer corporation tax. In the case of sole traders income tax is not directly connected with the business, as the calculation of it depends on whether the sole trade is married or not, the number of dependants that he may have and their ages, the amount and type of other income received by him, etc. It should therefore be charged to the Drawings Account.

The income tax charged upon a partnership is also subject to the personal situation of the partners. The actual apportionment of the tax between the partners must be performed by someone who has access to the personal tax computations, it most certainly is not apportioned in the partners' profit-sharing ratios. When the apportionment has been made each partner should have the relevant amount debited to his Drawings Account.

Sole traders and partnerships are not liable to corporation tax.

Income tax does, however, come into the accounts of limited companies in that the company, when paying charges such as debenture interest or some sorts of royalties, will deduct income tax from the amount to be paid to the debenture holder or royalty owner. This figure of income tax is then payable by the company to the Inland Revenue. This means simply that the company is acting as a tax collector on behalf of the Inland Revenue. Suppose the company has 1,000 different debenture holders, then it is far easier for the Inland Revenue if the company pays only the net amount (i.e. the amount of debenture interest less income tax) due to each debenture holder and then pays the income tax deducted, in one figure, to the Inland Revenue. This saves the Inland Revenue having to trace 1,000 debenture holders and then collect the money from them. It obviously cuts down on the bad debts that the Inland Revenue might suffer, it makes it more difficult to evade the payment of income tax, and all this plus the fact that it makes it cheaper for the Inland Revenue to administer the system.

For the rest of this book it will be assumed that the standard rate of income tax is 30 per cent. This rate will obviously differ from time to time. In addition where an individual has a high income he/she will pay rates of income tax which will exceed 30 per cent. However, a company will deduct income tax at the standard rate, even though individual debenture holders may have to pay income tax at higher rates, or indeed pay no income tax at all.

This means that if a company had 8 per cent debentures amounting to £100,000 then, assuming that the debenture interest was payable in one amount, cheques amounting to a total of £5,600 (8 per cent of £100,000 = £8,000 less 30 per cent income tax, £2,400 = £5,600), will be paid to the debenture holders. A cheque for £2,400 will then be paid to the Inland Revenue by the company. Assume that debenture holder AB is liable on his income to income tax at the rate of 30 per cent, and that he receives interest of £70 net (i.e. £100 gross less income tax £30), on his debenture of £1,250 then he has already suffered his rightful income tax by deduction at the source, He will thus not get a further bill from the Inland Revenue for the £30 tax, he has aleady suffered the full amount due by him, and the company will have paid the £30 income tax as part of the total income tax cheque of £2,400.

On the other hand debenture holder CD may not be liable to income tax because his income is low, or that he has a large number of dependants or other such circumstance for which he obtains liability from having to pay any income tax. If he has a debenture of £1,000 he will receive a cheque for interest amounting to £56 (i.e. £80 gross less income tax £24). As he is not liable to income tax, but as £24 of his money has been included in the total cheque paid by the company to the Inland Revenue of £2,400, then he will be able to claim a refund of £24 from the Inland Revenue. Such a claim is made direct to the Inland Revenue, the company has nothing to do with the refund.

With another debenture holder, EF, this person is liable to a very high rate of income tax, say 75 per cent, on his income. If he has a debenture of £25,000, then the company will pay a cheque to him of £1,400 (£2,000 gross less income tax £600). In fact he is really liable to £1,500 income tax (£2,000 at 75 per cent) on this income. As £600 income tax has been taken from his and handed over by the company, included in the total cheque of £2,400 income tax paid to the Inland Revenue by the company, then eventually the Inland Revenue will send an extra demand for income tax of £900 (£1,500 liable less £600 already paid). The company will have nothing to do with this extra demand.

Of course, a company may well have bought debentures or own royalties, etc., in another company. This may mean that the company not only pays charges, such as debenture interest, but also receives similar items from other companies. The company will receive such items net after income tax has been deducted. When the company both receives and pays such items, it may set off the tax already

suffered by it from such interest, etc., received against the tax
collected by it from its own charges, just paying the resultant net
figure of income tax to the Inland Revenue.

The figures of charges to be shown as being paid or received by
the company in the company's own Profit and Loss Account are the
gross charges, i.e. the same as they would have been if income tax had
never been invented. An exhibit will now be used to illustrate this
more clearly.

Exhibit 15.3

RST Ltd has 7 per cent debentures amounting to £10,000 and has
bought a £4,000 debenture of 10 per cent in a private company, XYZ
Ltd. During the year cheques amounting to £490 (£700 less 30 per
cent) have been paid to debenture holders, and a cheque of £280 (£400
less 30 per cent) has been received from XYZ Ltd. Instead of paying
over the £210 income tax deducted on payment of debenture interest,
RST Ltd waits until the cheque is received from XYZ Ltd, and then
pays a cheque for £90 (£210 collected by it less £120 already suffered
by deduction by XYZ Ltd) to the Inland Revenue in settlement.

Debenture Interest Payable

	£		£
Cash	490	Profit and Loss	700
Income Tax	210		
	700		700

Debenture Interest Receivable

	£		£
Profit and Loss	400	Cash	280
		Income Tax	120
	400		400

Income Tax

	£		£
Unquoted Investment Income	120	Debenture Interest	210
Cash	90		
	210		210

It may well have been the case that, although the income tax had
been deducted at source from both the payment out of the company,
and the amount received, no cash has been paid specifically to the

Inland Revenue by the company by the balance sheet date. This means that the balance of £90 owing to the Inland Revenue will be carried down as a credit balance and will be shown under Current Liabilities in the balance sheet.

Corporation Tax and the Imputation System

When a dividend is paid by a company, this is done without any specific deduction of tax of any kind from the dividend payment. However, the dividend has been paid out of the balance of profits remaining after corporation tax has been charged. In addition, although this has not been deducted specifically from the dividend cheques, a sum equal to $\frac{3}{7}$ of the dividend has to be paid as Advance Corporation Tax. The final part of what is called the Imputation System is that the recipient of the dividend is entitled to a tax credit. The tax credit will equal $\frac{3}{7}$ of the actual amount of the dividend received.

This works out in this way. An individual, not a company, who has 700 shares of £1 each in a company will receive a dividend cheque for £70 if the company pays a dividend of 10 per cent on its shares. When he declares the income on his tax return he will have to show the figure of the actual income received plus a tax credit equal to $\frac{3}{7}$ of that figure, i.e. in this case £70 + $\frac{3}{7}$ of £70 = £100. Assuming an income tax rate of 30 per cent he would normally have to pay £30 income tax on this income of £100, but he is able to set off the tax credit he is entitled to, making a liability of nil. On the other hand, if his personal reliefs are such that he would not have to pay any income tax at all, then he will be able to get a refund of the £30 tax credit from the Inland Revenue. If his income is so great that he has to pay a higher rate of income tax than 30 per cent, then the Inland Revenue will send him a tax demend for the extra income tax.

When it comes to companies buying shares in other companies there are a few differences. Some terminology is necessary here. 'Franked Investment Income' consists of the dividend received, plus the tax credit, by a UK resident company from another UK resident company. A 'Franked Payment' is a dividend, plus the relevant advance corporation tax, payable by a UK resident company. During the accounting period the company will set the tax portion of the franked investment income against the tax portion of the franked payment, and will pay only the balance as advance corporation tax. This means that if company A pays a dividend of £3,500 then normally it would have to pay advance corporation tax of £1,500 ($\frac{3}{7}$ of £3,500). If then company A receives a dividend from company B of £560, there will also be a tax credit of £240 ($\frac{3}{7}$ of £560). The amount of advance corporation tax will therefore be restricted to £1,500 − £240 = £1,260. In the relatively rare instance where the franked investment income exceeds the franked payment, then the excess of the tax portion of the income can be set off against the advance corporation tax payable in the next accounting period.

Although the payments of advance corporation tax are affected as stated, the full payment of corporation tax liability will be affected only as regards the allocation of it between the advance corporation tax part and the mainstream part. The dividends shown as being proposed or as being receivable are shown in the profit and loss and appropriation accounts at the actual figures paid or received. There is thus no form of double entry made for the tax credit, this just does not come into the final accounts at all. Exhibit 15.4 now illustrates the various items discussed so far in this chapter.

Exhibit 15.4

The following are relevant to GB Ltd for the year ended 31 December 19-7.

(a) There are 8 per cent debentures amounting to £20,000. The debenture interest was paid on 31 December less income tax of 30 per cent.

(b) GB Ltd had bought debentures of £5,000 in a private company giving debenture interest at the rate of 9 per cent. A cheque for the year's interest, less income tax at the rate of 30 per cent, is received on 31 December 19-7.

(c) Any income tax owing to the Inland Revenue has not been paid before the year-end.

(d) A dividend of 25 per cent is proposed for the year 19-7 on the 100,000 ordinary shares of £1 each.

(e) GB Ltd had bought 30,000 ordinary shares of £1 each in HH Ltd. On 30 November 19-7 HH Ltd declares and pays a dividend of 14 per cent. HH Ltd is a 'related' company, a term which will be explained later in chapter 18.

(f) The corporation tax liability for the year 19-7 is expected to be £40,000. The tax will be payable in 19-8.

G.B. Ltd. Profit and Loss Account for the year ended 31 December 19-7
(extracts)

		£	£
Debenture Interest	(a)		1,600
Gross Profit			xxxx
			xxxx
Income from shares in related companies	(e)	4,200	
Other interest receivable	(b)	450	4,650
Profit on ordinary activities before taxation			xxxx
Tax on profit or loss on ordinary activities	(f)		40,000
Profit on ordinary activities after taxation			xxxxx
Dividend Proposed	(d)		25,000

Balance Sheet as at 31 December 19-7 (extracts)

		£
Current Liabilities		
Proposed Ordinary Dividends	(d)	25,000
Corporation Tax Payable	(f)	40,000
Income Tax owing (a) £480 − (b) £135		345

Corporation Tax owing at the Balance Sheet Date

Where Corporation Tax is due and payable within twelve months, then it should be shown as a current liability.

For a company which started trading before 1 April, 1965, as already explained, there can be two years Corporation Tax owing, as the following example shows:
A Company Ltd. Balance Sheet date 31 December 19-7.
Corporation Tax on profits for year to 31 December 19-6 is due and payable 1 January 19-8 £10,000.
Corporation Tax on profits for year to 31 December 19-7 is due and payable 1 January 19-9 £15,000.

Accordingly, the £10,000 Corporation Tax due, as it is payable within 12 months is a current liability in the 19-7 balance sheet, whilst the £15,000 Corporation Tax according to SSAP 8 should be described as 'Corporation Tax Payable on 1 January 19-9' and shown as a separate non-current liability.

However, there is one futher complication. ACT normally does not mean an extra expense to the company, it is simply making an earlier payment of part of the Corporation Tax bill. If therefore a dividend of £4,200 for A Ltd on the 19-7 profits was payable in January 19-8, then ACT based on $\frac{3}{7}$ of that figure, i.e. £1,800 would be payable to the Inland Revenue in April 19-8. This is really a partial prepayment of the total £15,000 bill for Corporation Tax. As the £1,800 ACT is payable only 4 months from the balance sheet date then part of the total of £15,000 should be shown as a current liability, leaving £13,200 as a separate non-current liability. This is specified in SSAP 8.

Deferred Taxation

Quite frequently the profits on which the corporation tax is assessable and the profits per the accounts are markedly different. This is especially the case when tax regulations from time to time allow free depreciation of assets, i.e. a far greater amount will be given as capital allowances than would be shown as depreciation in the Profit and Loss Account. This can mean a relatively small amount of corporation tax payable for this year, even though the accounting profits would suggest a much higher figure. Another example would be that of gains on disposals of fixed assets, where the tax is 'rolled over' and payable on some event happening in the future.

SSAP 15: Accounting for Deferred Taxation states that the difference between these two figures would be best shown as an extra charge in the Profit and Loss Appropriation Account, and credited to a Deferred Taxation Account. In the balance sheet the balance in the Deferred Taxation Account should not be put with Reserves or with current liabilities, for it is neither of these. It should instead be shown as a separate item and must not be shown as part of shareholders' funds.

The the accounting net profit for the year might be £250,000, but because of the company being able to claim extra capital allowances when compared with depreciation charges, the taxable profits are £140,000. The rate of corporation tax is taken as being 50 per cent. This means that corporation tax chargeable will be £140,000 × 50 per cent = £70,000. The deferred taxation charge should therefore be £250,000 − £140,000 = £110,000 at 50 per cent = £55,000.

Profit and Loss Appropriation Account for the year ended . . .

		£
Profit on ordinary activities before taxation		250,000
Tax on profit on ordinary activities:		
Corporation Tax	70,000	
Deferred Taxation	55,000	
		125,000
Profit on ordinary activities after taxation		125,000

Balance Sheet as at . . .

Deferred Taxation	55,000
(Current Liabilities)	
Corporation Tax owing	70,000

When in future years the corporation tax payable is higher than it would normally be on comparable accounting profits, transfers of requisite amount will be made back to the Profit and Loss Appropriation Account. The Deferred Taxation Account will be debited and the Profit and Loss Appropriation credited.

This book has been concerned only with the double-entry aspect of Deferred Taxation. SSAP 15 will have to be read in detail for a fuller understanding.

Exercises

15.1. BG Ltd has a trading profit for the year ended 31 December 19-7, before dealing with the following items, of £50,000. You are to complete the Profit and Loss Account and Appropriation Account and show the balance sheet extracts.

(a) The standard rate of income tax is taken as being 30 per cent.
(b) BG Ltd had £40,000 of 9 per cent debentures. It sent them cheques for debenture interest for the year less income tax on 31 December 19-7.
(c) BG Ltd had bought £10,000 of 11 per cent debentures in another company. It received a year's interest, less income tax, on 30 December 19-7.
(d) No cheque has been paid to the Inland Revenue for income tax.
(e) BG Ltd had bought 15,000 ordinary shares of £1 each in MM Ltd. MM Ltd paid a dividend to BG Ltd of 20 per cent on 30 November 19-7. M.M. Ltd is a 'related company'.
(f) BG Ltd had a liability for Corporation Tax, based on the profits for 19-7, of £24,000.
(g) BG proposed a dividend of 30 per cent on its 70,000 ordinary shares of £1 each, out of the profits for 19-7.
(h) Transfer £5,000 to General Reserve.
(i) Unappropriated profits brought forward from last year amounted to £9,870.

15.2A. KK Ltd has a trading profit, before dealing with any of the undermentioned items, for the year ended 31 December 19-9 of £200,000. You are to complete the Profit and Loss and Appropriation Account for the year and balance sheet extracts as at the end of the year.

(a) The standard rate of income tax is taken as being 30 per cent.
(b) KK Ltd has bought £80,000 of 10 per cent debentures in another company. KK Ltd receives its interest, less income tax, for the year on 15 December 19-9.
(c) KK has issued £150,000 of 8 per cent debentures, and pays interest, less income tax for the year on 20 December 19-9.
(d) No cheque has been paid to the Inland Revenue for income tax.
(e) KK Ltd has a liability for Corporation Tax, based on the year's profits for 19-9, of £97,000.
(f) KK Ltd owns 60,000 ordinary shares of £1 each in GHH Ltd, and receives a cheque for the dividend of 20 per cent in November 19-9. GHH Ltd is neither a subsidiary company nor a related company.
(g) KK Ltd proposed a dividend of 15 per cent on the 100,000 ordinary shares of £1 each, payable out of the profits for 19-9.
(h) Transfer £20,000 to General Reserve.
(i) Unappropriated profits brought forward from last year amounted to £19,830.

16

Provisions, Reserves and Liabilities

A 'provision' is an amount written off or retained by way of providing for depreciation, renewals or diminution in value of assets; or retained by way of providing for any known liability of which the amount cannot be determined with 'substantial' accuracy. This therefore covers such items as Provisions for Depreciation. A 'liability' is an amount owing which can be determined with substantial accuracy.

Sometimes, therefore, the difference between a provision and a liability hinges around what is meant by 'substantial' accuracy. Rent owing at the end of a financial year would normally be known with precision, this would obviously be a liability. Legal charges for a court case which has been heard, but for which the lawyers have not yet submitted their bill, would be a provision. The need for the distinction between liabilities and provision will not become obvious until Chapter 18, where the requirements of the Companies Acts regarding disclosures in the Final Accounts are examined.

A 'Revenue Reserve' is where an amount has been voluntarily transferred from the Profit and Loss Appropriation Account by debiting it, thus reducing the amount of profits left available for cash dividend purposes, and crediting a named Reserve Account. The reserve may be for some particular purpose, such as a Foreign Exchange Reserve Account created just in case the firm should ever meet a situation where it would suffer loss because of devaluation of a foreign currency, or it could be a General Reserve Account.

Such transfers are, in fact, an indication to the shareholders that it would be unwise at that particular time to pay out all the available profits as dividends. The resources represented by part of the profits should more wisely and profitably be kept in the firm, at least for the time being. Revenue Reserves can be called upon in future years to help swell the profits shown in the Profit and Loss Appropriation Account as being available for dividend purposes. This is effected quite simply by debiting the particular Reserve Account and crediting the Profit and Loss Appropriation Account.

A General Reserve may be needed because of the effect of inflation. If the year 19-3 a firm needs a working capital of £4,000, the volume of trade remains the same for the next three years but the price level increases by 25 per cent, then the working capital requirements will now be £5,000. If all the profits are distributed the firm will still only have £4,000 working capital which cannot possibly finance the same volume of trade as it did in 19-3. Transferring annual amounts of profits to a General Reserve instead of paying them out as dividends is one way to help overcome this problem. On the other hand it may just be the prudence concept asserting itself, with a philosophy of 'It's better to be safe than sorry', in this case to restrict dividends because the funds they would withdraw from the business may be needed in a moment of crisis. This is sometimes overdone, with the result that the firm has excessive amounts of liquid funds being inefficiently used, whereas if they were paid out to the shareholders, who after all are the owners, then the shareholders could put the funds to better use themselves.

This then leaves the question of the balance on the Profit and Loss Appropriation Account, if it is a credit balance. Is it a Revenue Reserve? There is no straightforward answer to this, the fact that it has not been utilized for dividend purposes could mean that it has been deliberately held back and as such could be classified as a Revenue Reserve. On the other hand, there may be a balance on the account just because it is inconvenient to pay dividends in fractions of percentages.

A Capital Reserve is normally quite different from a Revenue Reserve. It is a reserve which is not available for transfer to the Profit and Loss Appropriation Account to swell the profits shown as available for cash dividend purposes. Most Capital Reserves can never be utilized for cash dividend purposes; notice the use of the word 'cash', as it will be seen later that Bonus Shares may be issued as a 'non-cash' dividend.

The ways that Capital Reserves are created must therefore be looked at.

1. Created in Accordance with the Companies Acts

The Companies Acts state that the following are Capital Reserves and can never be utilized for the declaration of dividends payable in cash.

(a) Capital Redemption Reserve. See Chapter 13.

(b) Share Premium Account. See Chapter 12.

(c) Revaluation Reserve. Where an asset has been revalued then an increase is shown by a debit in the requisite asset account and a credit in the Revaluation Account. The recording of a reduction in value is shown by a credit in the asset account and a debit in the Revaluation Account.

2. *Created by Case Law*

The Companies Act 1981 defined realised profits, albeit a rather complicated definition, and generally it can be said that if a company keeps to 'generally accepted accounting principles' then this will be said to be realised profits. As accounting develops and changes there will obviously be changes made in the 'generally accepted accounting principles'. Any definitive list here would therefore be out of place, as items may well be changed from realised profits to unrealised profits, with the passage of time.

There will however, be law cases which will establish whether or not a profit has been realised and it therefore available for cash dividend purposes, i.e. the item could be transferred to a Capital Reserve account instead of a Revenue Reserve account and vice-versa. Most of the law cases arising before 1981, deciding which profits had to go to Capital Reserve and which to Revenue Reserve will still apply. These are all items which will be studied by students moving to more advanced studies at a later stage. The new definition will however give rise to further law cases.

Capital Reserves put to Use

These can only be used in accordance with the Companies Acts. The following description of the actions which can be taken assumes that in fact the articles of association are the same as Table A for this purpose, and that therefore there are no provisions in the articles to prohibit such actions.

(a) Capital Redemption Reserve (for creation, see Chapter 13)

(i)   To be applied in paying up unissued shares of the company as fully-paid shares. These are commonly called 'bonus shares', and are dealt with in Chapter 17.

(ii) Can be reduced only in the manner as to reduction of share capital (see Chapter 17).

(iii) Can be reduced, in the case of a private company, where the permissible capital payment is greater than the nominal value of shares redeemed/purchased, see chapter 13.

(b) Share Premium Account (for creation, see Chapter 12)

(i)   The same provision referring to bonus shares as exists with the Capital Redemption Reserve.

(ii) Writing off preliminary expenses.

(iii) Writing off expenses and commission paid on the issue of shares or debentures.

(iv) In writing off discounts on shares or debentures issued (for creation of these accounts, see Chapter 12)

(v)   Providing any premium payable on redemption or purchase of shares or debentures.

(c) Revaluation Reserve

Where the directors are of the opinion that any amount standing to the credit of the revaluation reserve is no longer necessary then the reserve must be reduced accordingly. An instance of this would be where an increase in the value of an asset had been credited to the revaluation account, and there had subsequently been a fall in the value of that asset.

The revaluation reserve may also be reduced where the permissible capital payment exceeds the nominal value of the shares redeemed/purchased.

(d) Profits prior to Incorporation (for creation, see Chapter 14)

These can be used for the issuing of bonus shares, in paying up partly paid shares, or alternatively they may be used to write down goodwill or some such similar fixed asset.

(e) Created by Case Law

These can be used in the issue of bonus shares or in the paying up of partly paid shares.

17

The Increase and Reduction of the Share Capital of Limited Companies

Alteration of Capital

A limited company may, if so authorized by its articles, and the correct legal formalities are observed, alter its share capital in any of the following ways:

1. Increasing its share capital by new shares, e.g. increase Authorized Share Capital from £5,000 to £15,000.

2. Consolidate and divide all or any of its share capital into shares of a larger amount than its existing shares, for instance to make 5,000 Ordinary Shares of £1 each into 1,000 Ordinary Shares of £5 each.

3. Convert all or any of its paid-up shares into stock, and reconvert that stock into shares of any denomination, e.g. 10,000 Ordinary Shares of £1 each made into £10,000 Ordinary Stock.

4. Subdivide all, or any, of its shares into shares of smaller denominations, e.g. 1,000 Ordinary Shares of £6 each made into 2,000 Ordinary Shares of £3 each, or 3,000 Ordinary Shares of £2 each, etc.

5. Cancel shares which have not been taken up. This is 'diminution' of capital, not to be confused with reduction of capital described later in the chapter. Thus a firm with an Authorized Capital of £10,000 and an Issued Capital of £8,000 can alter its capital to be Authorized Capital £8,000 and Issued Capital £8,000.

Bonus Shares

These are shares issued to existing shareholders free of charge.

If the articles give the power, and the requisite legal formalities are observed, the following may be applied in the issuing of bonus shares:

1. The balance of the Profit and Loss Appropriation Account.
2. Any other revenue reserve.
3. Any capital reserve, e.g. Share Premium.

This thus comprises all of the reserves.

The reason why this should ever be needed can be illustrated by taking a somewhat exaggerated example, shown in Exhibit 17.1.

Exhibit 17.1

A company, Better Price Ltd, started business fifty years ago with 1,000 Ordinary Shares of £1 each and £1,000 in the bank. The company has constantly had to retain a proportion of its profits to finance its operations, thus diverting them from being used for cash dividend purposes. Such a policy has conserved working capital.

The firm's Balance Sheet as at 31 December 19-7 is shown as:

Better Price Ltd

Balance Sheet as at 31 December 19-7
(before bonus shares are issued)

	£
Fixed Assets	5,000
Current Assets less Current Liabilities	5,000
	10,000
Share Capital	1,000
Reserves (including Profit and Loss Appropriation balance)	9,000
	10,000

If in fact an annual profit of £1,500 was now being made, this being 15 per cent on capital employed, and £1,000 could be paid annually as cash dividends, then the dividend declared each year would be 100 per cent, i.e. a dividend of £1,000 on shares of £1,000 nominal value. It is obvious that the dividends and the share capital have got out of step with one another. Employees and trade unions may well become quite belligerent, as owing to the lack of accounting knowledge, or even misuse of it, it might be believed that the firm was making unduly excessive profits. Customers, especially if they are the general public, may also be deluded into thinking that they were being charged excessive prices, or, even though this could be demonstrated not to be true because of the prices charged by competitors, they may well still have the feeling that they were somehow being duped.

In point of fact, an efficient firm in this particular industry or trade may well be only reasonably rewarded for the risks it has taken by making a profit of 15 per cent on capital employed. The figure of 100 per cent for the dividend is due to the very misleading convention in accounting in the U.K. of calculating dividends in relationship to the nominal amount of the share capital.

If it is considered, in fact, that £7,000 of the reserves could not be used for dividend purposes, due to the fact that the net assets should remain at £8,000, made up of Fixed Assets £5,000 and working capital

£3,000, then besides the £1,000 Share Capital which cannot be returned to the shareholders there are also £7,000 reserves which cannot be rationally returned to them. Instead of this £7,000 being called reserves, it might as well be called capital, as it is needed by the business on a permanent basis.

To remedy this position, as well as some other needs less obvious, bonus shares were envisaged. The reserves are made non-returnable to the shareholders by being converted into share capital. Each holder of one Ordinary Share of £1 each will receive seven bonus shares (in the shape of seven ordinary shares) of £1 each. The Balance Sheet, if the bonus shares had been issued immediately, would then appear:

Better Price Ltd.
Balance Sheet as at 31 December 19-7
(after bonus shares are issued)

	£
Fixed Assets	5,000
Current Assets *less* Current Liabilities	5,000
	10,000
Share Capital (£1,000 + £7,000)	8,000
Reserves (£9,000 − £7,000)	2,000
	10,000

When the dividends of £1,000 per annum are declared in the future, they will amount to $\dfrac{£1,000}{£8,000} \times \dfrac{100}{1} = 12.5$ per cent. This will cause less disturbance in the mind of employees, trade unions, and customers.

Of course the issue of bonus shares may be seen by any of the interested parties to be some form of diabolical liberty. To give seven shares of £1 each free for one previously owned may be seen as a travesty of social justice. In point of fact the shareholders have not gained at all. Before the bonus issue there were 1,000 shares that owned between them £10,000 of net assets. Therefore, assuming just for this purpose that the book 'value' is the same as any other 'value', each share was worth £10. After the bonus issue each previous holder now has eight shares for every one share he held before. If he had owned one share only, he now owns eight shares. He is therefore the owner of $\frac{8}{8,000}$ part of the firm, i.e. a one-thousandth part. The 'value' of the net assets are £10,000, so that he owns £10 of them, so his shares are worth £10. This is exactly the same 'value' as that applying before the bonus issue was made.

It would be useful in addition, to refer to other matters for comparison. Anyone who had owned a £1 share fifty years ago, then worth £1, would now have (if he was still living after such a long time) eight shares worth £8. A new house of a certain type fifty years ago might have cost £x, it may now cost £$8x$, the cost of a bottle of beer may now be y times greater than it was fifty years ago, a packet of cigarettes may be z times more and so on. Of course, the firm has brought a lot of trouble on itself by waiting so many years to capitalize reserves. It should have been done by several stages over the years.

This is all a very simplified, and in many ways an exaggerated version. There is, however, no doubt that misunderstanding of accounting and financial matters have caused a great deal of unnecessary friction in the past and will probably still do so in the future. Yet another very common misunderstanding is that the assumption the reader was asked to accept, namely that the Balance Sheet values equalled 'real values', is often one taken by the reader of a Balance Sheet. Thus a profit of £10,000 when the net assets book values are £20,000 may appear to be excessive, yet in fact a more realistic value of the assets may be saleable value, in which case the value may be £100,000.

The accounting entries necessary are to debit the Reserve Accounts utilized, and to credit a Bonus Account. The shares are then issued and the entry required to record this is to credit the share capital Account and to debit the Bonus Account. The Journal entries would be:

The Journal

	Dr	Cr
	£	£
Reserve Account(s) (show each account separately)	7,000	
Bonus Account		7,000
Transfer of an amount equal to the bonus payable in		
fully-paid shares		
Bonus Account	7,000	
Share Capital Account		7,000
Allotment and issue of 7,000 shares of £1 each, in satisfaction		
of the bonus declared		

Rights Issue

A company can also increase its share capital by making a Rights Issue. This is the issue of shares to existing shareholders at a price lower than the ruling market price of the shares.

The price at which the shares of a very profitable company are quoted in the Stock Exchange is usually higher than the nominal value of the shares. For instance, the market price of the shares of a company might be quoted at £2.50 while the nominal value per share is only £1.00. If the company has 8,000 shares of £1 each and declares a rights issue of one for every eight held at a price of £1.50 per share, it is obvious that it will be cheaper for the existing shareholders to buy the rights issue at this price instead of buying the same shares in the open market for £2.50 per share. Assume that all the rights issue were taken up, then the number of shares taken up will be 1,000 (i.e. 8,000 ÷ 8). And the amount paid for them will be £1,500. The Journal entries will be:

The Journal

	Dr	Cr
	£	£
Cash	1,500	
Share Capital		1,000
Share Premium		500
Being the rights issue of 1 for every 8 shares		
held at a price of £1.50 nominal value being £1.00.		

It is to be noted that because the nominal value of each share is £1.00 while £1.50 was paid, the extra 50p constitutes a share premium to the company.

Reduction of Capital

1. Where Capital is not Represented by Assets

Any scheme for the reduction of capital needs to go through the legal formalities via the shareholders and other interested parties, and must receive the consent of the court. It is assumed that all of this has been carried out correctly.

Capital reduction means in fact that the share capital, all of it if there is only one class such as ordinary shares, or all or part of it if there is more than one class of shares, has been subjected to a lessening of its nominal value, or of the called-up part of the nominal value.

Thus:

(a) A £4 share might be made into a £3 share.
(b) A £5 share might be made into a £1 share.
(c) A £3 share, £2 called up, might be made into a £1 share fully paid up.
(d) A £5 share, £3 called-up, might be made into a £3 share £1 called up.

Any any other variations.

Why should such a step be necessary? The reasons are rather like the issue of bonus shares in reverse. In this case the share capital has got out of step with the assets, in that the share capital is not fully represented by assets. Thus Robert Ltd may have a Balance Sheet as follows:

Robert Ltd
Balance Sheet as at 31 December 19-7

	£
Net Assets	30,000
Ordinary Share Capital	
10,000 Ordinary Shares of £5 each fully paid	50,000
Less Debit Balance − Profit and Loss Account	20,000
	30,000

The net assets are shown at £30,000, it being felt in this particular firm that the book value represented a true and fair view of their 'actual value'. The company will almost certaintly be precluded from paying dividends until the debit balance on the Profit and Loss Appropriation Account has been eradicated and a credit balance brought into existence. Some firms, in certain circumstances, may still pay a dividend even thought there is a debit balance, but it is to be assumed that Robert Ltd is not one of them. If profits remaining after taxation are now running at the rate of £3,000 per annum, it will be more than seven years before a dividend can be paid. As the normal basic reason for buying shares is to provide income, although there may well enter another reason such as capital appreciation, the denial of income to the shareholders for this period of time is serious indeed.

A solution would be to cancel, i.e. reduce, the capital which was no longer represented by assets. In this case there is £20,000 of the share capital which can lay no claim to any assets. The share capital should therefore be reduced by £20,000. This is done by making the shares into £3 shares fully paid instead of £5 shares. The Balance Sheet would become:

Robert Ltd
Balance Sheet as at 31 December 19-7

	£
Net Assets	30,000
	30,000
Ordinary Share Capital	30,000
	30,000

Now that there is no debit balance on the Profit and Loss Appropriation Account the £3,000 available profit next year can be distributed as dividends.

Of course, the firm of Robert Ltd is very much a simplified version. Very often both preference and ordinary shareholders are involved and sometimes debenture holders as well. Even creditors occasionally sacrifice part of the amount owing to them, the idea being that the increase in working capital so generated will help the firm to achieve prosperity, in which case the creditors hope to enjoy the profitable contact that they used to have with the firm. The whole of these capital reduction schemes are matters of negotiation between the various interested parties. For instance, preference shareholders may be quite content for the nominal value of their shares to be reduced if the rate of interest they receive is increased. As with any negotiation the various parties will put forward their points of view and discussions will take place, until eventually a compromise solution is arrived at. When the court's sanction has been obtained, the accounting entries are:

(*a*) For amounts written off assets.
Debit Capital Reduction Account.
Credit Various Asset Accounts.

(*b*) For reduction in liabilities (e.g. creditors).
Debit liability accounts.
Credit Capital Reduction Account.

(*c*) The reduction in the share capital.
Debit Share Capital Accounts (each type).
Credit Capital Reduction Account.

(*d*) If a credit balance now exists on the Capital Reduction Account.
Debit Capital Reduction Account (to close).
Credit Capital Reserve.

It is very unlikely that there would ever be a debit balance on the Capital Reduction Account, as the court would very rarely agree to any such scheme which would bring about that result.

Capital Reduction schemes for private companies will be used less frequently with the advent of Section 54. Companies Act 1981, giving powers to companies to purchase their own shares. The new powers given there will normally be more suitable for private companies.

2. Where Some of the Assets Are No Longer Needed

Where some of the firm's assets are no longer needed, probably due to a contraction in the firm's activities, a company may find itself with a surplus of liquid assets. Subject to the legal formalities being observed, in this case the reduction of capital is effected by returning cash to the shareholders, i.e.:

(i) Debit Share Capital Account (with amount returnable).
Credit Sundry Shareholders.

(ii) Debit Sundry Shareholders.

   Credit Bank (amount actually paid).

Such a scheme could be objected to by the creditors if it affected their interests.

Exercises

17.1. Deflation Ltd, which had experienced trading difficulties, decided to reorganize its finances.

On 31 December 19-5 a final trial balance extracted from the books showed the following position:

	£	£
Share Capital, authorized and issued:		
150,000 6 per cent Cumulative Preference Shares of £1 each		150,000
200,000 Ordinary Shares of £1 each		200,000
Share Premium Account		40,000
Profit and Loss Account	114,375	
Preliminary Expenses	7,250	
Goodwill (at cost)	55,000	
Trade Creditors		43,500
Debtors	31,200	
Bank Overdraft		51,000
Leasehold Property (at cost)	80,000	
,, ,, (provision for depreciation)		30,000
Plant and Machinery (at cost)	210,000	
,, ,, ,, (provision for depreciation)		62,500
Stock in Hand	79,175	
	577,000	577,000

Approval of the Court was obtained for the following scheme for reduction of capital:

1. The preference shares to be reduced to £0.75 per share.
2. The ordinary shares to be reduced to £0.125 per share.
3. One £0.125 ordinary share to be issued for each £1 of gross preference dividend arrears; the preference dividend had not been paid for three years.
4. The balance on share premium account to be utilized.
5. Plant and machinery to be written down to £75,000.
6. The profit and loss account balance, and all intangible assets, to be written off.

At the same time as the resolution to reduce capital was passed, another resolution was approved restoring the total authorized capital to £350,000, consisting of 150,000 6 per cent cumulative preference shares of £0.75 each and the balance in ordinary shares of £0.125 each. As soon as the above resolutions had been passed 500,000 ordinary shares were issued at par, for cash, payable in full upon application.

You are required:

(a) to show the journal entries necessary to record the above transactions in the company's books, and
(b) to prepare a Balance Sheet of the company, after completion of the scheme.

(Institute of Chartered Accountants)

17.2. The Balance Sheet of Planners Ltd on 31 March 19-6 was as follows:

Balance Sheet

	£	£
Goodwill		20,000
Fixed Assets		100,000
		120,000
Current Assets:		
Stock	22,000	
Work in Progress	5,500	
Debtors	34,000	
Bank	17,500	
		79,000
Capital Expenses:		
Formation Expenses		1,000
		200,000
Issued Share Capital:		
120,000 Ordinary Shares of £1 each		120,000
50,000 6 per cent Cumulative Preference Shares of £1 each		50,000
		170,000
Less Profit and Loss Account Debit Balance		40,000
		130,000
6 per cent Debentures		50,000
Current Liabilities:		
Creditors		20,000
		200,000

The dividend on the preference shares is £9,000 in arrears. A scheme of reconstruction was accepted by all parties and was completed on 1 April 19-6.

A new company was formed, Budgets Ltd, with an authorized share capital of £200,000, consisting of 200,000 ordinary shares of £1 each. This company took over all the assets of Planners Ltd. The purchase consideration was satisfied partly in cash and partly by the issue, at par, of shares and debentures by the new company in accordance with the following arrangements:

1. The creditors of the old company received, in settlement of each £10 due to them, £7 in cash and three fully paid ordinary shares in the new company.
2. The holders of preference shares in the old company received seven fully paid ordinary shares in the new company to every eight preference shares in the old company and three fully paid ordinary shares in the new company for every £5 of arrears of dividend.
3. The ordinary shareholders in the old company received one fully paid share in the new company for every five ordinary shares in the old company.
4. The holders of 6 per cent debentures in the old company received £40 cash and £60 6 per cent debentures issued at par for every £100 debenture held in the old company.

5. The balance of the authorised capital of the new company was issued at par for cash and was fully paid on 1 April 19-6.

6. Goodwill was eliminated, the stock was valued at £20,000 and the other current assets were brought into the new company's books at the amounts at which they appeared in the old company's balance sheet. The balance of the purchase consideration represented the agreed value of the fixed assets.

You are required to show:

(a) The closing entries in the Realisation Account and the Sundry Shareholders Account in the books of Planners Ltd.

(b) To show your calculation of:
(i) The Purchase Consideration for the Assets, and (ii) the agreed value of the fixed assets.

(c) The summarised balance sheet of Budgets Ltd as on 1 April 19-6.

17.3. On 31 March 19-6 the following was the Balance Sheet of Finer Textiles Ltd:

Balance Sheet

	£	£
Fixed Assets:		
Goodwill and Trade Marks as valued	225,000	
Plant and Machinery (at cost *less* depreciation)	214,800	
Furniture and Fittings (at cost *less* depreciation)	12,600	
		452,400
Current Assets:		
Stock-in-Trade	170,850	
Sundry Debtors	65,100	
Cash in Hand	150	
		236,100
		688,500
Authorized Capital:		
150,000 7 per cent Preferences Shares of £1 each	150,000	
2,100,000 Ordinary Shares of £0.5 each	1,050,000	
		1,200,000
Issued and Fully Paid Capital:		
150,000 7 per cent Preference Shares of £1 each	150,000	
1,200,000 Ordinary Shares of £0.5 each	600,000	
		750,000
Capital Reserve		48,000
		798,000
Deduct Profit and Loss Account (debit balance)		183,900
		614,100
Current Liabilities:		
Sundry Creditors		31,800
Bank Overdraft		42,600
		688,500

The following scheme of capital reduction was sanctioned by the Court and agreed by the shareholders:

(i) Preference shares were to be reduced to £0.75 each.
(ii) Ordinary shares were to be reduced to £0.2 each.
(iii) The capital reserve was to be eliminated.
(iv) The reduced shares of both classes were to be consolidated into new ordinary shares of £1 each.
(v) An issue of £150,000 8 per cent Debentures at par was to be made to provide fresh working capital.
(vi) The sum written off the issued capital of the company and the capital reserve to be used to write off the debit balance of the Profit and Loss Account and to reduce fixed assets by the following amounts:

	£
Goodwill and trade marks	210,000
Plant and machinery	45,000
Furniture and fittings	6,600

(vii) The bank overdraft was to be paid off out of the proceeds of the debentures which were duly issued and paid in full.

A further resolution was passed to restore the authorized capital of the company to 1,200,000 ordinary shares of £1 each.

Prepare journal entries (cash transactions to be journalized) to give effect to the above scheme and draw up the Balance Sheet of the company after completion of the scheme.

17.4A. The summarized Balance Sheet of Owens Ltd at 31 December 19-9 was as follows:

	£
Freehold Premises	60,000
Plant	210,000
Stock	64,000
Debtors	70,000
Development Expenditure	75,000
Cash at Bank	6,000
Profit and Loss Account	85,000
	570,000
Issued Capital:	
150,000 6 per cent Preference Shares of £1 each	150,000
300,000 Ordinary Shares of £1 each	300,000
Creditors	120,000
	570,000

A capital reduction scheme has been sanctioned under which the 150,000 preference shares are to be reduced to £0.75 each, fully paid, and the 300,000 ordinary shares are to be reduced to £0.10 each, fully paid.

Development expenditure and the debit balance on Profit and Loss Account are to be written off, the balance remaining being used to reduce the book value of the plant.

Prepare the journal entries recording the reduction scheme and the balance sheet as it would appear immediately after the reduction. Narrations are not required in connection with journal entries.

18

The Final Accounts of Limited Companies: Profit and Loss Accounts

When a company draws up its own Final Accounts, purely for internal use by the directors and the management, then it can draft them in any way which is considered most suitable. Drawing up a Trading and Profit and Loss Account and Balance Sheet for the firm's own use is not necessarily the same as drawing up such accounts for examination purposes. If a firm wishes to charge something in the Trading Account which perhaps in theory ought to be shown in the Profit and Loss Account, then there is nothing to prevent the firm from so doing. The examinee, on the other hand, must base his answers on accounting theory and not on the practice of his own firm.

When it comes to publication, i.e. sent to the shareholder or to the Registrar of Companies, then the Companies Act, 1981, Schedule 1, lays down the information which *must* be shown and also *how* it should be shown. Prior to the 1981 Act, provided the necessary information was shown it was completely up to the company exactly *how* it was shown. The provisions of the 1981 Act bring the United Kingdom into line with the Fourth Directive of the EEC, and therefore the freedom previously available to companies on *how* to show the information has been taken away from them. There are however some advantages to be gained from such standardisation.

The 1981 Act however does give companies the choice of two alternative formats (layouts) for balance sheets, and four alternative formats for profit and loss accounts. As the reader of this chapter will most probably be studying this for the first time, it would be inappropriate to give all the details of all the formats. Only the far more advanced student would need such details. In this book therefore the reader will be show an internal profit & loss account which can easily be adapted to cover publication requirements under the 1981 Act, also a balance sheet.

All companies, even the very smallest, have to produce accounts for shareholders giving the *full* details required by the 1981 Act. 'Small' and 'medium' companies, as later defined, can however file 'modified' accounts with the Registrar of Companies. These will be examined later.

The format that will be used for the published profit and loss account in this book, out of the four formats which could be used, is Format 1. The reasons for this choice are that it is in a vertical style, which is much more modern and also more likely to gain extra marks from examiners, and in addition is much more like common UK practice before the 1981 Act. An example of Format 2, also in vertical style, is shown as Exhibit 18.5. Formats 3 and 4 are in horizontal style and are not shown in this book.

The Companies Act 1981, Schedule 1, shows Format 1 as in Exhibit 18.1.

Exhibit 18.1
Profit and loss account formats
Format 1

1. Turnover
2. Cost of sales
3. Gross profit or loss
4. Distribution costs
5. Administrative expenses
6. Other operating income
7. Income from shares in group companies
8. Income from shares in related companies
9. Income from other fixed asset investments
10. Other interest receivable and similar income
11. Amounts written off investments
12. Interest payable and similar charges
13. Tax on profit or loss on ordinary activities
14. Profit or loss on ordinary activities after taxation
15. Extraordinary income
16. Extraordinary charges
17. Extraordinary profit or loss
18. Tax on extraordinary profit or loss
19. Other taxes not shown under the above items
20. Profit or loss for the financial year

Obviously this is simply a list, and it does not show where sub-totals should be placed. The important point is that the items 1 to 20 have to be displayed in that order. Obviously if some items do not exist for the company in a given year then those headings will be omitted from the pubished profit and loss account. Thus if the company has no type of investments then items 7, 8, 9, 10 and 11 will not exist, so, that item 6 will be followed by item 12 in that company's published profit and loss account. The actual numbers on the left hand side of items do not have to be shown in the published accounts.

Exhibit 18.2 shows a Trading and Profit and Loss Account drawn up for internal use by the company. This could be drawn up in any way as far as the law is concerned because the law does *not* cover accounts prepared solely for the company's internal use. If the internal accounts were drawn up in a completely different fashion to those needed for publication, then there would be quite a lot of work to do to re-assemble the figures, into a profit and loss account for publication. In Exhibit 18.2 the internal accounts have been drawn up in a style which makes it much easier to get the figures for the published profit and loss account. As examination questions may ask for both (i) internal and (ii) published accounts, it makes it simpler for the students if the internal *and* published accounts follow a similar order of display.

Exhibit 18.2 (Accounts for internal use)

Block plc

Trading & Profit & Loss Account for the year ended 31 March 19-8

	£	£
Turnover		765,000
Less Cost of Sales:		
Stock 1 April 19-7	105,000	
Add Purchases	460,000	
	565,000	
Less Stock 31 March 19-8	126,000	439,000
Gross Profit		326,000
Distribution Costs:		
Salaries & Wages	50,000	
Motor Vehicles Costs: Distribution	21,000	
General Distribution Expenses	15,000	
Depreciation: Motors	4,000	
Machinery	3,000	93,000
Administrative Expenses:		
Salaries & Wages	44,000	
Directors' Remuneration	20,000	
Motor Vehicle Costs: Administrative	8,000	
General Administrative Expenses	31,000	
Auditors' Remuneration	2,000	
Depreciation: Motors	3,000	
Machinery	2,000	110,000	203,000
		123,000
Other Operating Income: Rents Receivable		7,000
		130,000
Income from shares in related companies	2,500	
Income from shares from non-related companies	1,500	
Other Interest Receivable	1,000	5,000
		135,000
Interest Payable:		
Loans Repayable within five years	500	
Loans Repayable in ten years time	1,500	2,000
Profit on ordinary activities before taxation		133,000
Tax on Profit on ordinary activities		48,000
Profit on ordinary activities after taxation		85,000
Undistributed profits brought forward from last year		55,000
		140,000
Transfer to General Reserve	15,000	
Proposed ordinary dividend	60,000	75,000
Undistributed profits carried forward to next year		65,000

Exhibit 18.3 (Accounts for publication)

Block plc

Profit and Loss Account for the year ended 31 March 19-8

		£	£
1.	Turnover		765,000
2.	Cost of Sales		439,000
3.	Gross Profit		326,000
4.	Distribution Costs	93,000	
5.	Administrative Expenses	110,000	203,000
			123,000
6.	Other Operating Income		7,000
			130,000
8.	Income from Shares in Related Companies	2,500	
9.	Income from Other Fixed Asset Investments	1,500	
10.	Other Interest Receivable	1,000	5,000
			135,000
12.	Interest Payable:		2,000
	Profit on Ordinary Activities before Taxation		133,000
13.	Tax on Profit on Ordinary Activities		48,000
14.	Profit for the year on Ordinary Activities after Taxation		85,000
	Undistributed Profits from last year		55,000
			140,000
	Transfer to General Reserve	15,000	
	Proposed Ordinary Dividend	60,000	75,000
	Undistributed Profits Carried to Next Year		65,000

Exhibit 18.2 is redrafted into a form suitable for publication and shown as Exhibit 18.3. The following notes are applicable.

The figures on the left hand side of Exhibit 18.3 do *not* have to be published. They are shown for the benefit of the reader of this book.

It would be legally possible for the internal accounts, as shown in Exhibit 18.2 to be published just as they are, because all the items are shown in the correct order. This would not have been possible if the internal accounts were drafted in a completely different order. However, the Companies Acts do not force companies to publish full accounts, as a company's competitors may thereby be given information which would lead to them being placed in a better competitive position against the company. The law therefore states the minimum information which must be disclosed, a company can show more than the minimum should it so wish.

Format Item 1. Turnover is defined as the amounts derived from the provision of goods and services falling within the company's ordinary activities, net after deduction of V.A.T. and trade discounts.

Format: Items 2, 4 and 5. The figures for Cost of Sales, Distribution costs and Administrative expenses must include any depreciation charges connected with these functions. In the case of

Block plc, because of the type of business, there are depreciation charges as part of Distribution costs and Administration expenses but not for Cost of Sales.

Format Item 6. This is operating income which does not fall under Item 1. Such items as rents receivable, royalties receivable might be found under this heading. It all depends on what the 'ordinary activities' of the company are, as Item 6 is for operating 'outside' the ordinary activities.

Format Item 7. When the reader reaches Chapter 27 of this book he will be introduced to holding companies and subsidiaries. Such companies are under 'common' control, i.e. the holding company owns sufficient shares to 'control' the activities of the subsidiary. The holding companies and all its subsidiaries are a 'group'. Any dividends received by a company from its investments in shares in any member of the 'group' have to be shown separately.

Format Item 8. The term 'related company' is a new term introduced by the 1981 Companies Act. It has virtually replaced the term 'associated company' previously used. A 'related company' is defined as a non-group company in which an investor company holds a long-term 'qualifying capital interest' (i.e. an interest in voting equity shares) for the purpose of securing a contribution to the investor's own activities by the exercise of control or influence. Where the equity stake exceeds 20 per cent, there is a presumption of such influence unless the contrary is shown.

Format Item 12. This includes bank interest on loans and overdrafts, debenture interest etc.

In the published Profit & Loss Account for Block plc there are no items per the format numbered 7, 11, 15, 16, 17, 18 and 19. After item 20, Profit for the year, there are several more lines, those of unappropriated profits brought forward and carried forward, transfer to reserves and proposed dividends. Although the format omits them, they are in fact required according to the detailed rules accompanying the Format. This also applies to the line 'Profit on Ordinary Activities before Taxation.

It would have been possible to amalgamate items, for instance 4 and 5 could have been shown as one item as 'Net Operating Expenses £203,000'. In this case included in the notes appended to the accounts would be an item showing how the figure of £203,000 was made up.

In the notes attached to the profit and loss account, Section 53 Companies Act 1981, requires that the following be shown separately:

(a) Interest on bank loans, overdrafts and other loans
 (i) repayable within 5 years from the end of the accounting period
 (ii) finally repayable after 5 years from the end of the accounting period.
(b) Amounts set aside for redemption of share capital and for redemption of loans.

(c) Rents from land, if material.

(d) Costs of hire of plant and machinery.

(e) Auditors Remuneration, including expenses.

Section 55 requires a note, where a company carries on business of two or more classes differing substantially from each other, of the amount of turnover for each class of business and the division of the profit and loss before taxation between each class. Information also has to be given of the turnover between different geographical markets.

Section 56, requires notes concerning numbers of employees, wages and salaries, social security costs and pension costs.

Exhibit 18.4 gives a Profit and Loss Account for a company which has amounts for each of items 1 to 20 inclusive. In addition the extra lines are shown, although they were omitted from the Format 1 in the Companies Act. The monetary figures are given so that the reader can see where sub-totals can be shown.

Exhibit 18.4

Profit and Loss Account: Format 1

		£	£000's £
1.	Turnover		800
2.	Cost of sales		500
3.	Gross profit or loss		300
4.	Distribution costs	60	
5.	Administrative expenses	40	
			100
			200
6.	Other operating income		30
			230
7.	Income from shares in group companies	20	
8.	Income from shares in related companies	10	
9.	Income from other fixed asset investments	5	
10.	Other interest receivable and similar income	15	
			50
			280
11.	Amounts written off investments	4	
12.	Interest payable and similar charges	16	
			20
	Profit or loss on ordinary activities before taxation		260
13.	Tax on profit or loss on ordinary activities		95
14.	Profit or loss on ordinary activities after taxation		165
15.	Extraordinary income	16	
16.	Extraordinary charges	4	
17.	Extraordinary profit or loss	12	
18.	Tax on extraordinary profit or loss	5	
			7
			172
19.	Other taxes not shown under the above items		8
20.	Profit or loss for the financial year		164
	Undistributed Profits from last year		60
			224
	Transfers to Reserves	40	
	Dividends Paid and Proposed	100	140
	Undistributed Profits Carried to Next year		84

Allocation of Expenses

It will be obvious under which heading most expenses will be shown whether they are

(i)   Cost of Sales, or

(ii) Distribution Costs, or

(iii) Administrative Expenses

However, some items are not so easy to allocate with certainty as the Companies Acts do not define these terms. Some companies may choose one heading for a particular items, whilst another company will choose to include that item under another heading. These items can now be examined.

(a)   Discounts Received. These are for prompt payment of amounts owing by us. Where they are for payments to suppliers of goods they could be regarded as either being a reduction in the cost of goods, or alternatively as being a financial recompense, i.e. the reward for paying money on time. If regarded in the first way it would be deducted from Cost of Sales, whereas the alternative approach would be to deduct it from Administrative Expenses.

However, these discounts are also deducted when paying bills in respect of Distribution Costs or Administrative Expenses, and it would also be necessary to deduct from these headings if the Cost of Sales deduction approach is used. As this raises complications in the original recording of discounts received, it would be more suitable in this book if all cash discounts received are deducted in arriving at the figure of Administrative Expenses.

(b)   Discounts Allowed. To be consistent in dealing with discounts, this should be included in Administrative Expenses.

(c)   Bad Debts. These could either be regarded as an expense connected with sales, after all they are sales which are not paid for. The other point of view is that for a debt to become bad, at least part of the blame must be because the proper administrative procedures in checking on customers' creditworthiness has not been thorough enough. In this book all bad debts will be taken as being part of Administrative Expenses.

Exhibit 18.5

The previous exhibit, 18.4, is now shown as it might appear in Format 2.

Profit and Loss Account: Format 2

		£	£	£000's£
1.	Turnover			800
2.	Change in stocks of finished goods and in Work in Progress			45
3.	Own work capitalised			25
4.	Other operating income			30
				900
5.	(a) Raw materials and consumables	290		
	(b) Other external charges	190	480	
6.	Staff costs:			
	(a) Wages and salaries	110		
	(b) Other pension costs	12	122	
7.	(a) Depreciation and other amounts written off tangible and intangible fixed assets	50		
	(b) Exceptional amounts written off current assets	10	60	
8.	Other operating charges		8	670
				230
9.	Income from shares in group companies		20	
10.	Income from shares in related companies		10	
11.	Income from other fixed asset investments		5	
12.	Other interest receivable and similar income		15	50
				280
13.	Amounts written off investments		4	
14.	Interest payable and similar charges		16	20
	Profit or loss on ordinary activities before taxation			260
15.	Tax on profit or loss on ordinary activities			95
16.	Profit or loss on ordinary activities after taxation			165
17.	Extraordinary income		16	
18.	Extraordinary charges		4	
19.	Extraordinary profit or loss		12	
20.	Tax on extraordinary profit or loss		5	7
				172
21.	Other taxes not shown under the above items			8
22.	Profit or loss for the financial year			164
	Undistributed Profits from last year			60
				224
	Transfers to Reserves		40	
	Dividends Paid and Proposed		100	140
	Undistributed Profits Carried to Next Year			84

Note: Obviously the author has had to invent figures for items 2, 3, 5, 6, 7 and 8, as it would be impossible to deduce them from the figures shown in Exhibit 18.4.

Exercises

18.1 From the following selected balance of Rogers plc as at 31 December 19-2 draw up (i) A Trading and Profit and Loss Account for internal use, and (ii) a Profit and Loss Account for publication.

	£
Profit and Loss Account as at 31 December 19-1	15,300
Stock 1 January 19-2	57,500
Purchases	164,000
Sales	288,000
Returns Inwards	11,500
Returns Outwards	2,000
Carriage Inwards	1,300
Wages & Salaries (see note b)	8,400
Rent & Rates (see note c)	6,250
General Distribution Expenses	4,860
General Administrative Expenses	3,320
Discounts Allowed	3,940
Bad Debts	570
Debenture Interest	2,400
Motor Expenses (see note d)	7,200
Interest Received on Bank Deposit	770
Income from shares in related companies (gross)	660
Motor Vehicles at cost: Administrative	14,000
Distribution	26,000
Equipment at cost: Administrative	5,500
Distribution	3,500
Royalties Receivable	1,800

Notes:

(a) Stock at 31 December 19-2 £64,000.

(b) Wages and Salaries are to be apportioned: Distribution Costs ⅓rd, Administrative Expenses ⅔rds.

(c) Rent and Rates are to be apportioned: Distribution Costs 60%, Administrative Expenses 40%.

(d) Apportion Motor Expenses equally between Distribution Costs and Administrative Expenses.

(e) Depreciate Motor Vehicles 25% and Equipment 20% on cost.

(f) Accrue auditors remuneration of £500.

(g) Accrue Corporation Tax for the year on ordinary activity profits £30,700.

(h) A sum of £8,000 is to be transferred to General Reserve.

(i) An ordinary dividend of £30,000 is to be proposed.

240

18.2. You are given the following selected balances of Federal plc as at 31 December 19-4. From them draw up (i) a Trading and Profit and Loss Account for the year ended 31 December 19-4 for internal use and (ii) A Profit and Loss Account for publication.

	£
Stock 1 January 19-4	64,500
Sales	849,000
Purchases	510,600
Carriage Inwards	4,900
Returns Inwards	5,800
Returns Outwards	3,300
Discounts Allowed	5,780
Discounts Received	6,800
Wages (putting goods into saleable condition)	11,350
Salaries and Wages: Sales and Distribution staff	29,110
Salaries and Wages: Administrative Staff	20,920
Motor Expenses (see note c)	15,600
Rent & Rates (see note d)	25,000
Investments in related companies (market value £66,000)	80,000
Income from shares in related companies	3,500
General Distribution Expenses	8,220
General Administrative Expenses	2,190
Bad Debts	840
Interest from Government Securities	1,600
Haulage Costs: Distribution	2,070
Debenture Interest Payable	3,800
Profit and Loss Account: 31 December 19-3	37,470
Motor Vehicles at cost: Distribution and Sales	75,000
Administrative	35,000
Plant & Machinery at cost: Distribution and Sales	80,000
Administrative	50,000
Production	15,000
Directors' Remuneration	5,000

Notes:

(a) The production department puts goods bought into a saleable condition.

(b) Stock at 31 December 19-4 £82,800.

(c) Apportion Motor Expenses: Distribution ⅔rds, Administrative ⅓rd.

(d) Apportion Rent and Rates: Distribution 80%, Administrative 20%.

(e) Write £14,000 off the value of Investments in related companies.

(f) Depreciation Motor Vehicles 20% on cost, Plant and Machinery 10% on cost.

(g) Accrue auditors' remuneration £2,000.

(h) Accrue Corporation Tax on ordinary activity profits £74,000.

(i) A sum of £20,000 is to be transferred to Debenture Redemption Reserve.

(j) An ordinary dividend of £50,000 is to be proposed.

18.3A. The following balance have been extracted from the books of Falconer plc as on 31 August 19-4. From them draw up (i) A Trading and Profit and Loss Account, for internal use, for the year ended 31 August 19-4, also (ii) A Profit and Loss Account for publication for the year.

	£
Purchases	540,500
Sales	815,920
Returns Inwards	15,380
Returns Outwards	24,620
Carriage Inwards	5,100
Wages – Productive	6,370
Discounts Allowed	5,890
Discounts Received	7,940
Stock 31 August 19-3	128,750
Wages & Salaries: Sales and Distribution	19,480
Wages & Salaries: Administrative	24,800
Motor Expenses: Sales and Distribution	8,970
Motor Expenses: Administrative	16,220
General Distribution Expenses	4,780
General Administrative Expenses	5,110
Rent and Rates (see note c)	9,600
Directors' Remuneration	12,400
Profit and Loss Account: 31 August 19-3	18,270
Advertising Costs	8,380
Bad Debts	1,020
Hire of Plant and Machinery (see note b)	8,920
Motor Vehicles at cost: Sales & Distribution	28,000
Administrative	36,000
Plant and Machinery: Distribution	17,500
Debenture Interest Payable	4,800
Income from Shares in group companies	12,800
Income from Shares in related companies	10,500
Preference Dividend Paid	15,000
Profit on disposal of investments	6,600
Tax on profit on disposal of investments	1,920

Notes:

(a) Stock at 31 August 19-4 £144,510.

(b) The hire of plant and machinery is to be apportioned: Productive £5,200, Administrative £3,720.

(c) Rent and Rates to be apportioned: Distribution ⅔rds, Administrative ⅓rd.

(d) Motors are to be depreciated at 25% on cost, Plant and Machinery to be depreciated at 20% on cost.

(e) Auditors remuneration of £1,700 to be accrued.

(f) Corporation Tax on profit from ordinary activities for the year is estimated at £59,300.

(g) Transfer £25,000 to General Reserve.

(h) Ordinary dividend of £60,000 is proposed.

242

18.4A. From the following balances of Danielle plc you are to draw up (i) A Trading and Profit and Loss Account for the year ended 31 December 19-6, for internal use, and (ii) A Profit and Loss Account for publication:

	£
Plant and Machinery, at cost (see note c)	275,000
Bank Interest Receivable	1,850
Discounts Allowed	5,040
Discounts Received	3,890
Hire of Motor Vehicles: Sales and Distribution	9,470
Hire of Motor Vehicles: Administrative	5,710
Licence Fees Receivable	5,100
General Distribution Expenses	11,300
General Administrative Expenses	15,800
Wages and Salaries: Sales and Distribution	134,690
Administrative	89,720
Directors' Remuneration	42,000
Motor Expenses (see note e)	18,600
Stock 31 December 19-5	220,500
Sales	880,000
Purchases	405,600
Returns Outwards	15,800
Returns Inwards	19,550
Profit and Loss Account as at 31 December 19-5	29,370

Notes:

(a) Stock at 31 December 19-6 £210,840.

(b) Accrue Auditor's Remuneration £3,000.

(c) Of the Plant and Machinery, £150,000 is Distributive in nature, whilst £125,000 is for Administration.

(d) Depreciate Plant and Machinery 20% on cost.

(e) Of the Motor Expenses ⅔rds is for Sales and Distribution and ⅓rd for Administration.

(f) Corporation Tax on Ordinary Profits is estimated at £28,350.

(g) Proposed ordinary dividend is £50,000.

(h) A sum of £15,000 is to be transferred to General Reserve.

19

The Final Accounts of Limited Companies: Balance Sheets

The Companies Act 1981 sets out two formats for the balance sheet, one vertical and one horizontal. The method chosen for this book is that of Format 1 because this most resembles U.K. practice. As it is the vertical style format it will also be looked upon with favour by examiners.

Format 1 is shown as Exhibit 19.1. Monetary figures have been included to illustrate it more clearly.

Exhibit 19.1

Balance Sheet – Format 1   £000's

	£	£	£
A. CALLED UP SHARE CAPITAL NOT PAID*			10
B. FIXED ASSETS			
I Intangible assets			
1. Development costs	20		
2. Concessions, patents, licences, trade marks and similar rights and assets	30		
3. Goodwill	80		
4. Payments on account	5	135	
II Tangible assets			
1. Land and buildings	300		
2. Plant and machinery	500		
3. Fixtures, fittings, tools and equipment	60		
4. Payments on account and assets in course of construction	20	880	
III Investments			
1. Shares in group companies	15		
2. Loans to group companies	10		
3. Shares in related companies	20		
4. Loans to related companies	5		
5. Other investments other than loans	30		
6. Other loans	16		
7. Own shares	4	100	1,115
C. CURRENT ASSETS			
I Stock			
1. Raw materials and consumables	60		
2. Work in progress	15		
3. Finished goods and goods for resale	120		
4. Payments on account	5	200	

II	Debtors		
	1. Trade debtors	200	
	2. Amounts owed by group companies	20	
	3. Amounts owed by related companies	10	
	4. Other debtors	4	
	5. Called up share capital not paid*	–	
	6. Prepayments and accrued income**	–	234
III	Investments		
	1. Shares in group companies	40	
	2. Own shares	5	
	3. Other investments	30	75
IV	Cash at Bank and in Hand		26
			535
D. PREPAYMENTS AND ACCRUED INCOME			15
			550

E. CREDITORS: AMOUNTS FALLING DUE WITHIN ONE YEAR

1. Debenture loans	5	
2. Bank loans and overdrafts	10	
3. Payments received on account	20	
4. Trade creditors	50	
5. Bills of exchange payable	2	
6. Amounts owed to group companies	15	
7. Amounts owed to related companies	6	
8. Other creditors including taxation and social security	54	
9. Accruals and deferred income***	–	162

F. NET CURRENT ASSETS (LIABILITIES)	388
G. TOTAL ASSETS LESS CURRENT LIABILITIES	1,513

H. CREDITORS: AMOUNTS FALLING DUE AFTER MORE THAN ONE YEAR

1. Debenture loans	20	
2. Bank loans and overdrafts	15	
3. Payments received on account	5	
4. Trade creditors	25	
5. Bills of exchange payable	4	
6. Amounts owed to group companies	10	
7. Amounts owed to related companies	5	
8. Other creditors including taxation and social security	32	
9. Accruals and deferred income***	–	116

I. PROVISIONS FOR LIABILITIES AND CHARGES

1. Pensions and similar obligations	20	
2. Taxation, including deferred taxation	40	
3. Other provisions	4	64

J. ACCRUALS AND DEFERRED INCOME*		20	200
			1,313

K. CAPITAL AND RESERVES

I	Called up share capital		1,000
II	Share premium account		100
III	Revaluation reserve		20
IV	Other reserves:		
	1. Capital redemption reserve	40	
	2. Reserve for own shares	10	
	3. Reserves provided for by the articles of association	20	
	4. Other reserves	13	83
V	PROFIT AND LOSS ACCOUNT		110
			1,313

(*); (**); (***) These items may be shown in either of the two positions indicated.

It should be noted that various items can be shown in alternative places, i.e.

CALLED UP SHARE CAPITAL NOT PAID, either in position A or position CII 5.

PREPAYMENTS AND ACCRUED INCOME, either CII 6 or as D.
ACCRUALS AND DEFERRED INCOME, either E9 or H9, or in total as J.

Items preceded by letters or Roman numerals must be disclosed on the face of the balance sheet, e.g. B. Fixed Assets, (K) II Share Premium Account, whereas those shown with Arabic numerals (you may call them ordinary numbers, 1, 2, 3, 4, etc) may be combined where they are not material or the combination facilitates assessment of the company's affairs. Where they are combined the details of each item should be shown in the notes accompanying the accounts. The actual letters, roman numerals or arabic numbers do *not* have to be shown on the face of the published balance sheets.

The following also apply to the balance sheet in Format 1.

BI Intangible assets. These are assets not having a 'physical' existence as compared with tangible assets which do have a physical existence. For instance you can see and touch the tangible assets of land and buildings, plant and machinery etc, whereas Goodwill does not exist in a physical sense.

For each of items under Fixed Assets, whether they are Intangible Assets, Tangible Assets or Investments, the notes accompanying the accounts must give full details of (i) cost, at beginning and end of financial year (ii) effect on that item of acquisitions, disposals, revaluations etc. during the year and (iii) full details of depreciation, i.e. accumulated depreciation at start of year, depreciation for year, effect of disposals on depreciation in the year and any other adjustments.

All fixed assets, including property and goodwill must be depreciated over the period of the useful economic life of each asset. Prior to this many companies had not depreciated property because of rising money values of the asset. Costs of research must not be treated as an asset, and development costs may be capitalised only in special cases. Any hire-purchase owing must not be deducted from the assets concerned. Only goodwill which has been purchased can be shown as an asset, internally generated goodwill must not be capitalised. (this does not refer to goodwill in consolidated accounts, see chapter 28).

Where an asset is revalued, normally this will be fixed assets being shown at market value instead of cost, any difference on revaluation must be debited or credited to a revaluation reserve, see K.III in the Format.

Investments shown as CIII will be in respect of those not held for the long-term.

Two items which could previously be shown as assets, (i) preliminary expenses, there are the legal expenses etc in forming the company, and (ii) expenses of and commission on any issue of share or debentures, must not now be shown as assets. They can be written off against any Share Premium Account balance, alternatively they should be written off to profit and loss account.

Full details of each class of share capital, and of authorised capital, will be shown in notes accompanying the balance sheet.

Choice of Formats

The Act leaves the choice of a particular format for the Balance Sheet and the Profit and Loss Account to the directors. Once adopted the choice must be adhered to in subsequent years except in the case that there are special reasons for the change. If a change is made then full reasons for the change must be stated in the notes attached to the accounts.

Fundamental Accounting Principles

The Companies Act 1981 sets out the accounting principles (or 'valuation rules' as they are called in the Fourth Directive of the EEC) to be followed when preparing company financial statements.

The following principles are stated in the Act, the reader can be referred to Chapter 10 of Business Accounting 1 for a fuller discussion of some of them.

(a)   A company is presumed to be a going concern.
(b)   Accounting policies must be applied consistently from year to year.
(c)   The prudence concept must be followed.
(d)   The accruals concept must be observed.
(e)   Each component item of assets and liabilities must be valued separately. As an instance of this, if a company has five different types of stock, each type must be valued separately at the lower of cost and net realisable value, rather than be valued on an aggregate basis.
(f)   Amounts in respect of items representing assets or income may *not* be set off against items representing liabilities or expenditure. Thus an amount owing on a hire-purchase contract cannot now be deducted from the value of the asset in the balance sheet, although this was often done before the 1981 Act.

Definition of Realised Profits

Schedule 1 (90) of the Act defines realised profits. The definition is worded in a tortuous and circular way, and will not be repeated here. What it means is that the accounts should comply with generally accepted accounting principles at the time in the UK. If that is done then all is well. This means that it leaves the determination of accounting principles, and consequently of profits, to the accountancy profession.

True and Fair View

If complying with the requirements of the 1981 Act would cause the accounts not to be 'true and fair' then the directors must set aside such requirements. This should not be done lightly, and it would not be common to find such instances.

Directors' Report

A directors' report must accompany the accounts. The main contents can be summarised thus:

(1) A fair review of the development of the company's business during the financial year (and of any subsidiaries) and of the position at the end of it.

(2) Names of directors at any time in the period.

(3) Proposed dividend.

(4) Proposed transfers to reserves.

(5) Principal activities of the company (and of any subsidiaries) and of any significant changes

(6) Significant changes in fixed assets.

(7) Indication of the difference between book and market values of land and buildings.

(8) (i) Particulars of important events since the end of the financial year.

(ii) Indication of likely future developments.

(iii) Indication of activities in the field of research and development.

(9) Details of directors' shareholdings and debentures in the company at start and close of the year.

(10) Details of U.K. political and charitable donations.

(11) Where average number of employees over 250, give details of employment and training of disabled people.

(12) Details of acquisition and disposal of a company's own shares.

Reporting Requirements for Small and Medium Companies

Small and medium sized companies do not have to file a full set of final accounts with the registrar of companies. They could, if they wished, send a full set of final accounts, but what they *have* to file is a minimum of 'modified accounts'. They would still have to send a full set to their own shareholders, the 'modified accounts' refer only to those filed with the Registrar.

The definition of 'small' and 'medium' companies is if, for the financial year in question and the previous year, the company comes within the limits of at least 'two' of the following three criteria:

CRITERIA	SIZE	
	Small	Medium
Balance Sheet Total (i.e. total assets)	£700,000	£2,800,000
Turnover	£1,400,000	£5,750,000
Average number of employees	50	250

Modified Accounts of Small Companies

(a) Neither a profit and loss account nor a directors' report has to be filed with the Registrar.

(b) A modified balance sheet showing only those items to which a letter or Roman numeral are attached (see Format 1, Exhibit 19.1) has to be shown. For example the total for CI Stocks has to be shown, but *not* the figures for each of the individual items comprising this total.

Modified Accounts of Medium Companies

(a) The Profit and Loss Account per Format 1 does not have to show item 1 Turnover or item 2 Cost of Sales. It will therefore begin with the figure of Gross Profit or Loss.

(b) The analyses of turnover and profit normally required as notes to the accounts need not be given.

(c) The balance sheet, however, must be given in full.

Exercises

19.1. The following balances remained in the books of Owen Ltd on 31 December 19-1, *after* the Profit & Loss Account and Appropriation Account had been drawn up. You are to draft the balance sheet as at 31 December 19-1 in accordance with the Companies Act 1981.

	Dr. £	Cr. £
Ordinary Share Capital: £1 shares		50,000
Preference Share Capital: 50p shares		25,000
Calls Account (Ordinary Shares)	150	
Development Costs	3,070	
Goodwill	21,000	
Land and Buildings − at cost	48,000	
Plant and Machinery − at cost	12,500	
Provision for Depreciation Buildings		16,000
Provision for Depreciation: Plant and Machinery		5,400
Shares in Related Companies	35,750	
Stock: Raw Materials	3,470	
Stock: Finished Goods	18,590	
Debtors: Trade	17,400	
Amounts Owed by Related Companies	3,000	
Prepayments	1,250	
Debentures (see note 1)		10,000
Bank Overdraft (repayable within 6 months)		4,370
Creditors: Trade (payable within 1 year)		12,410
Bills Payable (see note 2)		3,600
Share Premium		20,000
Capital Redemption Reserve		5,000
General Reserve		4,000
Profit and Loss Account		8,400
	164,180	164,180

Notes:

1. Of the debentures £6,000 is repayable in 3 months time, whilst the other £4,000 is repayable in 5 year's time.

2. Of the Bills Payable, £1,600 is in respect of a bill to be paid in 4 months time and £2,000 for a bill payable in 18 months time.

3. The depreciation charged for the year was: Building £4,000, Plant and Machinery £1,800.

250

19.2. After the profit and loss, appropriation account has been prepared for the year ended 30 September 19-4, the following balances remain in the books of Belle Works PLC. You are to draw up a balance sheet in accordance with the Companies Act 1981.

	£	£
Ordinary Share Capital		70,000
Share Premium		5,000
Revaluation Reserve		10,500
General Reserve		6,000
Foreign Exchange Reserve		3,500
Profit and Loss		6,297
Patents Trade Marks and Licences	1,500	
Goodwill	17,500	
Land and Buildings	90,000	
Provision for Depreciation: Land and Buildings		17,500
Plant and Machinery	38,600	
Provision for Depreciation: Plant and Machinery		19,200
Stock of Raw Materials: 30 September 19-4	14,320	
Work in Progress: 30 September 19-4	5,640	
Finished Goods: 30 September 19-4	13,290	
Debtors: Trade	11,260	
Debtors: Other	1,050	
Prepayments and Accrued Income	505	
Debentures (redeemable in 6 months time)		6,000
Debentures (redeemable in 4½ years time)		12,000
Bank Overdraft (repayable in 3 months)		3,893
Trade Creditors (payable in next 12 months)		11,340
Trade Creditors (payable after 12 months)		1,260
Bills of Exchange (payable within 12 months)		4,000
Corporation Tax (payable in 9 months time)		14,370
National Insurance (payable in next month)		305
Pensions Contribution Owing		1,860
Deferred Taxation		640
	193,665	193,665

19.3. J.P. Matthew PLC are wholesalers. The following is their trial balance as at 31 December 19-4:

	Dr. £	Cr. £
Ordinary Share Capital: £1 shares		150,000
Share Premium		10,000
General Reserve		8,000
Profit and Loss Account as at 31 December 19-3		27,300
Stock: 31 December 19-3	33,285	
Sales		481,370
Purchases	250,220	
Returns Outwards		12,460
Returns Inwards	13,810	
Carriage Inwards	570	
Carriage Outwards	4,260	
Warehouse Wages	50,380	
Salesmens Salaries	32,145	
Administrative Wages and Salaries	29,900	
Plant and Machinery (see note ii)	62,500	
Motor Vehicle Hire (see note iii)	9,600	
Provision for Depreciation: Plant and Machinery		24,500
Goodwill	47,300	
General Distribution Expenses	2,840	
General Administrative Expenses	4,890	
Directors' Remuneration	14,800	
Rents Receivable		3,600
Trade Debtors	164,150	
Cash at Bank and in Hand	30,870	
Trade Creditors (payable before 31 March 19-5)		28,290
Bills of Exchange Payable (payable 28 February 19-5)		6,000
	751,520	751,520

Notes:
  (i) Stock at 31 December 19-4 £45,890. It consists of goods for resale.
 (ii) Plant and Machinery: Apportion Distributive 60%, Administrative 40%.
(iii) Of the Motor Vehicle hire, £6,200 is for distributive purposes, the remainder being administrative.
(iv) Depreciate Plant and Machinery 20% on cost.
 (v) Accrue auditors' remuneration £600.
(vi) Corporation Tax for the year, payable 1st October 19-5 will be £29,100.
(vii) There is a proposed ordinary dividend of £50,000 for the year.

You are to draw up (a) A Trading and Profit and Loss Account for the year ended 31 December 19-4 for internal use, and (b) A Profit and Loss Account for publication also a Balance Sheet as at 31 December 19-4 for publication.

19.4A. The following balances remained in the records of Wilson Ltd on 31 December 19-3, *after* the Profit and Loss Appropriation Account had been drawn up. You are to draft the balance sheet as at 31 December 19-3 to comply with the Companies Act 1981.

	Dr.	Cr.
	£	£
Preference Share Capital: £1 shares		100,000
Ordinary Share Capital: £1 shares		150,000
Share Premium		35,000
Machinery Replacement Reserve		7,000
Calls Account (Preference Shares)	220	
Goodwill	30,000	
Plant and Machinery	185,650	
Provision for Depreciation: Plant and Machinery		68,500
Fixtures and Fittings	49,375	
Provision for Depreciation: Fixtures and Fittings		14,115
Payments on account of Plant and Machinery	3,550	
Shares in Related Companies (Long-Term)	112,360	
Stocks of Raw Materials	58,175	
Finished Goods Stock	38,240	
Trade Debtors	51,160	
Debtors: Related Companies	3,080	
Bank	15,428	
Cash	1,312	
Debentures (redeemable in 9 months time)		10,000
Debentures (redeemable in 5 years time)		22,000
Trade Creditors (payable in 19-4)		13,070
Bills Payable (all payable in 19-4)		1,575
Corporation Tax (payable 1 October 19-4)		48,022
Bills Payable (payable in 19-5)		1,950
Proposed Ordinary Dividend		25,000
Profit and Loss Account		52,318
	548,550	548,550

Note: During the year the depreciation charged was Plant and Machinery £24,000: Fixtures and Fittings £2,115.

19.5A. A balance sheet for Holmes PLC is to be drafted from the following balances as at 31 March 19-6. These were listed *after* the Profit and Loss Appropriation Account had been drafted.

	Dr. £	Cr. £
Ordinary Share Capital: £1 shares		26,000
Preferred Ordinary Share Capital: 50p shares		15,000
Preference Shares: £1 shares		10,000
General Reserve		7,500
Foreign Exchange Reserve		2,300
Profit and Loss Account		6,682
Development Costs	3,800	
Concessions, patents and licences	1,850	
Land and Buildings at cost	127,419	
Provision for Depreciation: Buildings		114,100
Plant and Machinery at cost	15,170	
Provision for Depreciation: Plant and Machinery		7,260
Shares in related companies	12,650	
Loans to related companies	15,100	
Other investments other than loans	2,890	
Stock: Raw Materials	7,391	
Work in Progress	8,422	
Trade Debtors	14,895	
Other debtors	2,310	
Short term investments: shares in other companies	15,400	
Cash at Bank	5,620	
Cash in Hand	155	
Provisions for Pension Funds		4,000
Trade Creditors		5,615
Owing to related companies		1,380
Debentures (redeemable 31 March 19-9)		6,400
Bills of Exchange Payable (see note)		4,170
Corporation Tax (payable 1 January 19-7)		14,195
Deferred Taxation		2,470
Proposed Dividends		6,000
	233,072	233,072

Notes:
(*a*) Bills of Exchange are payable £2,000 on 30 June 19-6 and £2,170 on 1 January 19-8.
(*b*) Depreciation charged for the year to 31 March 19-6: Buildings £7,800, Plant and Machinery £1,540.

19.6A. The trial balance of Payne Peerbrook PLC as on 31 December 19-6 is as follows:

	Dr. £	Cr. £
Preference Share Capital: £1 shares		50,000
Ordinary Share Capital: 50p shares		60,000
General Reserve		45,000
Exchange Reserve		13,600
Profit and Loss Account as on 31 December 19-5		19,343
Stock 31 December 19-5	107,143	
Sales		449,110
Returns Inwards	11,380	
Purchases	218,940	
Carriage Inwards	2,475	
Wages (putting goods into a saleable condition)	3,096	
Wages: Warehouse Staff	39,722	
Wages and Salaries: Sales staff	28,161	
Wages and Salaries: Administrative staff	34,778	
Motor Expenses (see note ii)	16,400	
General Distribution Expenses	8,061	
General Administrative Expenses	7,914	
Debenture Interest	10,000	
Royalties Receivable		4,179
Directors' Remuneration	18,450	
Bad Debts	3,050	
Discounts Allowed	5,164	
Discounts Received		4,092
Plant and Machinery at cost (see note iii)	175,000	
Provision for Depreciation: Plant and Machinery		58,400
Motor Vehicles at cost (see note ii)	32,000	
Provision for Depreciation: Motors		14,500
Goodwill	29,500	
Development Costs	16,320	
Trade Debtors	78,105	
Trade Creditors		37,106
Bank Overdraft (repayable any time)		4,279
Bills of Exchange payable (all due within 1 year)		6,050
Debentures (redeemable in 5 years time)		80,000
	845,659	845,659

Notes:

(i) Stock of Finished Goods on 31 December 19-6 £144,081.

(ii) Motor Expenses and Depreciation on Motors to be apportioned: Distribution ¾ths, Administrative ¼th.

(iii) Plant and Machinery depreciation to be apportioned. Cost of Sales ⅕th: Distribution ⅗ths: Administrative ⅕th.

(iv) Depreciate the following fixed assets on cost: Motor Vehicles 25%, Plant and Machinery 20%.

(v) Accrue Corporation Tax on profits of the year £14,150. This is payable 1 October 19-7.

(vi) A preference dividend of £5,000 is to be paid and an ordinary dividend of £10,000 are to be proposed.

You are to draw up:

(a) A Trading and Profit and Loss Account for the year ended 31 December 19-6 for internal use, and

(b) A Profit and Loss account for publication, also a Balance Sheet as at 31 December 19-6.

20

Investment Accounts

It is possible to envisage a situation where the only external investment made by a firm is in the form of money in an account with a Savings Bank, which had (say) an interest rate of 5 per cent per annum. Interest is calculated to 31 December each year and a cheque for the interest is sent to the account holder to arrive on 31 December. Such a type of account adhering to these dates would be very rare in practice. However, with such an account the accounting entries needed by the investing firm would be very simple indeed. If £400 was invested by a firm in such an account on 1 January 19-4 and eventually withdrawn on 31 December 19-7, then assuming that the firm's financial year was equated with the calendar year, the Cash Book for each year would be debited with £20 while each year's Investment Income Account would be credited with £20. The balance of the Investment Income Account, £20, would be transferred to the credit side of the Profit and Loss Account for each of the years ended 31 December 19-4, 19-5, 19-6 and 19-7. On the withdrawal of the £400 the Cash Book would be debited with £400 and the credit entry would be made in the Investment Account, thereby cancelling the original debit entry made when the cash was invested.

Most investments, however, are not of this sort, and have complicating factors. Investments can be divided into two main classes, government stocks and investments in limited companies, the latter may take the form of shares, stock or debentures. In this chapter government stocks will be dealt with first. Taxation will be ignored until it is mentioned specifically.

Government Stocks

With government stock the price is always quoted for that of £100 nominal value. Prices on the Stock Exchange will vary in accordance with supply and demand. Thus, Treasury 3 per cent Stock may be shown as 45. This means that on the Stock Exchange the price for £100 nominal value of the stock was £45. The purchaser of the stock will receive interest at the rate of £3 each year as interest payable is always based on the nominal value and not the Stock Exchange value.

Interest is payable at regular intervals depending on the stock concerned. Taking a government stock which carried interest at 5 per cent per annum, interest may be payable quarterly on 31 March, 30 June, 30 September and 31 December. Imagine that a man was willing to sell stock of £1,200 nominal value at 80, i.e. for £960 (£80 for £100 nominal value, therefore £80 × 12 = £960 for £1,200 nominal value). The purchaser is to receive the whole of the next interest on 31 March, this being £1,200 at 5 per cent per annum for three months = £15. The seller has received interest up to 31 December, the day before he sold the stock. Ownership of stock and ownership of interest have therefore both been on the same time scale. If market conditions do not change, consider the case of a man who is to sell the stock on 1 February, and the purchaser was still to receive all of the £15 interest on 31 March. The seller will not want to sell at the same price, for as January's interest is not to be received by him, the ownership of the stock and the right to receive interest have moved on to a different time scale. The seller is not now merely selling stock, he is also selling the right to one month's interest in addition. He would therefore now want £960 + one month's interest £5 = £965. When the purchaser pays £965 he will want to record the purchase in his own books. He will accordingly split this price as to £960 paid for the stock, a capital item, and the cost of income £5. When the full quarter's interest £15 is received, the £5 cost will be deducted in the income calculation leaving net income for the period as £10. This accords with the evidence, as two months' ownership for February and March is worth £1,200 × 5 per cent per annum × two months = £10. The seller would also apportion the selling price £1,205 as to £1,200 for the stock and £5 for the interest. The £5 interest would then be shown as investment income in his books. This is in fact, saying that where the interest is bought and sold as part of a total price, then interest received is not equal to interest accrued. The apportionment of cost and selling price is the way by which investment income can be equated with the duration of the ownership of the investment, i.e. fifteen months' ownership should show fifteen months' investment income.

Where the price of the stock does not include the right to the next instalment of interest it is stated to be *ex div* or e.d.; this stands for excluding dividend. Where it does include the right to receive the next instalment of interest, irrespective of how long the stock has been owned it is known as *cum div,* meaning including dividend. All prices are *cum div* unless stated specifically to be *ex div*.

Because of the necessity to keep income separate from the capital cost of the investment, each Investment Account has a column for income and a column for capital. In addition a column is used to show the nominal value of the stock, this being used for convenience and does not form part of the double-entry system. Brokerage charges and stamp duties are part of the capital cost of the investment and are included in the cheque paid to the firm's stockbrokers. Brokerage charges on sale are deducted from the cheque remitted by the stockbrokers for the sale proceeds, so that as the sale price is brought in net they have been effectively charged.

Exhibit 20.1

Brent Ltd bought £10,000 3 per cent Government Stock at 40 *ex div* on 1 January 19-6, the cheque for the stock £4,000 plus brokerage charges £100 being £4,100. The interest is received on 31 March, 30 June, 30 September and 31 December 19-6. During 19-7 interest is received on 31 March, and all the stock is sold for 43 *cum div* on 31 May, the cheque being £4,190, made up of £4,300 total proceeds *less* £110 brokerage charges. The financial year end of Brent Ltd is 31 December.

The following shows the entries in the Investment Account for the years ended 31 December 19-6 and 19-7.

Investment – 3 per cent Government Stock

	Nominal	Income	Capital				Nominal	Income	Capital
	£	£	£				£	£	£
19-6					**19-6**				
Jan 1 Cash	10,000		4,100		Mar 31 Cash			75	
Dec 31 Investment Income					Jun 30 ,,			75	
to Profit and Loss		300			Sep 30 ,,			75	
					Dec 31 ,,			75	
					,, 31 Balance c/d	10,000			4,100
	10,000	300	4,100			10,000	300	4,100
19-7					**19-7**				
Jan 1 Balance b/d	10,000		4,100		Mar 31 Cash			75	
Dec 31 Investment Income					May 31 ,,	(A) 10,000	50	4,140
to Profit and Loss		125			Sale Proceeds			
,, 31 Profit on sale to								
Profit and Loss			40					
	10,000	125	4,140			10,000	125	4,140

(A) As the stock is sold *cum div,* Brent Ltd is therefore including in the selling price the value of two months' interest for April and May = $\frac{2}{12} \times 3$ per cent × £10,000 = £50. The £4,190 sale price is accordingly apportioned £50 as to income and £4,140 as to capital.

To illustrate matters further, Exhibit 20.2 shows an investment where there are both extra purchases and sales of part of the investment.

Exhibit 20.2

On 1 January 19-4 Green Ltd bought £4,000 6 per cent Government Stock at £90, the cheque of £3,680 paid being £3,600 for the stock and £80 for the brokerage charges. Interest is receivable each year on 31 March, 30 June, 30 September, and 31 December.

include the cheque ... the ... stockbrokers. Brokerage charges on sale are deducted from the cheque remitted by the stockbrokers for the sale proceeds ... so that a lesser sum is brought in ... less their brokerage ... respectively charged ...

Exhibit 20...

Brent Ltd bought £10,000 6 per cent Government Stock at 40 ex div on 1 January 19-4, the cheque for the stock £4,000 plus brokerage charges £100 being £4 100. The interest is received on 31 March, 30 September and 31 December. During 19-5 interest is received on 31 March, and all the stock is sold for £3 cum div on 31 May, the cheque raising £4,000 less tax of £2,300 total proceeds less £110 brokerage charges. The year-end of Brent Ltd is 31 December.

The following shows the ... the Investment Account for the years ended 31 December.

Investment – 6 per cent Government Stock

Date	Detail	Nominal £	Income £	Capital £		Date	Detail	Nominal £	Income £	Capital £
19-4						19-4				
Jan 1	Cash	4,000		3,680		Mar 31	Cash		60	
Dec 31	Investment Income to Profit and Loss		240			Jun 30	"		60	
						Sep 30	"		60	
						Dec 31	"		60	
						Dec 31	Balance c/d	4,000		3,680
		4,000	240	3,680				4,000	240	3,680
19-5						19-5				
Jan 1	Balance b/d	4,000		3,680		Feb 1	Cash Sale proceeds	(A)		945
Jun 1	Adjustment for sale at ex div price (B)		10			Mar 31	Cash Sale proceeds	(B)	5	1,710
Dec 31	Investment Income to Profit and Loss (C)		115			Jun 1	Adjustment for sale at ex div price			10
						30	Cash (£3,000 × 6% × 3 months)		45	
						Sep 30	Cash (£1,000 × 6% × 3 months)		15	
						Dec 31	Cash (£1,000 × 6% × 3 months)		15	
						Dec 31	Profit and Loss – Loss on Sale of Investments	(D)		95
						Dec 31	Balance c/d	1,000		920
		4,000	125	3,680				4,000	125	3,680
19-6						19-6				
Jan 1	Balance b/d	1,000		920		Mar 31	Cash (£6,000 × 6% × 3 months)		90	
Feb 1	Cash	5,000	25	4,345		Jun 1	Adjustment of purchase at ex div price	(E)	5	
Jun 1	..	1,000		910		30	Cash (£6,000 × 6% × 3 months)		90	
.. 1	Adjustment of purchase at ex div price (E)			5		Sep 30	Cash (£7,000 × 6% × 3 months)		105	
Dec 31	Investment Income to Profit and Loss (F)		370			Dec 31	Cash (£7,000 × 6% × 3 months)		105	
						Dec 31	Balance c/d	7,000		6,180
		7,000	395	6,180				7,000	395	6,180
19-7										
Jan 1	Balance b/d	7,000		6,180						

(A) As the stock is sold cum div, Brent Ltd is therefore including in the selling price the value of two months' interest for April and May = £x 6 per cent × £10,000 = £50. The £4,100 sale proceeds accordingly apportioned as to income and £... as to capital.

To illustrate matters further, Exhibit 20.2 shows an investment where there is both extra purchase and sale, or part of the investment.

Exhibit 20...

On 1 January, Brent Ltd bought £... 6 per cent Government Stock at £90 at a nominal value of £3,680 plus ... £3,200 for the stock and £80 for the charges; interest is receivable each year on 31 March, 30 September, and 31 December.

On 1 February 19-5 £1,000 nominal value of the stock is sold *cum div,* the net proceeds being £950.

1 June 19-5, £2,000 nominal value sold *ex div,* net proceeds after brokerage being £1,710.

1 February 19-6, £5,000 nominal value bought *cum div,* the cost including brokerage being £4,370.

1 June 19-6, £1,000 nominal value bought *ex div,* cost including brokerage being £910.

On page 258 is the Investment Account in Green's books for the financial years ended 31 December 19-4, 19-5 and 19-6. Taxation is ignored.

Notes:

(A) The sale proceeds £950 represent the sale of the right to one month's interest, £1,000 × 6 per cent per annum for one month = £5, plus the right to the actual stock itself. This must therefore be the balance of the net sale proceeds, £950 – £5 = £945.

(B) The sale at an *ex div* price means that Green Ltd will receive interest for June on this £2,000 of stock even though the stock itself had passed out of Green Ltd's ownership. The actual net sale price is therefore £1,720, which is made up of £1,710 actually received plus £10 for the right to one month's interest retained. This is adjusted by debiting the Income column with £10 to cancel the income which was not equated with ownership, and crediting the Capital column with £10 representing the actual reduction in the sale price caused by selling at an *ex div* price. Note (C) will illustrate the validity of debiting the income column, as without this entry the amount of investment income transferred to the Profit and Loss Account would not agree with the facts relating to the duration of the investment and the rate of interest.

(C) The correctness of this can be proved if the interest actually accrued during ownership is calculated:

		£
6 per cent per annum on £4,000 for one month	=	20
6 per cent per annum on £3,000 for four months	=	60
6 per cent per annum on £1,000 for seven months	=	35
		115

(D)

	£	£
Cost of £1,000 nominal value of stock £3,680 × ¼ =	920	
Sold on 1 February 19-5 for	945	25 profit
Cost of £2,000 nominal value of stock £3,680 × ½ =	1,840	
Sold on 1 June 19-5 for (adjusted net sale price)	1,720	120 loss
		95 net loss

(E) The stock bought on 1 June 19-6 for £910 *ex div* meant that June's ownership would not bring in any interest on this stock. The price paid for the stock would have been reduced by the amount of June's interest, i.e. £1,000 at 6 per cent per annum for one month = £5. The true price paid therefore was £915. This is represented by a debit of £5 in the Capital column, while a credit of £5 in the Income column is made to show that ownership of fixed interest stock does in fact bring in a return of interest in accordance with the length of ownership.

(F) This can be proved to be correct.

	£
£1,000 at 6 per cent per annum for one month =	5
£6,000 at 6 per cent per annum for four months =	120
£7,000 at 6 per cent per annum for seven months =	245
	370

Investment in Limited Companies

In the cases where stocks, shares or debentures carry a fixed rate of interest the treatment is the same as with Government Stocks. However, where the investment is not of the fixed interest type, e.g. ordinary shares, the next dividend receivable is not known on purchase or sale. On the declaration of the next dividend an adjustment can be made, so that the account will contain the same balances as it would have done if the next dividend had been known, and the necessary apportionments taken place at sale or purchase rather than wait until the dividend had been declared. In theory these adjustments should always be made, but in practice they are usually ignored where the purchase and sale of investments do not constitute the main business of the firm.

Exercises

20.1. The following transactions of Trust Ltd took place during the year ended 30 June 19-7:

19-6

1 July	Purchased £12,000 4 per cent Consolidated Loan (interest payable 1 February and 1 August) at 60½ *cum div*.
12 July	Purchased 2,000 ordinary shares of £0.5 each in Abee Ltd for £4,000.
1 August	Received half-year's interest on 4 per cent Consolidated Loan.
15 August	Abee Ltd made a bonus issue of three ordinary shares for every two held. Trust Ltd sold 2,500 of the bonus shares for £1 each.
1 October	Purchased 5,000 ordinary shares of £1 each in Ceedee Ltd at £0.775 each.

19-7

2 January	Sold £3,000 4 per cent Consolidated Loan at 61 *ex div*.
1 February	Received half-year's interest on 4 per cent Consolidated Loan.
1 March	Received dividend of 18 per cent on shares in Abee Ltd.
1 April	Ceedee Ltd made a 'rights' issue of one share for every two held at £0.5 per share. 'Rights' sold on market for £0.25 per share.
1 June	Received dividend of 12½ per cent on shares in Ceedee Ltd.

You are required to write up the relevant investment accounts as they would appear in the books of Trust Ltd for the year ended 30 June 19-7, bringing down the balances as on that date.

Ignore brokerage and stamp duty.

(*Institute of Chartered Accountants*)

20.2. On 31 March 19-5 the investments held by Jowetts of Mayfair Ltd included 6,000 Ordinary shares of £1 each fully paid in Composite Interest Ltd, such shares appearing in the books at £7,200. It is not the practice of Jowetts of Mayfair Ltd to make apportionments of dividends received or receivable.

Jowetts of Mayfair Ltd sold 1,000 shares on 31 May 19-5 for £1,965. On 20 September 19-5 Composite Interest Ltd:

(*a*) Issued by way of a bonus issue three fully paid shares for every five held on 31 August 19-5.

(*b*) It gave the right to shareholders to apply for one share for every two actually held on 31 August 19-5, the price to be £1.05 per share payable in full on application.

The shares issued under (*a*) and (*b*) were not to participate in the dividend for the year ended 31 August 19-5.

The bonus shares were received. For the rights issue 1,800 shares were taken up and paid for on 30 September 19-5. The rights on the remaining shares were sold for £0.3 per share, the money for this being received on 15 November 19-5.

On 17 December 19-5 Composite Interest Ltd declared and paid a final dividend of 20 per cent for the year ended 31 August 19-5, and on 15 March 19-6 an interim dividend of 5 per cent for the year ended 31 August 19-6.

Show the investment account for the year ended 31 March 19-6 as it would appear in the books of Jowetts of Mayfair Ltd.

Expenses of sale are to be ignored.

20.3A. Stag Ltd is an investment company making up its accounts to 31 December in each year.

The following transactions have been extracted from the company's records for 19-9.

19-9

1 January	Purchased 1,000 ordinary shares of £0.25 each in Bull Ltd at £1.75 per share.
12 February	Purchased £2,000 ordinary stock in Bear Ltd for £1,500.
1 March	Received dividend of 20 per cent on shares in Bull Ltd.
24 April	Bull Ltd made a bonus issue of one share for every four held.
2 May	Received dividend of $2\frac{1}{2}$ per cent on ordinary stock in Bear Ltd.
10 May	Bull Ltd announced a rights issue of two ordinary shares for every five held on that date, at £1.25 per share. Rights sold on market for £0.5 per share.
1 August	Applied for £5,000 $7\frac{1}{4}$ per cent Loan stock in Bear Ltd issued at £98 per cent, and payable half on application and the balance in two equal instalments on 1 October and 1 December. The application was successful.
16 September	Received dividend of 30 per cent on shares in Bull Ltd.
1 October	Paid instalment on loan stock in Bear Ltd.
20 November	Received dividend of 3 per cent on ordinary stock in Bear Ltd.
1 December	Paid final instalment on loan stock in Bear Ltd.

You are required to write up the accounts for the investments in Bull Ltd and Bear Ltd as they would appear in the books of Stag Ltd for the year ended 31 December 19-9, bringing down the balances as on that date.

Ignore stamp duty, brokerage and taxation.

(Institute of Chartered Accountants)

20.4A. H.M. Ltd bought £10,000 nominal of Peatshire 6 per cent Loan Stock at 92 *cum div* on 30 April 19-8. Interest on the stock is paid half-yearly on 30 June and 31 December. £4,000 of the stock was sold at 94 *ex div* on 30 November 19-8.

H.M. Ltd prepares final accounts annually to 31 March.

Prepare the investment account in the company's ledger from the date of the purchase to 1 April 19-9.

Ignore brokerage, stamp duty and taxation and make apportionments in months.

20.5A. On 1 April 19-7, F.R.Y. Ltd purchased 10,000 ordinary shares of £1 each, fully paid, in T.L.S. Ltd at a cost of £20,500.

On 1 September 19-7, T.L.S. Ltd declared and paid a dividend of 15 per cent on its ordinary shares for the year ended 30 June 19-7.

On 1 November 19-7, T.L.S. Ltd gave its eight members the right to subscribe for one ordinary share for every eight held on 1 November 19-7, at a price of £1.5 per share, payable in full on application.

On 15 November 19-7, F.R.Y. Ltd purchased for £0.4 per share the rights of another shareholder in T.L.S. Ltd to subscribe for 750 shares under the rights issue.

On 30 November 19-7 F.R.Y. Ltd applied and paid for all the shares in T.L.S. Ltd to which it was then entitled.

On 8 September 19-8, T.L.S. Ltd declared and paid a dividend for the year ended 30 June 19-8, of 15 per cent on all ordinary shares, including those issued in 19-7.

On 1 October 19-8, F.R.Y. Ltd sold 4,500 ordinary shares in T.L.S. Ltd for £9,875.

The accounting year of F.R.Y. Ltd ends on 31 December.

F.R.Y. Ltd does not make apportionments of dividends received or receivable. When part of a holding of shares is sold, it is the practice of this company to calculate the cost of the shares sold as an appropriate part of the average cost of all the shares held at the date of the sale.

You are required to show the investment account in the books of F.R.Y. Ltd for the two years ended 31 December 19-7, and 31 December 19-8, bringing down the balance at the end of each year.

Ignore taxation.

(Chartered Institute of Secretaries and Administrators)

21

Contract Accounts

The span of production differs between businesses, and some fit into the normal pattern of annual accounts easier than others do. A farmer's accounts are usually admirably suited to the yearly pattern, as the goods they produce are in accordance with the seasons, and therefore repeat themselves annually. With a firm whose production span is a day or two the annual accounts are also quite suitable.

On the other hand, there are businesses whose work does not conform to a financial year's calculation of profits. Assume that a firm of contractors has only one contract being handled, and that is the total construction of a very large oil refinery complex. This might take five years to complete. Not until it is completed can the actual profit or loss on the contract be correctly calculated. However, if the company was formed especially with this contract in mind, the shareholders would not want to wait for five years before the profit could be calculated and dividends paid. Therefore an attempt is made to calculate profits yearly. Obviously, most firms will have more than one contract under way at a time, and also it would be rare for a contract to take such a long time to complete.

For each contract an account is opened. It is, in fact, a form of Trading Account for each contract. Therefore if the firm has a contract to build a new technical college it may be numbered Contract 71. Thus a Contract 71 Account would be opened. All expenditure traceable to the contract will be charged to the Contract Account. This is far easier than ascertaining direct expenses in a factory, as any expenditure on the site will be treated as direct, e.g. wages for the manual workers on the site, telephone rental for telephones on the site, hire of machinery for the contract, wages for the timekeepers, clerks, etc., on the site.

The contractor is paid by agreement on the strength of architects' certificates in the case of buildings, or engineers' certificates for an engineering contract. The architect, or engineer, will visit the site at regular intervals and will issue a certificate stating his estimate of the value of the work done, in terms of the total contract price (the sale price of the whole contract). Thus he may issue a certificate for £10,000. Normally the terms governing the contract will contain a clause concerning retention money. This is the amount, usually stated as a percentage, which will be retained, i.e. held back, in case the contract is not completed by a stated date, or against claims for faulty workmanship, etc. A 10 per cent retention in the case already mentioned would lead to £9,000 being payable by the person for whom the contract was being performed.

The administration overhead expenses not traceable directly to the sites are sometimes split on an arbitrary basis and charged to each contract. Of course, if there was only one contract, then all the overhead expenses would quite rightly be chargeable against it. On the other hand if there are twenty contracts being carried on, any apportionment must be arbitrary. No one can really apportion on a 'scientific' basis the administration overhead expenses of the managing director's salary, the cost of advertising to give the firm the right 'image', the costs of running accounting machinery for the records of the whole firm, and these are only a few of such expenses. In a fashion similar to the departmental accounts principle in Chapter 33 of book 1, it sometimes give misleading results, and it is therefore far better left for the administrative overhead expenses which are obviously not chargeable to a contract to be omitted from the Contract Accounts. The surplus left on each Contract Account is thus the 'contribution' of each contract to administrative overhead expenses and to profit.

Exhibit 21.1

Contract 44 is for a school being built for the Blankshire County Council. By the end of the year the following items have been charged to the Contract Account:

	Contract 44
Wages – Labour on Site	£5,000
Wages – Foremen and	
Clerks on the Site	600
Materials	4,000
Sub-contractors on the Site	900
Other Site Expenses	300
Hire of Special Machinery	400
Plant Bought for the Contract	2,000

The entries concerning expenditure traceable direct to the contract are relatively simple. These are charged to the Contract Account. These can be seen in the Contract Account shown on the next page.

Architects' certificates have been received during the year amounting to £14,000, it being assumed for this example that the certificate related to all work done up to the year end. A retention of 10 per cent is to be made, and the Blankshire County Council has paid £12,600. The £14,000 has been credited to a holding account called an Architects' Certificates Account, and debited to the Blankshire County Council Account. The total of the Architects' Certificates Account now needs transferring to the Contract 44 Account. It is, after all, the 'sale' price of the work done so far, and the Contract Account is a type of Trading Account. The £12,600 received has been debited to the Cash Book and credited to Blankshire County Council Account, which now shows a balance of £1,400, this being equal to the retention money.

The cost of the stock of the materials on the site unused is not included in the value of the architects' certificates and is therefore carried forward to the next year at cost price. The value of the plant at the end of the year is also carried forward. In this case the value of the cost of the plant not yet used is £1,400. This means that £2,000 has been debited for the plant and £1,400 credited, thus effectively charging £600 for depreciation. Assume that the stock of unused materials cost £800.

The Contract 44 Account will now appear:

Contract 44

	£		£
Wages – Labour on Site	5,000	Architects' Certificates	14,000
Wages – Foreman and Clerks		Stock of Unused	
on the Site	600	Materials c/d	800
Materials	4,000	Value of Plant c/d	1,400
Sub-contractors on the Site	900		
Other Site Expenses	300		
Hire of Special Machinery	400		
Plant Bought for the Contract	2,000		

The different between totals of the two sides (Credit side £16,200, Debit side £13,200) can be seen to be £3,000. It would be a brave man indeed who would assert that the profit made to date was £3,000. The contract is only part completed, and costly snags may crop up which would dissipate any potential profit earned, or snags may have developed already, such as subsidence, which has remained unnoticed as yet. The concept of prudence now takes over. The normal custom is, barring any evidence to the contrary, for the apparent profit (in the case £3,000) to have the following formula applied to it:

$$\text{Apparent profit} \times \tfrac{2}{3} \times \frac{\text{Cash received}}{\text{Work certified}} = \text{Amount which can be utilized for dividends, etc.}$$

In this case this turns out as $£3,000 \times \tfrac{2}{3} \times \dfrac{12,600}{14,000} = £1,800$.

There are variations on the formula under differing circumstances, but it is the formula which is usually propounded as being the most suitable.

Why two-thirds? Why not three-quarters? This is a fair question, and all that can be said is that the rule of thumb method devised years ago happened to be two-thirds. This was acceptable to accountants and businessmen. Just as technology has changed so also the two-thirds rule needs re-examination in a rapidly changing world. Modern techniques of building and engineering have undoubtedly minimized errors and snags compared with the past, therefore a much higher figure than two-thirds may now be quite justifiable.

The Contract 44 Account can now be completed:

Profit and Loss Account

	£
Profits from contracts:	
Contract 43	
Contract 44	1,800
Contract 45	

Balance Sheet (extracts)

	£
Plant (Contract 44 part)	1,400
Stock (Contract 44 part)	800
	£
Profit reserve on Contract 44	1,200

Contract 44

	£		£
Wages – Labour on Site	5,000	Architects' Certificates	14,000
Wages – Foreman and Clerks		Stock of Unused	
on the Site	600	Materials c/d	800
Materials	4,000	Value of Plant c/d	1,400
Sub-contractors on the Site	900		
Other Site Expenses	300		
Hire of Special Machinery	400		
Plant Bought for the			
Contract	2,000		
Profit to the Profit and Loss			
Account	1,800		
Reserve (the part of the			
apparent profit not yet			
recognized as earned) c/d	1,200		
	16,200		16,200
Stock of Unused Materials		Reserve b/d	1,200
b/d	800		
Value of Plant b/d	1,400		

In the case shown there has been an apparent profit of £3,000, but the action would have been different if instead of revealing such a profit, the Contract Account had in fact shown a loss of £3,000. In such a case it would not be two-thirds of the loss to be taken into account but the whole of it. Thus £3,000 loss would have been transferred to the Profit and Loss Account. This is in accordance with the concept of prudence which states that profits may be underestimated but never losses.

It is in fact not always the case that an engineer or architect will certify the work done up to the financial year end. He may call several days earlier than the year end. The cost of work done, but not certfied at the year end, will therefore need carrying down as a balance to the next period when certification will take place.

SSAP includes the valuation of long-term contract work in progress. The contents of this chapter do in fact conform to the statements made in SSAP 9.

Before SSAP 9 many contractors had only taken profit into account when the contract was completed. The advent of SSAP 9 has brought in anticipation of profit before completion of contract, although prudence is still very much the guiding concept.

Exercises

21.1. The final accounts of Diggers Ltd are made up to 31 December on each year. Work on a certain contract was commenced on 1 April 19-5 and was completed on 31 October 19-6. The total contract price was £174,000, but a penalty of £700 was suffered for failure to complete by 30 September 19-6.

The following is a summary of receipts and payments relating to the contract:

	During 19-5	During 19-6
Payments:		
Materials	25,490	33,226
Wages	28,384	45,432
Direct Expenses	2,126	2,902
Purchase of Plant on 1 April 19-5	16,250	–
Receipts		
Contract Price (*less* penalty)	52,200	121,100
Sale, on 31 October 19-6, of all plant purchased on 1 April 19-5	–	4,100

The amount received from the customer in 19-5 represented the contract price of all work certified in that year less 10 per cent retention money.

When the annual accounts for 19-5 were prepared it was estimated that the contract would be completed on 30 September 19-6, and that the market value of the plant would be £4,250 on that date. It was estimated that further expenditure on the contract during 19-6 would be £81,400.

For the purposes of the annual accounts, depreciation of plant is calculated, in the case of uncompleted contracts, by reference to the expected market value of the plant on the date when the contract is expected to be completed, and is allocated between accounting periods by the straight-line method.

Credit is taken, in the annual accounts, for such a part of the estimated total profit, on each uncompleted contract, as corresponds to the proportion between the contract price of the work certified and the total contract price.

You are required to prepare a summary of the account for this contract, showing the amounts transferred to profit and loss account at 31 December 19-5 and 31 December 19-6.

21.2. Stannard and Sykes Ltd are contractors for the construction of a pier for the Seafront Development Corporation. The value of the contract is £300,000, and payment is by engineer's certificate subject to a retention of 10 per cent of the amount certified, this to be held by the Seafront Development Corporation for six months after the completion of the contract.

The following information is extracted from the records of Stannard and Sykes Ltd.

	£
Wages on site	41,260
Materials delivered to site by supplier	58,966
Materials delivered to site from store	10,180
Hire of Plant	21,030
Expenses charged to Contract	3,065
Overheads charged to Contract	8,330
Materials on site at 30 November 19-8	11,660
Work certified	150,000
Payment received	135,000
Work in progress at cost (not the subject of a certificate to date)	12,613
Wages accrued 30 November 19-8	2,826

You are to prepare the Pier Contract Account to 30 November 19-8, and to suggest a method by which profit could be prudently estimated.

(*Association of Certified Accountants*)

21.3A. Cantilever Ltd was awarded a contract to build an office block in London and work commenced at the site on 1 May 19-5.

During the period to 28 February 19-6, the expenditure on the contract was as follows:

	£
Materials issued from stores	9,411
Materials purchased	28,070
Direct expenses	6,149
Wages	18,493
Charge made by the company for administration expenses	2,146
Plant and machinery purchased on 1 May 19-5, for use at site	12,180

On 28 February 19-6, the stock of materials at the site amounted to £2,164 and there were amounts outstanding for wages £366 and direct expenses £49.

Cantilever Ltd has received on account the sum of £64,170 which represents the amount of Certificate No. 1 issued by the architects in respect of work completed to 28 February 19-6, after deducting 10 per cent retention money.

The following relevant information is also available:

1. the plant and machinery has an effective life of five years, with no residual value, and

2. the company only takes credit for two-thirds of the profit on work certified.

You are required:

(a) to prepare a contract account for the period to 28 February 19-6, and

(b) to show your calculation of the profit to be taken to the credit of the company's Profit and Loss Account in respect of the work covered by Certificate No. 1.

(*Institute of Chartered Accountants*)

21.4A. You are required to prepare the contract account for the year ended 31 December 19-0, and show the calculation of the sum to be credited to the profit and loss account for that year.

On 1 April 19-0 MN Ltd commenced work on a contract which was to be completed by 30 June 19-1 at an agreed price of £520,000.

MN Ltd's financial year ended on 31 December 19-0, and on that day expenditure on the contract totalled £263,000 made up as under:

	£
Plant	30,000
Materials	124,000
Wages	95,000
Sundry expenses	5,000
Head office charges	9,000
	263,000

Cash totalling £195,000 had been received by 31 December 19-0 representing 75 per cent of the work certified as completed on that date, but in addition, work costing £30,000 had been completed but not certified.

A sum of £9,000 had been obtained on the sale of materials which had cost £8,000 but which had been found unsuitable. On 31 December 19-0 stocks of unused materials on site had cost £10,000 and the plant was valued at £20,000.

To complete the contract by 30 June 19-1 it was estimated that:

1. the following additional expenditures would be incurred:

	£
Wages	64,000
Materials	74,400
Sundry expenses	9,000

2. further plant cost £25,000 would be required;

3. the residual value of all plant used on the contract at 30 June 19-1 would be £15,000;

4. head office charges to the contract would be at the same annual rate plus 10 per cent.

It was estimated that the contract would be completed on time but that a contingency provision of £15,000 should be made. From this estimate and the expenditure already incurred, it was decided to estimate the total profit that would be made on the contract and to take to the credit of the profit and loss account for the year ended 31 December 19-0, that proportion of the total profit relating to the work actually certified to that date.

(*Institute of Cost and Management Accountants*)

22

Value Added Statements

A great deal of discussion has taken place in recent years about the desirability of not simply interpreting results in terms of profits only. One way of doing this is in terms of the value added by the business itself to the resources acquired by it in transforming them into the final product. The production of such 'value added statements' was recommended in the Corporate Report (1975).

Such value added can be taken to represent in monetary terms, the net output of an enterprise. This is the difference between the total value of its output and the value of the inputs of materials and services obtained from other enterprises. The value added is seen to be due to the combined efforts of capital, management and employees, and the statement shows how the value added has been distributed to each of these factors. (see Profit and Loss Account from which this has been derived on the next page).

Growth Ltd.

Statement of Value Added for the year ended 31 December 19-1

	£	£
Turnover		765,000
Bought in materials and services		346,000
Value Added		419,000
Applied the following way		
To pay employees wages, pensions and other benefits		220,000
To pay providers of capital		
Interest on loans	2,000	
Dividends to Shareholders	60,000	62,000
To pay government		
Corporation Tax Payable		44,000
To provide for maintenance and expansion of assets:		
Depreciation	74,000	
Retained Profits	19,000	93,000
		419,000

The reader can see that the retained profits £19,000 is made up of the increase in undistributed profits (£59,000 − £55,000) £4,000 + transfer to general reserve £15,000 = £19,000.

The value added statement can be seen to be a means of reporting the income for all the groups which contribute to an organisation's performance. It is therefore relevant to the information needed by all of these groups, something which is not well served by an ordinary profit and loss account.

As an example the Profit and Loss Account of Growth Ltd has been restated in value added terms:

Growth Ltd.

Profit and Loss Account for the year ended 31 December 19-1

	£	£
Turnover		765,000
Cost of Sales*		439,000
Gross Profit		326,000
Distribution Costs*	93,000	
Administrative Expenses*	108,000	201,000
		125,000
Interest Payable		2,000
Profit on Ordinary Activities before Taxation		123,000
Tax on Profit on Ordinary Activities		44,000
Profit for the year on Ordinary Activities after Taxation		79,000
Undistributed Profits from last year		55,000
		134,000
Transfer to General Reserve	15,000	
Proposed Ordinary Dividend	60,000	75,000
Undistributed Profits Carried to Next Year		59,000

Note: Costs* include:	£
Wages, pensions and other employee benefits	220,000
Depreciation	74,000
All other costs were bought in from outside	346,000
(£439,000 + £93,000 + £108,000)	£640,000

23

SSAP 10: Statement of Source and Application of Funds

In volume 1 the reader was introduced to Flow of Funds Statements. The present chapter deals specifically with SSAP 10, which requires that all audited financial accounts of enterprises with a turnover of more than £25,000 per annum should be accompanied by a funds statement. For the purpose of SSAP 10 'funds' are working capital, consequently cash flow statements are excluded.

The following *minimum* information (if appropriate and material) has to be shown:

(a) net profit or loss, with adjustments for items not using or providing funds,
(b) dividends paid,
(c) acquisitions and disposals of fixed and other non-current assets,
(d) funds raised for long term capital, e.g. shares, loan capital,
(e) redemptions and purchase of long term capital,
(f) changes in working capital, analysed between component parts, and movements in net liquid funds.

The basic layout, without figures, is now shown in Exhibit 23.1.

Exhibit 23.1

Statement of Source and Application of Funds
Year ended . . .

	£	£
Source of funds		
Profit before tax		x
Adjustments for items not involving the movement of funds: Depreciation		x
Total generated from operations		x
Funds from other sources		
Issue of shares for each	x	
Issue of loan capital	x	x
		x
Application of funds		
Dividends paid	x	
Tax paid	x	
Purchase of fixed assets	x	x
Increase/decrease in working capital		x
Increase/Decrease in stocks	x	
Increase/Decrease in debtors	x	
Decrease/Increase in creditors	x	
Movement in net liquid funds:		
Increase/Decrease in		
Cash Balances	x	
Short-term investments	x	x	x

The basic layout cannot be adhered to for all possible items. For instance, if there had been no purchase of fixed assets, but instead there had been a sale of fixed assets, then 'Sale of fixed assets' would appear under 'Funds from other sources'.

Two examples will now be worked through, Exhibit 23.2 and 23.3. Some points must be stressed:

(i) It is taxation *paid,* not taxation charged, that is needed.
(ii) It is dividends *paid,* not dividends proposed, that is needed.
(iii) Do *not* include any profit on sales of fixed assets, such profit is already automatically included in any figure of sales of fixed assets.
(iv) Look for other adjustments to the starting figure of profit before tax which do not involve movement by funds, e.g. provisions for bad debts.

Exhibit 23.2

PQ Ltd.
Balance Sheets as at 31 December

	19-6 £	19-6 £	19-7 £	19-7 £
Fixed Assets at cost	3,200		4,000	
Less Depreciation	1,200	2,000	1,600	2,400
Current Assets				
Stock	4,218		5,654	
Debtors	1,560		1,842	
Bank	840		695	
	6,618		8,191	

Less Current Liabilities	£	£	£	£	£	£
Creditors	922			988		
Taxation	306			410		
Proposed Dividend	500	1,728	4,890	750	2,148	6,043
			6,890			8,443

Finance by:		
Issued Share Capital		5,000	6,000
Profit and Loss Account		1,890	2,443
		6,890	8,443

PQ Ltd
Profit and Loss Account for the year ended 31 December 19-7

	£
Profit on ordinary activities before taxation	
(after charging depreciation £400)	1,713
Tax on profit on ordinary activities	410
	1,303
Undistributed profits from last year	1,890
	3,193
Proposed Dividend	750
Undistributed Profits carried to next year	2,443

PQ Ltd
Statement of Source and Application of Funds
Year ended 31 December 19-7

		£	£
Source of Funds			
Profit before tax			1,713
Add depreciation			400
Total generated from operations			2,113
Funds from other sources			
Issue of shares for cash			1,000
			3,113
Application of funds			
Dividend paid	(B)	500	
Tax paid	(C)	306	
Purchase of fixed assets		800	1,606
Increase in working capital		(A)	1,507
Increase in stocks		1,436	
Increase in debtors		282	
Increase in creditors	(D)	(66)	
		1,652	
Decrease in Cash balances		145 (A)	1,507

Notes
(A) Obviously if the statement has been drawn up correctly, then it should balance, in this case at £1,507 for each of these two figures.
(B) Dividend *paid*. This year's proposed dividend is £750 and the item shown as owing in the balance sheet is also £750. Therefore the dividend *paid* is that shown as owing at 31.12.19-6 £500.
(C) Tax shown as owing at 31.12.19-6 £306 has obviously been paid in the year, leaving only this year's taxation shown as owing.
(D) An increase in creditors would help reduce working capital, therefore shown in brackets, i.e. it is deducted from the other figures.

A more complicated example will now be shown in Exhibit 23.3.

Exhibit 23.2

ST Ltd.

Balance Sheets as at 31 December   19-7   19-8

	£	£	£	£	£
Fixed Assets at cost		5,600		8,300	
Less Depreciation		2,300	3,300	3,150	5,150
Current Assets					
Stock		7,204		5,516	
Debtors	3,120		3,994		
Less Provision for Bad Debts	210	2,910	180	3,814	
Cash		60		90	
		10,174		9,420	
Less Current Liabilities					
Creditors	1,520		1,416		
Taxation	580		735		
Proposed Dividend	800		1,200		
Bank Overdraft	105	3,005	7,169	629	3,980	5,440
			10,469		10,590
Financed by:					
Issued Share Capital			4,000		6,000
Profit and Loss Account			3,469		4,090
Loan Capital			3,000		500
			10,469		10,590

ST Ltd.

Profit and Loss Account for the year ended 31 December 19-8

	£
Profit on ordinary activities before taxation*	2,556
Tax on profit on ordinary activities	735
	1,821
Undistributed profits from last year	3,469
	5,290
Proposed dividend	1,200
Undistributed Profits carried to next year	4,090

*Includes profit on fixed assets sold of £85. The items sold had cost £1,120, had been depreciated £740, and were sold for £465.

The change in provision for bad debts had also been taken into account before arriving at profit of £2,556.

In getting the figures together for the Statement of Source and Application of Funds, some figures need to be deduced so that the profit figure can be adjusted. These are (*a*) Cost of fixed assets bought and (*b*) Depreciation charged. To find these it is necessary to reconstruct (*a*) the Fixed Asset Account and (*b*) the Depreciation Account. The figures needed will be those necessary to balance the accounts. *(In a real company these figures would be readily available, but examiners are fond of making students deduce the figures instead).*

Workings:

Fixed Assets Account

19-8		£	19-8		£
Jan 1	Balance b/fwd	5,600	Dec 31	Assets Disposal	1,120
Dec 31	Bank (missing figure)	3,820	,, 31	Balance c/fwd	8,300
		9,420			9,420

Provision for Depreciation Account

19-8		£	19-8		£
Dec 31	Assets Disposal	740	Jan 1	Balance b/fwd	2,300
,, 31	Balance c/fwd	3,150	Dec 31	Profit & Loss (missing figure)	1,590
		3,890			3,890

Now that the cost of fixed assets, and of the depreciation has been calculated, the preparation of the statement can be done.

ST Ltd,
Statement of Source and Application of Funds
Year ended 31 December 19-8

	£	£
Source of Funds		
Profit before tax		2,556
Add Depreciation		1,590
		4,146
Less Reduction in Provision for Bad Debts	30	
,, Profit on Fixed Assets	85	115
Total generated from operations		4,031
Funds from other sources		
Issue of shares for cash	2,000	
Sale of fixed assets	465	2,465
		6,496
Application of funds		
Dividends paid	800	
Tax paid	580	
Purchase of fixed assets	3,820	
Repayment of loan capital	2,500	7,700
Decrease in working capital		(1,204)
Decrease in stocks	(1,688)	
Increase in debtors	874	
Decrease in creditors	104	
	(710)	
Decrease in net liquid funds*	(494)	(1,204)

*Increase in overdraft 629 − 105 = 524 less increase in cash 30 = 494 net.

Exercises

23.1. Draw up a flow of funds statement, in accordance with SSAP 10, for the year 19-5 from the following information:

JJ Ltd.
Balance Sheets at 31 December

	19-4			19-5	
	£	£	£	£	£
Fixed Assets at cost		8,650		10,170	
Less Depreciation		2,890	5,760	3,905	6,265
Current Assets					
Stock		3,720		3,604	
Debtors		4,896		5,001	
Bank		544		–	
		9,160		8,605	
Less Current Liabilities					
Creditors	2,072		1,854		
Bank Overdraft	–		116		
Taxation	856		620		
Proposed Dividend	500	3,428	5,732	600	3,190	5,415
			11,492		12,680
Financed by:					
Issued Share Capital			10,000		10,000
Issued Share Capital			1,492		2,680
			11,492		12,680

Profit & Loss Account for the year ended 31 December 19-5

	£
Profit on ordinary activities before taxation (after charging depreciation £1,015)	2,408
Tax on profit on ordinary activities	620
	1,788
Undistributed profits from last year	1,492
	3,280
Proposed Dividend	600
Undistributed Profits carried to next year	2,680

23.2A. Draw up a flow of funds statement, in accordance with SSAP 10, for the year 19-8 from the following:

TX Ltd.
Balance Sheets as at 31 December

	19-7			19-8		
	£	£	£	£	£	£
Fixed Assets at cost		6,723			7,418	
Less Depreciation		2,946	3,777		3,572	3,846
Current Assets						
Stock		6,012			8,219	
Debtors	4,192			4,381		
Less Provision for Bad Debts	200	3,992		240	4,141	
Cash		100			35	
		10,104			12,395	
Less Current Liabilities						
Creditors	2,189			2,924		
Taxation	622			504		
Proposed Dividend	1,200			750		
Bank Overdraft	416	4,427	5,677	294	4,472	7,923
			9,454			11,769
Debentures			3,000			2,000
			6,454			9,769
Issued Share Capital			6,000			7,500
Profit and Loss Account			454			2,269
			6,454			9,769

Profit & Loss Account for the year ended 31 December 19-8

	£
Profit on ordinary activities before taxation*	3,069
Tax on profit on ordinary activities	504
	2,565
Undistributed profits from last year	454
	3,019
Proposed Dividend	750
Undistributed Profits carried to next year	2,269

*Includes loss on fixed assets sold of £114. The items sold had cost £2,070, had been depreciated £1,290 and were sold for £666.

24

Discounting Techniques

This chapter is an introduction to those areas of business decision where interest is an important item for consideration. Interest is the charge for borrowing money or the return from lending it. In more general terms since money can be freely borrowed or lent it may be considered as the cost of using or holding money. Since interest charges vary with time it follows that the interest factor will be important when deciding on things involving money flows spread out over periods of time.

Few people would hesitate if offered £1,000 now or £1,000 in twelve months' time to accept £1,000 now. However, if the offer was £900 now, or £1,000 at the end of twelve months, the decision might well be different. The increment of £100 in the year is equivalent to interest of 11.1 per cent on the capital sum of £900. If the recipient could obtain a return of more than 11.1 per cent he would be wise to take the £900 immediately. If, however, he were unable to find an outlet at a higher rate of interest he may well be advised to take £1,000 at the end of the year.

As in other areas of accountancy the problem of uncertainty plays an important part in decisions where the interest factor is concerned. Many of the decisions which have to be made involve areas which cannot be precisely calculated. Forecasts of future cash flows from profits for example, or the future trends of interest rates, can never be exact. For this reason it is frequently argued that detailed calculations involving interest are a waste of time. While it is fair to say that the results given by the processes described in this chapter can never be more accurate than the information on which they are based, they do give a logical decision based on the facts as presented.

In order to understand the basis on which interest calculations are made, a brief summary is included in the chapter covering the more important formulae for the calculation of interest.

Simple Interest

Simple interest is the return on a capital sum for one period of time. In practice, simple interest rarely applies other than for short periods of one year or less. Expressed as a formula simple interest (Is) is

$$Is = P \times r \times t$$

where P is the amount of the principal capital sum, $r =$ the rate of interest, $t =$ the length of time.

Example. £200 invested for six months at 5 per cent per annum

$$Is = 200 \times \tfrac{5}{100} \times \tfrac{6}{12} = £5$$

The total amount of the principal capital sum plus interest identified as A can be expressed by adapting the formula:

$$A = P + (Prt)$$

or

$$A = P(1 + rt)$$

Example. What amount would £200 invested at 5 per cent per annum accumulate to at the end of six months?

$$A = 200 \left[1 + (\tfrac{5}{100} \times \tfrac{6}{12})\right] = £205$$

Present Value

By adapting the formula again it is possible to calculate the present value of a future sum where a given rate of interest is earned on the money. Present value is a term used widely in the context of this chapter and means the value at the present moment, of future sums of money after allowing for interest. In our simple interest calculation the principal capital sum is the same as the present value. The present value is the principal capital sum which if it were invested now would accumulate at the given interest rate to the future amount which we have called A. The amount of the present value will, of course, be lower than the future amount, since

$$A = P(1 + rt)$$

and

$$P = \frac{A}{(1 + rt)}$$

Example. You have the prospect of receiving £205 at the end of six months. What is the present value of this money if the current rate of interest is 5 per cent per annum?

$$P = \frac{205}{\left[1 + (\tfrac{5}{100} \times \tfrac{6}{12})\right]}$$
$$P = £200$$

Compound Interest

Compound interest is the return on, or increase in, a capital sum for more than one time period, assuming that at the end of each time period the return or increase (i.e. interest) is added to the capital sum at the end of that time period and earns a return in all subsequent periods.

Example. What would £100 invested at 5 per cent per annum compound interest accumulate to at the end of three years?

Using the simple formula developed previously:

$$P(1 + r \times t) = A$$
End of Year 1 £100 $(1 + 0.05 \times 1)$ = £105
End of Year 2 £105 $(1 + 0.05 \times 1)$ = £110.25
End of Year 3 £110.25 $(1 + 0.05 \times 1)$ = £115.7625

Expressing the above calculation as a general formula would show:

End of Year 1 $P(1 + rt)$
End of Year 2 $P(1 + rt)(1 + rt)$ or $P(1 + rt)^2$
End of Year 3 $P(1 + rt)(1 + rt)(1 + rt)$ or $P(1 + rt)^3$

If n is taken as the number of periods during which the principal sum accumulates at interest and instead of using rt we use i as the rate of interest per time period, the compound interest formula can be written $A = P(1 + i)^n$ (*note:* if the rate of interest is 5 per cent per annum and the time period is for three months $i = 5$ per cent $\times \frac{3}{12} = 1.25$ per cent and $n = 3$).

Example. What would £500 invested at 6 per cent per annum accumulate to at the end of two years?

$$A = P(1 + i)^n = 500 (1 + 0.06)^2 = £561.8$$

In order to simplify calculations tables are available which show the amount to which £1 will accumulate at given rates of interest for different periods of time.

An example of a compound interest table is shown in Exhibit 24.1 and a more extensive one in the Appendix to this book. The figures shown by the tables can be checked as follows:

Example. To what amount would £1 accumulate in three years at 4 per cent per annum?

$$A = 1 (1 + 0.04)^3 = 1.1249$$

Compound Sum of £1

Year	1%	2%	3%	4%	5%	6%	7%	8%	9%	10%
1	1·010	1·020	1·030	1·040	1·050	1·060	1·070	1·080	1·090	1·100
2	1·020	1·040	1·061	1·082	1·102	1·124	1·145	1·166	1·188	1·210
3	1·030	1·061	1·093	1·125	1·158	1·191	1·225	1·260	1·295	1·331
4	1·041	1·082	1·126	1·170	1·216	1·262	1·311	1·360	1·412	1·464
5	1·051	1·104	1·159	1·217	1·276	1·338	1·403	1·469	1·539	1·611

Exhibit 24.1

Reading from the table the figure shown against year 3 under the 4 per cent column is $1·125$ (note that these tables are rounded to three places of decimals). This figure can be employed as a multiplier to calculate any required sums invested for three years at 4 per cent. Thus £400 for three years at 4 per cent would be –

$$£400 \times 1.125 = £450$$

Present Value

As an extension of the basic formula it will often be important to know the present value of a future sum of money which has been invested at a given rate of compound interest for a known number of periods.

Since we know that

$$A = P(1 + i)^n$$

then

$$P = \frac{A}{(1 + i)^n}$$

Tables are commonly available to show the present value of an amount of £1 at various rates of interest over given periods of time. An example is included in the Appendix.

Example. Find the present value of £1,500 due at the end of four years at 6 per cent per annum interest:

$$P = \frac{A}{(1 + i)^n} = \frac{1,500}{(1 + 0.06)^4} = £1,188.12$$

or using the tables

$$£1,500 \times 0.792 = £1,188$$

This result can be tested by working out what sum £1,188.12 would accumulate to over four years at 6 per cent. The answer should be £1,500.

$$A = P(1 + i) = 1,188.12(1 + 0.06)^4 = £1,500$$

or using tables

$$£1,188 \times 1.262 = £1,500$$

Annuities

An annuity is a series, or one of a series, of equal payments at fixed intervals. For example, rent payable every month, quarter or year, is one form of annuity. The term annuity originated in the field of insurance where in exchange for a lump sum payment or a series of premiums a regular payment would be made to the annuitant during his life. Regular payments such as rents or purchase by instalments occur frequently in business and it is, therefore, useful to know something about the calculation of annuities.

In practice there are a number of different kinds of annuity varying mainly in the details of when the regular payments are made, for example at the beginning or end of the period. In this chapter attention is centred entirely on the Ordinary Annuity in which the equal periodic payments occur at the end of the period. In practice, with a little thought it will be possible to handle most situations with a knowledge of how to calculate an Ordinary Annuity.

Formula for the Amount of an Ordinary Annuity

The amount of an annuity of £1 per period for three periods at 5 per cent interest might be determined as follows:

The first rent payment of £1 accumulates at 5 per cent interest for two periods and grows to:
$$£1(1+0.05)^2 = £1.1025$$

The second rent payment of £1 accumulates at 5 per cent interest for one period and grows to: £1.05

The third rent is due at the end of the annuity period £1.00

These add up to £3.1525

To develop the formula for the annuity we need to examine the relationship between compound interest, and an annuity of the amount of the interest. If £1 is invested for two periods at 5 per cent interest we have shown above that it will accumulate to £1.1025. Deducting the original investment from this amount we are left with the compound interest on £1 for two period as £0.1025. This amount is simply the amount of an annuity of 5 per cent of £1 for two period at 5 per cent.

This can be set down as:
$$0.05 \times \text{Annuity} = 1\,(1+0.05)^2 - 1$$
or
$$\text{Annuity} = 1\frac{(1+0.05)^2 - 1}{0.05} = \frac{(1.05)^2 - 1}{0.05}$$

Substituting generalized letters into the formula
$$\text{Annuity} = R\frac{(1+i)^n - 1}{i}$$

Where R = the annuity per period.

As in previous examples tables are available calculated on the basis of £1 to assist calculations; see the Appendix.

Example. A company plans to invest £1,000 at the end of the year for each of the next five years at an interest rate of 5 per cent per annum. How much will have accumulated at the end of the fifth year?

$$£1,000 \frac{(1+0.05)^5 - 1}{.05} = £5,525.631$$

or using tables

$$£1,000 \times 5.526 = £5,526$$

It will frequently be useful to know the amount required by way of periodic rents to acccumulate to a known future sum, for example when establishing a sinking fund.

It has already been established that where the amount of an annuity $= A$

$$A = R \frac{(1+i)^n - 1}{i}$$

Thus,
$$R = \frac{Ai}{(1+i)^n - 1}$$

Example. A company wishes to set aside equal annual amounts at the end of each year of the next four years, to accumulate to a fund of £5,000 for the replacement of assets. The amounts set aside will be invested at 6 per cent per annum interest. What amounts should be set aside?

$$R = \frac{Ai}{(1+i)^n - 1} = \frac{5,000\,(0.06)}{(1.06)^4 - 1} = £1,142.9578$$

The figure can be proved correct by the table below worked (as would be normal) to the nearest £1.

	Deposit £	Interest £	Increase in fund £	Balance of fund £
End of year 1	1,143	–	1,143	1,143
End of year 2	1,143	69	1,212	2,355
End of year 3	1,143	141	1,284	3,639
End of year 4	1,143	218	1,361	5,000

If reference is made to Chapter 7 a table has been prepared showing the amounts required to be set aside annually to accumulate to an amount of £1. This can be proved by using the formula.

Example. What amount invested annually at 5 per cent per annum will provide £1 in five years time?

$$R = \frac{Ai}{(1+i)^n - 1} = \frac{1\,(0.05)}{(1.05)^5 - 1} = £0.180975 \text{ (as per table)}$$

The Present Value of Annuities

It will often be necessary to calculate the present value of an annuity to evaluate a business problem. The present value of an annuity is the amount which if it were invested now at compound interest would be just sufficient to allow for the withdrawal of equal amounts (rents) at the end of a fixed number of periods. For example, we may wish to know whether to pay £135 cash now for a television or five instalments of £30 over the next two-and-a-half years instead. By converting the five instalments to a present cash value we can make direct comparison with the £135 cash price. If the present value of the annuity is more than £135 we should choose to pay cash. If, however, it comes to less than £135 the instalment method is cheaper. The result obtained will depend on the rate of interest used in the calculation.

The present value of an annuity will be equal to the sum of the present values of every individual rent payment. This can be illustrated in the above example, assuming 8 per cent rate of interest. The calculation shows it better at this rate of interest to pay by instalment.

				Present Value		
				Multiplier from		
Period	*£*			*Tables*		*£*
1	30	×		0.962	=	28.86
2	30	×		0.925	=	27.75
3	30	×		0.889	=	26.67
4	30	×		0.855	=	25.65
5	30	×		0.822	=	24.66
						133.59

(*Note:* when taking a half-yearly period the annual rate of interest is halved. The multiplier is therefore from the 4 per cent column of the Present Value tables.)

The formula for finding the present value of an ordinary annuity is developed as follows:

Compound discount (equivalent to compound interest) is the amount by which the total investment at compound interest will exceed the original capital. On the basis of £1:

$$\text{Discount} = 1 - \frac{1}{(1+i)^n}$$

By the same process of argument that was used when developing the formula for an ordinary annuity, it can be shown that the compound discount on £1 at 5 per cent is equal to 5 per cent of the present value of an annuity of £1. Thus

$$i \times \text{Present Value} = 1 - \frac{1}{(1+i)^n}$$

$$\text{Present Value} = \left[\frac{1 - \frac{1}{(1+i)^n}}{i} \right]$$

Tables are given in the Appendix to show the present values of an annuity of £1.

Example (details per previous example). The present value of five half-yearly payments of £30 at 8 per cent per annum would be:

$$R \left[\frac{1 - \frac{1}{(1+i)^n}}{i} \right] = 30 \left[\frac{1 - \frac{1}{(1+0.04)^5}}{0.04} \right] = \text{£}133.57$$

or using the tables $30 \times 4.452 = \text{£}133.56$.

Finally, to prove that the present value of an annuity is the amount which if it were invested now at compound interest would be just sufficient to allow for the withdrawal of equal amounts at the end of a fixed number of periods, we can show that the present value of £133.57 just calculated would fulfil this condition for withdrawals of £30 over five half-yearly periods with interest at 8 per cent per annum.

		£
Start		133.57
Period 1	Interest	5.34 (133.57 at 8 per cent for 6 months)
	Payment	(30.00)
Balance		108.91
Period 2	Interest	4.35
	Payment	(30.00)
Balance		83.26
Period 3	Interest	3.33
	Payment	(30.00)
		56.59
Period 4	Interest	2.26
	Payment	(30.00)
Balance		28.85
Period 5	Interest	1.15
	Payment	(30.00)
Balance		00.00

Applications to Business Situations

The interest formulae which have been described in this chapter are useful over a wide range of business situations and accounting problems. While it will not be possible in this one chapter to examine in detail the whole range of applications, some of the more important ones are described. For convenience these can be dealt with under the following headings:

1. Investment Decisions related to the question of whether capital expenditure is justified by the probable future returns, and in the selection of alternatives.
2. Accounting problems of valuing assets and calculation of appropriations to sinking funds and depreciation.
3. Leasing where there may be decisions as to whether to lease or buy and also how to record leases in the accounts.

Investment Decisions

One of the most important areas in which interest plays a role is where a decision has to be made about whether or not to invest business funds. In general no business wishes to invest money in a project unless the return or profit is considered to be sufficient. The decision as to whether a return is adequate in the light of the risks to be undertaken is a management and not an accounting decision. What the accountant should do is to show as accurately as he can the relationship between the cost of the project and the returns expected from it.

The comparison between a capital investment and the flow of funds which arise from that investment can be made in a number of ways. For example a company which has the opportunity to install a new machine costing £2,100 which will produce net income of £100 (after charging depreciation) per annum over three years and will then be scrapped without value, must decide whether the investment is a paying proposition. One common method would be to compare the average capital outlay with the average profit. In practice, firms interpret these things differently, but average capital will often be taken as the average of the opening and closing capital investment, i.e.

$$\frac{£2,100 + 0}{2} = £1,050$$

The average profit will usually be calculated by taking an arithmetic average of each year's profit. £100 + £100 + £100 = £300 ÷ 3 = £100.

The average profit expressed as a percentage of the average capital employed would then be:

$$\frac{£100}{£1,050} \times \frac{100}{1} = 9.4 \text{ per cent}$$

The management of the company would then have to decide whether or not a 9.4 per cent return was adequate. This method of appraisal is often known as the Accounting Rate of Return Method.

Another method of assessing the information is to work out the time period in which the outlay on the project is recouped from the cash flows originating from it. The Cash Flow which arises from a project will rarely be exactly the same as the accounting profit. One main item of difference is depreciation. Cash outflow usually only takes place at the point when a fixed asset is bought and paid for. Depreciation is an allocation against profit of this original cost, over the assets life. After the initial purchases however, no cash payments take place and depreciation can thus be called a non-cash expense. In this example the original outlay is £2,100 and the cash flows are:

Year 1 Profit £100 + the non-cash expense (Depreciation)   £700 = £800
Year 2   ,,   £100,, the   ,,   ,,   ,,   £700 = £800
Year 3   ,,   £100,, the   ,,   ,,   ,,   £700 = £800

The original outlay of £2,100 would be recouped during year 3. Assuming cash flows evenly during the year it would take $2\frac{5}{8}$ years to recover the whole original outlay. Companies using this method, which is known as the 'Payback Method', have a standard time within which they expect to be paid back. If the Standard Payback period required was three years, then this project would be acceptable.

One major disadvantage of the Accounting Rate of Return and the Payback Methods is that they ignore the cost of money over time (i.e. the time value of money). Another disadvantage is that the Payback Method ignores the cash flows after the payback period while the Accounting Rate of Return is based on accounting profit which can be distorted by changes in accounting policies adopted. Let us assume that the company concerned has to pay on average for borrowing capital, an amount equivalent to a 6 per cent rate of interest. Knowing this rate of interest it is possible to convert the future cash flows from the project to a present value at the start of the project. If the present value of the net future cash inflows exceed the capital outlay it can be said that the project is worthwhile, or at least will yield a real profit. It is important to note that it is cash flows that matter when considering the cost of money over time and not profit as such. The profit figure includes many items which are allocated to a period quite independently of when the expense or revenue is paid or received.

The present values of the cash inflows in the example are as follows:

Year	£		*Multiplier from present value of £1 tables at 6 per cent*		£
1	800	×	0.943	=	754.4
2	800	×	0.890	=	712.0
3	800	×	0.840	=	672.0
					2,138.4

(Note in this example the calculation could have been reduced by using the present value of an annuity table for an annuity of £800 for three years at 6 per cent − £800 × 2.673 = £2,138.4.)

By comparison with the outlay of £2,100 the project is worthwhile. The project has a net present value of £38.04 which is the discounted value of the cash flows arising from the project, i.e. £2,138.04 less the present worth of the capital outlays. So long as the net present value of the cash inflows exceeds the present value of the capital outlays thus giving a positive value to net present worth, the project will be worthwhile. It must be noted, however, that if the company's cost of capital were only 1 per cent higher, the present value would be £2,099 and the same project would be unacceptable. This method of evaluating an investment project is known as the Present Value Method.

The present value information may be expressed also as an index comparing the present value of the capital outlay with the present value of the other cash flows. In the example shown, the index would be $\frac{2,138.4}{2,100}$ = 1.018. This is known as the profitability index. The profitability index may be useful in comparing projects. For example, an investment with capital outlay £100 may give rise to other cash flows with a net present value of £300. The index is 3.00. A comparable capital outlay of £1,000,000 may produce net cash inflows with present value £1,000,500 which is an index of 1.0005. Thus whilst the net present value of the second project at £500 is higher than that of the first £300, the index shows that the ratio of return to capital outlay is better in the first project with an index of 3.00 compared to only 1.0005 in the second.

Another method of evaluating this information which is similar to the present value method just examined is one that seeks to find out which rate of interest would, if applied in the present value method, exactly equate the present value of the net cash inflows with the capital outlay. This can only be done by a trial and error process:

Year	Cash Flow	6 per cent		7 per cent	
	£		£		£
1	800	0.943	754.4	0.935	748.0
2	800	0.890	712.0	0.873	698.4
3	800	0.840	672.0	0.816	652.8
			2,138.4		2,099.2

When starting a problem of this sort from scratch it is necessary to choose two widely dispersed rates of interest in order to obtain an idea of where the final rate lies. For example, in the problem just examined we might have taken 5 per cent and 15 per cent. The present values from these rates would be £2,178 and £1,827 respectively and from this we could see that the solution will be nearer to the 5 per cent end. Notice that the higher the interest rate the lower will be the present value and vice versa. By successive trials our answer will be located between 6 per cent and 7 per cent. Unfortunately, the number we are looking for does not happen to be a whole number. Often it will be sufficient to take the nearest whole number rate of interest which in our example would be 7 per cent. If a more exact rate is required it can be calculated by what is known as interpolation. Starting from the lower rate of interest of 6 per cent we add $\frac{38 \cdot 4}{39 \cdot 2}$ths of the 1 per cent difference between 6 per cent and the higher rate of 7 per cent. The denominator of 39.2 is the difference between 2138.4 and 2,099.2. The numerator of 38.4 is the difference between the present value at 6 per cent £2,138.4 and the required present value of £2,100.

$$6 \text{ per cent} + \frac{38 \cdot 4}{39 \cdot 2} \times 1 \text{ per cent} = 6 \cdot 98 \text{ per cent}$$

This method of assessing projects is known as the Yield or Internal Rate of Return Method.

In comparing the results given by the different methods we have examined it can be seen that a discrepancy arises between the Accounting Rate of Return result at $9 \cdot 4$ per cent and the Yield result at $6 \cdot 98$ per cent. If the company's cost of capital were 7 per cent we should accept the project using the Accounting Rate of Return since that is higher. However, since the yield is only $6 \cdot 98$ per cent and the net present worth at 7 per cent is negative we should reject this project. By ignoring the cost of capital the Accounting Rate of Return is giving an incorrect result. The Present Value and Yield methods will give the same answer in all except a few special cases. The Payback Method is unsatisfactory because it ignores the total profit receivable from a project. If, for example, two projects are compared, both costing £1,000 but one yielding £500 per annum for three years and the other yielding £500 per annum for four years the payback period in both would be the same although the second alternative is clearly preferable. The payback method can be a useful supplement, however, to the present value or the yield methods for a company that is short of funds. If two projects give approximately the same yield, the one with quickest payback will be preferable.

So far in the example used, the decision has been whether a project is worth while or not, based on its cost, and the expected returns from it. The same methods are equally useful in deciding between two or more alternative investments, the project giving the highest present value of yield being the most desirable. No mention has been made of the impact that taxation will have in investment decisions. Provided it is remembered that we are dealing with cash flows and the tax is included in the year in which it is actually paid or refunded, then no special problems arise. An approximation which is often employed is to assume that cash flows occur at the end or beginning of each period (rather than throughout the period as will happen in practice). Whilst this assumption is not usually likely to cause serious distortion, and simplifies calculation, for some purposes half-yearly or shorter periods may be used for discounting.

Example. Enterprise Ltd is considering two alternative investments for increasing its plant capacity.

	Project 1 5 years		Project 2 6 years	
Project Life	£		£	
Investment in Equipment (scrap value nil) at beginning of first year	70,000		120,000	
Investment in Working Capital at beginning of first year (recoverable at the end of the projects life)	30,000		30,000	
Estimated Profits before taxation				
Year 1	10,000		15,000	
Remainder of life	20,000	per annum	27,000	per annum
Depreciation	14,000	per annum	20,000	per annum
Taxation in year of payment				
Year 2 (refund)	(2,000)		(3,000)	
Remainder of life	6,000	per annum	7,000	per annum

The company estimate that its cost of capital is 10 per cent per annum. It will be assumed that cash flows arise at the end of the year unless otherwise stated.

Using the Present Value Method of appraisal, it is useful to set out the problem as shown in Exhibits 24.2 and 24.3.

The solution to this problem in Exhibits 24.2 and 24.3 shows that the Net Present Worth of Project (2) £44,795 is higher than that for Project (1) £27,722. On this criteria the company would choose Project (2) although Project (1) would be worthwhile if it were not an alternative. The Internal Rate of Return and the Profitability Index, however, are marginally higher for Project (1) than for Project (2). The directors will have to decide whether they prefer Project (2) with its higher Investment and Net Present Worth of Project (1) which with a smaller Investment and Net Present Worth but which has a slightly higher yield. The decision will take into account the resources available to the firm, the risks associated with the two projects, also the alternative investment opportunities which might be available for the £50,000 difference in capital investment.

Exhibit 24.2

Project 1 (Outflows are shown in brackets)

Year	0	1	2	3	4	5	Totals of columns 0-5
Capital Flows							
Equipment	(70,000)						
Working Capital	(30,000)					30,000	
1 Total Capital Flow	(100,000)					30,000	
2 Discount Factors – 10 per cent	1.00					0.621	
3 = 1 × 2 Discounted Capital Flow	(100,000)					18,630	(81,370)
Other Flows							
Profit	—	10,000	20,000	20,000	20,000	20,000	
Depreciation	—	14,000	14,000	14,000	14,000	14,000	
Taxation	—	–	2,000	(6,000)	(6,000)	(6,000)	
4 Total Other Flows		24,000	36,000	28,000	28,000	28,000	
5 Discount Factors		0.909	0.826	0.751	0.683	0.621	
6 = 4 × 5 Discounted Other Flows		21,816	29,736	21,028	19,124	17,388	109,092
7 = 3 + 6 Total Discounted Flow	(100,000)	21,816	29,736	21,028	19,124	36,018	27,722

Summary: Net Present Worth at 10 per cent interest £27,722.
Internal Rate of Return (yield) = 19.2 per cent (Net Present Worth at 18 per cent £3,022; at 20 per cent (£2,000)).

Profitability Index = 1·341 $\left(\dfrac{109,092}{81,370} \right)$

Exhibit 24.3

Project 2 (Outflows are shown in brackets)

Year	0	1	2	3	4	5	6	Totals of Columns 0–6
Capital Flows								
Equipment	(120,000)							
Working Capital	(30,000)						30,000	
1 Total Capital Flow	(150,000)						30,000	
2 Discount Factors – 10 per cent	1.00						0.564	
3 = 1 × 2	(150,000)						16,920	(133,080)
Other Cash Flows								
Profit	—	15,000	27,000	27,000	27,000	27,000	27,000	
Depreciation	—	20,000	20,000	20,000	20,000	20,000	20,000	
Taxation			3,000	(7,000)	(7,000)	(7,000)	(7,000)	
4 Total Other Cash Flows		35,000	50,000	40,000	40,000	40,000	40,000	
5 Discount Factors		0.909	0.826	0.751	0.683	0.621	0.564	
6 = 4 × 5		31,815	41,300	30,040	27,320	24,840	22,560	177,875
7 = 3 + 6 Total Discounted Cash Flow	(150,000)	31,815	41,300	30,040	27,320	24,840	39,480	44,795

Summary: Net Present Worth at 10 per cent interest £44,795.
Internal Rate of Return (yield) = 18.97 per cent (Net Present Worth at 18 per cent £3,925; at 20 per cent (£4,175).

$$\text{Profitability Index} = 1\cdot 337 \left(\frac{177\cdot 875}{133\cdot 080}\right)$$

The methods of appraisal discussed in this part of the chapter describe the discounted cash flow approach to investment decision taking. We have not, however, considered many of the practical problems which surround such decisions. For example, there are often great difficulties in estimating what future cash flows will be. There will also be considerable uncertainty associated with future estimates which may be hard to quantify. It is by no means easy to determine the appropriate rate of interest to use in the calculations. In general terms it may be said that the company's cost of capital should be used as the rate of interest for present value calculations, or as the minimum acceptable rate when the internal rate of return is assessed. This still leaves the problem of defining the company's 'cost of capital'. Above all, in most management decisions the problem of investment is complicated by the many interrelationships involved. One decision can have implications for very many different parts of the business and the best solution for all the different parts may be hard to arrive at. Despite these problems this method of assessment is very valuable because it requires a disciplined approach to estimating the results of investment and does not forget the importance of interest where cash flows are spread of several periods of time.

Accounting Problems

Depreciation

In Chapter 7 a description was included of the calculation of the equal amounts of depreciation required to be set aside each year in a sinking fund, to accumulate with interest to a given sum in the future. From the descriptions given in the earlier section in this chapter it should be apparent that this is nothing more than a straightforward annuity calculation.

Example. Facts as in Exhibit 3, Chapter 7.

Required: to find the amount of an annuity that will amount to £10,000 at the end of five years invested at 5 per cent per annum.

From Table 3 it can be seen that a £1 annuity will amount to £5.526 over five years. The annuity which will amount to £10,000 will therefore be

$$\frac{£10,000}{5.526} = £1,810 \text{ (to the nearest whole £1)}$$

Alternatively the formula could have been employed as shown earlier in this chapter:

$$R = \frac{Ai}{(1+i)^n - 1} = \frac{£10,000(0.05)}{(1.05)^3 - 1} = £1,810$$

The calculation can be proved as follows:

Year	Sinking Fund amount set aside	5 per cent Interest	Total Depreciation	Cumulative total
	£		£	£
1	1,810	–	1,810	1,810
2	1,810	90	1,900	3,710
3	1,810	185	1,995	5,705
4	1,810	285	2,095	7,800
5	1,810	390	2,200	10,000

It is also possible to use the same calculation as a basis for allocating depreciation over the life of an asset without in fact investing funds, in sinking fund investments. The total depreciation column in the above table shows how the original cost of an asset costing £10,000 would be spread over its working life. (The appropriate rate of interest would be the return expected on the asset.)

Another depreciation method employing similar concepts to the sinking fund method is one, in fact, called the 'Annuity Method'. In this method besides the basic depreciation charge an additional cost is worked out and charged against profit.

This is an interest charge for using the asset during the year and is equal to the rate of return from the asset times the investment at the beginning of the year.

Example. Taking the facts as they were presented in the previous example the position would be:

Year	Book Value of Asset at beginning of year £	Basic Depreciation £	Interest on book value of assets using 5 per cent return £	Total depreciation including interest £
1	10,000	1,810	500	2,310
2	8,190	1,900	401	2,310
3	6,290	1,995	315	2,310
4	4,295	2,095	215	2,310
5	2,200	2,200	110	2,310
		10,000	1,550	11,550

In this example, since the rate of return on the asset is taken at the same rate as the interest used on the sinking fund method, the total depreciation charge works out to an equal amount each year. The interest on the book value of assets is a charge applying only within the business itself. It will be charged therefore as depreciation in one section of the Profit and Loss Account and credited in another, as interest received. The net effect is therefore the same as the sinking fund method of depreciation. Using T accounts to record the transactions the position shown would be:

Depreciation Fund

	Year		£
	1	A	1,810
	2	B	1,900
	3	C	1,995
	4	D	2,095
	5	E	2,200
			10,000

Internal Interest Revenue

Year		£	Year		£
1	Profit and Loss	500	1	A	500
2		410	2	B	410
3		315	3	C	315
4		215	4	D	215
5		110	5	E	110

Depreciation Expense

Year		£	Year		£
1	A	2,310	1	Profit and Loss	2,310
2	B	2,310	2		2,310
3	C	2,310	3		2,310
4	D	2,310	4		2,310
5	E	2,310	5		2,310

Profit and Loss Account (Extract)

Year 1

	£		£
Depreciation Expense	2,310	Internal Interest	500

Year 2

	£		£
Depreciation Expense	2,310	Internal Interest	410

Year 3

	£		£
Depreciation Expense	2,310	Internal Interest	315

Year 4

	£		£
Depreciation Expense	2,310	Internal Interest	215

Year 5

	£		£
Depreciation Expense	2,310	Internal Interest	100

Both the sinking fund and the annuity methods of depreciation have taken account of the importance of the cost of money over time.

The depreciation has been allocated over the life of the asset in a way which charges profits in the later years of the asset's life with a higher cost. This is not unreasonable if the asset concerned yields an equal profit over its life. This will be illustrated in the following example which uses basically the same facts that were illustrated in the earlier examples.

In order for the annuity method of depreciation to be applied, for this purpose it is necessary that the rate of return or interest used should be the one which discounts the future cash flow from profits to a present value equivalent to the original investment, i.e. the present value of an annuity of £2,310 for five years at 5 per cent = £10,000. In normal practice the investment figure of £10,000 and the cash flows of £2,310 would be known quantities. It would then be necessary by examination of the present value of annuity tables to establish that the rate of return was 5 per cent. (This figure would be used in subsequent calculations).

Example. An asset costing £10,000 is to be depreciated over a five-year life in which the profit yielded is £2,310 per annum before depreciation. The following results are shown if straight-line depreciation is used.

Year	Asset at w.d.v. at beginning of year	Depreciation	Profit after depreciation	Profit as per cent assets at w.d.v.
	£	£	£	
1	10,000	2,000	310	3.1
2	8,000	2,000	310	3.87
3	6,000	2,000	310	5.17
4	4,000	2,000	310	7.75
5	2,000	2,000	310	15.5
		10,000	1,550	

It is clear that where straight-line depreciation is used the return on assets increases from 3.1 per cent to 15.5 per cent over the five years, without any alteration in efficiency of the business whatever. By comparison figures where sinking fund depreciation is employed are as follows:

Year	Asset at w.d.v. at beginning of year	Depreciation	Profit after depreciation	Profit as per cent assets at w.d.v.
	£	£	£	
1	10,000	1,810	500	5
2	8,190	1,900	410	5
3	6,290	1,995	315	5
4	4,295	2,095	215	5
5	2,200	2,200	110	5
		10,000	1,550	

The sinking fund and annuity methods in these circumstances are yielding an answer to one of the problems of depreciation accounting, namely the distortion of reported net profit in relation to the net assets employed. Unfortunately, however, there is implicit in sinking fund and annuity methods an assumption that the cash flows, and correspondingly depreciation, occur evenly over the life of the asset. In practice, this rarely happens apart from items such as leases where the rents are exactly known.

Present Value

The theoretical answer to this problem lies in the use of the present value techniques already explored earlier in the chapter. Not only could the depreciation problem be solved but also that of the valuing of fixed assets. In order to solve the problem two things must be known, firstly the future cash flows which would originate from the asset, and secondly, the appropriate rate of interest representing cost of capital to the firm.

Example. A business expects cash flows from an investment costing £456.8 amounting to £200 per annum for three years. The company's cost of capital is 10 per cent.

The cash flows converted to present value at a rate of interest of 10 per cent would be:

Year		Present value factor	Present value
	£		£
1	200	0.909	181.8
2	200	0.826	165.2
3	200	0.751	150.2
			497.2

At the end of year 1 the Present Value of the Investment

$$£200 \times 0.909 \quad £181.8$$
$$£200 \times 0.826 \quad £165.2$$
$$£347.0$$

At the end of year 2 the Present Value of the Investment

$$£200 \times 0.909 \quad = £181.8$$

The amount to be written off each year can be computed as follows.

Year	Present value at beginning of year	Present value at end of year	Reduction in present value
	£	£	£
1	497.2	347.0	150.2
2	347.0	181.8	165.2
3	181.8	–	181.8
			497.2

The reduction in present value figures incorporate both a charge for true depreciation, which would be the same as the present value figures of the cash flow each year, i.e. the capital cost expired in the year

Year	Depreciation
1	£181.8
2	£165.2
3	£150.2

together with an adjustment for the interest on the capital employed. The interest factor is shown as follows:

Year	Reduction in present value	Depreciation	Interest factor
	£	£	
1	150.2	181.8	+31.6
2	165.2	165.2	–
3	181.8	150.2	−31.6

These figures can be proved in detail in the following way:

Year	Present value of cash flows	Interest at 10 per cent	Present value + interest	Interest at 10 per cent	Present value + Interest	Interest at 10 per cent
	£	£	£	£	£	£
1	181.8	18.18				
2	165.2	16.52	181.72	18.17		
3	150.2	15.02	165.22	16.52	181.74	18.17
		49.72		34.69		18.17

Year 1	Interest Expense 18.1	Interest Revenue 49.7 = +31.6
Year 2	Interest Expense 34.7	Interest Revenue 34.7 = 0
Year 3	Interest Expense 49.7	Interest Revenue 18.1 = −31.6

In the accounts of the company this would be presented as follows:

Year	Cash Flow	Depreciation	Income before Interest	Interest Expense	Income	Interest Revenue	Net Income
	£	£	£	£	£	£	£
1	200	181.8	18.2	18.2	−	49.7	49.7
2	200	165.2	34.7	34.7	−	34.7	34.7
3	200	150.2	49.7	49.7	−	18.2	18.2

The Return on net assets would be equal each year as shown below:

Year 1 $\dfrac{\text{Net Income}}{\text{Net Whole Value of Asset}}$ $\dfrac{49.7}{497.2}$ = 10 per cent

Year 2 $\dfrac{\text{Net Income}}{\text{Net Value of Asset}}$ $\dfrac{34.7}{347.0}$ = 10 per cent

Year 3 $\dfrac{\text{Net Income}}{\text{Net Value of Asset}}$ $\dfrac{18.2}{181.8}$ = 10 per cent

The Accounting entries to record the interest expense and revenue would be as shown in the T accounts below:

Interest Expense		Interest Revenue		Deferred Interest	
Year 1 18.2		Year 1 49.7	Year 1 31.6	−	
Year 2 34.7		Year 2 34.7	−	−	
Year 3 49.7		Year 3 18.2	−		Year 3 31.6

One important point has been overlooked in the analysis so far. It has been assumed that the assets should be valued in the accounts at the figure for the present value of future cash flows and depreciated accordingly. However, since this figure exceeds the cost value of the asset by £40.4 the method could be unacceptable where assets were required to be recorded at cost. In this circumstance it would be necessary to create a capital reserve for the amount of unrealized profit on revaluation of the asset. In the Balance Sheet this would be recorded as follows:

	£
Assets (valued on the basis of the Present Value of future Cash Flows)	497
Less Reserve for unrealized profits	40
Asset at Cost Value	457

The problem would arise at the end of the first and subsequent years of calculating the balance of unrealized profit. The way to do this is to calculate the interest rate that would exactly equate the future cash flows with the cost of the asset (as in the yield or discounted cash flow calculation). Trial and error methods give the following result:

Year	Cash Flow	Present Value Factor 15 per cent	Present Value
	£		£
1	200	0.870	174.0
2	200	0.756	151.2
3	200	0.658	131.6
			456.8

Having established that with a cost of capital of 15 per cent the present value of future cash flows would equal the cost of investment, the allocation of net income should be recalculated for the project using the 15 per cent interest rate.

This would amount to:

Year	Net Income at 15 per cent Interest
1	68.4
2	48.8
3	26.0
	143.2

If this is then compared with the net income with a 10 per cent rate of interest, the difference gives the expected profit that has been realized:

Year	Net Income at 15 per cent Interest	Net Income at 10 per cent Interest	Net Income Realised
	£	£	£
1	68	50	18
2	49	35	14
3	26	18	8
	143	103	40

At the end of year 1 the reserve for unrealised profit would be £22 and at the end of year 2 £8.

At the beginning of this section of the chapter the ideas put forward were described as a theoretical solution, since the uncertainty of predicting future cash flows creates great practical problems. The method nevertheless provides a most satisfactory model for the depreciation of assets. The depreciation charge is correctly spread out over the life of the asset in proportion to the return obtained from it, and proper allowance is made for the cost of money over time. Not only this but a valuation is placed upon the asset exactly related to the future returns expected from it, and the relationship between net profit and the net book value of the asset will not be distorted by the depreciation charge. The main advantage in understanding the present value method is as a standard for criticism of other methods, it also offers some useful advantages in the preparation of information for the management of a business.

Leasing

Leasing is an important method for many organisations to acquire assets. Things as diverse as motor vehicles, televisions, computers, machinery and buildings are commonly leased rather than bought. In a lease the lessor owns the object and leases it to the user, the lessee. The agreement which is legally binding and non-cancellable usually covers the major part of the economic life of the asset. The lessee in exchange for the use of the asset agrees to pay a rental, keep the item in good condition, insure it and properly service it. The rental payments and other costs are fully chargeable against the taxable profits of the lessee. The lessor as owner of the assets can claim all Capital Allowances for tax purposes against his taxable profits.

Leasing is possible because of the different costs of capital and tax situations between lessors and lessees. For example a company wishing to obtain a computer costing £100,000 may find it attractive to lease because the financial institution funding the operating can borrow at much lower rates than the company and its marginal tax rates against which the capital allowances on the computer can be set are significantly higher for the financial institution than the company.

The problem facing an organisation therefore is to compare the relative attractiveness of obtaining the use of an asset by buying it outright funding from normal sources of capital or whether to lease it.

It should be noted that the calculations of interest rates and the apportionment of interest which now follow, appertaining to leases, will also apply to Hire Purchase contracts where the 'true rate' of interest is not known. In such cases the hire purchase contract states only the 'nominal' rate of interest.

The Interest Rate Implied in a Lease (or Hire Purchase)

In the type of decision which has to be made the purchase price of an asset is known, as are the rental terms. From this an interest rate can be derived: —

A computer costing £100,000 has an expected life of 5 years with no scrap value. It can be leased for £27,740 per annum. The interest rate is that at which: —

The Cost of the Item = Present Value of the annual rental payments

$100,000 = 27,740 \times x$ (where x is the factor for the present value of an annuity of £1 for 5 years)

$$\therefore x = \frac{100,000}{27,740} = 3.605$$

By looking across the tables for the present value of an annuity on the five year period it will be seen that 3.605 corresponds to a rate of interest of 12%.

If scrap values are involved the calculation would have to be made as in the trial and error method of calculating internal rate of return.

This calculation has ignored the impact of taxation which may be crucial in the ultimate choice between leasing or buying. In the example we have just examined the rental payments would be deducted from taxable income and the net of tax cost would therefore be reduced by the tax borne by the company on its profits. If the tax rate were 42% of profits then the net of tax cost of the lease could be 58% of £27,740 = £16,089 and the corresponding interest rate would be 58% × 12% = 6.96%. (This ignores possible time lags in obtaining tax relief).

This net of tax rate of interest can be compared with the organisations net of tax cost of capital.

Accounting for Leases

In accounting for finance leases the problem is to divide the rental payments into an interest component and a capital repayment element. The rental payments are as was previously mentioned intended to pay for the use of the asset and for the finance required to fund the transaction. To calculate the interest element each period it is necessary to work out the real rate of interest implied in the lease, from knowledge of the rental payments, the period of the ease and the cash value of the assets involved at the start of the period.

If we take a problem similar to that illustrated in ED29 the facts are as follows: —

1. A rental of £670 per quarter payable in advance.
2. 20 quarterly payments starting from 1st January 19-2.
3. The leased asset could be purchased for cash of £10,000 at the start of the lease.

In order to calculate the implied rate of interest it must be remembered that an ordinary annuity calculation relates to payments at the end of the period. In this case we have one payment of £670 at the start and an annuity of £670 for 19 periods. The interest rate at which the present value of these lease payments equals the cash value of £10,000 is the interest rate implied in the lease.

$$\text{Present Value of annuity} = R \left[\frac{1 - \dfrac{1}{(1+i)^n}}{i} \right]$$

$$\therefore 10,000 = 670 + 670 \left[\frac{1 - \dfrac{1}{(1+i)^{19}}}{i} \right]$$

$$\therefore 9,330 = 670 \left[\frac{1 - \dfrac{1}{(1+i)^{19}}}{i} \right]$$

$$i = .0332 \text{ or } 3.32\%$$

Note that the initial payment of £670 reduces the cash value of the machine to £9,330 and the calculation then as for an ordinary annuity for 19 periods.

To find the rate of interest using the table for the Present Value of an Annuity requires the initial payment to be dealt with as before. We need to find the interest rate where 9330 = 670 × factor for 19 periods

or

$$\text{factor for 19 periods} = \frac{9,330}{670} = 13.925$$

By interpolation 3%   14.324
.399   13.925
4%   13.134
1.190

$$\frac{.399}{1.190} = .335$$

i.e. 3.3%

Applying the rate of interest of 3.32% (which may in practice be rounded to 3.3%) to the lease data shows the following: –

Exhibit 24.4

Calculation of the Periodic Finance Charge in the Lease

Period	Capital sum at start of period £	Rental paid £	Capital sum during period £	Finance charge (3.32% per quarter) £	Capital sum at end of period £
1/19-2	10,000	670	9,330	310	9,640
2/19-2	9,640	670	8,970	298	9,268
3/19-2	9,268	670	8,598	285	8,883
4/19-2	8,883	670	8,213	273	8,486
1/19-3	8,486	670	7,816	259	8,075
2/19-3	8,075	670	7,405	246	7,651
3/19-3	7,651	670	6,981	232	7,213
4/19-3	7,213	670	6,543	217	6,760
1/19-4	6,760	670	6,090	202	6,292
2/19-4	6,292	670	5,622	187	5,809
3/19-4	5,809	670	5,139	171	5,310
4/19-4	5,310	670	4,640	154	4,794
1/19-5	4,794	670	4,124	137	4,261
2/19-5	4,261	670	3,591	119	3,710
3/19-5	3,710	670	3,040	101	3,141
4/19-5	3,141	670	2,471	82	2,553
1/19-6	2,553	670	1,883	63	1,946
2/19-6	1,946	670	1,276	42	1,318
3/19-6	1,318	670	648	22	670
4/19-6	670	670	–	–	
		£13,400		£3,400	

Finance charges for each year of the contract are therefore:

	£
19-2 (310 + 298 + 285 + 273)	1,166
19-3	954
19-4	714
19-5	439
19-6	127

The total picture for the five years is as follows:

	Total Rental £	less Finance Charge £	= Capital Repayment £
19-2	2,680	1,166	1,514
19-3	2,680	954	1,726
19-4	2,680	714	1,966
19-5	2,680	439	2,241
19-6	2,680	127	2,553

In the Balance Sheet of the Company the liability under finance leases would be: –

	Obligations under finance leases at start of year £	less	Capital Repayment £	=	Obligations under finance leases at end of year £
19-2	10,000		1,514		8,486
19-3	8,486		1,726		6,760
19-4	6,760		1,966		4,794
19-5	4,794		2,241		2,553
19-6	2,553		2,553		–

A small company may consider that the calculations involved in the actuarial method described are too complicated and a simple rule-of-thumb method may be used instead, known as the Rule of 78.

The term arises because it was originally applied over 1 year and 78 is the sum of the number of months from 1 to 12 inclusive. The first month would receive a proportion in reverse order to its position i.e. $\frac{12}{78}$, the second month would receive $\frac{11}{78}$ and so on till the twelfth month which would receive $\frac{1}{78}$ of the total.

Under this system it is clear that the early periods will receive a heavier allocation than later periods which is what happens when interest is allocated according to the actuarial method. The relationship between the two will however only be approximate since there is no direct relationship. The finance charge to which the proportion is applied is simply the difference between the total payments under the leasing agreement and the cash value of the asset at the start.

If we refer back to the illustration of the actuarial method in Exhibit 24.4 the allocation of the finance charge of £3,400 to the periods concerned using the rule of 78 would be as follows: –

	Rental payment number £	For Rule of 78 £	Allocation ×£3,400 £	Annual Allocation £
1/19-2	1	19	340	
2/19-2	2	18	322	
3/19-2	3	17	304	
4/19-2	4	16	286	1,252
1/19-3	5	15	268	
2/19-3	6	14	251	
3/19-3	7	13	233	
4/19-3	8	12	215	967
1/19-4	9	11	197	
2/19-4	10	10	179	
3/19-4	11	9	161	
4/19-4	12	8	143	680
1/19-5	13	7	125	
2/19-5	14	6	107	
3/19-5	15	5	89	
4/19-5	16	4	72	393
1/19-6	17	3	54	
2/19-6	18	2	36	
3/19-6	19	1	18	
4/19-6	–	–	–	108
	190	190	3,400	3,400

Period 1/19-2 receives $\frac{19}{190} \times £3,400 = £340$ of the total finance

charge and so on. Note that because the payments are at the start of the period there is no allocation to period 4/19-6.

Comparison of the two methods of allocation is as follows: –

	Actuarial Method £	Rule of 78 £
19-2	1,166	1,252
19-3	954	967
19-4	714	680
19-5	439	393
19-6	127	108
	3,400	3,400

Exercises

24.1. The managing director of your firm has obtained the terms on which three different firms would manufacture a special machine. These are:

Firm A   £2,000 payable on delivery
£500 payable at the end of the following four years
Total £4,000

Firm B   £1,000 payable on delivery
£3,500 payable at the end of five years from delivery
Total £4,500

Firm C   Nothing payable on delivery
£800 at the end of each of the following four years
£1,000 at the end of the fifth year after delivery
Total £4,200

He says, obviously, the offer from Firm A is the best one. Would you agree with him or would you recommend one of the other offers, and if so, which one? You are required to show all your workings to substantiate your decision.

The average cost of capital to the firm is 6 per cent per annum.

308

24.2. Consider three investment projects A, B and C, all costing £300 to initiate, having a life of three years with income arising end-year on average, and the residual value of the assets being zero. Depreciation both for tax purposes and accounting purposes is on the straight-line basis of £100 per year. Tax is at the rate of 50 per cent and is levied and collected simultaneously at the end of each year. The details of earnings, depreciation, tax and profitability are given below:

Years	1	2	3
Project A	£	£	£
Gross Earnings	250	250	250
Depreciation	100	100	100
Profits before Tax	150	150	150
Tax at 50 per cent	75	75	75
Profits after Tax	75	75	75
Project B			
Gross Earnings	150	250	350
Depreciation	100	100	100
Profits before Tax	50	150	250
Tax at 50 per cent	25	75	125
Profits after Tax	25	75	125
Project C			
Gross Earnings	350	250	150
Depreciation	100	100	100
Profits before Tax	250	150	50
Tax at 50 per cent	125	75	25
Profits after Tax	125	75	25

(*a*) Calculate:
(i) The 'Payback Period' for each project.
(ii) The 'Rate of Return' (defined for this exercise as the ratio of average profit to average capital) for each project.
(iii) The 'Net Present Value' for each project; with a cost of capital of 10 per cent.
(*b*) If projects A, B and C were mutually exclusive indicate which one you would choose giving your reasons.

24.3. On 1 December 19-1 J. Sanda acquires a building for £26,485, payable 20 per cent down and the balance in twenty equal annual instalments which are to include interest at 7 per cent on a compound annual basis. What equal instalments will have to be paid for the building?

24.4. Machinery can be leased for five years at a rental of £52,760 per annum. The cash price is £200,000. What is the implied interest rate?

24.5. A leasing firm wishes to quote for supplying a machine with a cash cost of £60,000. The period of the lease would be for five years and the rate of interest required 16%.

Assuming five annual rental payments at the end of each year — what amount would each rental need to be?

24.6. A leasing company is leasing a machine which had a cash cost of £60,000 for 5 annual rentals of £18,326 per annum payable at the end of the year. (Refer to question 24.5 for implied rate of interest). Calculate the interest element in each rental payment using a) the annuity method, b) the rule of 78.

24.7A. A man has the choice of investing £8,000 in one of two policies.

Policy 1 yields an income of £2,000 per year for 5 years then £1,000 per year for a further 5 years.

Policy 2 yields an income of £1,600 per year for the 10 years.

If the market rate of interest was 10 per cent what would you advise the man to do?

What would be the effect if the market rate of interest was 20 per cent?

24.8A. A firm has to select between two investment projects, D and G. The relavant information is:

Cash inflows at year end

Project D	Project G
1,500	900
1,800	600
1,500	600
1,200	600
900	300
	300

Project A costs £4,200, all incurred at the beginning of the period.

Project B cost £300 at the beginning of the period, and £300 at the end of each subsequent year. The present return on investment is 15 per cent.

Advise the firm as to which project should be undertaken.

24.9A. The XYZ Co Ltd is considering the replacement of three of its present machines with a single machine which has just come on to the market. Consideration of this proposition has arisen because of the necessity to spend £5,000 on exceptional maintenance on the present machines. The three machines which would be replaced were purchased two years ago for £1,500 each, and are being depreciated over 12 years on a straight-line basis with an estimated final scrap value of £600 each. The current second hand market value of each of the machines is £1,000.

The annual operating costs for each of the existing machines are

	£	£
Material		60,000
Labour – 1 operator at 1,800 hours		1,350
Variable Expenses		925
Maintenance (excluding any exceptional expenditure)		2,000
Fixed Expenses:		
Depreciation	75	
Fixed factory overhead absorbed	2,700	
		2,775

The new machine has an estimated life of 10 years and will cost £100,000 as follows:

	£
Purchase Price (scrap value in 10 years £4,500)	87,000
Installation Costs	13,000

The estimated annual operating costs for all the existing output on the new machine are:

	£	£
Material		162,000
Labour:		
2 operators at 1,500 hours	3,000	
1 operator's assistant at 1,500 hours	900	
		3,900
Variable Expenses		2,275
Maintenance		4,500
Fixed Expenses		
Depreciation	9,550	
Fixed Factory overhead absorbed	7,800	
		17,350

The company's cost of capital is 10 per cent and products are evaluated in rate of return terms. In addition to satisfying the profitability test, projects must also satisfy a financial viability test, in that they must pay for themselves within a maximum period of 5 years.

You are required to:
(a) Advise management on the profitability of this proposal by applying the discounted cash flow – Trial and Error Yield Technique.
(b) Subject the proposal to a financial viability test and
(c) Comment briefly on two other factors that could influence this decision.

Notes:
1. Taxation is to be ignored.
2. Assume that residual value is received on the last day of a machine's working life.

24.10A. A company wishes to decide whether it should buy or lease a new piece of equipment. The cash price is £69,000 and the rentals £25,650 per annum for the expected life of four years. Assuming the company's cost of capital were 10% should it lease or buy − ignoring taxation.

24.11A. If a finance company leases equipment which has a cash price of £69,000 for four annual rentals of £25,650 how should it allocate the finance charge using *a*) Rule of 78, *b*) the annuity method. (Refer to question 24.10A for the implied interest).

25

Statements of Standard Accounting Practice

Introduction

The external users of accounts need to be able to be sure that reliance can be placed by them on the methods used by a business in calculating its profits and balance sheet values. In the late 1960's there was a general outcry that the standards used by different businesses were showing vastly different profits on similar data. In the U.K. a controversy had arisen following the takeover of AEI Ltd by GEC Ltd. In fighting the takeover bid made by GEC, the AEI directors had produced a forecast, in the 10th month of their financial year, that the profit before tax for the year would be £10 million. After the takeover the accounts of AEI for that same year showed a loss of £4½ million. The difference was attributed to being £5 million as 'matters substantially of fact' and £9½ million to 'adjustments which remain matters substantially of judgement'.

There was a general outcry in the financial pages of the national press against the failure of the accounting profession to lay down consistent principles for businesses to follow.

In December 1969 the Institute of Chartered Accountants in England and Wages issued a 'Statement of Intent in Accounting Standards in the 1970's.' The council of the institute then laid down a five point plant to advance accounting standards. Since then the other main accountancy bodies have joined with the institute in helping to produce standards.

Prior to the issuing of any standard a great deal of preparatory work is done which culminates in the publication of an Exposure Draft (ED). Copies of the exposure draft are then sent to those with a special interest in the topic. The accountancy journals also give full details of the exposure drafts. After full and proper consultation, when it is seen to be desirable, an accounting standard on the topic may then be issued.

There is however no general law compelling people to observe the standards. The only method of ensuring compliance with the standards is through the professional bodies using their own disciplinary procedures on their members.

This book deals with the main outlines of all SSAP's issued to the date that the book was written. It does not deal with all the many detailed points contained in the SSAP's and ED's. It would be a far larger book if this was attempted. Students at the later stages of their professional examinations will need to get full copies of all the SSAP's and study them thoroughly.

This chapter now deals with all of the existing SSAP's which are not specifically dealt with elsewhere.

International Accounting Standards

The International Accounting Standards Committee (IASC) was established in 1973. Representatives from each of the founder members, which includes the UK, sit on the committee as well as co-opted members from other countries.

The need for an IASC has been said to be mainly:

(i)   The considerable growth in international investment. This means that it is desirable to have similar methods the world over so that investment decisions are acided.

(ii) The growth in multi-national firms. These firms have to produce accounts covering a large number of countries. Standardisation between countries makes the accounting work that much easier and reduces costs.

(iii) As quite a few countries now have their own standard setting bodies it is desirable that their efforts should be harmonised.

(iv) For poor countries which cannot afford to have standard setting bodies, the IASC can help them by letting them use the international standards instead of setting their own standards.

In the United Kingdom the SSAP's have precedence over International Accounting Standards. In fact most of the provisions of International Accounting Standards are incorporated in existing SSAP's.

Disclosure of Accounting Policies (SSAP 2)

SSAP 2 simply states that the fundamental accounting concepts, accounting bases and accounting policies should normally be observed. These were covered in chapter 10 of volume one. In any case where they are not observed, then SSAP 2 states that the accounts should give adequate details of the variation from normal procedures.

Accounting for Value Added Tax (SSAP 5)

All that needs to be noted here is that chapter 18, volume one of this book, fully complies with SSAP 5. There is no need here to go into further detail.

Extraordinary Items and Prior Year Adjustments (SSAP 6)

Normal trading profit or loss has always had to be taken into the profit and loss account. However, previous to SSAP 6, there had always been the possibility that 'extraordinary' items affecting profit and loss could avoid the profit and loss account and be carried direct to reserves. In this way they would not be exposed to the view of the readers of the accounts. SSAP 6 seeks to remedy this deficiency. All extraordinary items, with certain specified exceptions, now have to go through the Profit and Loss Account.

In addition prior year adjustments, before this SSAP, were often dealt with by adjusting the Reserves. These now have to pass through the Profit and Loss Account and their nature and size disclosed.

Extraordinary items, for the purposes of this statement, are those items which derive from events or transactions outside the ordinary activities of the business and which are both material and expected not to recur frequently or regularly. They do not include items which, though exceptional on account of size and incidence (and which may therefore require separate disclosure), derive from the ordinary activities of the business. Neither do they include prior year items merely because they relate to a prior year.

Extraordinary items derive from events outside the ordinary activities of the business; they do not include items of abnormal size and incidence which derive from the ordinary activities of the business. The classification of items as extraordinary will depend on the particular circumstances − what is extraordinary in one business will not necessarily be extraordinary in another. Subject to this, examples of extraordinary items could be the profits or losses arising from the following:

(*a*) the discontinuance of a significant part of a business;
(*b*) the sale of an investment not acquired with the intention of resale;
(*c*) writing off intangibles, including goodwill, because of unusual events or developments during the period; and
(*d*) the expropriation of assets.

Prior year adjustments, that is prior year items which should be adjusted against the opening balance of retained profits or reserves, are rare and limited to items arising from changes in accounting policies and from the correction of fundamental errors. They are discussed in the paragraphs that follow. The majority of prior year items however should be dealt with in the profit and loss account of the year in which they are recognised and shown separately if material. They arise mainly from the corrections and adjustments which are the natural result of estimates inherent in accounting and more particularly in the periodic preparation of financial statements. Estimating future events and their effects requires the exercise of judgement and will require reappraisal as new events occur, as more experience is acquired or as additional information is obtained. Since a change in estimate arises from new information or developments it should not be given retrospective effect by a restatement of prior years. Sometimes a change in estimate may have the appearance of a change in accounting policy and care is necessary in order to avoid confusing the two. For example, the future benefits of a cost may have become doubtful and a change may be made from amortising the cost over the period of those benefits to writing it off when incurred. Such a change should be treated as a change in estimate and not as a change in accounting policy. Prior year items are not extraordinary merely because they relate to a prior year; their nature will determine their classification.

Accounting for Research and Development (SSAP 13)

SSAP 13 is concerned with this topic. It divides research and development expenditure under three headings:

(a) Pure (or basic) research: original investigation undertaken in order to gain new scientific or technical knowledge and understanding. Basic research is not primarily directed towards any specific practical aim or application;

(b) Applied research: original investigation undertaken in order to gain new scientific or technical knowledge and directed towards a specific practical aim or objective;

(c) Development: the use of scientific or technical knowledge in order to produce new or substantially improved materials, devices, products, processes, systems or services prior to the commencement of commercial production.

Expenditure incurred on pure and applied research can be regarded as part of a continuing operation required to maintain a company's business and its competitive position. In general, one particular period rather than another will not be expected to benefit and therefore it is appropriate that these costs should be written off as they are incurred.

The development of new and improved products is, however, distinguishable from pure and applied research. Expenditure on such development is normally undertaken with a reasonable expectation of specific commercial success and of future benefits arising from the work, either from increased revenue and related profis or from reduced costs. On these grounds it may be argued that such expenditure should be deferred to be matched against the future revenue.

It will only be practicable to evaluate the potential future benefits of development expenditure if:

(a) there is a clearly defined project: and

(b) the related expenditure is separately identifiable.

(1)

The outcome of such a project would then need to be examined for:

(a) its technical feasibility; and

(b) its ultimate commercial viability considered in the light of factors such as: \) (2)

    (i) likely market conditions (including competing products);

    (ii) public opinion;

    (iii) consumer and environmental legislation.

Furthermore a project will only be of value:

(a) if further development costs to be incurred on the same project together with related production, selling and administration costs will be more than covered by related future revenues; and \) (3)

(b) adequate resources exist, or are reasonably expected to be available, to enable the project to be completed and to provide any consequential increases in working capital.

The elements of uncertainty inherent in the considerations set out in paragraphs marked as (1) and (2) are considerable. There will be a need for different persons having differing levels of judgement to be involved in assessing the technical, commercial and financial viability of the project. Combinations of the possible different assessments which they might validly make can produce widely differing assessments of the existence and amounts of future benefits.

If these uncertainties are viewed in the context of the concept of prudence, the future benefits of most development projects would be too uncertain to justify carrying the expenditure forward. Nevertheless, in certain industries it is considered that there are numbers of major development projects that satisfy the stringent criteria set out in paragraphs (1) (2) and (3). Accordingly, where expenditure on development projects is judged on a prudent view of available evidence to satisfy these criteria, it may be carried forward and amortised over the period expected to benefit.

At each accounting date the unamortised balance of development expenditure should be examined project by project to ensure that it still fulfils the criteria in paragraphs (1) (2) and (3). Where any doubt exists as to the continuation of those circumstances the balance should be written off.

Fixed assets may be acquired or constructed in order to provide facilities for research and/or development activities. The use of such fixed assets will usually extend over a number of accounting periods and accordingly they should be capitalised and written off over their usual life.

Since the appearance of SSAP 13 in December 1977 the treatment of Research and Development Costs has been brought into law. The Companies Act 1981 specifically states that costs of research cannot be treated as assets. As far as development costs are concerned, the 1981 Act states:

In any amount is included in a company's balance sheet in respect of development costs the following information shall be given in a note to the accounts –

(a) the period over which the amount of those costs originally capitalised is being or is to be written off; and

(b) the reasons for capitalising the development costs in question.

Accounting for Post-Balance Sheet Events (SSAP 17)

Quite often there will be events occurring after a balance sheet date which will provide evidence of the value of assets, or of the amounts of liabilities, as at the balance sheet date. Obviously any event up to the balance sheet date will have affected the balance sheet. Then, once the board of directors have formally approved the accounts it becomes impossible to alter the accounts. However, there is the period between the balance sheet during which events may throw some light upon the valuation of assets or amounts of liabilities. SSAP 17 directs is attention to such events during this period.

SSAP 17 brings in two new terms – 'adjusting events' and 'non-adjusting events'.

Adjusting Events

These are events which provide additional evidence relating to conditions existing at the balance sheet date. They require changes in amounts to be included in financial statements. Examples of adjusting events are now given:

(a) *Fixed assets.* The subsequent determination of the purchase price or of the proceeds of sale of assets purchased or sold before the year end.

(b) *Property.* A valuation which provides evidence of a permanent diminution in value.

(c) *Investments.* The receipt of a copy of the financial statements or other information in respect of an unlisted company which provides evidence of a permanent diminution in the value of a long-term investment.

(d) *Stocks and work in progress.*

    (i) The receipt of proceeds of sales after the balance sheet date or other evidence concerning the net realisable value of stocks.

    (ii) The receipt of evidence that the previous estimate of accrued profit on a long-term contract was materially inaccurate.

(e) *Debtors.* The renegotiation of amounts owing by debtors, or the insolvency of a debtor.

(f) *Dividends receivable.* The declaration of dividends by subsidiaries and associated companies relating to periods prior to the balance sheet date of the holding company.

(g) *Taxation.* The receipt of information regarding rates of taxation.

(h) *Claims.* Amounts received or receivable in respect of insurance claims which were in the course of renegotiation at the balance sheet date.

(i) *Discoveries.* The discovery of errors or frauds which show the that the financial statements were incorrect.

Non-Adjusting Events

These are events which arise after the balance sheet date and concern conditions which did not exist at that time. Consequently they do not result in changes in amounts in financial statements. They may, however, be of such materiality that their disclosure is required by way of notes to ensure that financial statements are not misleading. Examples of non-adjusting events which may require disclosure are now given:

(a) *Mergers* and acquisitions.

(b) *Reconstructions* and proposed reconstructions.

(c) *Issues* of shares and debentures.

(d) *Purchases and sales of fixed assets* and investments.

(e) *Loss of fixed assets* or stocks as a result of a catastrophe such as fire or flood.

(f) *Opening new trading activities* or extending existing trading activities.

(g) *Closing a significant part of the trading activities* if this was not anticipated at the year end.

(h) *Decline in the value* of property and investments held as fixed assets, if it can be demonstrated that the decline occurred after the year end.

(i) *Changes in rates of foreign exchange.*

(j) *Government action,* such as nationalisation.

(k) *Strikes* and other labour disputes.

(l) *Augmentation of pension benefits.*

Accounting for Contingencies (SSAP 18)

The definition given in SSAP 18 is 'Contingency is a condition which exists at the balance sheet date, where the outcome will be confirmed only on the occurrence or non-occurrence of one or more uncertain future events. A contingent gain or loss is a gain or loss dependent on a contingency'.

The over-riding concern is the concept of prudence. Quite simply, if one is in doubt then contingent losses must be taken into account but contingent gains are left out. If there is a material contingent loss then it should be accrued if it can be estimated with reasonable accuracy. Otherwise it should be disclosed by way of notes to the accounts.

Accounting for Investment Properties (SSAP 19)

Under the accounting requirements of SSAP 12 'Accounting for depreciation', fixed assets are generally subject to annual depreciation charges to reflect on a systematic basis the wearing out, consumption or other loss of value whether arising from use, effluxion of time or obsolescence through technology and market changes. Under those requirements it is also accepted that an increase in the value of such a fixed asset does not generally remove the necessity to charge depreciation to reflect on a systematic basis the consumption of the asset.

A different treatment is, however, required where a significant proportion of the fixed assets of an enterprise is held not for consumption in the business operations but as investments, the disposal of which would not materially affect any manufacturing or trading operations of the enterprise. In such a case the current value of these investments, and changes in that current value, are of prime importance rather than a calculation of systematic annual depreciation. Consequently, for the proper appreciation of the financial position, a different accounting treatment is considered appropriate for fixed assets held as investments (called in this standard 'investment properties').

Investment properties may be held by a company which holds investments as part of its business such as an investment trust or a property investment company.

Investment properties may also be held by a company whose main business is not the holding of investments.

Where an investment property is held on a lease with a relatively short unexpired term, it is necessary to recognise the annual depreciation in the financial statements to avoid the situation whereby a short lease is amortised against the investment revaluation reserve whilst the rentals are taken to the profit and loss account.

This statement requires investment properties to be included in the balance sheet at open market value. The statement does not require the valuation to be made by qualified or independent valuers; but calls for disclosure of the names or qualifications of the valuers, the bases used by them and whether the person making the valuation is an employee or officer of the company. However, where investment properties represent a substantial proportion of the total assets of a major enterprise (e.g. a listed company) the valuation thereof would normally be carried out:

(a) annually by persons holding a recognised professional qualification and having recent post-qualification experience in the location and category of the properties concerned; and

(b) at least every five years by an external valuer.

26

Budgeting and Budgetary Control

Part One: An Introduction

It can be stated that management control is needed to try to ensure that the organisation achieves its objectives. Once the objectives have been agreed, plans should be drawn up so that the progress of the firm can be directed towards the ends specified in the objectives. Now it must not be thought that plans can be expressed only in accounting terms, for example quality of the product might be best shown in engineering terms, or social objectives shown in a plan concerned with employee welfare. But some of the objectives, such as the attainment of a desired profit, or of the attainment of a desired growth in assets can be expressed in accounting terms. When a plan is expressed quantitively it is known as a ''budget'' and the process of converting plans into budgets is known as ''budgeting''. In this book we are concerned primarily with budgets shown in monetary terms, i.e. financial budgets.

The budgeting process may be quite formal in a large organisation with committees set up to perform the task. On the other hand in a very small firm the owner may jot down his budget on a piece of scrap paper or even on the back of a used envelope. Some even manage without writing anything down at all, they have done the budgets in their heads and can easily remember them. This book is concerned with budgeting in a formal manner.

Budgets and People

Probably in no other part of accounting is there a greater need for understanding other people than in the processes of budgeting. Budgets are prepared to try to guide the firm towards its objectives. There is no doubt that some budgets that are drawn up are even more harmful to a firm than if none were drawn up at all.

Budgets are drawn up for control purposes, that is an attempt to control the direction that the firm is taking. Many people, however, look upon them, not as a guide, but as a straightjacket. We can look at a few undesirable actions that can result from people regarding budgets as a straightjacket rather than as a guide.

(a) The sales manager refuses to let a salesman go to Sweden in response to an urgent and unexpected request from a Swedish firm. The reason — the overseas sales expenses budget has already been spent. The result — the most profitable order that the firm would have received for many years is taken up instead by another firm.

(b) The works manager turns down requests for overtime work, because the budgeted overtime has already been exceeded. The result — the job is not completed on time, and the firm has to pay a large sum under a penalty clause in the contract for the job which stated that if the job was not finished by a certain date then a penalty of £20,000 would become payable.

(c) Towards the end of the accounting year a manager realises that he has not spent all of his budget for a particular item. He then launches on a spending spree, completely unnecessary items being bought, on the basis that "If I don't spend this amount this year they will cut down next year when I will really need the money." The result: a lot of unusable and unnecessary equipment.

(d) The education budget has been spent, therefore the education manager will not let anyone go on courses for the rest of the year. The result: the firm starts to fall behind in an industry which is highly technical, the staff concerned become fed up, and the better ones start to look for jobs in other firms which are more responsive to the need to allow personnel to keep in touch with changing technology.

Studies have shown that the more that managers are brought into the budgeting process, then the more successful budgetary control is likely to be. A manager on whom a budget is imposed, rather than a manager who had an active part in the drafting of his budget, is more likely to pay less attention to the budget and use it unwisely in the control process.

Having sounded the warning that needs to be borne in mind constantly when budgeting, we can now look at the positive end of budgeting — to see the advantages of a good budgetary control system.

Budgets and Profit Planning

The methodology of budgetary control is probably accountancy's major contribution to management. Before we get down to the mechanics of constructing budgets we should first of all look at the main outlines of drafting budgets.

When the budgets are being drawn up the two main objectives must be uppermost in the mind of top management, that is that the budgets are for:

(a) Planning. This means a properly co-ordinated and comprehensive plan for the whole business. Each part must interlock with the other parts.

(*b*) Control. Just because a plan is set down on paper does not mean that the plan will carry itself out. Control is exercised via the budgets, thus the name budgetary control. To do this means that the responsibility of managers and budgets must be so linked that the responsible manager is given a guide to help him to produce certain desired results, and the actual achieved results can be compared against the expected, i.e. actual compared with budget.

Preparation of Estimates

The first thing to establish is what the limiting factors are in a firm. It may well be the fact that sales cannot be pushed above a certain amount, otherwise it might be the fact that the firm could sell as much as it can produce, but the productive capacity of the firm sets a limit. Whatever the limiting factor is, there is no doubt that this aspect of the firm will need more attention than probably any other. There would not, for instance, be much point in budgeting for the sale of 1,000 units a year if production could not manufacture more than 700, or to manufacture 2,000 a year if only 1,300 of them could be sold.

There is no doubt that usually the most difficult estimate to make is that of sales revenue. This can be done by using one of two methods:

(i) Make a statistical forecast on the basis of the economic situation conditions applying reference to the goods sold by the company, and what is known about the actions of competitors.

(ii) The opposite is to make an internal forecast. This is usually done by asking each salesman, or group of salesmen, to estimate the sales in their own areas, and then total the estimates. Sometimes the salesmen are not asked at all.

Now we should remember that much of the subject matter that you have read about, or are currently reading in Economics, is very relevant here. A knowledge of elasticity of demand, whether the product is a complementary product, e.g. the price of egg-cups is linked to the demand for eggs, whether it is a substitute, e.g. that a rise in the price of butter may induce housewives to turn to other commodities instead, is very relevant in this area. Factors such as whether the firm has a monopoly, whether the firm has many small customers, a few large customers, or even one large customer, are of crucial importance. Estimating sales revenue is very much a matter of taking all the economic factors into account allied to other factors.

The sales budget is, however, more than just a sales forecast. Budgets should show the actions that management is taking to influence future events. If an increase in sales is desired the sales budget may show extra sales, which may well be an indication of the action that management is going to take by means of extra television advertising, making a better product, or to give retailers better profit margins and push up sales in that way.

The Production Budget

The production budget stems from the sales budget, but the first question that has to be settled is that of the level of the stock of finished goods which will be held by the firm.

If sales are even over the year, then production can also be in keeping with the sales figure, and the stock figure can remain constant. Suppose that the firm sells 50 units every month, then the firm can produce 50 units per month. In almost every firm, a stock level will have to be maintained, the amount of stock will be dependent on factors such as amount of storage space, the estimated amount needed to cater for breakdowns in production or for delays in receiving raw materials etc. Nonetheless, if the stock level was to be a minimum of 70 units it would still mean that production was at the rate of 50 units per month.

On the other hand sales may not be constant. Sales may average 50 units per month, but the figures may well be as follows:

January	20 units	February	30 units	March	60 units
April	80 units	May	70 units	June	40 units

This would mean that if production levels were kept at 50 units per month the stock levels would usually have to be more than 100 units, whilst if the stock levels were to be kept at 100 units minimum the production figures each month would equal the sales figures. We can now compare the two levels of production.

(a) Even Production Flow

The problem here is to find the stock level that the firm would need on 1st January if (i) sales are as shown, (ii) the stock must not fall below 100 units, (iii) production is to be 50 per units per month. It can be found by trial and error. For instance, if you decided to see that would happen if the firm started off with 100 units in stock at 1st January you would find that, after adding production and deducting sales each month, the stock level would fall to 90 units in May. As 100 units of stock is the minimum needed you would need to start off on 1st January with 110 units. The method is that if you start off your calculation with an estimated figure of stock, which must at least be the minimum figure required, then if you find that the lowest figure of stock shown during the period is 10 units less than the minimum stock required, go back and add 10 units to the stock to be held on 1st January. If the lowest figure is 30 units less than required add 30 units to the 1st January stock, and so on. We can now look at the figures in Exhibit 26.1.

Exhibit 26.1

UNITS	January	February	March	April	May	June
Opening Stock	110	140	160	150	120	100
Add Units Produced	50	50	50	50	50	50
	160	190	210	200	170	150
Less Sales	20	30	60	80	70	40
Closing Stock	140	160	150	120	100	110

Before we look at the implications of maintaining an even production flow we can look at another example. Try and work it out for yourself before looking at the answer in Exhibit 26.2. The Sales are expected to be January 70, February 40, March 50, April 120, May 140 and June 70. The stock level must not fall below 120 units and an even production flow of 80 units is required. What stock level would there have to be on 1st January?

Exhibits 26.2

UNITS	January	February	March	April	May	June
Opening Stock	140	150	190	220	180	120
Add Units Produced	80	80	80	80	80	80
	220	230	270	300	260	200
Less Sales	70	40	50	120	140	70
Closing Stock	150	190	220	180	120	130

It is more important in many firms to ensure a smooth production flow than to bother unduly about stock levels, assuming that the minimum stock level is always attained. If the work is skilled then that type of labour force may take several years to become trained, and skilled labour in many industries does not take kindly to being sacked and re-employed as the demand for the goods fluctuates. This is not always true with skilled labour, for instance in the building industry such craftsmen as bricklayers may go to a builder until he has completed a contract such as building a college, a hospital, or a housing estate, and then leave and go to another employer on the completion of the job.

On the other hand, a skilled engineer concerned with the manufacturer of say, diesel engines, would not expect to be fired and re-employed continuously. The bricklayer has a skill that is easily transferable to many other building employers in an area, whereas the diesel engineer may have only one firm within fifty miles of his home where he can perform his skills properly. A man employed as labourer might work on a building site in one part of a year and then transfer as a labourer to an engineering factory as a labourer in another part of the year. Whether a firm could carry on production with widely uneven production levels depends so much on the type of firm and the type of labour involved. A firm would only sack skilled labour which it needed again shortly if it could persuade the men or women to come back when required. If the people who had been sacked were likely to find other employment, and not return to the firm when required, then this would mean that the firm would probably keep them on its payroll and production would continue and stocks of finished goods would begin to pile up. Many firms do in fact realise their social obligations by only laying off workers when no other alternative is at all reasonable. In many organisations there are probably more workers from time to time than the firm actually needs — this is known as "organisational slack", so that there is a leeway between the increasing of production and having to take on extra workers.

(b) Uneven Production Levels

Some firms by their very nature will have uneven production levels, and this will be accepted by their labour force. An ice-cream firm would find sales at the highest levels in summer, tailing off in winter. It is not really possible to build up stocks of ice-cream very much in the winter for summer sales! Even if it could be done technically, the costs of refrigerating large quantities of ice-cream for several months could hardly be economic. The large labour force used in the summer months will probably include quite a few students occupying their vacation periods profitably, and not able anyway to work at the job all the year round even if they wanted to. Such a kind of firm will normally have a far greater relationship between current stock levels and current sales than a firm which has even production levels.

The calculation of the quantity to be produced is then:

Opening Stock + Units Produced − Sales = Closing Stock

This means that if the opening stock will be 80 units, the sales are expected to be 100 units and the desired closing is 50 units it becomes:

	units
Opening Stock	80
Add Production	?
Less Sales	100
Closing Stock	50

Production will, therefore, be the missing figure, i.e. 70 units (80 + Production 70 = 150 for sale less actually sold 100 = closing stock 50).

Exhibit 26.3 shows the units to be produced if the following information is known — Stock required 1st January 40, at end of each month, January 60, February 110, March 170, April 100, May 60, June 20. Sales are expected to be January 100, February 150, March 110, April 190, May 70, June 50.

Exhibit 26.3

UNITS	January	February	March	April	May	June
Opening Stock	40	60	110	170	100	60
Production required(?)	120	200	170	120	30	10
	160	260	280	290	130	70
Less Sales	100	150	110	190	70	50
Closing Stock	60	110	170	100	60	20

Linked with the production budget will be a materials purchase budget. It may well be that an order will have to be placed in January, received in March and issued to production in April. The purchase of materials will have to be planned as scientifically as possible.

Exercises

26.1. What would the production levels have to be for each month if the following data was available:

Units	19-5	Jan.	Feb.	March	April	May	June
(i)	Stock levels wanted at the end of each month	690	780	1,100	1,400	1,160	940
(ii)	Expected sales each month	800	920	1,090	1,320	1,480	1,020
(iii)	The stock level at 1 January, 19-5 will be 740 units.						

26.2. For the year ended 31 December, 19-9 the sales of units are expected to be:

January	110	July	70
February	180	August	30
March	170	September	170
April	150	October	110
May	120	November	150
June	100	December	190

The opening stock at 1 January 19-9 will be 140 units. The closing stock desired at 31 December, 19-9 is 150 units.

(a) What will production be per month if an even production flow is required and stock levels during the year could be allowed to fall to zero?

(b) Given the same information plus the constraint that stock levels must never fall below 80 units, and that extra production will be undertaken in January 19-9 to ensure this, what will be the January production figure?

26.3. What stock should be held by a firm on 1 January 19-7 if the following data is available:

Units	19-7	Jan.	Feb.	Mar.	April	May	June
(i)	Sales expected to be	160	190	300	180	110	290
(ii)	Production expected to be	200	220	240	260	280	300
(iii)	Desired stock level at 30 June, 19-7 is 430 units.						

26.4A. For the year ended 31 December, 19-6 the sales of units are expected to be:

January	70	July	20
February	90	August	30
March	60	September	60
April	40	October	70
May	30	November	90
June	20	December	50

The opening stock at 1 January, 19-6 will be 120 units. The closing stock desired at 31 December, 19-6 is 150 units.

(a) What will production be per month if an even production flow is required and stock levels during the year could be allowed to fall to zero?

(b) Given the same information plus the constraint that stock levels must never fall below 110 units, and that extra production will be undertaken in January 19-6 to ensure this, what will the January production figure be?

26.5A. A firm wants to maintain an even production flow for the first six months of 19-4 followed by an even production flow of 20 units per month greater for the last six months of 19-4.

Opening stock of units at 1 January, 19-4 are	50
Closing stock of units wanted at 31 December, 19-4	120
Sales of units during the year	650

How many units should be manufactured per month (a) January to June 19-4, (b) July to December 19-4?

26.6A. What stock should be held by a firm on 1 July, 19-7 if the following data is available:

Units	19-7	July	Aug.	Sept.	Oct.	Nov.	Dec.
(i)	Sales expected to be	100	140	180	270	190	130
(ii)	Production expected to be	160	200	220	250	210	180

(iii) Desired stock level at 31 December, 19-7 is 320 units.

Part Two: Cash Budgets

It is no use budgeting for production and for sales if sometime during the budget period the firm runs out of cash funds. When talking about cash in budgets we are also usually including bank funds, and therefore in this book we will not be differentiating between cash and cheque payments or between cash and cheques received. Cash is, therefore, also budgeted for, so that any shortage of cash can be known in advance and action taken to obtain permission for a loan or a bank overdraft to be available then, rather than wait until the shortage or deficiency occurs. Bank managers, or anyone concerned with the lending of money, certainly resent most strongly one of their customers needing a bank overdraft without prior warning, when in fact the customer could have known if he had drawn up a cash budget in advance which revealed the need for cash funds on a particular date.

The finance needed may not just be by way of borrowing from a bank or finance house, it may well be a long-term need that can only be satisfied by an issue of shares or debentures. Such issues need planning well in advance, and a cash budget can reveal (a) that they will be needed (b) how much is needed and (c) when it will be needed.

We can now look at a very simple case. Without being concerned in this first exhibit with exactly what the receipts and payments are for, just to keep matters simple at this stage, we can see the dangers that are inherent in not budgeting for cash.

Exhibit 26.4

Mr. Muddlem had a meeting with his accountant on 1st July, 19x3. He was feeling very pleased with himself. He had managed to get some very good orders from customers, mainly because he was now allowing them extra time in which to pay their accounts. Sprite, the accountant, said, "Can you afford to do all that you are hoping to do?"

Muddlem laughed, "Why, I'll be making so much money I won't know how to spend it."

"But have you got the cash to finance everything?" asked Sprite.

"If I'm making a good profit then of course I'll have the cash," said Muddlem. "I know the bank manager says that any bank overdraft could not be more than £1,000, but I doubt if I need it."

"Don't let us rely on guesses," says Sprite. "Let's work it out."

After an hour's work the following facts emerge.

(a) Present cash balance (including bank balance) £800.

(b) Receipts from debtors will be: July £2,000, August £2,600, September £5,000, October £7,000, November £8,000, December £15,000.

(c) Payments will be: July £2,500, August £2,700, September £6,900, October £7,800, November £9,900, December £10,300.

This is then summarised:

	July £	August £	Sept. £	Oct. £	Nov. £	Dec. £
Balance at start of the month:	+800	+300	+200			
Deficit at the start of the month:				-1,700	-2,500	-4,400
Receipts	2,000	2,600	5,000	7,000	8,000	15,000
	2,800	2,900	5,200	5,300	5,500	10,600
Payments	2,500	2,700	6,900	7,800	9,900	10,300
Balance at end of the month:	+300	+200				+300
Deficit at the end of the month:			-1,700	-2,500	-4,400	

"I'm in an awkward position now," says Muddlem. "I just cannot borrow £4,400 nor can I cut down on my sales, and anyway I don't really want to as these new sales are very profitable indeed. If only I'd known this, I could have borrowed the money from my brother only last week but he's invested it elsewhere now."

"Come and see me tomorrow," says Sprite. "There may well be something we can do."

Fortunately for Muddlem his luck was in. He arrived to see his accountant the following morning waving a cheque. "My wife won £5,000 on a jackpot bingo last night," he said.

"Thank goodness for that, at least in future you'll learn to budget ahead for cash requirements. You can't be lucky all the time," says Sprite.

Timing of Cash Receipts and Payments

In drawing up a cash budget it must be borne in mind that all the payments for units produced would very rarely be at the same time as production itself. For instance the raw materials might be bought in March, incorporated in the goods being produced in April, and paid for in May. On the other hand the raw materials may have been in hand for some time, so that the goods are bought in January, paid for in February, and used in production the following August. Contrary to this, the direct labour part of the product is usually paid for almost at the same time as the unit being produced. Even here a unit may be produced in one week and the wages paid one week later, so that a unit might be produced on say 27th June and the wages for the direct labour involved paid for on 3rd July.

Similarly the date of sales and the date of receipt of cash will not usually be at the same time, except in many retail stores. The goods might be sold in May and the money received in August, or even paid for in advance so that the goods might be paid for in February but the goods not shipped to the buyer until May. This is especially true, at least for part of the goods when a cash deposit is left for specially made goods which will take sometime to manufacture. A simple example of this would be a made-to-measure suit on which a deposit would be paid at the time of order, the final payment being made when the completed suit is collected by the buyer.

Exhibit 26.5

A cash budget for the six months ended 30th June, 19x3 is to be drafted from the following information.
(*a*) Opening cash balance at 1st January, 19x3 £3,200.
(*b*) Sales; at £12 per unit: cash received three months after sale.

Units: 19-2			19-3								
Oct.	Nov.	Dec.	Jan.	Feb.	Mar.	April	May	June	July	Aug.	Sept.
80	90	70	100	60	120	150	140	130	110	100	160

(*c*) Production: in units.

19-2			19-3								
Oct.	*Nov.*	*Dec.*	*Jan.*	*Feb.*	*Mar.*	*April*	*May*	*June*	*July*	*Aug.*	*Sept.*
70	80	90	100	110	130	140	150	120	160	170	180

(*d*) Raw Materials used in production costs £4 per unit of production. They are paid for two months before being used in production.

(*e*) Direct Labour. £3 per unit paid for in the same month as the unit produced.

(*f*) Other variable expenses, £2 per unit, ¾ of the cost being paid for in the same month as production, the other ¼ paid in the month after production.

(*g*) Fixed Expenses of £100 per month are paid monthly.

(*h*) A Motor Van is to be bought and paid for in April for £800.

Schedules of payments and receipts are as follows:

PAYMENTS: (The month shown in brackets is the month in which the units are produced)

January	£	February	£
Raw Materials: 130 (March) × £4	520	140 (April) × £4	560
Direct Labour: 100 (January) × £3	300	110 (February) × £3	330
Variable: 100 (January) × ¾ × £2	150	110 (February) × ¾ × £2	165
90 (December) × ¼ × £2	45	100 (January) × ¼ × £2	50
Fixed:	100		100
	£1,115		**£1,205**

March	£	April	£
Raw Materials: 150 (May) × £4	600	120 (June) × £4	480
Direct Labour: 130 (March) × £3	390	140 (April) × £3	420
Variable: 130 (March) × ¾ × £2	195	140 (April) × ¾ × £2	210
110 (February) × ¼ × £2	55	130 (March) × ¼ × £2	65
Fixed:	100		100
Motor Van			800
	£1,340		**£2,075**

May	£	June	£
Raw Materials: 160 (July) × £4	640	170 (August) × £4	680
Direct Labour: 150 (May) × £3	450	120 (June) × £3	360
Variable: 150 (May) × ¾ × £2	225	120 (June) × ¾ × £2	180
140 (April) × ¼ × £2	70	150 (May) × ¼ × £2	75
Fixed:	100		100
	£1,485		**£1,395**

RECEIPTS: (The month shown in brackets is the month in which the sale was made)

			£
January	80 (October)	× £12	960
February	90 (November)	× £12	1,080
March	70 (December)	× £12	840
April	100 (January)	× £12	1,200
May	60 (February)	× £12	720
June	120 (March)	× £12	1,440

CASH BUDGET

	Jan. £	Feb. £	Mar. £	April £	May £	June £
Balance from previous month	3,200	3,045	2,920	2,420	1,545	780
Add Receipts (per schedule)	960	1,080	840	1,200	720	1,440
	4,160	4,125	3,760	3,620	2,265	2,220
Less Payments (per schedule)	1,115	1,205	1,340	2,075	1,485	1,395
Balance carried to next month	3,045	2,920	2,420	1,545	780	825

Exercises

26.7. R. Jeeves seeks your advice. He has exactly £1,000 cash with which to start a business. He has also received permission from a bank manager to have an overdraft of up to £10,000 during his first six months of business starting 1 January 19-8.

His plans for his first six months trading are:

(a) Payments for goods and supplies: January £5,500, February £7,200, March £9,700, April £10,500, May £9,600, June £6,900.

(b) Receipts from debtors will be: January £3,900, February £5,900, March £6,000, April £7,100, May £8,400, June £9,500.

(c) Loan receivable on 1 March £700 to be repaid in full plus £100 interest on 1 June 19-8.

(d) Drawings £300 per calendar month.

You are required to draw up a cash budget, showing the balances each month for the six months to 30 June 19-8. Also make any suitable comments.

26.8. Draw up a cash budget for N. Morris showing the balance at the end of each month, from the following information for the six months ended 31 December 19-2:

(a) Opening Cash (including bank) balance £1,200

(b) Production in units:

19-2									19-3	
April	May	June	July	Aug.	Sept.	Oct.	Nov.	Dec.	Jan.	Feb.
240	270	300	320	350	370	380	340	310	260	250

(c) Raw Materials used in production cost £5 per unit. Of this 80 per cent is paid in the month of production and 20 per cent in the month after production.

(d) Direct Labour costs of £8 per unit are payable in the month of production.

(e) Variable expenses are £2 per unit, payable one-half in the same month as production and one-half in the month following production.

(f) Sales at £20 per unit:

19-2									19-3
Mar.	April	May	June	July	Aug.	Sept.	Oct.	Nov.	Dec.
260	200	320	290	400	300	350	400	390	400

Debtors to pay their accounts three months after that in which sales are made.

(g) Fixed expenses of £400 per month payable each month.

(h) Machinery costing £2,000 to be paid for in October 19-2.

(i) Will receive a legacy £2,500 in December 19-2.

(j) Drawings to be £300 per month.

26.9A. B. Ukridge comes to see you in April 19-3. He is full of enthusiasm for a new product that he is about to launch on to the market. Unfortunately his financial recklessness in the past has led him into being bankrupted twice, and he has only just got discharged by the court from his second bankruptcy.

"Look here laddie," he says, "with my new idea I'll be a wealthy man before Christmas."

"Calm down," you say, "and tell me all about it."

Ukridge's plans as far as cash is concerned for the next six months are:

(a) Present cash balance (including bank) £5.

(b) Timely legacy under a will — being received on 1 May, 19-3, £5,000. This will be paid into the business bank account by Ukridge.

(c) Receipts from debtors will be: May £400, June £4,000, July £8,000, August £12,000, September £9,000, October £5,000.

(d) Payments will be: May £100, June £5,000, July £11,000, August £20,000, September £12,000, October £7,000.

You are required: (i) To draw up a cash budget, showing the balances each month, for the six months to 31 October, 19-3.

(ii) The only person Ukridge could borrow money from would charge interest at the rate of 100 per cent per annum. This is not excessive considering Ukridge's past record. Advise Ukridge.

26.10A. Draw up a cash budget for J. Clarke from the following information for the six months 1 July, 19-9 to 31 December, 19-9.

(a) Opening cash (includes bank) balance 1 July 19-9 £1,500.

(b) Sales at £20 per unit:

	April	May	June	July	Aug.	Sept.	Oct.	Nov.	Dec.
Units	110	120	140	160	180	190	130	80	70

Debtors will pay two months after they have bought the goods.

(c) Production in units:

	April	May	June	July	Aug.	Sept.	Oct.	Nov.	Dec.	Jan.
Units	150	170	180	200	130	110	100	90	70	60

(d) Raw materials cost £6 per unit and are paid for 3 months after the goods are used in production.

(e) Direct labour of £5 per unit is payable in the same month as production.

(f) Other variable expenses are £3 per unit. Two-thirds of this cost is paid for in the same month as production and one-third in the month following production.

(g) Fixed expenses of £150 per month are paid one month in arrears — these expenses have been at this rate for the past two years.

(h) A machine is to be bought and paid for in September for £6,000.

(i) Clarke will borrow £3,000 from a relative in December 19-9. This will be put into the business bank account immediately.

26.11A. Draw up a cash budget for L. Jones, showing clearly the balance at the end of each month, from the following information for the six months ended 30 June, 19-2:

(a) Opening cash (includes bank) balance £800.

(b) Production in units:

19-1			19-2						
Oct.	Nov.	Dec.	Jan.	Feb.	March	April	May	June	July
300	400	460	540	700	640	560	500	420	380

(c) Raw materials used in production cost £3 per unit. Of this one-third is paid one month before production and two-thirds in the same month as production.

(d) Direct labour costs of £5 per unit are payable in the same month as production.

(e) Variable expenses are £4 per unit, payable three-quarters in the same month as production and one-quarter in the month following production.

(f) Sales at £15 per unit:

19-1			19-2					
Oct.	Nov.	Dec.	Jan.	Feb.	Mar.	April	May	June
240	360	480	580	620	720	680	520	360

Debtors to pay their accounts: one-fifth as a deposit in the months of the sale and the remainder two months later.

(g) Fixed expenses are £300 per month payable each month.

(h) Extensions to the premises costing £6,000 are to be paid for in February 19-2.

(i) An income tax refund of £3,700 will be received in June 19-2.

Part Three: Co-ordination of Budgets

The various budgets have to be linked together and a "Master Budget", which is really a budgeted set of Final Accounts drawn up. We have in fact looked at the Sales, Production and Cash Budgets. There are, however, many more budgets for parts of the organization, for instance there may be:

(i) A selling expense budget,

(ii) An administration expense budget,

(iii) A manufacturing overhead budget,

(iv) A direct labour budget,

(v) A purchases budget,

and so on. In this book we do not wish to get entangled in too many details, but in a real firm with a proper set of budgeting techniques there will be a great deal of detailed backing for the figures that are incorporated in the more important budgets.

Now it may be that when all the budgets have been co-ordinated, or slotted together, the Master Budget shows a smaller profit than the directors are prepared to accept. This will mean recasting budgets to see whether a greater profit can be earned, and if at all possible the budgets will be altered. Eventually there will be a Master Budget that the directors can agree to. This then gives the target for the results that the firm hopes to achieve in financial terms. Remember that there are other targets such as employee welfare, quality product etc. that cannot be so expressed.

The rest of this chapter is concerned with the drawing up of budgets for an imaginary firm, Walsh Ltd., culminating in the drawing up of a Master Budget.

To start with we can look at the last Balance Sheet of Walsh Ltd. as at 31st December, 19-4. This will give us our opening figures of stocks of raw materials, stock of finished goods, cash (including bank) balance, creditors, debtors etc.

Walsh Ltd.
Balance Sheet as at 31 December 19-4

		Depreciation	
Fixed Assets	Cost	to date	Net
	£	£	£
Machinery	4,000	1,600	2,400
Motor Vehicles	2,000	800	1,200
	6,000	2,400	3,600

Current Assets

Stocks: Finished Goods (75 units)		900
Raw Materials		500
Debtors (19x4 October £540 + November £360 + December £450)		1,350
Cash and Bank Balances		650
		3,400

Less Current Liabilities

Creditors for Raw Materials (November £120 + December £180)	300	
Creditors for Fixed Expenses (December)	100	400
Working Capital		3,000
		6,600

Financed by:

Share Capital: 4,000 shares £1 each	4,000
Profit & Loss Account	2,600
	6,600

The plans for the six months ended 30th June, 19-5 are as follows:

(i) Production will be 60 units per month for the first four months, followed by 70 units per month for May and June.

(ii) Production costs will be (per unit):

	£
Direct Materials	5
Direct Labour	4
Variable Overhead	3
	£12

(iii) Fixed overhead is £100 per month, payable always one month in arrears.

(iv) Sales, at a price of £18 per unit, are expected to be:

	January	February	March	April	May	June
No. of units	40	50	60	90	90	70

(v) Purchases of direct materials (raw materials) will be:

	January	February	March	April	May	June
	£	£	£	£	£	£
	150	200	250	300	400	320

(vi) The creditors for raw materials bought are paid two months after purchase.

(vii) Debtors are expected to pay their accounts three months after they have bought the goods.

(viii) Direct Labour and variable overhead are paid in the same month as the units are produced.

(ix) A machine costing £2,000 will be bought and paid for in March.

(x) 3,000 shares of £1 each are to be issued at par in May.

(xi) Depreciation for the six months: Machinery £450, Motor Vehicles £200.

We must first of all draw up the various budgets and then incorporate them into the Master Budget. Some of the more detailed budgets which can be dispensed with in this illustration will be omitted.

Materials Budget

	Jan.	Feb.	March	April	May	June
Opening Stock £	500	350	250	200	200	250
Add Purchases £	150	200	250	300	400	320
	650	550	500	500	600	570
Less Used in Production:						
Jan.—April 60 × £5	300	300	300	300		
May and June 70 × £5					350	350
Closing Stock £	350	250	200	200	250	220

Production Budget (in units)

	Jan.	Feb.	March	April	May	June
Opening Stock (units)	75	95	105	105	75	55
Add Produced	60	60	60	60	70	70
	135	155	165	165	145	125
Less Sales	40	50	60	90	90	70
Closing Stock	95	105	105	75	55	55

Production Cost Budget (in £'s)

	Jan.	Feb.	March	April	May	June	Total
Materials Cost £	300	300	300	300	350	350	1,900
Labour Cost £	240	240	240	240	280	280	1,520
Variable Overhead £	180	180	180	180	210	210	1,140
	720	720	720	720	840	840	4,560

Creditors Budget

	Jan.	Feb.	March	April	May	June
Opening Balance £	300	330	350	450	550	700
Add Purchases £	150	200	250	300	400	320
	450	530	600	750	950	1,020
Less Payments £	120	180	150	200	250	300
Closing Balance £	330	350	450	550	700	720

Debtors Budget

	Jan.	Feb.	March	April	May	June
Opening Balances	1,350	1,530	2,070	2,700	3,600	4,320
Add Sales £	720	900	1,080	1,620	1,620	1,260
	2,070	2,430	3,150	4,320	5,220	5,580
Less Received £	540	360	450	720	900	1,080
Closing Balances £	1,530	2,070	2,700	3,600	4,320	4,500

Cash Budget

	Jan.	Feb.	March	April	May	June
Opening Balance £	+650	+550	+210			+1,050
Opening Overdraft £				−2,010	−2,010	
Received (see schedule) £	540	360	450	720	3,900	1,080
	1,190	910	660	1,290	1,890	2,130
Payments (see schedule) £	640	700	2,670	720	840	890
Closing Balance £	+550	+210			+1,050	+1,240
Closing Overdraft £			−2,010	−2,010		

Cash Payments Schedule

	Jan.	Feb.	March	April	May	June
Creditors for goods bought two months previously £	120	180	150	200	250	300
Fixed Overhead £	100	100	100	100	100	100
Direct Labour £	240	240	240	240	280	280
Variable Overhead £	180	180	180	180	210	210
Machinery £			2,000			
£	640	700	2,670	720	840	890

Cash Receipts Schedule

	Jan.	Feb.	March	April	May	June
Debtors for goods sold three months previousl £	540	360	450	720	900	1,080
Shares Issued £					3,000	
					3,900	

Master Budget
Forecast Operating Statement for the Six months ended 30 June 19-5

		£
Sales		7,200
Less Cost of Goods Sold:		
Opening Stock of Finished Goods	900	
Add Cost of Goods Completed	4,560	
	5,460	
Less Closing Stock of Finished Goods	660	4,800
Gross Profit		2,400
Less:		
Fixed Overhead	600	
Depreciation: Machinery	450	
Motors	200	650
		1,250
Net Profit		1,150

Forecast Balance Sheet as at 30 June 19-5

Fixed Assets

	Cost £	Depreciation to date £	Net £
Machinery	6,000	2,050	3,950
Motor Vehicles	2,000	1,000	1,000
	8,000	3,050	4,950

Current Assets

Stocks: Finished Goods	660	
Raw Materials	220	
Debtors	4,500	
Cash and Bank Balances	1,240	
	6,620	
Less Current Liabilities:		
Creditors for Goods	720	
Creditors for Overheads	100	820
Working Capital		5,800
		10,750

Financed By:

Share Capital	7,000
Profit and Loss Account (2,600 + 1,150)	3,750
	10,750

Capital Budgeting

The plan for the acquisition of fixed assets such as machinery, buildings etc. is usually known as a Capital Budget. Management will evaluate the various possibilities open to it, and will compare the alternatives. This is a very important part of budgeting. So far in this book it has been assumed that any capital budgeting has already been done.

Exercises

26.12. D. Smith is to open a retail shop on 1 January, 19-4. He will put in £25,000 cash as Capital. His plans are as follows:

(i)   On 1 January 19-4 to buy an pay for Premises £20,000, Shop Fixtures £3,000, Motor Van £1,000.

(ii) To employ two assistants, each to get a salary of £130 per month, to be paid at the end of each month. (P.A.Y.E. tax, National Insurance contributions etc. are to be ignored.)

(iii) To buy the following goods (shown in units):

	Jan.	Feb.	March	April	May	June
Units	200	220	280	350	400	330

(iv) To sell the following number of units:

	Jan.	Feb.	March	April	May	June
Units	120	180	240	300	390	420

(v)   Units will be sold for £10 each. One-third of the sales are for cash, the other two-thirds being on credit. These latter customers are expected to pay their accounts in the second month following that in which they received the goods.

(vi) The units will cost £6 each for January to April inclusive, and £7 each thereafter. Creditors will be paid in the month following purchase. (Value stock-in-trade on F.I.F.O. basis.)

(vii) The other expenses of the shop will be £150 per month payable in the month following that in which they were incurred.

(viii)Part of the premises will be sub-let as an office at a rent of £600 per annum. This is paid in equal instalments in March, June, September and December.

(ix) Smith's cash drawings will amount to £250 per month.

(x)   Depreciation is to be provided on Shop Fixtures at 10 per cent per annum and on the Motor Van at 20 per cent per annum.
You are required to:

(a) Draw up a Cash Budget for the six months ended 30 June, 19-4, showing the balance of cash at the end of each month.

(b) Draw up a forecast Trading and Profit and Loss Account for the six months ended 30 June 19-4 and a Balance Sheet as at that date.

26.13. Newman and Harris are to form a private limited company in the name of Craft Limited. They tell you that their plans for their first six months of trading for the period 1 January 19-4 to 30 June 19-4 are:

(a) Harris will put £20,000 into the business bank account on 1 January 19-4. He will be issued with 20,000 ordinary shares of £1 each at par.

(b) Newman will put £40,000 into the business bank account on 1 January 19-4. He will then be issued with 32,000 ordinary shares of £1 each at par, and a 7 per cent debenture of £8,000.

(c) Sales, all on credit, will be; January £12,000; February £16,000; March £28,000; April £22,000; May £24,000; June £26,000. All debtors will pay their accounts three months after that in which they buy the goods.

(d) Purchases, all on credit, will be: January £48,000; February £16,000; March £18,000; April £20,000; May £14,000; June £10,000. Creditors will be paid in the month following that in which the goods are bought.

(e) Wages and salaries will be £800 per month, payable on the last day of each month.

(f) Newman and Harris are to be the only directors. They are to be paid directors' remuneration totalling £1,200 per month, payable on the last day of each month.

(g) The first debenture interest will be paid on 31 December 19-4.

(h) Premises costing £30,000 will be occupied on 1 January 19-4 and will be paid for in February 19-4.

(i) All other expenses of £600 per month for the first five months and £840 for June are to be paid in the month following that in which they are incurred.

(j) Equipment will be bought on 1 January 19-4 for £12,000, payment being made of £6,000 in March 19-4 and £6,000 in June 19-4.

(k) Stock-in-Trade at 30 June 19-4 will be £21,800.

(l) Depreciation is to be written off the equipment at the rate of 20 per cent per annum.

You are required to:

(i) Draft a cash budget, showing clearly the bank balance at the end of each month.

(ii) Draft the budgeted Trading and Profit and Loss Account for the six months ended 30 June 19-4 and a Balance Sheet as at that date.

Ignore Taxation.

26.14. The following is a summary of the Trading and Profit and Loss Accounts of Blakes Ltd. for the 6 months to 31 May 19-8, and a Balance Sheet as at that date.

Trading and Profit and Loss Account

Stock	13,600	Sales	72,000
Purchases	55,000	Stock	11,000
Gross Profit	14,400		
	83,000		83,000
Wages and Salaries	5,800	Gross Profit	14,400
Administration expenses	3,600		
Net Profit	5,000		
	14,400		14,400

Balance Sheet

Fixed Assets	9,000	Issued Share Capital	10,000
Stock	11,000	(Ordinary £1 shares)	
Debtors	9,600	Profit and Loss Account	15,070
Bank	5,400	Trade Creditors	9,330
		Administration Expenses	
		outstanding	600
	£35,000		£35,000

At a meeting of the directors the following forward projections for the 6 months to 30 November 19-8 were agreed to:

1. Rate of gross profit to be reduced from 20% to 16⅔% of sales. The period of credit is to be increased from 1 month to 2 months, and it is expected that every customer will pay for the goods 2 months after the date of sale. It is expected that sales will be increased immediately from £12,000 to £18,000 each calendar month.

2. It is assumed that Blakes Ltd. will pay for all purchases 1 month after purchase. The stock is to be increased to £20,000 by the end of November. Purchases each month are of an equal amount.

3. Wages and Salaries will be £1,100 per calendar month payable each month.

4. Administration expenses will be £720 per calendar month, and it is expected that on the last day of each month there will be one month's expenses owing.

5. The firm is to issue 5,000 Ordinary Shares of £1 each in September at a premium of 25p. payable in full on application. The issue is expected to be a success.

6. Further finance is expected to be by bank overdraft. All sums received are to be paid into the bank and all payments made by cheque. No discounts will be received or allowed.

You are required to prepare a summary of the company's bank account for each of the six months, the Trading and Profit and Loss Account for the same period and a summary of the Balance Sheet as at the last day. Depreciate fixed Assets at the rate of 10 per cent per annum.

342

26.15A B. Cooper is going to set up a new business on 1 January, 19-8. He estimates that his first six months in business will be as follows:

(i)   He will put £10,000 into a bank account for the firm on 1 January, 19-8.

(ii)   On 1 January, 19-8 he will buy Machinery £2,000, Motor Vehicles £1,600 and Premises £5,000, paying for them immediately out of the business bank account.

(iii) All purchases will be effected on credit. He will buy £2,000 goods on 1 January and he will pay for these in February. Other purchases will be rest of January £3,200, February, March, April, May and June £4,000 each month. Other than the £2,000 worth bought in January all other purchases will be paid for two months after purchase.

(iv)   Sales (all on credit) will be £4,000 for January and £5,000 for each month after that. Debtors will pay for the goods in the third month after purchase by them.

(v)   Stock-in-trade on 30 June, 19-8 will be £2,000.

(vi)   Wages and Salaries will be £150 per month and will be paid on the last day of each month.

(vii) General Expenses will be £50 per month, payable in the month following that in which they were incurred.

(viii) He will receive a legacy of £5,500 on 21 April, 19-8. This will be paid into the business bank account immediately.

(ix)   Insurance covering the 12 months of 19-8 will be paid for by cheque on 30 June, 19-8, £140.

(x)   Rates will be paid as follows: for the three months to 31 March, 19-8 by cheque on 28 February, 19-8: for the 12 months ended 31 March, 19-9 by cheque on 31 July 19-8. Rates are £360 per annum.

(xi)   He will make drawings of £80 per month by cheque.

(xii) He has substantial investments in public companies. His bank manager will give him any overdraft that he may require.

(xiii) Depreciate Motors 20 per cent per annum, Machinery 10 per cent per annum.

You are required to:

(a)   Draft a cash budget (includes bank) month by month showing clearly the amount of bank balance or overdraft at the end of each month.

(b)   Draft the projected Trading and Profit and Loss Account for the first six month's trading, and a Balance Sheet as at 30 June, 19-8.

26.16A. The balance sheet of Gregg Ltd. at 30 June, 19-6 was expected to be as follows:

Balance Sheet 30 June, 19-6

Fixed Assets	Cost	Depreciation to date	Net
Land and Buildings	40,000	—	40,000
Plant and Machinery	10,000	6,000	4,000
Motor Vehicles	6,000	2,800	3,200
Office Fixtures	500	220	280
	56,500	9,020	47,480

Current Assets		
Stock-in-Trade: Finished Goods	1,800	
Raw Materials	300	
Debtors (19-6 May £990 + June		
£900)	1,890	
Cash and Bank Balances	7,100	11,090
		£58,570
Financed By:		
Share Capital		50,000
Profit and Loss Account		7,820
		57,820
Current Liabilities		
Creditors for Raw Materials		
(April £240 + May £140 + June £160)	540	
Creditors for variable overhead	210	750
		£58,570

The plans for the six months to 31 December 19-6 can be summarised as:

(i) Production costs per unit will be:

	£
Direct Materials	2
Direct Labour	5
Variable overhead	3
	£10

(ii) Sales will be at a price of £18 per unit for the three months to 30 September and at £18.5 subsequently. The number of units sold would be:

	July	Aug.	Sept.	Oct.	Nov.	Dec.
Units	60	80	100	100	90	70

All sales will be on credit, and debtors will pay their accounts two months after they have bought the goods.

(iii) Production will be even at 90 units per month.

(iv) Purchases of direct materials — all on credit — will be:

July	Aug.	Sept.	Oct.	Nov.	Dec.
£	£	£	£	£	£
220	200	160	140	140	180

Creditors for direct materials will be paid three months after purchase.

(v) Direct labour is paid in the same month as production occurs.

(vi) Variable overhead is paid in the month following that in which the units are produced.

(vii) Fixed overhead of £90 per month is paid each month and is never in arrears.

(viii)A machine costing £500 will be bought and paid for in July. A motor vehicle costing £2,000 will be bought and paid for in September.

(ix) A debenture of £5,000 will be issued and the cash received in November. Interest will not start to run until 19-7.

(x) Provide for depreciation for the six months: Motor Vehicles £600, Office Fixtures £30, Machinery £700.

You are required to draw up as a minimum:

(a) Cash Budget, showing figures each month.

(b) Debtors Budget, showing figures each month.

(c) Creditors Budget, showing figures each month.

(d) Raw Materials Budget, showing figures each month.

(e) Forecast Operating Statement for the six months.

(f) Forecast Balance Sheet as at 31 December, 19-6.

In addition you may draw up any further budgets you may wish to show the workings behind the above budgets.

26.17A. The balance sheet of Brahms Ltd. at 31 December, 19-4 was expected to be:

Balance Sheet 31 December, 19-4

Assets Employed:		Depreciation	
Fixed Assets	Cost	to date	Net
Plant and Machinery	20,000	7,000	13,000
Motor Vehicles	8,000	3,000	5,000
Office Equipment	1,000	400	600
	29,000	10,400	18,600
Current Assets			
Stock-in-Trade: Finished Goods		7,600	
Raw Materials		3,600	
Debtors (December)		4,500	
Cash and Bank Balances		700	16,400
			£35,000
Financed By:			
Share Capital			30,000
Profit and Loss Account			1,700
			31,700
Current Liabilities			
Creditors for fixed expenses		300	
Creditors for Raw Materials			
(November £1,400, December £1,600)		3,000	3,300
			£35,000

Plans for the six months ended 30 June, 19-5 are as follows:

(a) Sales will be at a price of £50 per unit. The number of units sold are expected to be:

	Jan.	Feb.	March	April	May	June
Units	80	70	120	150	130	100

All sales will be on credit. Debtors will pay their accounts in the month after purchase.

(b) Production will be at the rate of 100 per month for January, February and March, and 120 per month thereafter.

(c) Production costs per unit will be:

	£
Direct Material	20
Direct Labour	12
Variable overhead	6
	£38

(d) Purchases of direct materials — all on credit — will be:

January	February	March	April	May	June
£2,000	£1,800	£2,200	£2,800	£2,600	£2,400

Creditors for direct materials are paid two months after the goods are bought.

(e) Direct labour and variable overhead are paid in same month as production. Fixed expenses of £300 per month are paid one month after expenses incurred.

(f) Fixed expenses of £300 per month are paid one month in arrears.

(g) A machine costing £4,000 will be bought and paid for in February.

(h) Provide for depreciation for the 6 months: Plant and Machinery £1,400: Motor Vehicles £800, Office Equipment £50.

You are required to draw up as a minimum:

(i) Cash budget, showing figures for each month.

(ii) Debtors budget, showing figures each month.

(iii) Creditors budget, showing figures each month.

(iv) Raw materials budget, showing figures each month.

(v) Forecast Operating statement for the six months ended 30 June, 19-5.

(vi) Forecast Balance Sheet as at 30 June, 19-5. In addition you may wish to show the workings behind the above budgets.

Part Four: Further Thoughts on Budgets

The process of budgeting with the necessary participation throughout management, finally producing a profit plan, is now a regular feature in all but the smallest firms. Very often budgeting is the one time when the various parts of management can really get together and work as a team rather than just as separate parts of an organisation. When budgeting is conducted under favourable conditions, there is no doubt that a firm which budgets will tend to perform rather better than a similar firm that does not budget. Budgeting means that managers can no longer give general answers affecting the running of the firm, they have to put figures to their ideas, and they know that in the end their estimated figures are going to be compared with what the actual figures turn out to be.

It has often been said that the act of budgeting is possibly of more benefit than the budgets which are produced. However, the following benefits can be claimed for good budgeting:

(*a*) The strategic planning carried on by the board of directors or owners can be more easily linked to the decisions by managers as to how the resources of the business will be used to try to achieve the objectives of the business. The strategic planning has to be converted into action, and budgeting provides the ideal place where such planning can be changed into financial terms.

(*b*) Standards of performance can be agreed to for the various parts of the business. If sales and production targets are set as part of a co-ordinated plan, then the sales department cannot really complain that production is insufficient if they had agreed previously to a production level and this is being achieved, nor can production complain if its production exceeds the amount budgeted for and it remains unsold.

(*c*) The expression of plans in comparable financial terms. Some managers think mainly in terms of say units of production, or of tons of inputs or outputs, or of lorry mileage etc. The effect that each of them has upon financial results must be brought home to them. For instance a transport manager might be unconcerned about the number of miles that his haulage fleet of lorries covers until the cost of doing such a large mileage is brought home to him, often during budgeting, and it may then be and only then that he starts to search for possible economies. It is possible in many cases to use mathematics to find the best ways of loading vehicles, or of the routes taken by vehicles so that fewer miles are covered and yet the same delivery service is maintained. This is just one instance of many when the expression of the plans of a section of a business in financial terms sparks off a search for economies, when otherwise such a search may never be started at all.

(*d*) Managers can see how their work slots into the total activities of the firm. It can help to get rid of the feeling of "I'm only a number not a person", because he can identify his position within the firm and can see that his job really is essential to the proper functioning of the firm.

(*e*) The budgets for a firm cannot be set in isolation. This means that the situation of the business, the nature of its products and its work force etc., must be seen against the economic background of the country. For instance it is no use budgeting for extra labour when labour is in extremely short supply, without realising the implications, possibly that of paying higher than normal wage rates. Increasing the sales target during a "credit squeeze" needs a full investigation of the effect of the shortage of money upon the demand for the firms's goods and so on.

The charges made against budgeting are mainly that budgets bring about inflexibility, and that managers will not depart from budget even though the departure would bring about a more desirable result. Too many budgets are set at one level of sales or production when in fact flexible budgets (discussed later in this chapter) ought to be used. It is very often the case that budgeting is forced upon managers against their will, instead the firm should really set out first of all to do a "selling job" to convince managers that budgets are not the monsters so often thought. A trial run for part of a business is far superior than starting off by having a fully detailed budget set up right away for the whole of the business. Learning to use budgets is rather like learning to swim. Let a child get used to the water first and remove its fear of the water, then it will learn to swim fairly easily. For most children (but not all), if the first visit to the baths meant being pushed into the deep end immediately, then reaction against swimming would probably set in. Let a manager become used to the idea of budgeting, without the fear of being dealt with severely during a trial period, and most managers will then become used to the idea and participate properly.

Flexible Budgets

So far in this book budgets have been drawn up on the basis of one set of expectations, based on just one level of sales and production. Later, when the actual results are compared with the budgeted results expected in a fixed budget, they will have deviated for two reasons:

(1) Whilst the actual and budgeted volumes of production and sales may be the same there may be a difference in actual and budgeted costs.

(2) The volumes of actual and budgeted units of sales and production may vary, so that the costs will be different because of different volumes.

The variations, or variances as they are more commonly known, are usually under the control of different managers in the organisation. Variances coming under (1) will probably be under the control of the individual department. On the other hand variances under (2) are caused because of variations in plans brought about by top management because of changing sales, or at least the expectation of changing sales.

Budgets are used for control purposes, therefore a manager does not take kindly to being held responsible for a variance in his spending if the variance is caused by a type (2) occurrence if he is working on a fixed budget. The answer to this is to construct budgets at several levels of volume, and to show what costs etc. they should incur at different levels. For instance, if a budget had been fixed at a volume of 500 units and the actual volume was 550, then the manager would undoubtedly feel aggrieved if his costs for producing 550 units are compared with the costs he should have incurred for 500 units. Budgets which do allow for changing levels are called "Flexible Budgets".

To draft a full set of flexible budgets is outside the scope of this book, but an instance of one department's flexible budget for manufactured overhead can be shown in Exhibit 26.1.

Exhibit 26.1

Data Ltd.
Budget of Manufacturing Overhead, Department S.
(This would in fact be in greater detail)

Units	400	450	500	550	600
	£	£	£	£	£
Variable overhead	510	550	600	680	770
Fixed overhead	400	400	400	400	400
Total overhead (A)	£910	£950	£1,000	£1,080	£1,170
Direct Labour hours (B)	200	225	250	275	300
Overhead rates (A) divided by (B)	£4.55	£4.22	£4.0	£3.92	£3.9

Notice that the Variable costs in this case do not vary in direct proportion to production. In this case once 500 units production have been exceeded they start to climb rapidly. The flexible budget makes far greater sense than a fixed budget. For instance if a fixed budget had been agreed at 400 units, with variable overhead £510, then if production rose to 600 units the manager would think the whole system unfair if he was expected to incur only £510 variable overhead (the figure for 400 units). On the contrary, if the comparison was on a flexible budget then costs at 600 units production would instead be compared with £770 (the figure at 600 units).

27

Consolidated Accounts: Introduction

The owners of a company are its shareholders. The purchase of ordinary shares normally gives a person three main rights, these being proportionate to the number of shares held by him. These are:

(a) Voting rights.

(b) A right to an interest in the net assets of the company. (Net assets means assets less liabilities.)

(c) A right to an interest in the profits earned by the company.

Because of the voting rights the ordinary shareholder is normally entitled to vote at shareholders' meetings. Preference shares on the other hand do not normally have full voting rights, their votes usually being restricted to where their dividends are in arrears or where their special rights are being varied. The reader should also realise that debentures carry no right to vote at general meetings.

At shareholders' meetings the ordinary shareholder, by virtue of his voting rights, is able to show his approval or disapproval (in accordance with the number of shares owned by him) of the election of directors. The directors appoint the officers of the company and manage its affairs. Therefore any group of shareholders acting together, who between them own more than 50 per cent of the voting shares of the company, can control the election of directors and, as a consequence, they can control the policies of the company through the directors. This would also hold true if any one shareholder owned more than 50 per cent of the voting shares.

One company may hold shares in another company; therefore if one company wishes to obtain control of another company it can do so by obtaining more than 50 per cent of the voting shares in that company.

Holding Companies and Subsidiary Companies

A company, S Ltd, has an issued share capital of 1,000 ordinary shares of £1 each. On 1 January 19-6 H Ltd buys 501 of these shares from Jones, a shareholder, for £600. H Ltd will now have control of S Ltd because it has more than 50 per cent of the voting shares. H Ltd is called the 'holding' company and S Ltd is said to be its 'subsidiary' company.

Now just because the identity of S Ltd's shareholders has changed does not mean that the balance sheet of S Ltd will be drafted in a different fashion. Looking only at the balance sheet of S Ltd no one would be able to deduce that H Ltd owned more than 50 per cent of the shares, or even that H Ltd owned any shares at all in S Ltd. After obtaining control of S Ltd both H Ltd and S Ltd will continue to maintain their own sets of accounting records and to draft their own balance sheets. In fact if the balance sheets, of H Ltd and S Ltd are looked at, both before and after the purchase of the shares, then any differences can be noted.

Exhibit 27.1

(a) Before H Ltd acquired control of S Ltd.

H. Ltd Balance Sheet as at 31 December 19-5

	£	£
Fixed Assets		2,000
Current Assets:		
Stock-in-Trade	2,900	
Debtors	800	
Bank	1,300	
		5,000
		7,000
Share Capital		5,000
Profit and Loss Account		2,000
		7,000

S Ltd Balance Sheet as at 31 December 19-5

	£	£
Fixed Assets		400
Current Assets:		
Stock-in-Trade	400	
Debtors	200	
Bank	100	
		700
		1,100
Share Capital		1,000
Profit and Loss Account		100
		1,100

(b) After H Ltd acquired control of S Ltd the balance sheets would appear as follows before any further trading took place:

H Ltd Balance Sheet as at 1 January 19-6

	£	£
Fixed Assets		2,000
Investment in Subsidiary Company		600
Current Assets:		
Stock-in-Trade	2,900	
Debtors	800	
Bank	700	
		4,400
		7,000
Share Capital		5,000
Profit and Loss Account		2,000
		7,000

S Ltd Balance Sheet as at 1 January 19-6

	£	£
Fixed Assets		400
Current Assets:		
Stock-in-Trade	400	
Debtors	200	
Bank	100	
		700
		1,100
Share Capital		1,000
Profit and Loss Account		100
		1,100

The only differences can be seen to be those in the balance sheets of H Ltd. The bank balance has been reduced by £600, this being the cost of shares in S Ltd, and the cost of the shares now appears as 'Investment in Subsidiary Company £600'. The balance sheets of S Ltd are completely unchanged.

From the Profit and Loss Account point of view, the appropriation section of S Ltd would also be completely unchanged after H Ltd takes control. H Ltd would however see a change in its Profit and Loss Account when a dividend is received from S Ltd, in this case the dividends received would be shown as Investment Income on the credit side of the Profit and Loss Account. Remember that dividends payable are charged to the Appropriation section of the paying company's Profit and Loss Account, whilst dividends received are in the main part of the receiving company's Profit and Loss Account.

The Need for Consolidated Accounts

Imagine a shareholder of H Ltd receiving H Ltd's Balance Sheet and Profit and Loss Account annually. After H Ltd's acquisition of the shares in S Ltd then £600 would appear as an asset in H Ltd's Balance Sheet. As the shares of S Ltd are now not so readily marketable, remembering that over 50 per cent are owned by H Ltd, it would be normal to find the investment remaining at cost, i.e. £600. The Profit and Loss Account would show dividends received from S Ltd. The cost of the investment in S Ltd and the dividends received from S Ltd would be the only items referring to the subsidiary in the records of H Ltd.

Anyone investing in H Ltd is, because of its majority share-holding in S Ltd, therefore also investing in S Ltd as well. Therefore just as the other assets and liabilities change over the years in H Ltd and the shareholders are very much concerned with the changes, so also does the shareholder of H Ltd want to know about the changes in the assets and liabilities of S Ltd. He is not, however, a shareholder of S Ltd, and therefore is not automatically entitled to a set of final accounts of S Ltd annually. Correspondingly, if the situation was to stay put at that point, the shareholder of H Ltd would not get a proper accounting view of his investment. This is accentuated if in fact the holding company was one with 20 subsidiaries, owning a different percentage of the shares in each one, and with all kinds of inter-indebtedness and inter-company sales — all of which need special treatment as seen later in this book.

The only way that a shareholder in H Ltd can see clearly, in accounting terms, how his investment is progressing is for him to receive a consolidated set of the accounts of both companies showing the overall effect of his investment.

Different Methods of acquiring Control of one Company by Another

So far the acquisition of control in S Ltd was by H Ltd buying more than 50 per cent of the shares in S Ltd from Jones, i.e. buying shares on the open market. This is by no means the only way of acquiring control, so by way of illustration some of the other methods are now described.

(a) S Ltd may issue new shares to H Ltd amounting to over 50 per cent of the voting shares. H Ltd pays for the shares in cash.

(b) H Ltd could purchase over 50 per cent of the voting shares of S Ltd on the open market by exchanging for them newly issued shares of H Ltd.

Or, acting through another company:

(c) H Ltd acquires more than 50 per cent of the voting shares in S1 Ltd for cash, and then S1 Ltd proceeds to acquire all of the voting shares of S2 Ltd. S2 Ltd would then be a sub-subsidiary of H Ltd.

These are only some of the more common ways by which one company becomes a subsidiary of another company.

The Nature of a Group

Wherever two or more companies are in the relationship of holding and subsidiary companies then a 'group' is said to exist. When such a group exists then besides the Final Accounts of the Holding company itself, then to comply with legal requirements, there must be a set of Final Accounts prepared in respect of the group as a whole. These group accounts are usually known as 'consolidated accounts', because the accounts of all the companies have had to be consolidated together to form one Balance Sheet and one Profit and Loss Account.

Sometimes holding companies carry on trading as well as investing in their subsidiaries. There are however other holding companies that do not trade at all, the whole of their activities being concerned with investing in other companies.

Teaching Method

The method used in this book for teaching consolidated accounts is that of showing the reader the adjustments needed on the face of the consolidated balance sheet, together with any workings necessary shown in a normal arithmetical fashion. The reasons why this method of illustrating consolidated accounts has been chosen are as follows:

(a) The author believes that it is his job to try to help the reader understand the subject, and not just to be able to perform the necessary manipulations. He believes that, given understanding of what is happening, then the accounting entries necessary follow easily enough. Showing the adjustments on the face of the balance sheet gives a 'birds-eye view' so that it is easier to see what is happening, rather than trace one's way laboriously through a complex set of double entry adjustments made in ledger accounts.

(b) The second main reason is that this would be a much lengthier and more costly book if all of the double entry accounts were shown. It is better for a first look at consolidated accounts to be an introduction to the subject only, rather than be at one and the same time both an introduction and a very detailed survey of the subject. If the reader can understand the consolidated accounts shown in this book then he/she will have a firm foundation which will enable him/her to tackle the more difficult and complicated aspects of the subject.

Group Accounts (SSAP 14)

This SSAP deals with group accounts, or consolidated accounts are they are known in this book. The requirements of the SSAP are fully observed in what is written in the chapters which follow.

28

Consolidation of Balance Sheets: Basic Mechanics I

This chapter is concerned with the basic mechanics of consolidating balance sheets. The figures used will be quite small ones, as there is no virtue in obscuring the principles involved by bringing in large amounts. For the sake of brevity some abbreviations will be used. As the consolidation of the accounts of either two or three companies, but no more, will be attempted, then the abbreviations will be 'H' for the holding company, 'S1' the first subsidiary company, and 'S2' the second subsidiary company. Where there is only one subsidiary company it will be shown as 'S'. Unless started to the contrary, all the shares will be ordinary shares of £1 each.

It will make the problems of the reader far easier if relatively simple balance sheets can be used to demonstrate the principles of consolidated accounts. To this end the balance sheets which follow in the next few chapters will usually have only two sorts of assets, those of stock and cash at bank. This will save a great deal of time and effort. If every time a consolidated balance sheet was to be drawn up the reader had to deal with assets of Land, Buildings, Patents, Motor Vehicles, Plant and Machinery, Stock, Debtors and Bank balances, then this would be an unproductive use of time.

Rule 1

The first rule is that in consolidation like things cancel out each other. In fact 'Cancellation Accounts' are in fact what consolidation accounts are all about. It also helps the reader to see the issue more clearly if the consolidated balance sheet is constructed immediately after H has bought the shares in S. In fact this would not be done in practice, but it is useful to use the method from a teaching point of view.

Exhibit 28.1

100 per cent of the shares of S bought at balance sheet value.

H has just bought all the shares of S. Before consolidation the balance sheets of H and S appear as follows:

H Balance Sheet

	£
Investment in subsidiary S (A)	6
Bank	4
	10
Share Capital	10
	10

S Balance Sheet

	£
Stock	5
Bank	
	6
Share Capital (B)	6
	6

Now the consolidated balance sheet can be drawn up. The rule about like things cancelling out each other can now be applied. As can be seen, item (A) in H's balance sheet and item (B) in S's balance sheet are concerned with exactly the same thing, namely the 6 ordinary shares of S; and for the same amount, for the shares are shown in both balance sheets at £6. These are cancelled when the consolidated balance sheet is drafted.

H & S Consolidated Balance Sheet

	£
Stock	5
Bank (£4 + £1)	5
	10
Share Capital	10
	10

Exhibit 28.2

100 per cent of the shares of S bought for more than balance sheet value.

H Balance Sheet

		£
Investment in subsidiary S: 6 shares	(C)	9
Bank		1
		10
Share Capital		10
		10

S Balance Sheet

		£
Stock		5
Bank		1
		6
Share Capital	(D)	6
		6

Now (C) and (D) refer to like things, but the amounts are unequal. What has happened is that H has given £3 more than the book value for the shares of S. In accounting, where the purchase money for something exceeds the stated value then the difference is known as Goodwill. This is still adhered to in the consolidation of balance sheets. The consolidated balance sheet is therefore:

H and S Consolidated Balance Sheet

	£
Goodwill (C) £9 – (D) £6	3
Stock	5
Bank (£1 + £1)	2
	10
Share Capital	10
	10

Exhibit 28.3

100 per cent of the shares of S bought for less than balance sheet value.

H Balance Sheet

		£
Investment in subsidiary S: 6 shares	(E)	4
Stock		5
Bank		1
		—
		10
		═
Share Capital		10
		—
		10
		═

S Balance Sheet

		£
Stock		5
Bank		1
		—
		6
		═
Share Capital	(F)	6
		—
		6
		═

H has bought all of the shares of S, but has given only £4 for £6 worth of shares at balance sheet values. The £2 difference is the opposite of Goodwill. Contrary to what many people would think, this is not 'Badwill' as such a word is not an accounting term. The uninitiated might look upon the £2 as being 'profit' but your knowledge of company accounts should tell you that this difference could never be distributed as cash dividends. It is therefore a 'Capital Reserve' and will be shown accordingly in the consolidated balance sheet. The consolidated balance sheet therefore appears as:

H and S Consolidated Balance Sheet

	£
Stock (£5 + £5)	10
Bank (£1 + £1)	2
	—
	12
	═
Share Capital	10
Capital Reserve (F) £6 − (E) £4	2
	—
	12
	═

Cost of Control

In fact the expression 'Cost of Control' could be used instead of 'Goodwill'. This expression probably captures the essence of the purchase of the shares rather than calling it goodwill. It is precisely for the sake of gaining control of the assets of the company that the shares are bought. However the expression 'Goodwill' is more widely used and is correspondingly the one that will be used through the remainder of this book.

(You can now attempt Exercises 28.1, 28.2 and 28.3)

Rule 2

This states that, although the whole of the shares of the subsidiary have not been bought, nonetheless the whole of the assets of the subsidiary company (subject to certain inter-company transactions described later) will be shown in the consolidated balance sheet.

This rule comes about because of the choice made originally between two possible methods that could have been chosen. Suppose that H bought 75 per cent of the shares of S then the balance sheets could be displayed in one of two ways, e.g.

H and S Consolidated Balance Sheet

	£
Goodwill	xxxx
Assets of H: 100 per cent	xxxx
Assets of S: 75 per cent	xxxx
	xxxx
Share Capital of H	xxxx
	xxxx

H and S Consolidated Balance Sheet

	£
Goodwill	xxxx
Assets of H: 100 per cent	xxxx
Assets of S: 100 per cent	xxxx
	xxxx
Share Capital of H	xxxx
Claims of outsiders which equal 25 per cent of the assets of S	xxxx
	xxxx

It can be seen that both balance sheets show the amount of assets which H owns by virtue of its proportionate shareholding. On the other hand the second balance sheet gives a fuller picture, as it shows that H has control of all of the assets of S, although in fact it does not own all of them. The claims of outsiders comes to 25 per cent of S and obviously they cannot control the assets of S, whereas H, with 75 per cent, can control the whole of the assets even though they are not fully owned by it. The second balance sheet method gives rather more meaningful information and is the method that is actually used for consolidated accounts.

Assume that S has 6 shares of £1 each and that it has one asset, namely stock £6. H buys 4 shares for £1 each, £4. If the whole of the assets of S £6 are to be shown on the assets side of the consolidated balance sheet, and the cancellation of only £4 is to take place on the other side, then the consolidated balance sheet would not balance. Exhibit 28.4 shows this in detail before any attempt is made to get the consolidated balance sheet to balance.

Exhibit 28.4

H Balance Sheet

	£
Investment in subsidiary: 4 shares (bought today)	4
Stock	5
Bank	1
	10
Share Capital	10
	10

S Balance Sheet

	£
Stock	6
Share Capital	6

Now as the 2 extra shares have not been bought by H then they cannot be brought into any calculation of goodwill or capital reserve. H has in fact bought 4 shares with a balance sheet value of £1 each, £4, for precisely £4. There is therefore no element of goodwill or capital reserve. But on the other hand the consolidated balance sheet per Rule 2 must show the whole of the assets of S. This gives a consolidated balance sheet as follows:

H and S Consolidated Balance Sheet

	£
Stock (£5 + £6)	11
Bank	1
Share Capital	10

Quite obviously the balance sheet totals differ by £2. What is this £2? On reflection it can be seen to be the £2 shares not bought by H. These shares belong to outsiders, they are not owned by the group. These outsiders also hold less than 50 per cent of the voting shares of S, in fact if they owned more then S would not be a subsidiary company. The title given to the outside shareholders is the apt one therefore of 'Minority Interest'. As the whole of the assets of S are shown in the consolidated balance sheet then part of these assets are owned by the minority interest. This claim against the assets is therefore shown on the capital side of the consolidated balance sheet. The consolidated balance sheet becomes:

H and S Consolidated Balance Sheet

	£
Stock (£5 + £6)	11
Bank	1
	12
Share Capital	10
Minority Interest	2
	12

This therefore is the convention of showing the whole of the assets of the subsidiary (less certain inter-company transactions) in the consolidated balance sheet, with the claim of the minority interest shown on the other side of the balance sheet.

Exhibit 28.5

Where less than 100 per cent of the subsidiary's shares are bought at more than book value.

H Balance Sheet

	£
Investment in subsidiary: 6 shares (G)	8
Stock	11
Bank	1
	20
Share Capital	20
	20

S Balance Sheet

	£
Stock	7
Bank	3
	10
Share Capital (I)	10
	10

H has bought 6 shares only, but has paid £8 for them. As the book value of the shares is £6, the £2 excess must therefore be Goodwill. The cancellation is therefore £6 from (G) and £6 from (I), leaving £2 of (G) to be shown as Goodwill in the consolidated balance sheet. The remaining £4 of (I) is in respect of shares held by the minority interest.

H and S Consolidated Balance Sheet

	£
Goodwill	2
Stock (£11 + £7)	18
Bank (£1 + £3)	4
	24
Share Capital	20
Minority Interest	4
	24

Exhibit 28.6

Where less than 100 per cent of the shares in the subsidiary are bought at less than book value.

H Balance Sheet

	£
Investment in subsidiary: 7 shares (J)	5
Stock	13
Bank	2
	20
Share Capital	20
	20

S Balance Sheet

	£
Stock	9
Bank	1
	10
Share Capital (K)	10
	10

Seven shares of S have now been bought for £5. This means that £5 of (J) and £5 of (K) cancel out with £2 shown as Capital Reserve. The remaining £3 of (K) is in respect of the shares held by the minority interest and will be shown as such in the consolidated balance sheet.

H and S Consolidated Balance Sheet

	£
Stock (£13 + £9)	22
Bank (£2 + £1)	3
	25
Shares	20
Capital Reserve	2
Minority Interest	3
	25

(You can now attempt Exercises 23.6 and 23.7)

Taking over Subsidiaries with Reserves

So far, for reasons of simplification, the examples given have been of subsidiaries having share capital but no reserves. When reserves exist, as they do in the vast majority of firms, it must be remembered that they belong to the ordinary shareholders. This means that if H buys all the 10 shares of S for £15, and S at that point of time has a credit balance of £3 on its Profit and Loss Account and a General Reserve of £2, then what H acquires for its £15 is the full entitlement/rights of the 10 shares measured by/shown as:

	£
10 Shares	10
Profit and Loss	3
General Reserve	2
	15

This means that the £15 paid and the £15 entitlements as shown will cancel out each other and will not be shown in the consolidated balance sheet. This is shown by the balance sheets shown in Exhibit 28.7.

Exhibit 28.7
Where 100 per cent of the shares are bought at book value when the subsidiary has reserves.

H Balance Sheet

		£
Investment in subsidiary: 10 shares	(L)	15
Stock		11
Bank		2
		28
Share Capital		20
Profit and Loss		5
General Reserve		3
		28

S Balance Sheet

		£
Stock		9
Bank		6
		15
Share Capital	(M1)	10
Profit and Loss	(M2)	3
General Reserve	(M3)	2
		15

H and S Consolidated Balance Sheet

	£
Stock (£11 + £9)	20
Bank (£2 + £6)	8
	28
Share Capital	20
Profit and Loss	5
General Reserve	3
	28

The cost of the shares (L) £15 is cancelled out exactly against (M1) £10 + (M2) £3 + (M3) £2 = £15. These are therefore the only items cancelled out and the remainder of the two balance sheets of H and S are then combined to be the consolidated balance sheet.

Exhibit 28.8

Where 100 per cent of the shares are bought at more than book value when the subsidiary has reserves.

H Balance Sheet

	£
Investment in subsidiary: 10 shares (N)	23
Stock	7
Bank	5
	35
Share Capital	20
Profit and Loss	9
General Reserve	6
	35

S Balance Sheet

	£
Stock	15
Bank	2
	17
Share Capital (01)	10
Profit and Loss (02)	4
General Reserve (03)	3
	17

H paid £23 (N) for the entitlements (01) £10 + (02) £4 + (03) £3 = £17, so that a figure of £6 will be shown in the consolidated balance sheet for Goodwill.

H and S Consolidated Balance Sheet

	£
Goodwill	6
Stock (£7 + £15)	22
Bank (£5 + £2)	7
	35
	==
Share Capital	20
Profit and Loss	9
General Reserve	6
	35
	==

Exhibit 28.9

Where 100 per cent of the shares in the subsidiary are bought at below book value when the subsidiary has reserves.

H Balance Sheet

	£
Investment in subsidiary: 10 shares (P)	17
Stock	10
Bank	8
	35
	==
Share Capital	20
Profit and Loss	6
General Reserve	9
	35
	==

S Balance Sheet

	£
Stock	16
Bank	5
	21
	==
Share Capital (Q1)	10
Profit and Loss (Q2)	8
General Reserve (Q3)	3
	21
	==

H has paid £17 (P) for the benefits of (Q1) £10 + (Q2) £8 + (Q3) £3 = £21. This means that there will be a Capital Reserve of £21 − £17 = £4 in the consolidated balance sheet, whilst (P), (Q1), (Q2) and (Q3) having been cancelled out will not appear.

H and S Consolidated Balance Sheet

	£
Stock (£10 + £16)	26
Bank (£8 + £5)	13
	39
Share Capital	20
Profit and Loss	6
General Reserve	9
Capital Reserve	4
	39

Exhibit 28.10

Where less than 100 per cent of the shares are bought in a subsidiary which has reserves, and the shares are bought at the balance sheet value.

H Balance Sheet

	£
Investment in subsidiary: 8 shares (R)	24
Stock	15
Bank	6
	45
Share Capital	20
Profit and Loss	17
General Reserve	8
	45

S Balance Sheet

	£
Stock	21
Bank	9
	30
Share Capital (T1)	10
Profit and Loss (T2)	5
General Reserve (T3)	15
	30

The items (R) and the parts of (T1), (T2) and (T3) which are like things need to be cancelled out. The cancellation takes place from the share capital and reserves of S as follows:

	Total at acquisition date	Bought by H 80 per cent	Held by Minority Interest
	£	£	£
Share Capital	10	8	2
Profit and Loss	5	4	1
General Reserve	15	12	3
	30	24	6

The amount paid by H was £24, and as H acquired a total of £24 value of shares and reserves the cancellation takes place without there being any figure of Goodwill or Capital Reserve. The consolidated balance sheet therefore appears:

H and S Consolidated Balance Sheet

	£
Stock (£15 + £21)	36
Bank (£6 + £9)	15
	51
Share Capital	20
Profit and Loss	17
General Reserve	8
Minority Interest	6
	51

Partial Control at a Price not Equal to Balance Sheet Value

In Exhibit 28.10 the amount paid for the 80 per cent of the shares of S was equal to the balance sheet value of the shares in that it amounted to £24. Very rarely will it be so, as the price is normally different from balance sheet value. If an amount paid is greater than the balance sheet value then the excess will be shown as Goodwill in the consolidated balance sheet, whilst if a smaller amount than balance sheet value is paid then the difference is a Capital Reserve and will be shown as such in the consolidated balance sheet. Using the balance sheet figure of S in Exhibit 23.10 then if H had paid £30 for 80 per cent of the shares of S then the consolidated balance sheet would show a Goodwill figure of £6, whilst if instead £21 only had been paid then the consolidated balance sheet would show £3 for Capital Reserve.

When the acquisition of two subsidiaries brings out in the calculations a figure of Goodwill in respect of the acquisition of one subsidiary, and a figure for Capital Reserve in respect of the acquisition of the other subsidiary, then the net figure only will be shown in the consolidated balance sheet. For instance if H had acquired two subsidiaries S1 and S2 where the calculations showed a figure of £10 for Goodwill on the acquisition of S1 and a figure of £4 for Capital Reserve on the acquisition of S2, then the consolidated balance sheet would show a figure for Goodwill of £6. Given figures instead of £11 Goodwill for S1 and £18 Capital Reserve for S2 then the consolidated balance sheet would show a Capital Reserve of £7.

The final Exhibit in this chapter is a composite one, bringing in most of the points already shown.

Exhibit 28.11

Where two subsidiaries have been acquired, both with reserves, full control being acquired of one subsidiary and a partial control of the other subsidiary.

H Balance Sheet

	£
Investments in subsidiaries:	
S1 10 shares (U)	37
S2 7 shares (V)	39
Stock	22
Bank	2
	100
Share Capital	40
Profit and Loss	50
General Reserve	10
	100

S1 Balance Sheet

	£
Stock	19
Bank	11
	30
Share Capital (W1)	10
Profit and Loss (W2)	12
General Reserve (W3)	8
	30

S2 Balance Sheet

	£
Stock	42
Bank	18
	60
Share Capital (X1)	10
Profit and Loss (X2)	30
General Reserve (X3)	20
	60

With the acquisition of S1 H has paid £37 for (W1) £10 + (W2) £12 + (W3) £8 = £30, giving a figure of £7 for Goodwill. With the acquisition of S2 H has given £39 for 7/10ths of the following: (X1) £10 + (X2) £30 + (X3) £20 = £60 × 7/10ths = £42, giving a figure of £3 for Capital Reserve. As the net figure only is to be shown in the consolidated balance sheet then it will be Goodwill £7 − Capital Reserve £3 = Goodwill (net) £4.

H and S1 and S2 Consolidated Balance Sheet

		£
Goodwill		4
Stock (£22 + £19 + £42)		83
Bank (£2 + £11 + £18)		31
		118
Share Capital		40
Profit and Loss		50
General Reserve		10
Minority Interest:		
3/10ths of (X1)	3	
3/10ths of (X2)	9	
3/10ths of (X3)	6	
		18
		118

Now work through Exercises 28.10 and 28.11

Exercises

28.1. The following balance sheets were drawn up immediately H Ltd had acquired control of S Ltd. You are to draw up a consolidated balance sheet.

H Balance Sheet

	£
Investment in S: 100 shares	110
Stock	60
Bank	30
	200
Share Capital	200
	200

S Balance Sheet

	£
Stock	80
Bank	20
	100
Share Capital	100
	100

28.2. You are to draw up a consolidated balance sheet from the following balance sheets of H Ltd and S Ltd which were drawn up immediately H Ltd had acquired the shares in S Ltd.

H Balance Sheet

	£
Investment in S Ltd: 3,000 shares	2,700
Fixed Assets	2,000
Stock	800
Debtors	400
Bank	100
	6,000
Share Capital	6,000
	6,000

S Balance Sheet

	£
Fixed Assets	1,800
Stock	700
Debtors	300
Bank	200
	3,000
Share Capital	3,000
	3,000

28.3. Draw up a consolidated balance sheet from the following balance sheets which were drawn up as soon as H Ltd had acquired control of S Ltd.

H Balance Sheet

	£
Investment in S Ltd:	
60,000 shares	60,000
Fixed Assets	28,000
Stock	6,000
Debtors	5,000
Bank	1,000
	100,000
Share Capital	100,000
	100,000

S Balance Sheet

	£
Fixed Assets	34,000
Stock	21,000
Debtors	3,000
Bank	2,000
	60,000
Share Capital	60,000
	60,000

28.4A. H Ltd acquires all the shares in S Ltd and then the following balance sheets are drawn up. You are to draw up a consolidated balance sheet.

H Balance Sheet

	£
Investment in S Ltd	29,000
Fixed Assets	5,000
Stock	4,000
Debtors	3,000
Bank	1,000
	42,000
Share Capital	42,000
	42,000

S Balance Sheet

	£
Fixed Assets	12,000
Stock	6,000
Debtors	4,000
Bank	2,000
	24,000
Share Capital	24,000
	24,000

28.5A. Draw up a consolidated balance sheet from the balance sheets of H Ltd and S Ltd that were drafted immediately the shares in S Ltd were acquired by H Ltd.

H Balance Sheet

	£
Investment in S Ltd: 63,000 shares	50,000
Fixed Assets	18,000
Stock	5,000
Debtors	4,000
Bank	3,000
	80,000
Share Capital	80,000
	80,000

S Balance Sheet

	£
Fixed Assets	48,000
Stock	6,000
Debtors	5,000
Bank	4,000
	63,000
Share Capital	63,000
	63,000

28.6. H Ltd acquires 60 per cent of the shares in S Ltd. Balance Sheets are then drafted immediately. You are to draw up the consolidated balance sheet.

H Balance Sheet

	£
Investment in S Ltd: 1,200 shares	1,500
Fixed Assets	900
Stock	800
Debtors	600
Bank	200
	4,000
Share Capital	4,000
	4,000

S Balance Sheet

	£
Fixed Assets	1,100
Stock	500
Debtors	300
Bank	100
	2,000
Share Capital	2,000
	2,000

28.7. H Ltd acquires 95 per cent of the shares of S Ltd. The following balance sheets are then drafted. You are to draw up the consolidated balance sheet.

H Balance Sheet

	£
Investment in S: 2,850 shares	2,475
Fixed Assets	2,700
Stock	1,300
Debtors	1,400
Bank	125
	8,000
Share Capital	8,000
	8,000

S Balance Sheet

	£
Fixed Assets	625
Stock	1,700
Debtors	600
Bank	75
	3,000
Share Capital	3,000
	3,000

28.8A. H Ltd buys 66⅔ per cent of the shares in S Ltd. You are to draw up the consolidated balance sheet from the following balance sheets constructed immediately control had been achieved.

H Balance Sheet

	£
Investment in S: 600 shares	540
Fixed Assets	1,160
Stock	300
Debtors	200
Bank	100
	2,300
Share Capital	2,300
	2,300

S Balance Sheet

	£
Fixed Assets	400
Stock	200
Debtors	240
Bank	60
	900
Share Capital	900
	900

28.9A. After H Ltd acquired 75 per cent of the shares of S Ltd the following balance sheets are drawn up.

H Balance Sheet

	£
Investments in S Ltd: 1,200 shares	1,550
Fixed Assets	2,450
Stock	1,000
Debtors	800
Bank	200
	6,000
Share Capital	6,000
	6,000

S Balance Sheet

	£
Fixed Assets	800
Stock	400
Debtors	250
Bank	150
	1,600
Share Capital	1,600
	1,600

28.10. Immediately after H Ltd had acquired control of S1 Ltd and S2 Ltd the following balance sheets were drawn up. You are to draw up a consolidated balance sheet.

H Balance Sheet

	£
Investments in subsidiaries: S1 Ltd (3,000 shares)	3,800
S2 Ltd (3,200 shares)	4,700
Fixed Assets	5,500
Current Assets	2,500
	16,500
Share Capital	10,000
Profit and Loss Account	6,500
	16,500

S1 Balance Sheet

	£
Fixed Assets	2,200
Current Assets	1,300
	3,500
Share Capital	3,000
Profit and Loss Account	400
General Reserve	100
	3,500

S2 Balance Sheet

	£
Fixed Assets	4,900
Current Assets	2,100
	7,000
Share Capital	4,000
Profit and Loss Account	1,000
General Reserve	2,000
	7,000

28.11. Immediately after H Ltd had acquired control of S1 Ltd and S2 Ltd the following balance sheets were drawn up. You are to draw up a consolidated balance sheet.

H Balance Sheet

	£
Investment in subsidiaries:	
S1 Ltd (1,800 shares)	4,200
S2 Ltd (2,000 shares)	2,950
Fixed Assets	4,150
Current Assets	2,100
	13,400
Share Capital	10,000
Profit and Loss Account	2,000
General Reserve	1,400
	13,400

S1 Balance Sheet

	£
Fixed Assets	3,500
Current Assets	2,500
	6,000
Share Capital	3,000
Profit and Loss Account	1,200
General Reserve	1,800
	6,000

S2 Balance Sheet

	£
Fixed Assets	1,800
Current Assets	1,400
	3,200
Share Capital	2,000
Profit and Loss Account	500
General Reserve	700
	3,200

28.12A. Immediately after H Ltd had achieved control of S1 Ltd and S2 Ltd the following balance sheets are drawn up. You are to draw up the consolidated balance sheet.

H Balance Sheet

	£
Investment in subsidiaries:	
S1 4,000 shares	6,150
S2 6,000 shares	8,950
Fixed Assets	3,150
Current Assets	2,050
	20,300
Share Capital	15,000
Profit and Loss Account	2,000
General Reserve	3,300
	20,300

S1 Balance Sheet

	£
Fixed Assets	5,300
Current Assets	1,200
	6,500
Share Capital	4,000
Profit and Loss Account	1,100
General Reserve	1,400
	6,500

S2 Balance Sheet

	£
Fixed Assets	6,000
Current Assets	3,450
	9,450
Share Capital	7,000
Profit and Loss Account	1,400
General Reserve	1,050
	9,450

28.13A. The following balance sheets of H Ltd, S1 Ltd and S2 Ltd were drawn up as soon as H Ltd had acquired the shares in both subsidiaries. You are to draw up a consolidated balance sheet.

H Balance Sheet

	£
Investment in subsidiaries:	
S1 3,500 shares	6,070
S2 2,000 shares	5,100
Fixed Assets	2,030
Current Assets	1,400
	14,600
Share Capital	11,000
Profit and Loss Account	1,000
General Reserve	2,600
	14,600

S1 Balance Sheet

	£
Fixed Assets	4,800
Current Assets	2,400
	7,200
Share Capital	5,000
Profit and Loss Account	900
General Reserve	1,300
	7,200

S2 Balance Sheet

	£
Fixed Assets	2,800
Current Assets	900
	3,700
Share Capital	2,000
Profit and Loss Account	1,400
General Reserve	300
	3,700

29

Consolidation of Balance Sheets: Basic Mechanics II

In the last chapter the consolidation of balance sheets was looked at as if the consolidated balance sheets were drawn up immediately the shares in the subsidiary had been acquired. However, this is very rarely the case in practice, and therefore the consolidation of balance sheets must be looked at as at the time it actually takes place, i.e. at the end of an accounting period some time after acquisition has taken place. Correspondingly, the balance on the profit and loss account of the subsidiary, and possibly the balances on the other reserve accounts, will have altered when compared with the figures at the date of acquisition.

In chapter 28 the Goodwill, or Capital Reserve, was calculated at the date of acquisition, and this calculation will stay unchanged as the years go by. It is important to understand this. Say for instance that the calculation was made of Goodwill on 31 December 19-3 and that the figure was £5,000. Even if the calculation was made one year later, on 31 December 19-4, then the calculation must refer to the reserves, etc., as on 31 December 19-3 as this is when they were acquired, and so the figure of Goodwill will still be £5,000. This would be true even if 5 years went by before anyone performed the calculation. In practice therefore, once the figure of Goodwill has been calculated then there is absolutely no need to re-calculate it every year. However, in examinations the Goodwill figure will still have to be calculated by the student even though the consolidated balance sheet that he is drawing up is 5, 10 or 20 years after the company became a subsidiary. This has to be done because the previous working papers are not available to an examinee.

It would be outside the law and good accounting practice for any company to return its capital to the shareholders, unless of course special permission was granted by the court[1]. Similarly, if a holding company was to pay its money in acquiring a company as a subsidiary, and then distribute as dividends the assets that it had bought then this is really the same as returning its capital to its shareholders. This can best be illustrated by a simple example.

1. Since the 1981 Companies Act, see chapter 13, powers have been given to companies to purchase own shares.

H pays £15 to acquire 100 per cent of the shares of S, and the share capital of S consists of £10 of shares and £5 profit and loss account. Thus to acquire a capital asset, i.e. ownership of S, the holding company has parted with £15. If the balance of the profit and loss account of S was merely added to the profit and loss balance of H in the consolidated balance sheet then the £5 balance of S could be regarded as being distributable as cash dividends to the shareholders of H. As this £5 of reserves has been bought as a capital asset then such a dividend would be the return of capital to the shareholders of S, and to prevent this the balance of the profit and loss account of S on acquisition is capitalised, i.e. it is brought into the computation as to whether there is goodwill or capital reserve and not shown in the consolidated balance sheet as a profit and loss account balance. On the other hand the whole of any profit made by S since acquisition will clearly belong to H's shareholders as H owns 100 per cent of the shares of S.

Exhibit 29.1

Where the holding company holds 100 per cent of the subsidiary company's shares.

H acquires the shares on 31 December 19-4. The balance sheets one year later are as follows:

H Balance Sheet as at 31 December 19-5

	£
Investment in subsidiary: 10 shares bought 31/12/19-4 (A)	18
Stock	11
Bank	3
	32
Share Captial	20
Profit and Loss	12
	32

S Balance Sheet as at 31 December 19-5

		£
Stock		14
Bank		2
		16
Share Capital	(B)	10
As at 31/12/19-4	(C)	5
Profit for 19-5	(D)	1
		6
		16

The shares were acquired on 31 December 19-4, therefore the calculation of the Goodwill or Capital Reserve is as the position of those firms were at that point in time. Thus for (A) £18 the firm of H obtained the following at 31 December 19-4, Shares (B) £10 and Profit and Loss (C) £5 = £15. Goodwill therefore amounted to £3. The profit of S made during 19-5 is since acquisition and does not therefore come into the Goodwill calculation. The figure of (D) £1 is a reserve which belongs wholly to H, as H in fact owns all of the shares of S. This (D) £1 is added to the reserves shown in the consolidated balance sheet.

H Consolidated Balance Sheet as at 31 December 19-5

	£
Goodwill	3
Stock (£11 + £14)	25
Bank (£3 + £2)	5
	33
Share Capital	20
Profit and Loss (H £12 + S £1)	13
	33

Exhibit 29.2

Where the holding company holds 100 per cent of the shares of the subsidiary and there is a post acquisition loss.

H Balance Sheet as at 31 December 19-5

	£	£
Investment in subsidiary:		
10 shares bought 31/12/19-4 (E)		19
Stock		10
Bank		4
		33
Share Capital		20
Profit and Loss:		
As at 31/12/19-4	7	
Add Profit 19-5	6	
		13
		33

S Balance Sheet as at 31 December 19-5

			£
Stock			9
Bank			2
			11
			10
Share Capital	(F)		
Profit and Loss:		£	
As at 31/12/19-4	(G)	4	
Less Loss 19-5	(I)	3	
			1
			11

In calculating Goodwill, against the amount paid (E) £19 are cancelled the items (F) £10 and (G) £4, thus the Goodwill is £5. The loss (I) has been incurred since acquisition. A profit since acquisition, as in Exhibit 29.2, adds to the reserves in the consolidated balance sheet, therefore a loss must be deducted.

H Consolidated Balance Sheet as at 31 December 19-5

	£
Goodwill	5
Stock (£10 + £9)	19
Bank (£4 + £2)	6
	30
Share Capital	20
Profit and Loss (£13 − (I) £3)	10
	30

Exhibit 29.3

Where the holding company acquires less than 100 per cent of the shares of the subsidiary and there is a post acquisition profit.

H Balance Sheet as at 31 December 19-5

		£
Investment in subsidiary:		
8 shares bought 31/12/19-4	(J)	28
Stock		7
Bank		3
		38
Share Capital		20
Profit and Loss	£	
As at 31/12/19-4	10	
Add Profit 19-5	8	18
		38

S Balance Sheet as at 31 December 19-5

		£
Stock		28
Bank		2
		30

		£	
Share Capital	(K)		10
Profit and Loss:		£	
As at 31/12/19-4	(L)	15	
Add Profit 19-5	(M)	5	
	(N)		20
			30

H has given (J) £28 to take over 80 per cent of (K) + (L) i.e. 80 per cent of (£10 + £15) = £20. Therefore Goodwill is £8. The profit for 19-5 (M) £5 is also owned 80 per cent by H = £4, and as this has been earned since the shares in S were bought the whole of this belongs to the shareholders of H and is also distributable to them, therefore it can be shown with other Profit and Loss Account balances in the consolidated balance sheet.

The Minority Interest is 20 per cent of (K) £10 + (N) £20 = £6. It must be pointed out that, although the holding company splits up the profit and loss account balances into pre-acquisition and post-acquisition, there is no point in the Minority Interest doing likewise. It would however amount to exactly the same answer if they did, because 20 per cent of (K) £10 + (L) £15 + (M) £5 still comes to £6, i.e. exactly the same as 20 per cent of (N) £20 + (K) £10 = £6.

H Consolidated Balance Sheet as at 31 December 19-5

	£
Goodwill	8
Stock (£7 + £28)	35
Bank (£3 + £2)	5
	48

	£
Share Capital	20
Profit and Loss (H £18 + £4)	22
Minority Interest: (Shares £2 + Profit and Loss £4)	6
	48

If there had been a post-acquisition loss then this would have been deducted from H's balance of Profit and Loss Account £18 when the consolidated balance sheet was drawn up.

Exercises

29.1. H Ltd buys 100 per cent of the shares of S Ltd on 31 December 19-5. The balance sheets of the two companies on 31 December 19-6 are as shown, you are to draw up a consolidated balance sheet as at 31 December 19-6.

H Balance Sheet as at 31 December 19-6

	£	£
Investment in subsidiary:		
4,000 shares bought 31/12/19-5		5,750
Fixed Assets		5,850
Current Assets		2,400
		14,000
Share Capital		10,000
Profit and Loss Account:		
As at 31/12/19-5	1,500	
Add Profit for 19-6	2,500	
		4,000
		14,000

S Balance Sheet as at 31 December 19-6

	£	£
Fixed Assets		5,100
Current Assets		1,500
		6,600
Share Capital		4,000
Profit and Loss Account:		
As at 31/12/19-5	800	
Add Profit for 19-6	1,800	
		2,600
		6,600

29.2. H Ltd buys 70 per cent of the shares of S Ltd on 31 December 19-8. The balance sheets of the two companies on 31 December 19-9 are as follows. You are to draw up a consolidated balance sheet as at 31 December 19-9.

H Balance Sheet as at 31 December 19-9

	£	£
Investment in S Ltd:		
7,000 shares bought 31/12/19-8		7,800
Fixed Assets		39,000
Current Assets		22,200
		69,000
Share Capital		50,000
Profit and Loss Account:		
As at 31/12/19-8	4,800	
Add Profit for 19-9	9,200	
		14,000
General Reserve		5,000
		69,000

S Balance Sheet as at 31 December 19-9

	£	£
Fixed Assets		8,400
Current Assets		4,900
		13,300
Share Capital		10,000
Profit and Loss Account:		
As at 31/12/19-8	1,700	
Less Loss for 19-9	400	
		1,300
General Reserve (unchanged since 19-5)		2,000
		13,300

29.3A. H Ltd bought 55 per cent of the shares in S Ltd on 31 December 19-6. From the following balance sheets you are to draw up the consolidated balance sheet as at 31 December 19-7.

H Balance Sheet as at 31 December 19-7

	£	£
Investment in S Ltd: 2,750 shares		4,850
Fixed Assets		13,150
Current Assets		13,500
		31,500
Share Capital		30,000
Profit and Loss Account:		
As at 31/12/19-6	900	
Add Profit for 19-7	600	
		1,500
		31,500

S Balance Sheet as at 31 December 19-7

	£	£
Fixed Assets		4,600
Current Assets		3,100
		7,700
Share Capital		5,000
Profit and Loss Account:		
As at 31/12/19-6	700	
Add Profit for 19-7	500	
		1,200
General Reserve (unchanged since 19-3)		1,500
		7,700

29.4. H buys shares in S1 and S2 on 31 December 19-4. You are to draft the consolidated balance sheet as at 31 December 19-5 from the following:

H Balance Sheet as at 31 December 19-5

	£	£
Investments:		
S1: 6,000 shares		8,150
S2: 8,000 shares		11,400
Fixed Assets		21,000
Current Assets		12,000
		52,550
Share Capital		40,000
Profit and Loss Account:		
As at 31/12/19-4	2,350	
Add Profit for 19-5	5,200	
		7,550
General Reserve		5,000
		52,550

S1 Balance Sheet as at 31 December 19-5

	£	£
Fixed Assets		9,900
Current Assets		4,900
		14,800
Share Capital		10,000
Profit and Loss Account:		
As at 31/12/19-4	1,100	
Add Profit for 19-5	1,700	
		2,800
General Reserve (same as 31/12/19-4)		2,000
		14,800

S2 Balance Sheet as at 31 December 19-5

	£	£
Fixed Assets		6,000
Current Assets		4,000
		10,000
Share Capital		8,000
Profit and Loss Account:		
As at 31/12/19-4	500	
Less Loss for 19-5	300	
		200
General Reserve (same as 31/12/19-4)		1,800
		10,000

29.5A. H Ltd bought 40,000 shares in S1 Ltd and 27,000 shares in S2 Ltd on 31 December 19-2. The following balance sheets were drafted as at 31 December 19-3. You are to draw up a consolidated balance sheet as at 31 December 19-3.

H Balance Sheet as at 31 December 19-3

	£	£
Investments in subsidiaries:		
S1 Ltd 40,000 shares		49,000
S2 Ltd 27,000 shares		30,500
Fixed Assets		90,000
Current Assets		80,500
		250,000
Share Capital		200,000
Profit and Loss Account:		
As 31/12/19-2	11,000	
Add Profit for 19-3	16,000	
		27,000
General Reserve		23,000
		250,000

S1 Balance Sheet as at 31 December 19-3

	£	£
Fixed Assets		38,200
Current Assets		19,200
		57,400
Share Capital		50,000
Profit and Loss Account:		
As at 31/12/19-2	3,000	
Less Loss for 19-3	1,600	
		1,400
General Reserve (as at 31/12/19-2)		6,000
		57,400

S2 Balance Sheet as at 31 December 19-3

	£	£
Fixed Assets		31,400
Current Assets		14,600
		46,000
Share Capital		36,000
Profit and Loss Account:		
As at 31/12/19-2	4,800	
Add Profit for 19-3	3,400	
		8,200
General Reserve (as at 31/12/19-2)		1,800
		46,000

30

Inter-Company Dealings: Indebtedness and Unrealised Profit in Stocks

When a subsidiary company owes money to the holding company, then the amount owing will be shown as a debtor in the holding company's balance sheet and as a creditor in the subsidiary company's balance sheet. Such debts in fact have to be shown separately from other debts so as to comply with the Companies Acts. Such a debt between these two companies is however the same debt, and following the rule that like things cancel out, then the consolidated balance sheet will show neither debtor nor creditor for this amount as cancellation will have taken place. The same treatment would apply to debts owed by the holding company to the subsidiary, or to debts owed by one subsidiary company to another subsidiary company. The treatment is exactly the same whether the subsidiary is 100 per cent owned or not.

Exhibit 30.1

Where the subsidiary company owes money to the holding company.

H Balance Sheet

		£	£
Investment in subsidiary: 10 shares			10
Stock			13
Debtors:			
Owing from subsidiary	(A)	4	
Other debtors		7	
		—	11
Bank			1
			35
Share Capital			20
Profit and Loss			6
Creditors			9
			—
			35

S Balance Sheet

	£	£
Stock		6
Debtors		13
Bank		3
		22
Share Capital		10
Creditors:		
Owing to holding company	(B) 4	
Other creditors	8	
		12
		22

H & S Consolidated Balance Sheet

	£
Stock (£13 + £6)	19
Debtors (£7 + £13)	20
Bank (£1 + £3)	4
	43
Share Capital	20
Profit and Loss	6
Creditors (£9 + £8)	17
	43

Unrealised Profit in Stock-in-Trade

It is possible that companies in a group may not have traded with each other. In that case the stocks-in-trade at the balance sheet date will not include goods bought from another member of the group. Again it is also possible that the companies may have traded with each other, but at the balance sheet date all of the goods traded with each other may have been sold to firms outside the group, and the result is that none of the companies in the group will have any of such goods included in their stock-in-trade.

However, it is also possible that the companies have traded with each other, and that one or more of the companies has goods in its stock-in-trade at the balance sheet date which have been bought from another group member. If the goods had been traded between members of the group at cost price, then the consolidated balance sheet would not be altered just because of a change in the location of stocks-in-trade. This means that it would not offend accounting practice by adding together all of the stock figures and showing them in the consolidated balance sheet, as the total will be the total of the cost of the unsold goods within the group.

Conversely, goods are usually sold between members of the group at prices above the original cost price paid by the first member of the group to acquire them. If all of such goods are sold by group members to firms outside by the balance sheet date then no adjustments are needed in the consolidated balance sheet, because the goods will not then be included in the stocks-in-trade. It would however be more usual to find that some of the goods had not been sold by one of the companies at the balance sheet date, so that company would include these goods in its stock-in-trade in its own balance sheet. Suppose that the holding company H owns all the shares in S, the subsidiary, and that H had sold goods which had cost it £12 to S for £20. Assume in addition that S had sold none of these goods by the balance sheet date. In the balance sheet of S the goods will be included in stock-in-trade at £20, whilst the profits made by H will include the £8 profit recorded in buying the goods for £12 and selling them for £20. Although this is true from each company's point of view, it most certainly is not true from the group viewpoint. The goods have not passed to anyone outside the group, and therefore the profit of £8 has not been realized by the group.

Going back to basic accounting concepts, the realization concept states that profit should not be recognized until the goods have been passed to the customer. As the consolidated accounts are concerned with an overall picture of the group, and the profits have not been realized by the group, then such profits should be eliminated. Accordingly the figure of £8 should be deducted from the profit and loss account of H on consolidation, and the same amount should be deducted from the stock-in-trade of S on consolidation. This cancels an unrealized inter-group profit.

If H had sold goods which had cost it £12 to S, a 100 per cent owned subsidiary, for £20, and S had sold $\frac{3}{4}$ of the goods for £22 by the balance sheet date then the picture would be different. H will have shown a profit in its profit and loss account for these sales of £8. In addition S will have shown a profit in its profit and loss account for the sales made of £7, i.e. £22 − $\frac{3}{4}$ of £20. The two profit and loss accounts show total profits of £8 + £7 = £15. So far however, looking at the group as a whole, these goods have cost the group £12. Three-quarters of these have been sold to firms outside the group, so that cost of goods sold outside the group is $\frac{3}{4} \times$ £12 = £9, and as these were sold by S the profit realized by the group is £22 − £9 = £13. This is £2 less than that shown by adding up the separate figures for each company in the group. Thus the group figures would be over-stated by £2 if the separate figures were merely added together without any adjustment. In addition the stock-in-trade would be overvalued by £2 if the two separate figures were added together because the remaining stock-in-trade of S includes one-quarter of the goods bought from H, i.e. $\frac{1}{4} \times £20 = £5$, but the original cost of the group was $\frac{1}{4} \times £12 = £3$. The adjustment needed is that in the consolidation process £2 will be deducted from the profit and loss balance of H and £2 will be deducted from the stock-in-trade of S, thus removing any unrealized inter-group profits.

This could be expressed in tabular form as:

(a)	Cost of goods to H	£12
(b)	Sold to S for	£20
(c)	Sold by S, $\frac{3}{4}$ for	£22
(d)	Stock of S at balance sheet date at cost to S $\frac{1}{4}$ of (b)	£5
(e)	Stock of S at balance sheet date at cost to H $\frac{1}{4}$ of (a)	£3
(f)	Excess of S balance sheet value of stock over cost to group (d) − (e)	£2
(g)	Profit shown in H profit and loss account (b) − (a) = £8	
(i)	Profit shown in S profit and loss account (c) £22 − $\frac{3}{4}$ of (b) £15 = £7	
(j)	Profit shown in the profit and loss accounts of H and S = (g) + (i) = £15	
(k)	Actual profit made by the group dealing with outsiders (c) £22 less ($\frac{3}{4}$ of (a) £12)£9 = £13	
(l)	Profit recorded by individual companies exceeds profit made by the group's dealing with outsiders (j) − (k) = £2	

The action needed for the consolidated balance sheet is therefore to deduct (f) £2 from the stock figures of H and S, and to deduct (l) £2 from the profit and loss account figures of H and S.

Exhibit 30.2

Where the stock-in-trade of one company includes goods bought from another company in the group.

H Balance Sheet as at 31 December 19-3

	£	£
Investment in subsidiary:		
10 shares bought 31/12/19-2		16
Stock-in-Trade		24
Bank		6
		46
Share Capital		20
Profit and Loss Account:		
As at 31/12/19-2	8	
Profit for 19-3 (C)	18	
		26
		46

S Balance Sheet as at 31 December 19-3

	£	£
Stock-in-Trade (D)		22
Bank		3
		25
Share Capital		10
Profit and Loss Account:		
As at 31/12/19-2	6	
Profit for 19-3	9	
		15
		25

During the year H sold goods which had cost it £16 to S for £28, i.e. recording a profit for H of £12. Of these goods two-thirds had been sold by S at the balance sheet date, leaving one-third in stock-in-trade. This means that the stock-in-trade of S (D) includes £4 unrealized profit (⅓ × £12). The figure of H's profit for the year (C) £18 also includes £4 unrealized profit. When consolidating the two balance sheets £4 therefore needs deducting from each of those figures.

In Exhibit 30.2 the subsidiary has been wholly owned by the holding company. The final figures would have been exactly the same if it had been the subsidiary which had sold the goods to the holding company instead of vice-versa.

H Consolidated Balance Sheet as at 31 December 19-3

	£
Stock-in-Trade (S £22 − £4 + H £24)	42
Bank (H £6 + S £3)	9
	51
Share Capital	20
Profit and Loss Account (S £9 + H £8 + £18 − £4)	31
	51

Partially Owned Subsidiaries and Unrealised Profits

So far the examples looked at have been those where wholly owned subsidiaries have been concerned. The situation can be different when the subsidiary is only partly owned.

In Exhibit 30.2 the unrealized profit in stock-in-trade was £4, and in that case the subsidiary was 100 per cent controlled. Suppose that in fact the ownership of shares was 75 per cent then there would be more than one possibility:

(a) (i) That £4 is deducted from the stock-in-trade figure in the consolidated balance sheet, and correspondingly £4 is deducted from the profit and loss account of H when it is consolidated, there being no adjustment for minority interest, or

  (ii) That £4 is deducted from the stock-in-trade figure in the consolidated balance sheet. To correspond with this a proportion is deducted from the minority interest, in this case £4 × 25 per cent = £1, whilst the remaining holding company proportion of 75 per cent, £3, is deducted from H profit and loss account when consolidated.

(b) That the profit to be cancelled out be restricted to the proportion of control of the subisidiary. In this particular case the part of the profit to be cancelled out is restricted to 75 per cent, i.e. £3. This has to be deducted both from the stock-in-trade of S on consolidation and from the profit and loss account of H.

None of these methods is incorrect, and they are all in use. With (b) the view is taken that only part of the sale, in this case 75 per cent, is connected with the group, the other part of the sale of 25 per cent being to the minority interest and therefore this 25 per cent of profits can be said to be realized.

Obviously there are advocates for each of these methods. A student at his first acquaintance with consolidated accounts is more likely to want to master the basic mechanics, leaving the study of the suitability of certain methods until later in his course. The simplest to operate is certainly method (a) (i) and in point of fact it accords with the author's opinion of the best method. In using any of these methods the student should always indicate in his answer that he/she realizes that more than one method could have been used. An asterisk against this part of the answer with a brief note shown below the balance sheet is sufficient, but it is dangerous to omit such a note, as the specimen answer from which the examiner is marking may have used one of the other methods, and it would be quite easy for him to mark the answer as wrong if a note was not appended.

Exhibit 30.3

Where the stock-in-trade of one company includes goods bought from another company in the group, and the holding company does not have 100 per cent of the shares in the subsidiary.

H Balance Sheet as at 31 December 19-6

	£	£
Investment in subsidiary:		
8 shares bought 31/12/19-5		16
Stock-in-Trade		25
Bank		1
		42
Share Capital		20
Profit and Loss Account:		
As at 31/12/19-5	3	
Profit for 19-6	19	
		22
		42

S Balance Sheet as at 31 December 19-6

	£	£
Stock-in-Trade		27
Bank		3
		30
Share Capital		10
Profit and Loss Account:		
As at 31/12/19-5	5	
Profit for 19-6	15	
		20
		30

Included in the stock-in-trade of S at 31 December 19-6 are goods bought by H for £10 and sold to S for £15. S had not sold any of these goods before 31 December 19-6.

H and S Consolidated Balance Sheet as at 31 December 19-6

	Methods		
	(ai)	(aii)	(b)
Goodwill	4	4	4
Stock-in-Trade:			
(ai) (25 + 27 − 5)	47		
(aii) (25 + 27 − 5)		47	
(b) (25 + 27 − 4)			48
Bank	4	4	4
	55	55	56
Share Capital	20	20	20
Profit and Loss Account:			
(ai) (S 80% × 15 + H3 + 19 − 5)	29		
(aii) (S 80% × 15 + H3 + 19 − 4)		30	
(b) (S 80% × 15 + H3 + 19 − 4)			30
Minority Interest:			
(ai) (Shares 2 + P/Loss 20% × 20)	6		
(aii) (Shares 2 + P/Loss 20% × 20 = 4 − 1)		5	
(b) (Shares 2 + P/Loss 20% × 20 = 4)			6
	55	55	56

Exercises

30.1. You are to draw up a consolidated balance sheet from the following details as at 31 December 19-9.

H Balance Sheet as at 31 December 19-9

	£	£
Investment in subsidiary:		
1,000 shares bought 31/12/19-8		2,800
Fixed Assets		1,100
Stock		1,200
Debtors		2,100
Bank		200
		7,400
Share Capital		2,000
Profit and Loss Account:		
As at 31/12/19-8	1,500	
Profit for 19-9	2,200	
		3,700
General Reserve		800
Creditors		900
		7,400

S Balance Sheet as at 31 December 19-9

	£	£
Fixed Assets		1,200
Stock		900
Debtors		1,400
Bank		300
		3,800
Share Capital		1,000
Profit and Loss Account:		
As at 31/12/19-8	950	
Profit for 19-9	1,150	
		2,100
Creditors		700
		3,800

During the year H had sold goods which had cost £150 to S for £240. None of these goods had been sold by the balance sheet date.

At the balance sheet date H owes S £220.

30.2. Draw up a consolidated balance sheet as at 31 December 19-4 from the following:

H Balance Sheet as at 31 December 19-4

	£	£
Investment in subsidiary:		
6,000 shares bought 31/12/19-3		9,700
Fixed Assets		9,000
Stock		3,100
Debtors		4,900
Bank		1,100
		27,800
Share Capital		20,000
Profit and Loss Account:		
As at 31/12/19-4	6,500	
Loss for 19-5	2,500	
		4,000
Creditors		3,800
		27,800

S Balance Sheet as at 31 December 19-4

	£	£
Fixed Assets		5,200
Stock		7,200
Debtors		3,800
Bank		1,400
		17,600
Share Capital		10,000
Profit and Loss Account:		
As at 31/12/19-4	3,500	
Profit for 19-5	2,000	
		5,500
Creditors		2,100
		17,600

At the balance sheet date S owes H £600.

During the year H sold goods which had cost £300 to S for £500. Three-quarters of these goods had been sold by S by the balance sheet date.

30.3A. Draw up a consolidated balance sheet from the following details as at 31 December 19-8.

H Balance Sheet as at 31 December 19-8

	£	£
Investment in subsidiaries:		
S1 30,000 shares bought 31/12/19-7		39,000
S2 25,000 shares bought 31/12/19-7		29,000
Fixed Assets		22,000
Stock		26,000
Debtors		13,000
Bank		5,000
		134,000
Share Capital		100,000
Profit and Loss Account:		
As at 31/12/19-7	14,000	
Add Profit for 19-8	9,000	
		23,000
General Reserve		2,000
Creditors		9,000
		134,000

S1 Balance Sheet as at 31 December 19-8

	£	£
Fixed Assets		22,000
Stock		11,000
Debtors		8,000
Bank		3,000
		44,000
Share Capital		30,000
Profit and Loss Account:		
As at 31/12/19-7	8,000	
Less Loss for 19-8	5,000	
		3,000
General Reserve (as at 31/12/19-7)		4,000
Creditors		7,000
		44,000

S2 Balance Sheet as at 31 December 19-8

	£	£
Fixed Assets		21,000
Stock		9,000
Debtors		7,000
Bank		1,000
		38,000
Share Capital		30,000
Profit and Loss Account:		
As at 31/12/19-7	1,200	
Add Profit for 19-8	1,800	
		3,000
Creditors		5,000
		38,000

At the balance sheet date S2 owed S1 £500 and H owed S2 £900.

During the year H had sold goods costing £2,000 to S1 for £2,800. Of these goods one-half had been sold by the year end. He had also sold goods costing £500 to S2 for £740, of which none had been sold by the year end.

30.4A. You are to draw up a consolidated balance sheet as at 31 December 19-3 from the following:

H Balance Sheet as at 31 December 19-3

	£	£
Investment in subsidiaries:		
S1 75,000 shares bought 31/12/19-2		116,000
S2 45,000 shares bought 31/12/19-2		69,000
Fixed Assets		110,000
Stock		13,000
Debtors		31,000
Bank		6,000
		345,000
Share Capital		300,000
Profit and Loss Account:		
As at 31/12/19-2	22,000	
Less Loss for 19-3	7,000	
		15,000
General Reserve (as at 31/12/19-2)		7,000
Creditors		23,000
		345,000

S1 Balance Sheet as at 31 December 19-3

	£	£
Fixed Assets		63,000
Stock		31,000
Debtors		17,000
Bank		3,000
		114,000
Share Capital		75,000
Profit and Loss Account:		
As at 31/12/19-2	11,000	
Add Profit for 19-3	12,000	
		23,000
Creditors		16,000
		114,000

S2 Balance Sheet as at 31 December 19-3

	£	£
Fixed Assets		66,800
Stock		22,000
Debtors		15,000
Bank		4,000
		107,800
Share Capital		80,000
Profit and Loss Account:		
As at 31/12/19-2	12,800	
Less Loss for 19-3	2,400	
		10,400
General Reserve (as at 31/12/19-2)		6,400
Creditors		11,000
		107,800

At the balance sheet date S1 owed H £2,000 and S2 £500, and H owed S2 £1,800.

H had sold goods which had cost £2,000 to S2 for £3,200, and of these goods one-half had been sold by S2 by the year end.

31

Consolidated Accounts: Acquisition of Shares in Subsidiaries at Different Dates

Up to this point the shares bought in subsidiary companies have all been bought at one point in time for each company. However, it is a simple fact that shares are often bought in blocks at different points in time, and that the first purchase of shares in a company may not give the buyer a controlling interest.

For instance, a company S has an issued share capital of 100 ordinary shares of £1 each, and the only reserve of S is the balance of the profit and loss account which was £50 on 31 December 19-4, and two years later on 31 December 19-6 it was £80. H buys 20 shares on 31 December 19-4 for £36 and a further 40 shares on 31 December 19-6 for £79. There are two possibilities open when calculating pre-acquisition profits, and therefore Goodwill or Capital Reserve. These are:

(a) To calculate these on the basis of shares bought as at date of each purchase, i.e. as at 31 December 19-4 and 31 December 19-6.
(b) To calculate them on the basis of the shares held when control was achieved, i.e. as at 31 December 19-6.

This would give different answers which are now shown.

	£	£
Method (a)		
Shares bought 31/12/19-4	20	
Proportion of Profit and Loss Account as at 31/12/19-4: 20 per cent × £50	10	
	—	30
Share bought 31/12/19-6	40	
Proportion of Profit and Loss Account as at 31/12/19-6: 40 per cent × £80	32	
	—	72
		102

	£	£
Paid 31/12/19-4	36	
Paid 31/12/19-6	79	
	—	115

Goodwill therefore £115 − £102 =   £13

Method (b)

	£	£
Shares bought	60	
Profit and Loss Account of subsidiary of which control achieved 31/12/19-6: 60 per cent × £80	48	
	—	108

	£	£
Paid 31/12/19-4	36	
Paid 31/12/19-6	79	
	—	115

Goodwill therefore £115 − £108 = £7

There does not seem to be any doubt that method (a) would be preferable for examination purposes. In fact both methods are used in practice. It would seem that method (b) would be preferred in practice where the shares bought prior to control constituted a relatively small part of the issued share capital, especially if in the earlier stages eventual control was not visualized. On the other hand where the purchases are all part of an overall plan to gain control of the company then method (a) is preferred.

In addition it has been conveniently assumed so far that all shares have been bought exactly on the last day of an accounting period. This will just not be so, most shares being bought part way through an accounting period. Unless specially audited accounts are drawn up as at the date of acquisition there is no up-to-date figure of Profit and Loss Account as at the date of acquisition. As this is needed for the calculation of Goodwill or Capital Reserve the figure has to be obtained somehow. Naturally enough specially audited accounts would be the ideal for the purpose of the calculation, but if they are not available a second-best solution is necessary. In this instance the Profit and Loss balance according to the last balance sheet before the acquisition of the shares is taken, and an addition made (or deduction – if a loss) corresponding to the proportion of the year's profits that had been earned before acquisition took place. This is then taken as the figure of pre-acquisition profits for Goodwill and Capital Reserve calculations.

Exhibit 31.1

Calculation of pre-acquisition profits, and Goodwill, where the shares are bought part way through an accounting period.

H bought 20 of the 30 issued ordinary shares of S for £49 on 30 September 19-5. The accounts for S are drawn up annually to 31 December. The balance sheet of S as at 31 December 19-4 showed a balance on the Profit and Loss Account of £24. The profit of S for the year ended 31 December 19-5 disclosed a profit of £12.

	£	£
Shares bought		20
Profit and Loss Account:		
Balance at 31/12/19-4	24	
Add Proportion of 19-5 profits before acquisition 9/12 × £12	9	
	33	
Proportion of pre-acquisition profits		
20 shares owned out of 30, ⅔ × £		22
		42

Paid for shares £49
Therefore Goodwill is £49 − £42 = £7

Exercises

31.1. On 31 December 19-4, S Ltd had Share Capital £40,000 and Reserves of £24,000. Two years later the Share Capital has not altered but the Reserves have risen to £30,000. The following shares were bought by H Ltd 10,000 on 31 December 19-4 for £23,500, and on 31 December 19-6 14,000 for £31,000. Assuming that this completed an overall plan to gain control of the company you are to calculate the figure of Goodwill/Capital Reserve for the consolidated balance sheet as at 31 December 19-6.

31.2A. On 31 December 19-6, S Ltd had share Capital of £400,000 and Reserves of £260,000. Three years later the Share Capital is unchanged but the Reserves have risen to £320,000. The following shares were bought by H Ltd 100,000 on 31 December 19-6 for £210,000 and 200,000 on 31 December 19-9 for £550,000. This completed the plan to take control of the company. Calculate the figure of Goodwill/Capital Reserve for the consolidated balance sheet as at 31 December 19-9.

31.3. H Ltd bought 50,000 of the 80,000 issued ordinary £1 shares of S Ltd for £158,000 on 31 August 19-8. S Ltd accounts are drawn up annually to 31 December. The balance sheet of S Ltd on 31 December 19-7 showed a balance on the Profit and Loss Account of £36,000. The profit of S Ltd for the year ended 31 December 19-8 showed a profit of £42,000. Calculate the figure for the Goodwill/Capital Reserve to be shown in the consolidated balance sheet as at 31 December 19-8.

31.4A. On 1 January 19-1 S Ltd had a Share Capital of £300,000, a Profit and Loss Account balance of £28,000 and a General Reserve of £20,000. During the year ended 31 December 19-1 S Ltd made a profit of £36,000, none of which was distributed. H Ltd bought 225,000 shares on 1 June 19-1 for £333,000. Calculate the figure of Goodwill/Capital Reserve to be shown in the consolidated balance sheet as at 31 December 19-1.

32

Inter-Company Dividends

(a) Not from Pre-Acquisition Profits

These dividends are paid by one company to another. They will therefore be shown in the receiving company's own Profit and Loss Account as Investment Income, with a subsequent increase in its final Profit and Loss Appropriation Account balance and an equivalent increase in the bank balance. From the paying company's own accounts point of view, it has shown the dividend as a charge against its own Profit and Loss Appropriation Account, thus reducing the final balance on that account, and when paid there will be a reduction of the bank balance. If the dividend has been proposed, but not paid, at the accounting year end then it will be normal for the proposed dividend to be shown as a current liability in the subsidiary company's balance sheet, and as a current asset on the holding company's balance sheet as dividend owing from the subsidiary.

From the consolidated balance sheet point of view (making an assumption about pre-acquisition profit shown in detail later) no action is needed. It is a past event which is automatically cancelled when drafting the consolidated balance sheet as they are like things.

(b) If Paid from Pre-Acquisition Profits

In chapter 29 the company law principle that dividends should not be paid out of capital was reiterated. To prevent this happening the pre-acquisition profits were capitalized and brought into the Goodwill or Capital Reserve calculation. A company cannot circumvent the principle by buying the shares of a company, part of the purchase price being for the reserves of the subsidiary, and then utilizing those reserves by paying itself dividends, and consequently adding those dividends to its own profits and then declaring an increased dividend itself. The next two exhibits are drawn up to illustrate this.

Exhibit 32.1

Dividends paid from post-acquisition profits.

H buys 100 per cent of the shares of S on 31 December 19-4. In 19-5 S pays a dividend of 50 per cent = £5 which H receives. To simplify matters the dividend is declared for 19-5 and paid in 19-5.

H Balance Sheet as at 31 December 19-5

	£	£
Investment in subsidiary:		
10 shares bought 31/12/19-4		23
Stock		11
Bank		1
		35
Share Capital		20
Profit and Loss Account:		
As at 31/12/19-4	7	
Add Profit for 19-5 (including dividend of £5 from S)	8	
		15
		35

S Balance Sheet as at 31 December 19-5

	£	£
Stock		19
Bank		7
		26
Share Capital		10
Profit and Loss Account:		
As at 31/12/19-4	12	
Profit for 19-5	9	
Less Dividend paid to H	5	4
		16
		26

The dividend is £5 out of profits made since the acquisition of £9. The dividend can be treated as being from post-acquisition profits, and can therefore be shown in the Profit and Loss Account of H as Investment Income and so swell the profits of H available for dividend purposes.

H Consolidated Balance Sheet as at 31 December 19-5

	£
Goodwill (£23 − £10 − £12)	1
Stock (H £11 + S £19)	30
Bank (H £1 + S £7)	8
	39
	===
Share Capital	20
Profit and Loss Account:	
(H £7 + £8 + S £4)	19
	39
	===

Exhibit 32.2

Dividends paid from pre-acquisition profits.

H Balance Sheet as at 31 December 19-4

	£
Investment in subsidiary:	
10 shares bought 31/12/19-4	23
Stock	7
Bank	1
	31
	===
Share Capital	20
Profit and Loss Account	11
	31
	===

S Balance Sheet as at 31 December 19-4

	£
Stock	14
Bank	3
	17
	===
Share Capital	10
Profit and Loss Account	7
	17
	===

H Consolidated Balance Sheet as at 31 December 19-4
(immediately after acquisition)

	£
Goodwill (H £23 – S £10 – S £7)	6
Stock	21
Bank (H £1 + S £3)	4
	—
	31
	=
Share Capital	20
Profit and Loss Account	11
	—
	31
	=

The consolidated balance sheet already shown was drafted immediately after acquisition. The following balance sheets show the position one year later. It is helpful to remember that the calculation of goodwill does not alter.

H Balance Sheet as at 31 December 19-5

	£	£
Investment in subsidiary:		
(£23 originally calculated less dividend from pre-acquisition		
profits £7)		16
Stock		18
Bank		5
		—
		39
		=
Share Capital		20
Profit and Loss Account:		
As at 31/12/19-4	11	
Add Profit for 19-5 (does not include the dividend from S)	8	
	—	
		19
		—
		39
		=

S Balance Sheet as at 31 December 19-5

	£	£
Stock		8
Bank		2
		—
		10
		=
Share Capital		10
Profit and Loss Account:		
As at 31/12/19-4	7	
Add Profit for 19-5*	0	
	—	
Less Dividend paid	7	
	—	
		10
		=

*For simplicity the profit of S for 19-5 is taken as being exactly nil.

H Consolidated Balance Sheet as at 31 December 19-5

	£
Goodwill	6
Stock	26
Bank	7
	—
	39
	=
Share Capital	20
Profit and Loss (P £19)	19
	—
	39
	=

It will be noticed that when a dividend is paid out of pre-acquisition profits it is in fact a return of capital to the holding company. Accordingly the dividend is deducted from the original cost of the investment; it is a return of the purchase money rather than be treated as Investment Income of the holding company. A common practice of many examiners, or 'trick' if you prefer to call it that, would have been to treat the receipt as investment income instead of as a refund of capital. Thus the balance sheet of H as at 31 December 19-5 in this exhibit would have read 'Profit and Loss Account £26' instead of 'Profit and Loss Account £19', and the Investment would be shown at £23 instead of £16. This means that the examiner really wants the examinee to adjust what is in fact an incorrect balance sheet, so that the only way is to adjust the holding company's balance sheet before proceeding with the consolidation of the balance sheets of H and S.

Proposed Dividend at Date of Acquisition of Shares

Quite frequently there will be a proposed dividend as at the date of the acquisition of the shares, and the holding company will receive the dividend even though the dividend was proposed to be paid from profits earned before acquisition took place. The action taken is similar to that in Exhibit 32.2, in that it will be deducted from the price paid for the shares in order that the net effective price is calculated.

Exhibit 32.3

Shares acquired in a subsidiary at a date when a proposed dividend is outstanding.

H Balance Sheet as at 31 December 19-3

	£	£
Investment in subsidiary:		
10 shares bought 31/12/19-2	22	
Less Dividend from pre-acquisition profits	6	
	—	
		16
Stock		11
Bank		2
		—
		29
		=
Share Capital		20
Profit and Loss Account:		
As at 31/12/19-2	4	
Profit for 19-3	5	
	—	
		9
		—
		29
		=

S Balance Sheet as at 31 December 19-3

	£	£
Stock		19
Bank		4
		—
		23
		=
Share Capital		10
Profit and Loss Account:		
As at 31/12/19-2 (after deducting the proposed dividend £6)	5	
Add Profit for 19-3	8	
	—	
		13
		—
		23
		=

H Consolidated Balance Sheet as at 31 December 19-3

	£	£
Goodwill (see workings below)		1
Stock		30
Bank		6
		—
		37
		=
Share Capital		20
Profit and Loss Account:		
(H £9 + S £8)		17
		—
		37
		=

Calculation of Goodwill

	£	£
Paid		22
Less Shares taken over	10	
Less Profit and Loss balance at 31/12/19-2	5	
Less Dividend paid from pre-acquisition profits	6	
	—	21
Goodwill		1

Proposed Dividends

When dividend is proposed by a company it will be shown as a current liability in its balance sheet. This is just as true for a subsidiary company as it would be for a company which is not controlled by another company. It is common practice for the holding company to show a proposed dividend from a subsidiary for an accounting period as being receivable in the same accounting period. Thus the subsidiary will show the proposed dividend as a current liability and the holding company will show it as a current asset. However, as this is merely another form of inter-indebtedness the amounts owing must be cancelled out when drawing up the consolidated balance sheet. Where the subsidiary is owned 100 per cent by the holding company then the two items will cancel out fully.

When the subsidiary is only part-owned there is the question of the minority interest. The cancellation of the part of the proposed dividend payable to the holding company is effected, and the remainder of the proposed dividend of the subsidiary will be that part owing to the minority interest. This can be dealt with in two ways, both acceptable in accounting:

(*a*) The part of the proposed dividend due to the minority interest is added back to the minority interest figure in the consolidated balance sheet.

(*b*) To show the part of the proposed dividend due to the minority interest as a current liability in the consolidated balance sheet.

It must be borne in mind that nothing that has been said refers in any way to the proposed dividends of the holding company. These will simply be shown as a current liability in the consolidated balance sheet.

Method (*b*) would seem to be the better method. For instance, when considering the working capital or liquidity of the group it is essential that all current liabilities due to external parties should be brought into calculation. If the proposed dividend soon to be paid to persons outside the group was excluded, this could render the calculations completely invalid.

Exhibit 32.4

Where a subsidiary has proposed a dividend, and there is a minority interest share in the subsidiary.

This will be shown using method (*b*) just described.

H Balance Sheet as at 31 December 19-3

	£
Investment in subsidiary:	
6 shares bought 31/12/19-1	17
Stock	19
Proposed dividend receivable from S	3
Bank	1
	40
Share Capital	20
Profit and Loss Account	11
Proposed dividend (of the holding company)	9
	40

S Balance Sheet as at 31 December 19-3

	£
Stock	23
Bank	7
	30
Share Capital	10
Profit and Loss Account	15
Proposed Dividend	5
	30

Note: At the date of acquisition of the shares on 31 December 19-1 the profit
and loss account balance of S was £10, and there were no proposed dividends
at that date.

H Consolidated Balance Sheet as at 31 December 19-3

	£	£
Goodwill (see workings)		5
Stock		42
Bank		8
		55
Share Capital		20
Profit and Loss Account (see workings below)		14
Minority Interest:		
Shares	4	
Profit and Loss 2/5ths	6	
		10
Current Liabilities:		
Proposed dividends of Holding Company	9	
Owing to Minority Interest	2	
		11
		55

Workings:	£	£	£
Profit and Loss Account:			
H's Profit and Loss balance			11
S's Profit and Loss balance		15	
Less Owned by Minority Interest: 2/5ths × £15	6		
Less Pre-acquisition profits at 31/12/19-1 bought by holding company: 3/5ths × £10	6		
		12	
			3
			14
Goodwill:			
Paid			17
Less Shares bought		6	
Less Pre-acquisition profits 3/5ths × £10		6	
			12
			5

If method (*a*) had been used then the consolidated balance sheet would be as shown except for Minority Interest and Current Liabilities. These would have appeared:

	£	£
Minority Interest:		
Shares	4	
Profit and Loss	8	
		12
Current Liabilities:		
Proposed Dividend		9

Exercises

32.1. The following balance sheets were drawn up as at 31 December 19-7. The person drafting the balance sheet of H Ltd was not too sure of an item and has shown it as a suspense item.

H Balance Sheet as at 31 December 19-7

	£	£
Investment in subsidiary:		
20,000 shares bought 31/12/19-6		29,000
Fixed Assets		40,000
Current Assets		5,000
		74,000
Share Capital		50,000
Profit and Loss Account:		
As at 31/12/19-6	8,000	
Add Profit for 19-7	11,000	
		19,000
Suspense*		5,000
		74,000

*The suspense item consists of the dividend received from S in January 19-7.

S Balance Sheet as at 31 December 19-7

	£	£
Fixed Assets		17,000
Current Assets		10,000
		27,000
		20,000
Share Capital		
Profit and Loss Account:		
As at 31/12/19-6*	3,000	
Add Profit for 19-7	4,000	
		7,000
		27,000

*The balance of £3,000 is after deducting the proposed dividend for 19-6 of £5,000.

32.2A. The balance sheets of H Ltd and S Ltd were drawn up as at 31 December 19-4 as follows:

H Balance Sheet as at 31 December 19-4

	£	£
Investment in subsidiary:		
100,000 shares bought 31/12/19-3		194,000
Fixed Assets		250,000
Current Assets		59,000
		503,000
		400,000
Share Capital		
Profit and Loss Account:		
As at 31/12/19-3	39,000	
Add profit for 19-4*	64,000	
		103,000
		503,000

*The profit figure for 19-4 includes the dividend of £20,000 received from S Ltd for the year 19-3.

S Balance Sheet as at 31 December 19-4

	£	£
Fixed Assets		84,000
Current Assets		49,000
		133,000
Share Capital		100,000
Profit and Loss Account:		
As at 31/12/19-3*	11,000	
Add Profit for 19-4	22,000	
		33,000
		133,000

*The balance of £11,000 is after deducting the proposed dividend for 19-3 £20,000.

32.3. Draw up a consolidated balance sheet as at 31 December 19-9 from the following information.

H Balance Sheet as at 31 December 19-9

	£	£
Investment in subsidiary:		
30,000 shares bought 31/12/19-8		47,000
Fixed Assets		44,000
Current Assets		12,000
		103,000
Share Capital		80,000
Profit and Loss Account:		
As at 31/12/19-8	14,000	
Add Profit for 19-9	9,000	
		23,000
		103,000

S Balance Sheet as at 31 December 19-9

	£	£
Fixed Assets		36,000
Current Assets		21,000
		57,000
Share Capital		40,000
Profit and Loss Account:		
As at 31/12/19-8	4,000	
Add Profit for 19-9	7,000	
	11,000	
Proposed Dividend for 19-9	6,000	
		57,000

The proposed dividend of S has not yet been brought into the accounts of H Ltd.

32.4A. The balance sheets of H Ltd and S Ltd are as follows:

H Balance Sheet as at 31 December 19-4

	£	£
Investment in subsidiary:		
120,000 shares bought 31/12/19-3		230,000
Fixed Assets		300,000
Current Assets		75,000
		605,000
Share Capital		500,000
Profit and Loss Account:		
As at 31/12/19-3	64,000	
Add Profit for 19-4	41,000	
		105,000
		605,000

S Balance Sheet as at 31 December 19-4

	£	£
Fixed Assets		203,000
Current Assets		101,000
		304,000
Share Capital		200,000
Profit and Loss Account:		
As at 31/12/19-3	51,000	
Add Profit for 19-4	13,000	
		64,000
Proposed Dividend for 19-4		40,000
		304,000

The proposed dividend of S has not yet been brought into the accounts of H Ltd.

Draw up the consolidated balance sheet as at 31 December 19-4.

33

Consolidated Balance Sheets: Sundry Matters

Preference Shares

It should be remembered that preference shares do not carry voting powers under normal conditions, nor do they possess a right to the reserves of the company. Contrast this with ordinary shares which, when bought, will give the holding company voting rights and also a proportionate part of the reserves of the company.

This means that the calculation of Goodwill or Capital Reserve on the purchase of preference shares is very simple indeed. If 9 Preference Shares of £1 each are bought for £12 then Goodwill will be £3, while if 20 Preference Shares of £1 each are bought for £16 then the Capital Reserve will be £4. The amount of Goodwill or Capital Reserve on the purchase of preference shares is not shown separately from that calculated on the purchase of ordinary shares, instead the figures will be amalgamated to throw up one figure only on the consolidated balance sheet.

Preference Shares owned by the minority interest are simply shown as part of the minority interest figure in the consolidated balance sheet, each share being shown at nominal value.

Sale of Fixed Assets between Members of the Group

There is obviously nothing illegal in one company in the group selling items in the nature of fixed assets to another company in the group. If the sale is at the cost price originally paid for it by the first company, then no adjustment will be needed in the consolidated balance sheet. Rather more often the sale will be at a price different from the original cost price. The inter-company unrealized profit must be eliminated in a similar fashion to that taken for the unrealized profit in trading stock as described in Chapter 30.

If the fixed asset is shown at its cost to the group in the consolidated balance sheet rather than at the cost to the particular company, then obviously the depreciation figures on that fixed asset should be adjusted to that based on the group cost rather than of the cost of the particular company.

Exhibit 28.1

H Balance Sheet as at 31 December 19-6

	£	£
Investment in S:		
50 shares bought 31/12/19-5		95
Fixed Assets	78	
Less Depreciation	23	
	—	55
Current Assets		20
		170
Share Capital		100
Profit and Loss Account:		
As at 31/12/19-6	30	
For the year 19-6	40	
	—	70
		170

S Balance Sheet as at 31 December 19-6

	£	£
Fixed Assets	80	
Less Depreciation	20	
	—	60
Current Assets		35
		95
Share Capital		50
Profit and Loss Account:		
As at 31/12/19-5	20	
For the year 19-6	25	
	—	45
		95

During the year H Ltd had sold a fixed asset which had cost it £20 to S Ltd for £28. Of the figure of £20 depreciation in the balance sheet of S, £7 refers to this asset and £13 to the other assets. The rate of depreciation is 25 per cent. The £8 profit is included in the figure of £40 profit for 19-6 in the balance sheet of H.

This means that the figure of £8 needs cancelling from the asset costs in the consolidated balance sheet and from the Profit and Loss Account balance. In addition the figure of depreciation needs adjusting downward, from the £7 as shown on the balance sheet of S, to the figure of £5, i.e. 25 per cent depreciation based on the cost of the asset to the group. This in turn means that the figure of profit for S £25 needs increasing by £2, as, instead of the expense of £7 depreciation there will now be a reduced expense of £5. The consolidated balance sheet becomes:

H and S Consolidated Balance Sheet as at 31 December 19-6

	£	£
Goodwill		25
Fixed Assets	150	
Less Depreciation	41	
		109
Current Assets		55
		189
Share Capital		100
Profit and Loss Account:		
(H £70 − £8 + S £25 + £2)		89
		189

Revaluation of Fixed Assets

The consolidated balance sheet should give a picture that is not clouded by the method of drafting consolidated accounts. The consolidation process is looked at from the point of view that the holding company acquires shares in a company, and thereby achieves control of that company, and, in addition, it is recognized that the reserves are also taken over. It has been seen previously that the economic view is that of taking over the assets of another company, after all one does not buy such shares so that one possesses the share certificates, rather it is for the assets which are taken over and used. The consolidated balance sheet should therefore give the same picture as that which would have been recorded if, instead of buying shares, the assets themselves had been bought directly.

If, therefore, the fixed assets as shown in the balance sheet of the subsidiary were really valued at more than that figure when acquisition took place, then it would be better if the value of the fixed assets in the consolidated balance sheet was to be shown at that figure.

Such a revaluation can either be recorded in the separate accounts of the subsidiary companies themselves, or alternatively it can be brought into the workings when the consolidated balance sheet is drawn up.

It can be seen that, failing attention to the above, some rather strange results can occur. For instance, if H buys all the 10 shares of S for £18 when the reserves are £5, then the Goodwill calculation normally is:

	£	£
Cost		18
Less share	10	
Less reserves	5	
	—	15
		—
Goodwill		£3

However, H might have bought the shares of S because it thought that, instead of the value of £15 assets as shown on the balance sheet of S (represented on the other side of the balance sheet by Shares £10 and Reserves £5), the assets were really worth £17. In the eyes of H Ltd therefore it is giving £18 for physical assets worth £17 and the Goodwill figure is correspondingly £18 − £17 = £1. Assuming that the difference is in the recorded value of fixed assets, then the consolidated balance sheet will be showing a wrong picture if it shows Goodwill £3 and Asset £15. The revaluation upwards of the fixed assets by £2, and the consequent reduction of the Goodwill figure by £2 will redress the view.

Where there are depreciation charges on the revalued assets then this also will need adjusting.

Exhibit 28.2

H Balance Sheet as at 31 December 19-6

	£	£
Investment in subsidiary:		
30 shares bought 31/12/19-5		56
Fixed Assets	80	
Less Depreciation for the year	16	
	—	64
Current Assets		26
		—
		146
		—
Share Capital		100
Profit and Loss Account:		
As at 31/12/19-5	20	
Add Profit 19-6	26	
	—	46
		—
		146
		—

S Balance Sheet as at 31 December 19-6

	£	£
Fixed Assets	50	
Less Depreciation for the year	10	
	—	40
Current Assets		14
		—
		54
		═
Share Capital		30
Profit and Loss Account:		
As at 31/12/19-5	3	
Add Profit 19-6	21	
	—	24
		—
		54
		═

At the point in time when H bought the shares in S, the assets in S were shown at a value of £33 in the balance sheet of S. In fact however H valued the fixed assets as being worth £20 higher than that shown. The consolidated balance sheet will therefore show them at this higher figure. In turn the depreciation, which is at the rate of 20 per cent, will be £4 higher. The consolidated balance sheet therefore appears:

H and S Consolidated Balance Sheet as at 31 December 19-6

	£	£
Goodwill		3
Fixed Assets		
(£80 + £70)	150	
Less Depreciation (£16 + £14)	30	
	—	120
Current Assets		40
		—
		163
		═
Share Capital		100
Profit and Loss Account:		
(H £46 + S £21 − increased depreciation £4)		63
		—
		163
		═

Exercises

33.1. From the following balance sheets and further information you are to draw up a consolidated balance sheet as at 31 December 19-8.

H Balance Sheet as at 31 December 19-8

	£	£
Investment in S:		
200,000 shares bought 31/12/19-7		340,000
Fixed Assets	300,000	
Less Depreciation	100,000	
		200,000
Current Assets		103,000
		643,000
Share Capital		500,000
Profit and Loss Account:		
As at 31/12/19-7	77,000	
Add Profit for 19-8	66,000	
		143,000
		643,000

S Balance Sheet as at 31 December 19-8

	£	£
Fixed Assets	210,000	
Less Depreciation	40,000	
		170,000
Current Assets		102,000
		272,000
Share Capital		200,000
Profit and Loss Account:		
As at 31/12/19-7	40,000	
Add Profit for 19-8	32,000	
		72,000
		272,000

During the year H Ltd had sold a fixed asset, which had cost it £40,000, to S for £50,000. S has written off 20 per cent, i.e. £10,000 as depreciation for 19-8.

33.2A. From the following balance sheets and supplementary information you are to draw up a consolidated balance sheet as at 31 December 19-5.

H Consolidated Balance Sheet as at 31 December 19-5

	£	£
Investment in S:		
10,000 shares bought 31/12/19-4		23,000
Fixed Assets	84,000	
Less Depreciation	14,000	
		70,000
Current Assets		20,000
		113,000
Share Capital		75,000
Profit and Loss Account:		
As at 31/12/19-4	15,000	
Add Profit for 19-5	23,000	
		38,000
		113,000

S Consolidated Balance Sheet as at 31 December 19-5

	£	£
Fixed Assets	26,000	
Less Depreciation	10,000	
		16,000
Current Assets		12,000
		28,000
Share Capital		10,000
Profit and Loss Account:		
As at 31/12/19-4	6,000	
Add Profit for 19-5	7,000	
		13,000
General Reserve		
(as at 31/12/19-4)		5,000
		28,000

During the year H sold a fixed asset to S. It had cost H £3,000 and it was sold to S for £5,000. S had written off £500 as depreciation during 19-5.

33.3   *H Balance Sheet as at 31 December 19-7*

	£	£
Investment in S:		
60,000 shares bought on 31/12/19-6		121,000
Fixed Assets	90,000	
Less Depreciation for year	24,000	
		66,000
Current Assets		40,000
		227,000
Share Capital		150,000
Profit and Loss Account:		
As at 31/12/19-6	44,000	
Add Profit for 19-7	33,000	
		77,000
		227,000

S Balance Sheet as at 31 December 19-7

	£	£
Fixed Assets	70,000	
Less Depreciation for year	7,000	
		63,000
Current Assets		28,000
		91,000
Share Capital		60,000
Profit and Loss Account:		
As at 31/12/19-6	17,000	
Add Profit for 19-7	14,000	
		31,000
		91,000

When H Ltd bought the shares of S Ltd it valued the fixed assets at £95,000 instead of the figure of £70,000 as shown in the balance sheet of S.

Draw up a consolidated balance sheet as at 31 December 19-7.

33.4A. *H Balance Sheet as at 31 December 19-5*

	£	£
Investment in S:		
30,000 shares bought 31/12/19-4		53,400
Fixed Assets	60,000	
Less Depreciation for year	6,000	
		54,000
Current Assets		10,600
		118,000
Share Capital		80,000
Profit and Loss Account:		
As at 31/12/19-7	27,000	
Add Profit for 19-5	11,000	
		38,000
		118,000

S Balance Sheet as at 31 December 19-5

	£	£
Fixed Assets	40,000	
Less Depreciation for year	4,000	
		36,000
Current Assets		11,000
		47,000
Share Capital		30,000
Profit and Loss Account:		
As at 31/12/19-4	8,000	
Add Profit for 19-5	9,000	
		17,000
		47,000

When H Ltd took control of S Ltd it valued the fixed assets at 31/12/19-4 at £50,000 instead of £40,000 as shown.

Draw up the consolidated balance sheet as at 31 December 19-5.

34

Consolidation of the Accounts of a Vertical Group of Companies

A vertical group can be said to be one in which a holding company has a controlling interest in a subsidiary, then that subsidiary has a controlling interest in a sub-subsidiary. This can be extended further in a vertical chain of downward holdings.

As an example H Ltd might own 90 per cent of S1, and S1 in turn owns 60 per cent of S2. This means that H owns 90 per cent of 60 per cent of S2 = 54 per cent. In that case H owned more than 50 per cent of the sub-subsidiary S2. In point of fact the eventual ownership of the holding company might be less than 50 per cent, as follows, H Ltd owns 60 per cent of S which in turn owns 75 per cent of S2. This means that H owns 60 per cent of 75 per cent of S2 = 45 per cent. In both of these cases consolidated accounts will have to be prepared including both S1 and S2. The fact that in the second case H Ltd controlled less than 50 per cent of S2 is immaterial. The holding company subsidiary relationship exists where the sub-subsidiary is a subsidiary of the sub-subsidiary of the holding company, and all such companies need to be incorporated in the consolidated accounts.

There are in fact two different methods of consolidating the accounts. The first method follows the reasoning already given in this chapter which involves computing the holding company's interest in the sub-subsidiary company and taking that percentage of the capital and reserves of that company into the consolidation process. The second method recognizes the fact that if there are three companies H, S1 and S2, then S1 by law, because S2 is its subsidiary, must produce a consolidated balance sheet of S1 and S2. The technique therefore is to consolidate first the balance sheets of S1 and S2, and when that is done the balance sheet of H is then consolidated with the consolidated balance sheet of S1 and S2.

The recommended practice for students would be to use the first method. It is certainly simpler to apply, and it is finding increasing favour in practice. Given the necessarily simple type of examples in a basic text-book there does not in fact seem to be a great divergence of difficulty between the two methods, but this would not be so in more complicated examples.

Method A. Computation of the Holding Company's Indirect Interest

Exhibit 34.1

The following are the balance sheets of H Ltd, S1 Ltd and S2 Ltd.

H Balance Sheet as at 31 December 19-5

	£	£
Investment in S1 Ltd:		
8 shares bought 31/12/19-4		41
Stock		53
Bank		6
		100
Share Capital		40
Profit and Loss:		
As at 31/12/19-4	24	
Add Profit for 19-5	36	
		60
		100

S1 Balance Sheet as at 31 December 19-5

	£	£
Investment in S2:		
15 shares bought 31/12/19-4		25
Stock		8
Bank		2
		35
Share Capital		10
Profit and Loss:		
As at 31/12/19-4	5	
Add Profit for 19-5	10	
		15
General Reserve (as at 31/12/19-4)		10
		35

S2 Balance Sheet as at 31 December 19-5

	£	£
Stock		39
Bank		16
		55
Share Capital		20
Profit and Loss:		
As at 31/12/19-4	15	
Add Profit for 19-5	20	
		35
		55

The control of the companies can be summarized as:

	S1 Ltd	S2 Ltd
Group	80%	60%
Minority Interest	20%	40%

The proportion of S2 owned by the group can be seen to be 80 per cent of 75 per cent = 60 per cent, with the remainder 40 per cent held by the minority interest.

H and S1 and S2 Consolidated Balance Sheet

	£
Goodwill	20
Stock (£53 + £8 + £39)	100
Bank (£18 + £6)	24
	144
Share Capital	40
Profit and Loss:	
(H £60 + S1 £8 + S2 £12)	80
Minority Interests	24
	144

Workings:	£	£	£
Cost of Shares to Group: in S1 Ltd		41	
in S2 Ltd 80% of £25		20	
		—	61
Less Nominal Value of Shares held:			
In S1 Ltd		8	
In S2 Ltd 60% of £20		12	
		—	20
General Reserves S1 Ltd 80% of £10		8	
Profit and Loss Account:			
In S1 Ltd 80% of £5	4		
In S2 Ltd 60% of £15	9		
	—	13	
		—	41
			—
Goodwill per Consolidated Balance Sheet			20
			=

Minority Interests:	£	£	£
In S1 Ltd: Shares 20% of £10	2		
Profit and Loss 20% of £15	3		
	—	5	
General Reserve 20% of £10		2	
In S2 Ltd: Shares 40% of £20	8		
Profit and Loss 40% of £35	14		
	—	22	
		—	29
Less cost of shares in S2 to minority interest of S1, 20% of £25			5
Minority Interest as per Consolidated Balance Sheet			24
			=

Method B

This method first consolidates the balance sheet of S1 with that of S2. After this the resulting consolidated balance sheet of the S1 and S2 group is then consolidated with the balance sheet of H. The figures that are used are the same as for Exhibit 34.1.

Exhibit 34.2

S1 and S2 Consolidated Balance Sheet as at 31 December 19-5

	£
Stock (£8 + £39)	47
Bank (£2 + £16)	18
	—
	65
	=
Share Capital	10
Profit and Loss Account:	
(S1 £15 + S2 £15)	30
Capital Reserve	$1\frac{1}{4}$
General Reserve	10
Minority Interest	
(25% of £20 + £35)	$13\frac{3}{4}$
	—
	65
	=

H and S1 and S2 Consolidated Balance Sheet as at 31 December 19-5

	£
Goodwill (£21 − £1¼)	19¾
Stock (£53 + £47)	100
Bank (£18 + £6)	24
	143¾

	£
Share Capital	40
Profit and Loss Account (see below)	80
Minority Interest (see below)	23¾
	143¾

Goodwill (remember this is calculated as at 31/12/-4)	£	£
Cost		41
Shares	8	
Profit and Loss 8/10ths × S1 £5	4	
General Reserve 8/10ths × £10	8	
		20
Goodwill on acquisition by H of S1		21
Less Capital Reserve on acquisition by S1 and S2		1¼
		19¾

Minority Interests

General Reserve 2/10ths of £10	2
Shares of S1	2
Profit and Loss S1 and S2 2/10ths of £30	6
Minority Interest per consolidated balance sheet of S1 and S2	13¾
	23¾

Profit and Loss Account

H Balance Sheet		60
Per consolidated balance sheet of S1 and S2 8/10ths of £30	24	
Less Pre-acquisition profits of S1 (there was a £5 balance at acquisition date) 8/10ths of £5	4	
		20
		80

It can be seen that the only differences between the methods are the amounts of the minority interest and of the goodwill calculated on consolidation.

Exercises

34.1. From the following balance sheets you are to draft a consolidated balance sheet for the group of H, S1 and S2. Use Method A as described in the chapter.

H Balance Sheet as at 31 December 19-7

	£	£
Investment in S1:		
9,000 shares bought 31/12/19-6		23,000
Fixed Assets		99,000
Current Assets		25,000
		147,000
Share Capital		100,000
Profit and Loss Account:		
As at 31/12/19-6	15,000	
Add Profit for 19-7	22,000	
		37,000
General Reserve		10,000
		147,000

S1 Balance Sheet as at 31 December 19-7

	£	£
Investment in S2:		
3,500 shares bought 31/12/19-6		6,000
Fixed Assets		22,000
Current Assets		5,000
		33,000
Share Capital		10,000
Profit and Loss Account:		
As at 31/12/19-6	7,000	
Add Profit for 19-7	16,000	
		23,000
		33,000

S2 Balance Sheet as at 31 December 19-7

	£	£
Fixed Assets		6,000
Current Assets		3,000
		9,000
Share Capital		5,000
Profit and Loss Account:		
As at 31/12/19-6	1,000	
Add Profit for 19-7	3,000	
		4,000
		9,000

432

34.2A. From the following balance sheets prepare a consolidated balance sheet for the group H, S1 and S2. Use Method A as per the chapter.

H Balance Sheet as at 31 December 19-9

	£	£
Investment in S1:		
16,000 shares bought 31/12/19-8		39,000
Fixed Assets		200,000
Current Assets		40,000
		279,000
Share Capital		200,000
Profit and Loss Account:		
As at 31/12/19-8	43,000	
Add Profit for 19-9	36,000	
		79,000
		279,000

S1 Balance Sheet as at 31 December 19-9

	£	£
Investment in S2:		
7,000 shares bought 31/12/19-8		13,000
Fixed Assets		16,000
Current Assets		4,000
		33,000
Share Capital		20,000
Profit and Loss Account:		
As at 31/12/19-8	6,000	
Add Profit for 19-9	4,000	
		10,000
General Reserve (as at 31/12/19-8)		3,000
		33,000

S2 Balance Sheet as at 31 December 19-9

	£	£
Fixed Assets		10,500
Current Assets		5,500
		16,000
Share Capital		10,000
Profit and Loss Account:		
As at 31/12/19-8	1,000	
Add Profit for 19-9	5,000	
		6,000
		16,000

35

Consolidated Profit and Loss Accounts

The consolidated profit and loss account is drawn up to show the profit (or loss) of the whole of the companies in the group, treating the group as a single entity. If all of the subsidiaries are owned 100 per cent, and there are no inter-company dividends or unrealized profits in stock, then it is simply a case of adding together all of the separate profit and loss accounts to form the consolidated profit and loss account.

If on the other hand there is a minority interest in the subsidiary company/companies, then the whole of the profits of the separate companies are brought into account first of all, the whole of the corporation tax is deducted, and from the resultant figure the minority interest's share is deducted, leaving as a residual the profits after tax which belong to the group.

Exhibit 35.1

	H Ltd	S Ltd
	£	£
Profit on ordinary activities before Taxation	2,000	1,500
Less Tax on Profit on Ordinary Activities	800	600
Profits for the year on Ordinary Activities after Taxation	1,200	900

H owns 80 per cent of the shares of S Ltd

This means that the minority interest are entitled to 20 per cent of the profits of S Ltd after tax has been deducted, i.e. 20 per cent of £900 = £180. The consolidated profit and loss account therefore appears as:

	£
Profits on Ordinary Activities before Taxation	3,500
Less Tax on Profit on Ordinary Activities	1,400
Profits for the year on Ordinary Activities after Taxation	2,100
Less Profit attributable to minority interests	180
Profit for the year attributable to the shareholders of H Ltd	1,920

Appropriation of Group Profits

Once the group profit has been found then the appropriations out of that profit can be shown. It must be remembered that all entries referring to the dividends paid or proposed by S Ltd will be completely eliminated for the purposes of the consolidation. However, the dividends paid and proposed by the holding company itself will be shown in the consolidated profit and loss account. This can best be seen in Exhibit 35.2.

Exhibit 35.2

	H Ltd		S Ltd	
	£	£	£	£
Profits (before showing dividend receivable from S Ltd as revenue)		2,000		
Profits				1,200
Add Dividend receivable from S Ltd		200		
Net Profit (profits before tax)		2,200		1,200
Less Corporation Tax	900		450	
Proposed Dividends	500		200	
		1,400		650
Unappropriated Profits for the year		800		550

If S had been owned 100 per cent by H then the consolidated profit and loss account would appear as:

	£
Profit on ordinary activities before Taxation (£2,000 + £1,200)	3,200
Less Tax on Profit on Ordinary Activities	1,350
Profit for the year on ordinary activities after Taxation	1,850
Less Appropriations:	
Proposed Dividends	500
Unappropriated Profits for the year	1,350

On the other hand if S had been only partly owned, say 80 per cent, by H then the figures would appear as in Exhibit 35.3.

Exhibit 35.3

	H Ltd		S Ltd	
	£	£	£	£
Profits (before showing dividend receivable from S Ltd as revenue)		2,000		
Profits				1,200
Add Dividend receivable from S Ltd		160		
Net Profits (profits before taxation)		2,160		1,200
Less Corporation Tax	900		450	
Proposed Dividends	500		200	
		1,400		650
Unappropriated Profits for the year		760		550

This means that the minority interest are entitled to 20 per cent of (£1,200 profits less £450 tax) £750 = £150.

The Consolidated Profit and Loss Account will appear as:

	£
Profits on Ordinary Activities before Taxation	3,200
Less Tax on Profit on Ordinary Activities	1,350
Profit for the year on Ordinary Activities after Taxation	1,850
Less Profit attributable to minority interests	150
Profit for the year attributable to the shareholders of H Ltd	1,700
Less Appropriations:	
Proposed Dividends	500
Undistributed Profits carried forward to next year	*1,200

*Note: this can be reconciled with the figures per the separate companies accounts as follows:

	£	£
Per the Consolidated Profit and Loss Account		1,200
Minority Shareholders' Interest	150	
Less 20 per cent of Ordinary Dividend (included in the figure of £150 on the line above)	40	
		110
Per the Separate Accounts £550 + £760		1,310

Any transfer to Consolidated Reserves will be:

(*a*) Those of the Holding Company, plus
(*b*) The Group's share of the Subsidiary's Transfers to Reserves.

These can be seen in Exhibit 35.4.

	H		S	
	£	£	£	£
Profits (before dividend receivable from S)		3,000		
Profits				2,000
Add Dividend Receivable from S		300		
		3,300		2,000
Less Corporation Tax	1,400		800	
Proposed Dividend	1,000		400	
Transfers to General Reserve	550		600	
		2,950		1,800
Unappropriated Profits carried forward to next year		350		200

H Ltd owns 75 per cent of the shares of S Ltd

Profit on Ordinary Activities before Taxation	5,000
Less Tax on Profit on Ordinary Activities	2,200
Profit for the year on Ordinary Activities after Taxation	2,800
Less Profit attributable to Minority Interests	300
Profit for the year attributable to the shareholders of H Ltd.	2,500

Less Appropriations:		
Proposed Dividend	1,000	
Transfer to General Reserve (£550 + $\frac{3}{4}$ of £600)	1,000	
		2,000
Undistributed Profit carried forward to next year		*500

*Reconcilable with separate Profit and Loss Accounts:		
Per Consolidated Profit and Loss Account		500
Minority Shareholders' Interest	300	
Less 25 per cent of Ordinary Dividends (included in the figure of £300 on the last line)	100	
Less 25 per cent of transfer to General Reserve (25 per cent of £600)	150	
	250	50
Per the Separate Accounts (£350 + £200)		550

Exercises

35.1. From the following draw up the consolidated profit and loss account for the year ended 31 December 19-6.

	H		S	
	£	£	£	£
Profits		80,000		30,000
Add Dividend receivable from S		4,500		
		84,500		
Less Corporation Tax	35,000		14,000	
Proposed Dividend	30,000		6,000	
		65,000		20,000
		19,500		10,000

H owns 75 per cent of the shares in S.

35.2A. Draw up a consolidated profit and loss account from the following for the year ended 31 December 19-8.

	H		S	
	£	£	£	£
Profits		550,000		200,000
Dividend receivable from S		36,000		
		586,000		
Less Corporation Tax	254,000		98,000	
Proposed Dividend	180,000		60,000	
		434,000		158,000
		152,000		42,000

H owns 60 per cent of the shares of S.

35.3A. The following are summarized balance sheets of North Ltd, South Ltd, and West Ltd at 31 December 19-6.

	North Ltd	South Ltd	West Ltd
	£	£	£
Issued Share Capital (£1 Ordinary Shares)	100,000	25,000	15,000
Profit and Loss Account at 31 December 19-4	44,000	7,000	6,000
Net Profit (loss) 19-5	16,500	2,400	(3,000)
Net Profit (loss) 19-6	18,000	3,600	(1,200)
6 per cent debentures	—	5,000	—
Current liabilities	11,500	4,000	2,600
	190,000	47,000	19,400

Fixed assets	115,000	27,000	14,000
Current assets	31,000	9,000	5,400
25,000 ordinary shares in South Ltd at cost	39,000	–	–
10,000 ordinary shares in West Ltd at cost	–	11,000	–
£5,000 6 per cent debentures of South Ltd at cost	5,000	–	–
	190,000	47,000	19,400

North Ltd acquired its shares in South Ltd on 31 December 19-4, and South Ltd acquired its shares in West Ltd on 31 December 19-5.

The profit and loss account of South Ltd at 31 December 19-4 had been debited with a proposed dividend of £2,500. The dividend was paid on 1 March 19-5, and was included in the net profit of North Ltd for the year 19-5. No other dividends have been paid or proposed by any of the companies in the relevant years.

South Ltd issued the 6 per cent debentures on 1 July 19-6. The accrued interest for the six months to 31 December 19-6, has been deducted in the calculation of the net profit of South Ltd for 19-6, and has been included in the current liabilities of South Ltd, but no entry has been made in the books of North Ltd for the interest due on the debentures.

Prepare the consolidated balance sheet of the group at 31 December 19-6.

Give a short summary of your calculations for all items in the consolidated balance sheet, except share capital, fixed assets and current assets.

Ignore taxation.

(Institute of Bankers)

35.4A. The summarized balance sheet of Expansion Ltd, Flourish Ltd, and Growth Ltd at 31 December 19-0 were:

	Expansion Ltd	*Flourish Ltd*	*Growth Ltd*
	£	£	£
200,000 shares in Flourish Ltd at cost	240,000	–	–
180,000 shares in Growth Ltd at cost	–	252,000	–
Sundry Assets *minus* Current Liabilities	53,000	173,000	664,000
	293,000	425,000	664,000
Issued Share Capital (£1 Ordinary Shares)	120,000	200,000	300,000
Profit and Loss Account	63,000	13,000	59,000
Proposed Final Dividends	30,000	12,000	5,000
9 per cent debentures	80,000	200,000	300,000
	293,000	425,000	664,000

Details of profits and dividends for 19-9 and 19-0 are shown below:

	Expansion Ltd	Flourish Ltd	Growth Ltd
	£	£	£
Profit and Loss Account 31 December 19-8	48,000	31,000	
Net Profit 19-9	23,000	18,000	(not relevant)
Less Dividends for 19-9:			
Interim paid July 19-9	–	(15,000)	
Final paid Feb. 19-0	(15,000)	(5,000)	
Profit and Loss Account 31 December 19-9	56,000	29,000	83,000
Net Profit 19-0	37,000	34,000	21,000
Less Dividends for 19-0:			
Interim paid July 19-0	–	(38,000)	(40,000)
Final proposed	(30,000)	(12,000)	(5,000)
Profit and Loss Account, 31 December 19-0	63,000	13,000	59,000

In the above statement, dividends have been credited to net profit of the relevant company when, and not before, the dividends were received.

All debenture interest has been appropriately deducted in the calculation of net profit and there were no share issues in the relevant years.

On 31 December 19-8, Expansion Ltd acquired its shares in Flourish Ltd and, on 31 December 19-9, Flourish Ltd acquired its shares in Growth Ltd. Both acquisitions were 'ex dividend', so that dividends declared prior to acquisition can be ignored.

Required:
(*a*) The consolidated balance sheet of the group at 31 December 19-0. It is important that you submit your calculations of all items in the consolidated balance sheet. Ignore taxation.
(*b*) Brief comments on what you considered to be the advantages or disadvantages (to a user of the accounts) of the information which would be shown in the consolidated accounts, compared with accounts for Expansion Ltd alone.

35.5A. The summarized balance sheets of E.S.T. Ltd and its two subsidiary companies, H.R.D. Ltd and S.N.W. Ltd, at 31 December 19-7, were as under:

E.S.T. Ltd.

	£
Fixed Assets	85,000
Current Assets	62,000
16,000 Ordinary Shares in H.R.D. Ltd at cost *less* dividend for 19-5	19,800
30,000 Ordinary Shares in S.N.W. Ltd at cost	48,000
	214,800

Issued Share Capital (150,000 Ordinary Shares of £1 each)	150,000
Profit and Loss Account	26,800
Current Liabilities	38,000
	214,800

H.R.D. Ltd

	£	£
Fixed Assets		18,000
Current Assets		14,750
		32,750
Issued Share Capital (20,000 Ordinary Shares of £1 each)		20,000
Profit and Loss Account:		
Balance at 31/12/19-5	5,500	
Less Dividend for 19-5	2,000	
	3,500	
Net Profit, 19-6	1,500	
	5,000	
Less Net Loss, 19-7	1,250	
		3,750
Current Liabilities		9,000
		32,750

S.N.W. Ltd

	£	£
Fixed Assets		31,000
Current Assets		16,200
		47,200
Issued Share Capital (30,000 Ordinary Shares of £1 each)		30,000
Profit and Loss Account:		
Balance at 31/12/19-6	7,000	
Net Profit, 19-7	4,200	
		11,200
Current Liabilities		6,000
		47,200

E.S.T. Ltd acquired the shares in the subsidiaries as follows:

Date		Price
		£
31 December 19-5.	12,000 shares in H.R.D. Ltd	15,000
31 December 19-6.	4,000 shares in H.R.D. Ltd	6,000
31 December 19-6.	30,000 shares in S.N.W. Ltd	48,000

For the purpose of determining the price of the shares in S.N.W. Ltd, the fixed assets of that company were valued at £5,000 in excess of the amount at which they stood in the books. The fixed assets were not written up in the books of S.N.W. Ltd, and, in the accounts of that company for 19-7, depreciation was charged at 10 per cent of the book amount. In the consolidated accounts, the fixed assets of S.N.W. Ltd are to be brought in at their valuation at the date of acquisition of the shares, less depreciation, for the year 19-7, at the rate of 10 per cent of that amount.

You are required to prepare a consolidated balance sheet, as on 31 December 19-7.

Show you calculations.

Ignore taxation.

(Chartered Institute of Secretaries and Administrators)

35.6A. The following are the trial balances of A.T.H. Ltd, G.L.E. Ltd, and F.R.N. Ltd as on 31 December 19-8.

	A.T.H. £	G.L.E. £	F.R.N. £
Ordinary Share Capital (shares of £1 each, fully paid)	100,000	30,000	20,000
7 per cent Cumulative Preference Share Capital (shares of £1 each, fully paid)	–	–	5,000
Profit and Loss Account – balance at 31/12/19-7	15,600	6,000	1,900
Current Liabilities	20,750	15,900	18,350
Sales	194,000	116,000	84,000
Dividend received from G.L.E. Ltd	1,200	–	–
	331,550	167,900	129,250
Fixed Assets	45,000	29,000	25,000
Current Assets	46,000	27,500	22,500
24,000 Ordinary Shares in G.L.E. Ltd at cost	33,700	–	–
20,000 Ordinary Shares in F.R.N. Ltd at cost	21,250	–	–
Cost of Goods Sold	153,000	87,000	63,000
General Expenses	32,600	22,900	18,750
Dividend for 19-8, paid on 31/12/19-8	–	1,500	–
	331,550	167,900	129,250

A.T.H. Ltd acquired the shares in F.R.N. Ltd on 31 December 19-6, when the credit balance on the profit and loss account of F.R.N. Ltd was £700, and acquired the shares in G.L.E. Ltd on 31 December 19-7. No dividend was paid by either A.T.H. Ltd or G.L.E. Ltd for the year 19-7.

No dividend has been paid by F.R.N. Ltd for the years 19-6, 19-7 and 19-8 and none is proposed. The directors of A.T.H. Ltd propose to pay a dividend of £7,000 for 19-8.

The sales of G.L.E. Ltd for 19-8 (£116,000) include £1,000 for goods sold to F.R.N. Ltd and this amount has been debited to purchases account in the books of F.R.N. Ltd. All these goods were sold by F.R.N. Ltd during 19-8.

Required:

A consolidated trading and profit and loss account for the year 19-8 and a consolidated balance sheet as on 31 December 19-8 (not necessarily in a form for publication).

Ignore depreciation of fixed assets and taxation.

(Chartered Institute of Secretaries and Administrators)

35.7A. You are required to prepare a consolidated profit and loss account for the year ended 31 December 19-0, suitable for incorporation in the published accounts of A Limited, which will not include a separate profit and loss account for the holding company.

	A Ltd	B Ltd
	£	£
Profit and Loss Account, balance at 1/1/19-0	36,000	15,000
Trading Profit	71,000	40,000
Dividends (gross) from B Ltd		
Preference	5,400	–
Ordinary	7,500	–
	119,900	55,000
Depreciation	12,000	4,000
Debenture Interest	10,000	–
Directors' Emolument	7,000	3,000
Taxation	22,000	15,000
Dividends Paid:		
6 per cent Preference 30 June	–	3,000
31 December	–	3,000
Ordinary:		
Interim 30 June	12,000	5,000
Final 31 December	12,000	5,000
Profit and Loss Account, balance at 31/12/19-0	44,900	17,000
	119,900	55,000

The following information relates to share capital:

	A Ltd	B Ltd
	£	£
Ordinary Shares of £1 each fully paid	400,000	200,000
6 per cent Preference Shares of £1 each, fully paid		100,000
Shares in B Ltd held by A Ltd:		
Ordinary Shares acquired 1/7/19-0		150,000
Preference Shares acquired 1/1/19-0		90,000

Income and expenditure are deemed to accrue evenly throughout the year. All dividends are payable out of the current year's profits. The directors of B Ltd resigned on 1 July 19-0 and were replaced on that day by directors of A Ltd who are to receive the same remuneration as the former directors.

(Institute of Cost and Management Accountants)

36

Accounting for the Results of Associated Companies

In January 1971 the Institute of Chartered Accountants in England and Wales issued its first statement of standard accounting practice. This was concerned with investments in companies which were either 50 per cent owned or less than 50 per cent owned by the investing company. Where a company is more than 50 per cent owned then it will be a subsidiary company and the rules which govern consolidated accounts, as explained in the last few chapters, will apply. With the investments in other companies then before 1971 these have normally been brought into the investing company's accounts only by virtue of the amount of the dividends received or receivable at the accounting date, and the cost of the investment has been shown in the balance sheet. This accounting standard brought in another form of company, as 'Associated Company'.

The Definition given of 'Associated Company' was as follows:

A company (not being a subsidiary of the investing group or company) is an associated company of the investing group or company if:

(a) the investing group or company's interest in the associated company is effectively that of a partner in a joint venture or consortium.

or

(b) the investing group or company's interest in the associated company is for the long term and is substantial (i.e. not less than 20 per cent of the equity voting rights), and, having regard to the disposition of the other shareholdings, the investing group or company is in a position to exercise a significant influence over the associated company.

In both cases it is essential that the investing group or company participates (usually through representation on the board) in commercial and financial policy decisions of the associated company, including the distribution of profits.

The accounting standard states that the consolidation procedure normally used for subsidiaries should be extended to associated companies. Since the Companies Act 1948 has required the preparation of group accounts normally in the form of consolidated accounts there had been two important developments. Previous to 1948 subsidiary companies had been the main way by which companies had conducted an important part of their business through the medium of other companies. Since then there has been the growing practice of companies to conduct parts of their business through other companies (frequently consortium or joint venture companies) in which they have had a substantial but not controlling interest. The other is the importance which investors have come to attach to earnings, as distinct from dividends, the price/earnings ratio and earnings per share. As investors have become more sophisticated they have realized that the dividends themselves tell only part of the story, what is also of importance is how much has actually been earned in profits during the period.

This has meant that, if a company had subsidiaries and what are now defined as associated companies, then the results of each subsidiary for both dividends and profits would be brought fully into the consolidated accounts. The associated companies results could merely be shown by virtue of dividends received or receivable and the cost of the investment. Thus a full view of subsidiaries was given but only a partial view, very often a totally misleading one, was given of the associated companies. The accounting standard of 1971 was to correct such poor reporting by putting associated companies on what really is the same basis as for subsidiary companies.

Of course a holding company will already have to prepare consolidated accounts for itself and it subsidiaries. On the other hand where a company has no subsidiaries, but it has one or more associated companies, then it will have to adapt its profit and loss account, suitably title to incorporate the additional information. For an example of this see Exhibit 36.1.

The investing group or company should give particulars of the names of and its interests in companies treated as associated companies, and of any other companies in which it holds not less than 20 per cent of the equity voting rights but which are not treated as associated companies.

A revised Accounting Standard was issued in April 1982. The requirements fundamentally remain the same.

The 1981 Companies Act introduced the term 'related company'. Obviously all associated companies will fall within the definition of associated companies. The Accounting Standards has decided *not* to extend the requirements of the standard to include all related companies, as it believes that the principles of equity accounting should only be applied in the circumstances specified in the standard.

Exhibit 36.1

Example of a profit and loss account of a company without subsidiaries.

Profit and loss account of investing company.

	£'000	£'000
Turnover		2,000
Cost of sales		1,400
Gross profit		600
Distribution costs	175	
Administrative expenses	125	300
Profit on ordinary activities before taxation		300
Tax on profit on ordinary activities		85
Profit on ordinary activities after taxation		215
Dividends – proposed		80
Amount set aside to reserves		135

Supplementary statement incorporating results of associated companies:

	£'000
Share of profits less losses of associated companies	50
Less tax	15
Share of profits after tax of associated companies	35
Profit on ordinary activities after taxation (as above)	215
Profit attributable to members of the investing company	250
Dividends – proposed	80
Net profit retained (£35,000 by associated companies)	170

Note: The earnings per share figure would be based on £250,000.

37

Accounting Ratios: A Further View

In Chapters 32 and 45 of volume one, the reader was introduced to accounting ratios and to the interpretation of final accounts. The present chapter takes the reader one stage further. On occasion the reader will be required to look again at factors already dealt with volume one, but it may be in greater depth or with a different slant.

Accounting information summarises the economic performance and situation of a business. In order to make use of this information the user needs to analyse and interpret its meaning. When confronted with information it is useful to have a framework of analysis available to make an attempt to distil what is important from the mass of less important data.

A mechanic confronted with a car that is refusing to start has a set of routine checks which will by elimination help to identify the problem. Someone without the appropriate knowledge can feel helpless faced with the complex array of electrical and mechanical parts under the bonnet of a car.

A business is in many ways more complex than a motor car. In a car cause and effect can be traced through a mechanical sequence. A thorough check will show the fault and a repair can be made. If a business's sales decline however, the cause may be clearly identifiable on the other hand the problem may be due to a variety of causes, some of which are human problems and may not be so easily diagnosed. A business consists of people interacting amongst themselves as well as with the mechanical means of production at their disposal. The human behaviour element may not always lend itself to logical and systematic analysis.

Having said this however the first stage in analysis is the development of a systematic review of the accounting data. In this respect accounting ratios are relationships which bring together the results of activity which experience shows identify the key areas for success of the business.

The choice of ratios will be determined by the needs of the user of the information. In this chapter the ratios which are illustrated are divided into main groups which may be identified with the requirements of particular users. However this division whilst it is useful as an aid to our memory and in developing a logical approach should not be taken as a set of rigid rules. A supplier of goods on credit to a firm, will mainly be interested in his customers immediate ability to repay him, which will be measured by liquidity ratios, but he will also be interested in the overall future and prospects of the customer measured by the Profitability and other ratios.

The main parties interested in accounts include shareholders and potential shareholders, creditors, lenders, the Government for taxation and statistical purposes, potential take over bidders, employees particularly though their trade unions, as well as management. The interests of the various parties have been summarised in Exhibit 38.1 which divides the types of ratio into five main categories. In this book it is not possible to show all possibly useful ratios since these can run to many hundreds, rather generally useful common ratios are illustrated. In practice it is sensible to calculate as many ratios as appear useful for the required objective.

Exhibit 37.1

Examples of Parties with an immediate interest	Type of Ratio
Potential Suppliers of goods on credit; Lenders, e.g. Bank managers and debenture holders; Management.	*Liquidity (Credit Risk):* Ratios indicating how well equipped the business is to pay its way.
Shareholders (Actual and Potential); Potential take-over bidders; Lenders; Management; Competitive firms; Tax Authorities; Employees.	*Profitability:* How successfully is the business trading.
Shareholders (Actual and Potential); Potential take-over bidders; Management; Competitive Firms; Employees.	*Use of Assets:* How effectively are the assets of the firm utilised.
Shareholders (Actual and Potential); Potential take-over bidders; Management; Lenders and Creditors in assessing risk.	*Capital Structure:* How does the capital structure of the firm affect the cost of capital and the return to shareholders.
Shareholders (Actual and Potential); Potential take-over bidders; Management.	*Investment:* Show how the market prices for a share reflect a company's performance.

Exhibit 37.2 shows a set of accounts prepared for The Rational Company Ltd. The various types of ratio mentioned in Exhibit 37.1 will be illustrated using the data for The Rational Company Ltd.

Exhibit 37.2

The Rational Co. Ltd.
Profit and Loss Account for the year ended 31 December 19-1

	£	£
Turnover		900,000
Cost of Sales		780,000
Gross Profit		120,000
Distribution Costs	27,000	
Administrative Expenses	30,000	57,000
		63,000
Other Operating Income (Royalties)		4,700
		67,700
Interest Payable		15,700
Profit on Ordinary Activities before Taxation		52,000
Tax on Profit on Ordinary Activities		22,000
Profit for the year on Ordinary Activities after Taxation		30,000
Undistributed Profits from last year		107,400
		137,400
Preference Dividend paid	2,400	
Proposed Ordinary Dividend	15,000	17,400
Undistributed Profits Carried to Next Year		120,000

Rational Co. Ltd.
(Abridged Balance Sheet as at 31 December 19-1)

	Cost	Depreciation	Net
Fixed Assets	£	£	£
Land and Buildings	500,000	140,000	360,000
Plant	40,000	10,000	30,000
	540,000	150,000	390,000
Current Assets			
Stock		90,000	
Debtors		105,000	
Bank		15,000	
		210,000	
Less Current Liabilities			
Trade Creditors	21,000		
Bank Overdraft	32,000		
Current Taxation	22,000		
Proposed Ordinary Dividend	15,000	90,000	
Working Capital			120,000
			510,000
Debentures 7%			210,000
			300,000

Capital and Reserves
Called-up Share Capital

Ordinary Shares	150,000	
8% Preference Shares	30,000	180,000
Profit and Loss Account		120,000
		300,000

N.B. The Market Price of an ordinary share at 31 December 19-1 was
£3.

Liquidity Ratios

The analysis of credit risk was the historic starting point for formal
ratio analysis. With widely scattered markets a firm is frequently
asked to trade with companies it has little or no knowledge of. The
risks of supplying goods on credit to a strange company are fairly
obvious and in practice can be very hazardous. Many small businesses
have themselves been forced to wind up because a large customer has
failed to pay its debt. It is hardly surprising that firms specializing in
giving advice on credit risks should have come into existence. These
firms started the consistent use of ratios to analyze company balance
sheets. Usually they are operating as outsiders and therefore have to
rely on published information, in contrast to the management of a
business who can obtain much more detailed information about that
business. The following ratios are useful in the measurement of
liquidity:-

The Current Ratio

The Current Ratio measures Current Assets: Current Liabilities. In
general terms we are comparing assets which will become liquid in
approximately twelve months with liabilities which will be due for
payment in the same period.

In interpreting the ratio a creditor will want to see a sufficiently
large amount of current assets to cover liabilities and the eventuality
of losses. It is hard, however, to say exactly what is satisfactory since
factors of type of industry and overall size and reputation of the firm
will play a part. A commonly used rule of thumb would be 2:1, in
other words £2 of Current Asset for £1 of Current Liability, but many
very goods firms show a lower ratio, whilst some bad ones, by over
valuing assets, show a much higher ratio. Referring to Exhibit 38.2 the
Current Ratio is 210,000:90,000 = 2.3:1. This may also be conveniently
expressed by $\dfrac{210,000}{90,000} = 2.3$ times.

The Acid Test Ratio

In order to refine the analysis of the Current Ratio another ratio is used which takes only those current assets which are cash or will convert very quickly into cash. This will normally mean Cash and Debtors or Current Assets less Stock in Trade. The Acid Test Ratio may, therefore, be stated as:-

Current Assets less Stock in Trade : Current Liabilties.

The ratio calculated from Exhibit 38.2 is:-

$$\frac{120,000}{90,000} = 1.3 \text{ times.}$$

This shows that provided Creditors and Debtors are paid at approximately the same time, the company has sufficient liquid resources to meet its current liabilities. If a large proportion of the Current Assets had been in the form of Stock in Trade the liquid position might have been dangerously low.

The ratios shown under Credit Risk have been concerned with liquidity. A useful supplement to this type of analysis is provided by Cash Flow Statements which have been dealt with in another chapter. From the point of view of management, the forecast cash flow statement is the most useful statement for control of credit. For those outside the firm, however, this information is not usually available and they must rely on the ratios.

Profitability Ratios

Profitability is the end product of the policies and decisions taken by a firm, and is its single most important measure of success.

Gross Profit/Sales

From Exhibit 38.2 the ratio for the Rational Company Ltd. is $\dfrac{120,000}{900,000}$ = .133 or as a percentage on sales = 13.3 per cent.

It is impossible to state a rule of thumb for this figure which will vary considerably from firm to firm and industry to industry.

Net Profit (after Tax)/Sales

The same comments apply to Net Profit/Sales as to Gross Profit/Sales. The difference between the two ratios will be explained by measuring the ratios of sales to the Expenses in the Profit and Loss Account. The ratio from Exhibit 37.2 in $\dfrac{30,000}{900,000}$ = .033 = 3.3 per cent. This percentage of 3.3 indicates by how much the profit margin can decline before the firm makes losses.

Return on Capital Employed

Great care must be exercised in measuring ratios of profit to Capital Employed. There are no standard definitions and thus for comparability it is necessary to ensure that the same method is used over time for the same firm or between different firms. Another problem is inherent in comparing profit which arises over a period of time, with Capital Employed which is taken from the Balance Sheet and is thus measured at one point of time. For a proper evaluation the Capital Employed needs to be an average figure for the accounting period in which the profit was calculated. As an external analyst the only data available is at the beginning and end of the accounting period. Since the year end is by no means likely to be representative of the average for a period any calculated figure must be taken with caution. If for example an analyst knows that a major investment in fixed assets took place mid-way through the year he would tend to average the opening and closing figures. If little change has taken place then the year end figure may be used.

Net Profit (After Tax)/Total Assets

In this calculation of Return on Capital Employed the Total Assets are defined as all Fixed and other Non-Current Assets plus Working Capital. Working Capital is simply the figure reached by deducting Current Liabilities from Current Assets, (assuming that Current Assets exceed Current Liabilities). Using the data from Exhibit 37.2 the working capital is Current Assets £210,000 less Current Liabilities £90,000 = £120,000. The Total Assets are therefore Fixed Assets £390,000 + Working Capital £120,000 = £510,000 and the return is

$$\frac{\text{Net Profit (after tax)}}{\text{Total Assets}} = \frac{30,000}{510,000} = 5.88\%$$

One of the problems with using this approach to Return on Capital is that Net Profit after tax will already have had interest on debentures, loans and overdrafts charged against it and thus if this interest is significant the return on assets will be understated.

Similarly if the Assets of the business include items of an intangible nature such as Goodwill it is often felt that the return on assets is better related to tangible assets alone, since the accounting valuation of intangibles varies so much.

To answer these problems the following ratio is often used:-

Net Operating Profit/Operating Assets

The aim here is to be take the operating profit which is the outcome of operations before interest charges are made or any investment income is included. This profit will then be taken over Operating Assets which are the tangible assets used in the generation of the Operating Income. Operating Assets will not include intangibles nor investments in shares or other securities outside the firm, whether shown under a separate hearing or as Current Assets.

As with the previous calculation of Total Assets it is appropriate to take Working Capital as part of Operating Assets but in this definition it is frequently appropriate to exclude Bank Overdraft from Current Liabilities. Although from a legal point of view and from the Banks intention it is a Current Liability, since repayment can be demanded at short notice, in practice for a well run business the bank is usually happy to maintain an overdraft over extended periods of time. Unlike most of the other Current Liabilities interest is chargeable on overdrafts.

Thus this definition of Return on Capital Employed is Net Operating Profit: Tangible Operating Fixed Assets + (Working Capital + Overdraft). Referring to Exhibit 37.2 this is equal to £390,000 + £120,000 + £30,000 = £540,000. Which is equivalent to:-

Share Capital £180,000 + Reserves £120,000 + Debentures £210,000 + Bank overdraft £30,000 = £540,000

The Net Operating Profit which in Exhibit 37.2 = £67,700 is the profit obtained from the Capital Employed before paying interest or dividends to any of these sources of capital. This return on Capital Employed in the Rational Company Ltd. is therefore $\frac{67,700}{540,000} = 12.54$ per cent.

Net Profit (After Taxes)/Owners Equity

In this case the net profit after tax (less Preference Dividends) is compared with the Ordinary Shareholders stake in the business i.e. ordinary share capital plus reserves. From Exhibit 37.2 the ratio is

$$\frac{£27,600}{£270,000} = 10.2 \text{ per cent.}$$

In contrast to the previous ratio this one is not an overall measure of profitability but is specially concerned with the return an ordinary shareholder might expect.

SSAP 3 Earnings per share applies to all U.K. companies quoted on the stock exchanges. It is impossible to summarise the SSAP in a few words. Students at later stages of professional examinations should obtain the SSAP and read its detailed instructions.

Use of Assets Ratios

Although the way assets are utilized will effect profitability, these particular ratios deserve to be evaluated separately as they are of great importance. In effect they show how effectively management has been using the assets at their disposal.

A straightforward ratio between Assets and Sales can be used by the external analyst. For the Rational Co. Ltd we should show:—

Land and Buildings	: Sales	360,000 : 900,000	= 1 : 2.5
Plant	: Sales	30,000 : 900,000	= 1 : 30.0
Total Fixed Assets	: Sales	390,000 : 900,000	= 1 : 2.3
Stock in Trade	: Sales	90,000 : 900,000	= 1 : 10.0
Debtors	: Sales	105,000 : 900,000	= 1 : 8.6
Cash at Bank	: Sales	15,000 : 900,000	= 1 : 60.0
Total Current Assets	: Sales	210,000 : 900,000	= 1 : 4.3

It is often convenient to express these ratios in terms of 'per £1,000 of sales' to avoid too much "rounding off." For example Land and Buildings per £1,000 of sales would be £400, i.e. (360,000 ÷ 900).

A number of these activity ratios are sufficiently important to merit special mention and in some cases detailed development.

Sales/Fixed Assets

The ratio of Sales to Fixed Assets measures the utilisation a firm is obtaining from its investment in fixed plant. If the ratio is low it indicates that management may not be utilizing its plant very effectively. In the illustration from Exhibit 37.2, the ratio is = 2.3 times, or £433.3 per £1,000 of sales.

Stock Turnover

This important ratio is measured in the first instance by dividing Sales by Stock in Trade. Since Sales are at Selling Prices, the Stock should also be measured at selling price. Usually an easier way is to divide Sales at Cost Price (which is the Cost of Goods Sold total) by Stock in Trade at cost value. The stock figure used should be an average figure for the year. Whilst the true average will be known to management it will often not be available to outsiders. In this situation a very rough approximation is used by taking the average of the opening and closing stocks. if in the example in Exhibit 38.2, the stock at 1 January had been £50,000 and the stock at 31st December is £90,000 the average would be taken as

$$\frac{50,000 + 90,000}{2} = £70,000.$$

The Stock turnover therefore is

$$\frac{\text{Cost of Goods Sold}}{\text{Stock in Trade}} = \frac{780,000}{70,000} = 11.1 \text{ times.}$$

If the cost of Goods Sold is not known, it may be necessary to use the Sales figure instead. Although this is not a satisfactory basis, it may be better than nothing if like is compared with like. Notice that in this example Stock turnover = 10.0 times if the Sales figure is used.

Collection Period for Debtors

The resources tied up in debtors is an important ratio subject. We have already calculated the relationships of debtors to sales which in the example is 1:8.6. This means that for every £8.6 sold there is £1 of debtors outstanding.

This relationship is often translated into the length of time a debtor takes to pay. If we assume that the sales for Rational Ltd. are made over the whole of one year i.e. 365 days this means that on average a debt is outstanding for $365 \times \dfrac{1}{8.6} = 42.4$ days. Notice that it is assumed sales take place evenly over the year, and we have ignored holidays. However it is useful to know that our customers take about 6 weeks to pay!

In recent years the interest in productivity measurement has raised interest in many ratios which combine information which is not essentially part of the accounts with accounting data. Published Accounts for example are now required to show as supplementary information the average number of people employed by a limited Company. This information may be related to Sales to give an index of Sales per employee. For example if the average number employed by the Rational Company were 215 then sales per employee would be $\dfrac{900,000}{215} = £4,186$. This example is given as an illustration of the development of this type of measurement which may be a useful guide to assessment of a company's performance.

Capital Structure Ratios

The Capital Structure of a business is important because it has a significant influence on the risk to lenders, and on the return to shareholders.

In the first instance it is worthwhile to express the Balance Sheet in percentage terms. For the Rational Company using the main subtotals it would be as follows:

Balance Sheet at 31 December 19-1

		% of balance sheet totals
Fixed Assets		130
Current Assets	70	
Less Current Liabilities	30	40
		170
Less Debentures		70
		100
Ordinary Shares		50
Preference Shares		10
Profit and Loss Account		40
		100

Net Worth/Total Assets

From this it can be seen immediately that Ordinary Shares and Preference Shares with the Reserves, which total is often called Net Worth is providing 50 per cent of the financing of Fixed and Current Assets. Thus the ratio Net Worth: Fixed Assets + Current Assets is an important measure of the shareholder stake in a business. (300,000: 390,000 + 210,000 = 1:2).

Fixed Assets/Net Worth

From the Balance Sheet it is also easy to see that a high proportion of the assets (65%) are Fixed Assets. A comparison of the Fixed Assets with Net Worth shows whether the longer term investment usually involved in Fixed Assets is provided by Shareholders. In our example the ratio is £390,000 : £300,000 (or 65%:50%) = 1:0.77. This ratio shows that shareholders are not providing all the investment required to finance the fixed assets quite apart from current assets. The remainder of the funding of assets is provided by borrowing. The important thing here is to ensure that the borrowing is sufficiently long term to match the investment in fixed assets. If the company has to repay borrowing whilst all its resources are locked into assets which cannot easily be converted into cash it can only make repayment by fresh borrowing or new capital issues which may cause problems.

Fixed Assets/Net Worth and Long Term Loan

Provided the Mortgage Debenture has a reasonably long life the Rational Company provides reasonable cover of its Fixed Assets since Fixed Assets: Net Worth + Long Term Loan are in the ratio 1:1.31.

Coverage of Fixed Charges

This relationship is obtained by dividing net profit by any fixed interest charges or rentals. Since these charges are allowable expenses for tax purposes, the profit before tax will be used. From Exhibit 38.2 the interest charges are £15,700 with no rental expense. The available profit before tax is £52,000 + £15,700 = £67,700. The Fixed Charges are, therefore, covered

$$\frac{\text{Profit before tax} + \text{Fixed Charges}}{\text{Fixed Charges}} = \frac{67,000}{15,700} = 4.3 \text{ times.}$$

This is low enough to indicate a company which is high geared.

By 'high geared' is meant a company which has a high proportion of borrowing to net worth. A company with no gearing has all its funds provided by the ordinary shareholder. Gearing has also been measured indirectly in the ratio of Net Worth: Total Assets. The lower the proportion of funds provided from Net Worth, the higher the borrowing and hence gearing.

The coverage of fixed charges gives a very important measure of the extent to which the profit may decline before the company is not able to earn enough to cover the interest etc. it is legally obliged to pay. If charges are not paid legal steps will be taken against the company which usually end in it being taken over or wound up.

Borrowing/Net Worth

This ratio is the most direct measure of gearing since it indicates the proportions in which all funds are provided for the business. Borrowing is taken as all the long term and current liabilities of the business and Net Worth as Share Capital and Reserves. In this definition Preference Shares are included in net worth. Although the return to Preference Shareholders is a fixed rate interest there is no legal obligation for the company to pay it, hence the inclusion with Net Worth. If you are however looking at the effect of gearing on the return to ordinary shareholders it may then be appropriate to treat Preference Share Dividends as a fixed charge.

The Ratio for Rational Co. Ltd. is thus £210,000 + £90,000 : 300,000 = 1:1.

Investment Ratios

These ratios are important for the investor and financial manager who is interested in the market prices of the shares of a company on the Stock Exchange.

Dividend Yield

This measures the real rate of return on an investment in shares, as distinct from the declared dividend rate which is based on the nominal value of a share. The Yield is calculated as follows, illustrated from Exhibit 38.2:

$$\frac{\text{The Dividend per Share}}{\text{Market Price per Share}} = \frac{£1 \times 10 \text{ per cent}}{£3} = 3.3 \text{ per cent.}$$

Dividend Cover for Ordinary Shares

This indicates the amount of profit for an ordinary dividend and indicates the amount of profit retained in the business. The cover is:

$$\frac{\text{Net Profit for the year after Tax} - \text{Preference Dividend}}{\text{Dividend on Ordinary Shares}}$$
$$= \frac{£30,000 - 2,400}{15,000} = 1.8 \text{ times.}$$

Earnings Per Ordinary Share

As is implied by the name this ratio is

$$\frac{\text{Net Profit for the year after tax} - \text{Preference Dividend}}{\text{Number of Ordinary Shares}}$$
$$= \frac{£30,000 - 2,400}{150,000} = £0.18 \text{ per share}$$

The calculation of this important ratio is now covered by the Statement of Standard Accounting Practice 3.

The Price Earnings Ratio

Finally the Price Earnings Ratio relates the earnings per share to the price the shares sell at in the market. From Exhibit 37.2 the ratio is:

$$\frac{\text{Market Price}}{\text{Earnings per Share}} = \frac{£3}{£.18} = 16.7$$

This relationship is an important indicator to investor and financial manager of the market's evaluation of a share, and is very important when a new issue of shares is due since it shows the earnings the market expects in relation to the current share prices.

Summary of Ratios

Type of Ratio	Method of Calculation
LIQUIDITY	
Current Ratio	$\dfrac{\text{Current Assets}}{\text{Current Liabilities}}$
Acid Test Ratio	$\dfrac{\text{Current Assets less Stock in Trade}}{\text{Current Liabilities}}$
PROFITABILITY	
Gross Profit/Sales	$\dfrac{\text{Gross Profit}}{\text{Sales}}$
Net Profit after Tax/Sales	$\dfrac{\text{Net Profit after Tax}}{\text{Sales}}$
RETURN ON CAPITAL EMPLOYED	
Net Profit After Tax/Total Assets	$\dfrac{\text{Net Profit After Tax}}{\text{Fixed and Other Assets + Working Capital}}$
Net Operating Profit/Operating Assets	$\dfrac{\text{Net Operating Income}}{\text{Tangible Operating Fixed Assets + Working Capital and Overdraft}}$
Net Profit (after tax)/Owners Equity	$\dfrac{\text{Net Profit after tax less Preference Dividend}}{\text{Ordinary Share Capital + Reserves}}$
USE OF ASSETS	
Asset/Sales	$\dfrac{\text{Individual Asset Totals}}{\text{Sales}}$
Sales/Fixed Assets	$\dfrac{\text{Sales}}{\text{Fixed Assets}}$
Stock Turnover	$\dfrac{\text{Cost of Goods Sold}}{\text{Average Stock in Trade}}$
Collection Period for Debtors	$365 \times \dfrac{\text{Debtors}}{\text{Sales}}$

CAPITAL STRUCTURE

Net Worth/Total Assets

$$\frac{Ordinary\ Share\ Capital + Preference\ S.C. + Reserves}{Fixed\ Assets + Other\ Assets + Current\ Assets}$$

Fixed Assets/Net Worth

$$\frac{Fixed\ Assets}{Net\ Worth}$$

Fixed Assets/Net Worth and Long Term Loan

$$\frac{Fixed\ Assets}{Net\ Worth + Long\ Term\ Loan}$$

Coverage of Fixed Charges

$$\frac{Net\ Profit\ before\ tax\ and\ Fixed\ Charges}{Fixed\ Charges}$$

Borrowing/Net Worth

$$\frac{Long\ Term\ +\ Current\ Liabilities}{Net\ Worth}$$

INVESTMENT

Dividend Yield

$$\frac{Dividend\ per\ Share}{Market\ Price\ per\ Share}$$

Dividend Cover for Ordinary Shares

$$\frac{Net\ Profit\ after\ tax\ -\ Pref.\ Div.}{Ordinary\ Share\ Dividend}$$

Earnings per Ordinary share

$$\frac{Net\ Profit\ after\ tax\ -\ Pref.\ Div.}{Number\ of\ Ordinary\ Shares}$$

Price Earnings Ratio

$$\frac{Market\ Price\ per\ Share}{Earnings\ per\ Share}$$

Exercises

37.1A. Describe the five main groups of ratios and indicate who may be interested in each type.

37.2A. Explain what you think the following ratios indicate about a firm:
(a) Acid Test ratio.
(b) Net Operating Profit/Capital Employed.
(c) Collection Period for Debtors.
(d) Net Worth/Total Assets.
(e) Dividend Cover for Ordinary Shares.

37.3A. Stock Turnover is sometimes calculated by dividing sales by the average of the opening and closing stock in trade figures. What is wrong with this method of computation?

37.4. For each of the following items select the lettered item(s) which indicate(s) its effect(s) on the company's accounts. More than one item may be affected.

1. Declaration and payment of a dividend on Preference Share Capital.
2. Declaration of a proposed dividend on ordinary shares due for payment in one month.
3. Purchase of stock in trade for cash.
4. Payment of creditors.
5. Bad Debt written off against an existing provision for Bad and Doubtful Debts.

   Effect
A. Reduces working capital.
B. Increases working capital.
C. Reduces current ratio.
D. Increases current ratio.
E. Reduces acid test ratio.
F. Increases acid test ratio.

37.5A. Describe four ratios which might help you to assess the profitability of a company and explain their significance.

37.6. A limited company with 100,000 £1 Ordinary Shares as its Capital earns a profit after tax of £15,000. It pays a dividend of 10 per cent. The Market price of the shares is £1.50. What is the:

(*a*) Yield on Ordinary Shares?
(*b*) Earnings per share?
(*c*) Price/Earnings ratio?

37.7A. What ratios might be of particular interest to a potential holder of debentures in a limited company?

37.8. The following is a Trading and Profit and Loss Account of a small limited company engaged in manufacturing for the year ending 31 December 19-2:

	£'000	£'000
Sales (Credit)		150
Opening Stock	20	
Purchases (credit)	120	
	140	
Less Closing Stock	40	
	100	
Direct Manufacturing Expenses	20	
Overhead Expenditure	10	130
Net Profit		20

Balance Sheet at 31 December, 19-2

			£'000
Fixed Assets:	Cost	Aggreg. depr.	
Freehold Property	100	–	100
Plant and Machinery	40	20	20
	140	20	120
Current Assets:			
Stocks at cost		40	
Debtors		50	
Quoted Investments at cost		60	
Bank		20	
		170	
Less Current Liabilities:			
Corporation Tax	10		
Bills Payable	20		
Tax Creditors	60	90	80
			200
5 per cent Debentures			60
			140
Authorised and Issued Share Capital			100
Reserves			40
			140

Required

Select five major ratios and apply them to the above accounts and comment upon their relevance.

37.9A.
Ironsides Limited
Balance Sheet as at 31 December, 19-8

	£	£	£
Fixed Assets at cost			7,200,000
Depreciation			2,000,000
			5,200,000
Current Assets			
Stock		1,200,000	
Debtors		800,000	
Investments		600,000	
Cash		200,000	
		2,800,000	
Less Current Liabilities			
Creditors	280,000		
Taxation	520,000	800,000	
Working Capital			2,000,000
			7,200,000
6% Debenture		800,000	
5% Mortgage		2,000,000	
Bank Loan 8%		400,000	3,200,000
			4,000,000
Capital and Reserves			
Share Capital: Ordinary £1 shares			
Authorised		2,500,000	
Issued			2,400,000
General Reserve			1,600,000
			4,000,000

Condensed Profit and Loss Account for year ended 31 December, 19-9.

	£	£
Sales		12,000,000
Cost of Production		10,320,000
GROSS PROFIT		1,680,000
Other Expenses:		
Administration	120,000	
Selling	68,000	
Rent	112,000	
Depreciation	400,000	700,000
		980,000
Less Interest –		
Bank	32,000	
Mortgage	100,000	
Debenture	48,000	180,000
		800,000
Less Corporation Tax 45%		360,000
		440,000
Less Dividend		400,000
To General Reserve		£ 40,000

You are required to calculate for Ironsides Ltd. ten significant ratios and comment on the meaning.

37.10. The annual accounts of the Wholesale Textile Company Limited have been summarized for 19-1 and 19-2 as follows:

	Year 19-1		Year 19-2	
	£	£	£	£
Sales				
Cash	60,000		64,000	
Credit	540,000	600,000	684,000	748,000
Cost of sales		472,000		596,000
Gross margin		128,000		152,000
Expenses				
Warehousing		26,000		28,000
Transport		12,000		20,000
Administration		38,000		38,000
Selling		22,000		28,000
Debenture interest		—		4,000
		98,000		118,000
Net profit		30,000		34,000

	On 31 Dec. 19-1		On 31 Dec. 19-2	
	£	£	£	£
Fixed assets				
(*less* depreciation)		60,000		80,000
Current assets				
Stock	120,000		188,000	
Debtors	100,000		164,000	
Cash	20,000	240,000	14,000	366,000
Less Current liabilities				
Trade creditors		100,000		152,000
Net current assets		140,000		214,000
		200,000		294,000
Share Capital		150,000		150,000
Reserves and undistributed profit		50,000		84,000
Debenture loan		—		60,000
		200,000		294,000

You are informed that:—

1. All sales were from stocks in the company's warehouse.
2. The range of merchandise was not changed and buying prices remained steady throughout the two years.
3. Budgeted total sales for 19-2 were £780,000.
4. The debenture loan was received on 1 January, 19-2, and additional fixed assets were purchased on that date.

You are required to state the internal accounting ratios that you would use in this type of business to assist the management of the Company in measuring the efficiency of its operation, including its use of capital.

Your answer should name the ratios and give the figures (calculated to one decimal place) for 19-1 and 19-2, together with possible reasons for changes in the ratios for the two years. Ratios relating to capital employed should be based on the capital at the year end. Ignore taxation.

38

Interpretation of Final Accounts

The Interpretation of Final Accounts through the use of ratios can conveniently be divided into two parts. Firstly there is analysis by those outside the firm who are seeking to understand more from the published accounting data. On the other side there is management wishing to interpret a much fuller range of internal information in a meaningful way. In both situations current information will be assessed in relation to past trends of the same business and with comparative information for similar firms.

Comparisons Over Time

One of the most helpful ways in which accounting ratios can be used is to compare them with previous periods ratios for the same organisation. Taking as an example Net Profit after Tax/Sales results for the Rational Co. Ltd are as follows:—

	This year	1	2	3	4	5
		Years ago				
Net Profit after Tax/Sales	3.3	3.8	3.1	3.4	3.4	3.5

This years result acquires much more significance when compared to the previous five years. The appreciation of the trends is usually assisted by graphing the results as in Exhibit 38.1.

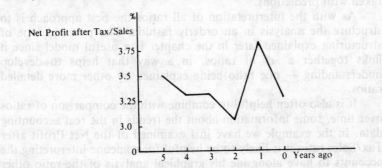

Exhibit 38.1

464

This graph very clearly illustrates how the net profit margin has fluctuated. In this type of case the ratio which is a comparative number is not expected to "grow" in the way that an expanding firm expects its Sales to grow. Thus for ratios an ordinary graph would normally be appropriate.

However when the ratio points have been plotted it can be helpful to insert a line of best fit to these points. Thus on the graph we drew of Net Profit After Tax/Sales a line of best fit gives a useful idea of the past trends of the ratio as in Exhibit 38.2.

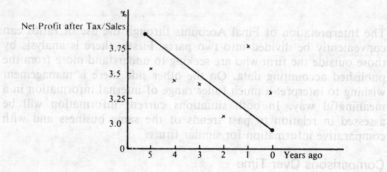

Exhibit 38.2

This can be drawn either by eye or better by using a statistical technique such as least squares.

It is very tempting to extend these trend lines into the future as a form of forecast. Past trends should not be used mechanically to predict the future. Only if you are sure that all conditions influencing a ratio are likely to remain constant next year should you extend the trend. Notice that in the graph we have just plotted the linear trend is relatively little influenced by the upturn in the current year. This improvement may in fact represent the start of an upward movement if we had sufficient information to explain it. Thus great care must be taken with predictions.

As with the interpretation of all ratios the best approach is to structure the analysis in an orderly fashion. The pyramid type of structuring explained later in the chapter is a useful model since it links together a set of ratios, in a way that helps to develop understanding — one ratio being explained by other more detailed ratios.

It is also often helpful to combine with the comparison of ratios over time, some information about the trends in the real accounting data. In the example we have just examined of the Net Profit after Tax/Sales ratio it is likely to be helpful for someone interpreting the accounts to have alongside his graphical analysis of the ratio other graphs showing the sales in £ and Net Profit after Tax in £. The ratio analysis must always be kept in the perspective of the real accounting results. The graphs of key figures from the Profit and Loss Account for example can usefully be developed on logarithmic scales to emphasise trends.

Comparisons with other firms

Comparisons over time are useful since they give a perspective on trends developing within a firm. However since firms operate in a competitive environment it is always necessary to have some basis of comparison with other organisations particularly those in the same type of business.

Whilst in principle inter-firm comparisons are very worthwhile there are considerable practical differences. Firstly in many cases organisations are not directly comparable with others in size or in the exact nature of business carried on. A large multinational company can be involved in a wide range of industries and countries of operation, as a whole therefore it is probably unique. Size can in itself have an important bearing on ratios. For example the Capital Structure Ratios of a large public company are not comparable with one which is small and privately owned. Secondly inter-company comparisons are frequently made misleading by differences in accounting methods and factors such as the age structure and location of assets.

Most of the difficulties mentioned can be overcome by a properly structured scheme of inter-firm comparison. Here firms agree to pool data and employ experts to ensure comparability of the data. However this type of scheme is only available internally for the management. For the external analyst relying on published data the development of accounting standards is helping to ensure a better basic source of information. The external analyst must by necessity look at the overall ratios for more general guidelines to a firm's performance.

External Analysis

The outsider is at some disadvantage in undertaking ratio analysis since he will have relatively little information about the underlying bases of accounting. He will, however, be able to obtain information which is now published, showing ratios by industry. These are calculated from the published accounts of public companies, and more limited information on accounts of private companies. This information would tend to be in a form similar to that shown in Exhibit 38.3, which is an abbreviated form of a broad schedule of ratios.

Using some information from Exhibit 37.2 in Chapter Thirty Seven, let us set up the information we have available to assess the Rational Co. Ltd. which is a Building and Civil Engineering Firm.

Exhibit 38.3

*Illustration of Published Ratios by Industry
Quoted Companies Year 19x0 and 19x1*

Industry Classification	Year	Financial Performance				Credit Control	
		P/CE %	NP/S %	S/FA times	S/ST times	CA/CL times	LA/CL times
Building and Civil Engineering	19-0	14.5	3.9	7.7	10.1	1.32	.96
	19-1	14.8	4.6	7.0	7.3	1.36	.93
Specialist Construction Contractors	19-0	14.5	5.3	6.0	9.8	1.55	1.15
	19-1	17.8	6.0	6.3	12.1	1.66	1.08

Notes: P. = Net Operating Profit   S.T. = Stock in Trade
          N.P. = Net Profit After Tax   C.A. = Current Assets
          C.E. = Capital Employed   C.L. = Current Liabilities
          S. = Sales   L.A. = Liquid Assets or Current Assets
          F.A. = Fixed Assets   Less Stock

The ratios shown are the median figures for the companies in the sample. In practice it would be common to show the two quartile figures as well.

Ratio	Rational Co. Ltd.		Industry Median for Building and Civil Engineering	
	19-0	19-1	19-0	19-1
Operating Profit/Capital Employed	13.2	11.7	14.5	14.8
Net Profit after Tax/Sales	3.8	3.3	3.9	4.6
Sales/Fixed Assets	3.1	2.3	7.7	7.0
Sales/Stock	13.5	12.9	10.1	7.3
Current Assets/Current Liabilities	2.2	2.3	1.32	1.36
Liquid Assets/Current Liabilities	1.1	1.3	.96	.93

Whilst it must be appreciated that we are working with only a few ratios and that ideally we would look at least at five year's information we might draw some tentative conclusions:

Operating Profit/Capital Employed is lower than the median figure for the industry. Looking further we see that Sales/Fixed Asset Ratio is considerably below average. The two ratios are closely linked since Sales is an important contributor to Profit and Fixed Assets are part of Capital Employed. Net Profit after tax to Sales is also below average but the company is utilizing its stock above the average level. Both the liquidity ratios are above average, which may mean from the company's point of view that too much resources are tied up in non-productive cash or debtor balances, which would also contribute to a low return on capital employed.

In practice we could also look at the quartile figures in addition to the median. Our conclusions from the analysis can only be tentative but there is an impression which develops even from the limited information we have looked at that all is not right with the Rational Co. Ltd. Profitability is below average and the explanation seems to lie in a low net profit margin, and low utlization of fixed assets plus too many liquid assets. The trend of profitability figures cannot be assessed from two years, and it would have been useful to see information covering as many years back such as will give a reasonable guide. In preparing the graphs of trends over time for the ratios it is often very useful to show the Industry Data on the same graph as that for the firm. Using the example previously illustrated the graph for the Rational Co. Ltd. Profit after Tax/Sales would be improved by adding the Industry Median figures as in Exhibit 38.4

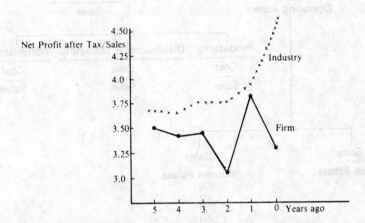

Exhibit 38.4

Internal Analysis

From a management point of view very useful information can be drawn from a detailed ratio analysis between companies using a full range of information not normally published. The Centre for Inter-firm Comparisons is a specialist organisation undertaking this work, maintaining secrecy as to the identity of participating firms, but ensuring that all firms taking parts prepare their information on a comparable basis. Several Trade Associations and Professional Bodies run similar schemes for their members. The Centre for Inter-firm Comparison have developed what is known as the "pyramid" approach to ratios. This simply means that a key ratio at the top of the pyramid is explained by more detailed ratios which branch out below.

468

One example is shown in Exhibit 38.5 developed from the key ratio Operating Profit/Operating Assets. Note that $\dfrac{\text{Operating Profit}}{\text{Operating Assets}}$ is the same as $\dfrac{\text{Sales}}{\text{Operating Assets}} \times \dfrac{\text{Operating Profit}}{\text{Sales}}$ (cancelling out Sales in the multiplication).

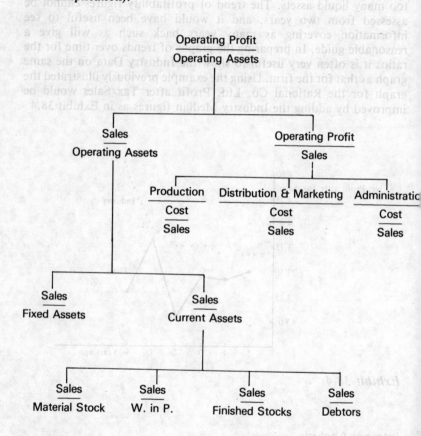

Exhibit 38.5

In a working scheme very many detailed ratios would be developed from the framework illustrated in this chapter. The main benefit usually arises by the more general comparison, but the detail allows backup research if things are going wrong.

The ratios are as follows:-

Ratio	Last Year	This Year
Return on assets		
1. Operating profit/Operating assets (%)	8.2	11.1
Profit margin on sales and turnover of assets		
2. Operating profit/sales (%)	6.7	5.8
3. Sales/Operating assets (times per year)	2.5	1.7
Departmental costs (as a percentage of sales)		
4. Production	71.0	70.9
5. Distribution and marketing	16.3	18.2
6. Administration	6.0	5.1
Asset utilisation (£'s per £1,000 of sales)		
3a. Operating assets	703	653
10. Current assets	593	480
11. Fixed assets	102	101
Current asset utilisation (£'s per £1,000 of sales)		
12. Material stocks	142	141
13. Work in progress	156	152
14. Finished stocks	152	94
15. Debtors	143	103

The results of our firm can now be appraised alongside the other companies in the sample. Our firm is identified by "C".

THE INTERIM COMPARISON

Ratio	A	B	C	D	E
Return on assets					
1. Operating profit/Operating assets (%)	17.2	14.5	11.1	8.6	3.9
Profit margin on sales and turnover of assets					
2. Operating profit/sales (%)	14.0	14.3	5.8	7.9	2.0
3. Sales/Operating assets (times per year)	1.3	1.1	1.7	1.0	2.4
Departmental costs (as a percentage of sales)					
4. Production	74.0	70.5	70.9	71.7	77.0
5. Distribution and marketing	8.5	12.2	18.2	14.2	16.0
6. Administration	3.5	3.0	5.1	6.2	5.0
Asset utilisation (£'s per £1,000 of sales)					
3a. Operating assets	842	908	653	1,030	500
10. Current assets	616	609	480	800	370
11. Fixed assets	250	320	101	241	160
Current asset utilisation (£'s per £1,000 of sales)					
12. Material stocks	131	120	141	172	84
13. Work in progress	148	120	132	175	140
14. Finished stocks	203	164	94	259	68
15. Debtors	134	205	123	194	78

Interpreting the Inter-firm Comparison we are able to see that our firm is below two other firms in return on operating assets. This can be traced to Operating Profit/Sales. Note that total departmental costs + operating profit as per cent sales = 100 per cent. The main factor in the profit being below firms A and B is high distribution and marketing costs. Action can be taken on these costs if appropriate.

Since firm C will have details of the general size and description of all the firms in the sample (although the names of firms are confidential) and knows that the Centre for Inter-firm Comparison makes sure that the figures used are comparable, very valuable information can be drawn for management.

When several periods data is available this type of information is much more readily appreciated in graphical form.

The Limitations of Ratio Analysis

The Advantages of ratio analyses which have been brought out in this text are that they provide a consistent and disciplined approach to the analysis of accounts. In addition they are a convenient method of comparing the performance of a particular firm with others and of seeing trends over time. Nonetheless there are dangers in accepting answers which appear to be put forward by ratios in too rigid a manner. The following points are relevant: —

1. Accounting Statements present a limited picture only of the business. The information included in accounts does not cover all aspects of the business.

2. The problem associated with differing bases of accounting are nowhere more important than in ratio analysis. In particular differences in valuing fixed assets, depreciation methods and in valuation of stock-in-trade can be mentioned. As you will appreciate from your study of accounting there is usually a variety of accounting methods which may be appropriate to a particular firm.

3. The accounts of large organisations frequently aggregate operations in different industries and an external analyst will not be able to split up the results of one sector from another.

4. Comparison of a firm which finances its fixed plant through rental, thus not showing it as an asset, with a firm which purchases its own assets will be difficult.

5. External analysis of balances can be misleading because the picture at that particular moment of time may not be representative of the year as a whole. For example firms frequently take stock when their stock levels are lowest. Average figures should be used but are not available externally.

6. Interpretation of a change in a ratio needs careful examination of changes in both numerator and denominator. Without a very full and detailed investigation some wrong conclusions can be drawn.

7. There is room for considerable difference between individual companies. It is wrong to lay down too rigid guidelines since what may be good for one successful firm may be wrong for another.

8. In general it is incorrect to compare small firms with very large firms. Many of the general industrial analyses of ratios are overall averages, and are, therefore, not strictly comparable to any particular firm.

The lesson is that whilst ratios are useful in indicating areas for investigation they cannot be relied upon to answer all the questions raised. Many of the limitations may, however, be reduced if a properly supervised scheme of inter-firm comparison is introduced.

Interpretation of Accounts for Employees

The interpretation which has been reviewed so far in this chapter has been for people with a good knowledge of the basis of accounting. Many firms have realised in recent years that it can be of great interest to their employees, if they attempt to make important features of the accounts generally available. Experience has tended to show that the average employee is very easily put off if too much detail is presented to him. Most firms attempt therefore to give a much more limited amount of information and to present it as imaginatively as possible in a special employee report. It is always far better to get over a limited amount of important information than to include so much detail that the message is obscured. Those who are interested can look for more detail in the main published accounts.

Firms have developed many different approaches in preparing their reports to employees. Many succeed by capturing interest through good graphics and design. Care must be taken however not to make these reports appear too trivial or condescending. There is a very wide range of approach between different firms many of which include cartoons and 'comic-strip' types of presentation to capture interest. Space is not available here to do justice to this type of presentation. Try to find examples of company reports in libraries.

472

Exercises

38.1A. During 19-3 the comparative financial data for three companies in the same industrial sector was as follows:

	Z.A. Ltd.	X.B. Ltd.	C.L. Ltd.
	£	£	£
Fixed Assets (net)	52,000	76,000	54,000
Current Assets—			
Stock	48,000	40,000	64,000
Debtors	30,000	56,000	80,000
Cash	42,000	24,000	16,000
	172,000	196,000	214,000
Less Current Liabilities			
Creditors	(24,400)	(44,600)	(64,000)
Proposed Dividends	(7,600)	(11,400)	(30,000)
	140,000	140,000	120,000
Issued Capital—			
6 per cent £1 Preference	10,000	40,000	—
£1 Ordinary Shares	70,000	60,000	120,000
Revenue Reserves	60,000	40,000	—
	140,000	140,000	120,000
Average Stock	50,000	72,000	60,000
Sales	250,000	240,000	800,000
Gross Profit	50,000	60,000	80,000
Net Profit	30,000	30,000	30,000

You are required:

(a) to write a report analysing and comparing the performance of the three companies;

(b) to advise a client with £5,000 to invest in shares of one of the three companies which company and which type of share to select.

38.2A. The Directors of Handbags Ltd. have asked you to assess the situation of their Company.

Preliminary investigations show the following results and median data from an Interfirm Association acting for the bag making industry of which Handbags Ltd. is a member.

	19-1 Interfirm % of Total	19-1 H Ltd. £000's £	19-2 Interfirm % of Total	19-2 H Ltd. £000's £	19-3 Interfirm % of Total	19-3 H Ltd. £000's £
Land and Buildings at Valuation	20	300	25	300	30	240
Plant and Machinery at Valuation	20	60	25	54	40	45
Stocks at cost						
Materials	20	45	15	90	10	90
Finished Goods	20	45	25	90	10	135
Debtors	10	45	10	60	5	90
Cash	10	45	—	6	5	—
	100%	£540	100%	£600	100%	£600
Share Capital	40	300	40	300	30	300
Capital Reserve	—	—	—	—	—	30
Reserves and P. & L.	10	90	20	60	30	—
10% Debentures	—	—	—	150	—	150
Creditors	50	150	40	90	40	120
	100%	£540	100%	£600	100%	£600

Note: Handbags Ltd. sold land (cost £60,000) for £90,000 in 19-3 to provide extra working capital.

PROFIT AND LOSS ACCOUNT DATA

	19-1		19-2		19-3	
	Interfirm % of Sales	H Ltd. £000's £	Interfirm % of Sales	H Ltd. £000's £	Interfirm % of Sales	H Ltd. £000's £
COST OF SALES						
Materials Consumed	20	180	20	165	15	150
Wages (Direct)	40	342	30	393	15	318
Depreciation of Plant (charged by a machine hour rate)	2	18	8	15	10	9
Power (fixed charge per unit consumed)	1	9	3	9	5	6
Other Variable Overheads (e.g. Salesmen's Commission)	2	18	4	15	5	12
Light, heat, salaries, etc.	14	135	18	129	18	144
Depreciation premises	1	9	2	9	2	6
OTHER DEBITS:						
Interest on Loan Capital	—	—	—	15	—	15
Taxation	8	84	6	—	12	—
Dividends	8	60	8	—	15	—
TOTAL DEBITS	96	855	99	750	97	660
SALES	100	900	100	720	100	600
DEFICIT for year	—	—	—	30	—	60
SURPLUS for year	4	45	1	—	3	—
BALANCES b/fwd	*	45	*	90	*	60
BALANCES c/f.	*	90	*	60	*	—
Bags sold		300,000		210,000		150,000
Average price per bag		£3		£3		£2.15

*Note it is not realistic to show interfirm balances as a per cent on sales.

Discuss the trends indicated and the preliminary conclusions you would draw from this data.

39

Alternatives to Historic Cost Accounting

The twentieth century has been a period of continual and unprecedented change and has witnessed enormous economic fluctuation. Two factors which seem to be inseparable from economic fluctuation are inflation in the monetary system and significant changes in the market values of real goods and services. The impact of changes in the buying power of the monetary unit and real changes in asset values are clearly both of very great importance to accounting. There has been no lack of those who recognise that historic cost accounting does not adequately deal with these two issues. The problem so far has been to provide a generally acceptable alternative. Indeed the attempts to provide an acceptable SSAP have produced unprecedented problems for the various accounting bodies concerned.

In this chapter no attempt will be made to describe the very detailed provisions which were set out in the provisional SSAP on "Accounting for Changes in the Purchasing Power of Money" and the subsequent SSAP16 on "Current Costing Accounting". It would appear that these attempts to provide comprehensive adjustments to the historic cost accounts have only won support from relatively few larger organisations. Simpler adjustments seem to be called for and the basic principles underlying such statements are all that is covered in this chapter.

Inflation and Accounts

Inflation is a change in the buying power of the currency unit. It is measured by taking a representative sample of goods and service on a periodic basis and establishing how much they cost in each period. If at three periods the cost of the sample was: –

Start	£100
end year 1	£105
ended year 2	£126

then the inflation measure would be on year 1 − 5 points on the base of 100 which is 5%. In year 2 the index measure moves 21 points which from the start of year 2 is $\dfrac{21}{105}$ or 20%. Index numbers to measure inflation are prepared by the Governments Statistical Service. The most commonly quoted and used index is the Retail Price index which measures the average household's consumption of goods and services. This index will not be the actual rate for any individual family − it is an average. Similarly it will have to take account of new circumstances such as the fact that in the year 1900 there were no televisions − whereas today they are a significant element in a family budget. What this means is that the measurement of inflation can only be very broadly based on certain assumptions. Accountants who are looking for precise measurement will be disappointed. However since inflation exists − without any doubt − it has been generally accepted that a very broad measure of consumers spending such as the Retail Price Index − is a reasonable guide − which is better than nothing, and can be used for the adjustment of accounting data.

The impact of inflation is to reduce the buying power of money. From the previously quoted example you would need £126 at the end of year 2 to buy what cost £100 at the start. If you hold cash throughout the period you simply lose value. In this example you have lost £26 from the start − as measured in the purchasing power units at the end of year 2.

In historic accounting terms using the same data the balance sheet would show:

Start		*Year 1*		*Year 2*	
Cash	100	Cash	100	Cash	100
Capital	100	Capital	100	Capital	100

To reflect inflation the capital would need to be

Year 1   Start Capital $100 \times \dfrac{105}{100} = £105$

Year 2   Year 1 Capital $105 \times \dfrac{126}{105} = £126$

To reflect this in the balance sheet would require the following: −

Start		*Year 1*		*Year 2*	
Cash	100	Cash	100	Cash	100
Capital	100	Capital adjusted	105	Capital adjusted	126
		Less Monetary		Less Monetary	
		Loss	5	Loss	26
			100		100

The next problem is to consider a business which instead of having its assets in monetary units which inevitably fixes its buying power − instead holds all resources in fixed assets or inventories.

These real assets do not have a fixed money face value, and their market price may well change upwards in an inflationary period, but it is unlikely that the market price change will exactly equal the inflation change. Nonetheless real asset values are often assumed to change in line with inflation − in which even the balance sheets would be shown as follows assuming that the asset is Inventory held from the start: −

Start		Year 1		Year 2	
Inventory	100	Inventory		Inventory	
		$100 \times \dfrac{105}{100} =$	105	$105 \times \dfrac{126}{105} =$	126
Capital	100	Capital adjusted	105	Capital adjusted	126

Notice that this final approach is really only an adjustment to capital assuming that if real assets are held − no inflation caused loss takes place. This may not of course be realistic since inflation could have an adverse impact on the value of some real assets.

Another issue arises when a business has liabilities in its accounts. If a firm obtains loans or creditors the amount due to them is invariably fixed in money terms whatever the inflation rate. If the business we have just reviewed funded its assets with Capital £50 and Loan £50 in the same period of inflation − then the result would be different since there would be a gain on the money owed. Firstly assume the asset is cash: −

Start		Year 1		Year 2	
Cash	100	Cash	100	Cash	100
Capital	50	Capital adjusted		Capital adjusted	
Loan	50	$50 \times \dfrac{105}{100} =$	52.5	$525 \times \dfrac{126}{105} =$	63.0
	100	Monetary		Monetary	
		Loss	5.0	Loss	26.0
		less gain on		less gain on	
		loan	2.5	2.5	loan	13.0	13.0
			50.0		50.0
		Loan	50.0	Loan	50.0
			100		100

The shareholders clearly gain the loss of buying power on the loan in each period. This will also be true if the assets are real rather than monetary. Taking the facts as before but including the loan: −

Start		Year 1		Year 2	
Inventory	100	Inventory	105	Inventory	126
Capital	50	Capital adjusted	52.5	Capital adjusted	63.0
Loan	50	add gain on loan	2.5	add gain on loan	13.0
	100		55.0		76.0
		Loan	50.0	Loan	50.0
			105.0		126.0

In an ongoing business the company will of course hold both monetary and real assets. The trading activity will also lead to fluctuating levels of working capital items. The adjustments will therefore have to take some account of the changes during the accounting year. However the basic elements of inflation accounting so far as the purchasing power unit is concerned are described.

Current Cost Accounting

As far as the adjustments just described are concerned no account is taken of the values of the specific assets owned by the organisation. Current Cost Accounting is an attempt to replace the historic values in traditional accounts with current market based values. In particular the following items will be adjusted: –

1)   Fixed assets will be shown at their 'value to the business' not depreciated historic cost.

2)   Depreciation will be based on the revised current values in 1).

3)   Inventories will be valued at 'value to the business' not historic cost (– although market realisable value will still provide a limit under the prudence concept).

4)   The Cost of Goods Sold will be calculated on the basis of 'value to the business' at the date of consumption (not of purchase).

Value to the Business

In a market there are two levels of value – the buying price and the selling price. For some things the difference may be small but often there is quite a significant gap. For many products there is a middleman or dealer who operates between the buyer and the seller and who takes some remuneration for his services. The more specialised and complex the product the larger the gap is likely to be between buying selling prices.

For example a firm in the textile industry may have ordered dyestuffs to their own colour specifications which cost £5,000 from the producer. If the firms finds that the order for which the dyestuffs were purchased has been cancelled it may wish to dispose of them. If the colours are non-standard nobody else may wish to buy them, their market price may be nothing and they will be scrapped.

The buying price on the market is generally called the Replacement Value of an asset. The price at which it can be sold in the market is its Realisable Value. For accounting purposes it has been proposed that the appropriate basis of value should be 'Value to the Business.' In order to determine this you need to decide what a business would do if it were deprived of the asset. If the business owns a machine which cost £5,000, what is its value? If in the event of the machine being irrepairably damaged the firm would buy another machine then its value is its replacement cost. If however the machine would not be replaced then its value would be based on Realisable Value, which is what it could be sold off for.

In a normal business where continuity of production and development exists you would expect most values to be based on Replacement Value. However with technological product change being very rapid it is sometimes the case that the replacement does not imply buying an identical item. When you replace something you buy the best thing available to satisfy your requirements. In other words you are concerned with the replacement of the services obtained from the asset not the asset in its own right. The judgement about replacement or realisation can only be made by the management. However it is judgement and therefore basically subjective in nature.

Accounting for Current Values

In normal practice the conversion from historic cost to current cost will be based on the use of an index number as in the examples for inflation. Here however the index should be specific for the type of asset concerned.

If a business owns a fixed asset bought four years ago for £10,000 and 60% depreciated the balance sheet under historic cost would be

	£	£
Fixed Asset at cost	10,000	
less Depreciation	6,000	4,000
		£
Capital		4,000

If the appropriate 'value to the business' price index for the particular index four years ago were 150 and this year it is 450 then the balance sheet values would be £10,000 $\times \dfrac{450}{150} = 30,000$ for the Asset

and £6,000 $\times \dfrac{450}{150} = 18,000$ for the Depreciation.

The new Balance Sheet would show: –

	£	£
Fixed Asset at valuation	30,000	
less Depreciation	18,000	12,000
		£
Capital		4,000
Revaluation Reserve		8,000
		12,000

The adjustments to Inventories and Purchases will be made in the same way and adjusted to the Revaluation Reserves.

The main impact of the Cost of Sales and Depreciation adjustments are likely to be in the Profit and Loss Account where historic values of cost are likely to be increased in periods of inflation thus reducing profits.

The attempt in SSAP16 to provide a comprehensive method of accounting for changes in prices combined the elements of Current Cost accounting in adjusting Fixed Assets and Depreciation and Inventories and Cost of Sales together, with some purchasing power adjustments on monetary working capital and also an adjustment related to the borrowing element (gearing). Criticism of this standard was based on its complexity, difficulty in obtaining asset values particularly for overseas assets, and lack of real impact on many businesses. A return to a very basic standard allowing individual firms to determine the best method for their own business now seems likely to be the way for the future and indeed is very much in line with the pragmatic traditions of accounting development.

Answers to Exercises

1.1 (a) Year 1 – Dr Stock 500 *add* Production Cost 1,600 *less* Stock 300, Gross Profit 1,200, Cr Sales 3,000.
Year 2 – Dr Stock 300, Production Cost 2,800 *less* Stock 700, Gross Profit 600, Cr Sales 3,000.
Year 3 – Dr Stock 700, Production Cost 1,600 *less* Stock 500, Gross Profit 1,200, Cr Sales 3,000.

(b) Year 1 – Dr Stock 1,000, Production Cost 1,600 *less* Stock 600, Gross Profit 1,000. Cr Sales 3,000.
Year 2 – Dr Stock 600, Production Cost 2,800 *less* Stock 1,400, Gross Profit 1,000, Cr Sales 3,000.
Year 3 – Stock 1,400, Production Cost 1,600 *less* Stock 1,000, Gross Profit 1,000, Cr Sales 3,000.

(c) The production cost method (in this case) would be used.

(d) Different production levels.

1.2 (a) (i) $\dfrac{20,000}{120,000} \times \dfrac{(360,000 + 570,000 + 72,000 + 48,000 + 30,000)}{1,080,000} = 180,000$

(ii) $\dfrac{20,000}{120,000} \times (360,000 + 570,000 + 30,000)\ 960,000 = 160,000.$

(b) Trading – Dr Factory Cost b/d 1,080,000 *less* Closing Stock 160,000 = Cost of Goods Sold 920,000, Gross Profit c/d 280,000. Cr Sales 1,200,000 Profit & Loss – Dr Expenses 120,000, Net Profit 160,000. Cr Gross Profit b/d 280,000.

(c) Trading – Dr Factory Cost b/d 1,080,000, Gross Profit c/d 360,000. Cr Sales 1,440,000 Profit & Loss – Dr Expenses 120,000, Extra Advertising 5,000, Net Profit 235,000. Cr Gross Profit b/d 360,000.

1.3 (a) FIFO (i) Article 1,375 + 450 + 4,800 + 2,800 + 5,400 + 500 = 15,325;
(ii) Category 1,875 + 8,400 + 6,100 = 16,375.

(b) LIFO (i) Article 1,250 + 400 + 4,600 + 2,800 + 5,400 + 400 = 14,850;
(ii) Category 1,650 + 8,100 + 6,100 = 15,850.

1.4 (a) 23,850 + net Sales 2,048 (cost) + Sale or return 200 = 26,098 overcast 140 − worthless 700 − Stationery 1,400 − net purchases 3,700 = adjusted figure 20,158.

(b) G.P. 158,000 + 250 − fall in stock (23,850 − 20,158) 3,692 = 154,558. N. Profit 31,640 + Stationery 1,400 + 250 − fall 3,692 = 29,598. Net Current Assets 24,600 + Stationery 1,400 + 250 − fall 3,692 = 22,558.

1.5 (a) Gross Profits Year (1) 6,000: (2) 16,000: (3) 31,000: (4) 76,000

(b) Gross Profits Year (1) 6,000: (2) 14,000: (3) 27,000: (4) 82,000

(c) Total profits 129,000 both. (d) per text.

1.6 (a) Gross Profits: LIFO 1,600: FIFO 1,000

Stock Valuation LIFO $400 \times 12 + 100 \times 10 + 400 \times 5 = 7,800$:

FIFO $400 \times 10 + 100 \times 12 + 400 \times 5 = 7,200$.

(b) Prudence: Cost and others. (c) see text.

2.1 (a) Bills Receivable Dr: 2,460 & 1,500. Cr: 3,960, Bank Dr. 3,960, Cr. 145 & 1,500 & 6. R. Johnson Dr 2,460, Cr. 2,460, Scarlet Dr. 1,500 & 1,500 & 6, Cr. 1,500 Discounting Charges Dr. 145 (b) JOHNSON'S BOOKS: Bills Payable Dr 1,500, Cr. 1,500, N. Gudgeon Dr. 1,500, Cr 1,500 & 1,500 & 6. Noting charges Dr. 6, SCARLET'S BOOKS: Bills Payable Dr. 2,460, Cr. 2,460. Gudgeon Dr. 2,460, Cr. 2,460, Bank Cr 2,460.

2.3 K.C. − Dr Balance b/f 960, Bank 960, Cr Bill Received 960, Bank 360, Bad debts 600.

Bills receivable − Dr KC 960, Cr Bank 960.

Bank − Dr Bill receivable 960, KC 360, Cr Discounting charges 12, KC (discounted bill) 960.

Discounting Charges − Dr Bank 12.

Bad Debts − Dr KC 600.

2.4 Debits 12,370 + 16,904 + 177 + 88 = 29,539.

Credits 105 + 407 + 15,970 + 1,230 + 306 + 129 + 604 + Balances c/d 10,788 = 29,539.

2.5 Debits 33 + 568 + 1,860 + 9,464 + 177 + 8,710 balances = 20,812.

Credits 8,570 + 11,375 + 800 + 20 + 47 = 20,812.

3.1 *Olliers Books* − J.V. Account: Dr Cash: 3 cars 900, Repairs 60, Profit 237, balance c/d 403, Cr Sales 1,600, After balancing down Dr Cash 403, Cr Balance b/d 403.

Avons Books − J.V. Account: Dr Rent 20, Adverts 10, Licence 36, Vehicle 100, Profit 237, Cr Balance c/d 403, After balanced down Dr Balance b/d 403, Cr Cash 403.

3.2 *Plants Books* − J.V. Account: Dr Rent 156, Labour planting 105, Fertilizing 36, Sundries 10, Labour 18, Fertilizer 29, Profit 266, Cr Balance c/d 620, after balancing down Dr Balance b/d 620, Cr Cash 620.

Hoe Books − J.V. Account: Dr Seeds 48, Motor expenses 17, Share profit 114, Cr Balance c/d 179, after balancing down Dr Balance b/d 179, Cr Cash 179.

Reap Books – J.V. Account: Dr Lifting 73, Sale expenses 39, Share profit 76, Balance c/d 799, Cr Sales proceeds 987, after balancing down Dr Cash (Plant) 620, (Hoe) 179, Cr Balance b/d 799.

Memo J.V. Account – Cr Sale proceeds 987, Dr Rent 156, Labour – Planting 105, Fertilizing 36, Sundry 18, Lifting 73, Fertilizer 29, Motor 17, Seeds 48, Sale expenses 39, Sundries 10, Profit Hoe 114, Plant 266, Reap 76.

4.1 *Consignment* – Dr Goods 3,000, Carriage 147, Insurance 93, Freight 240, Port charges 186 (total 3,666) Commission M.B. 175, Profit 270, Cr Sales 3,500, Stock c/d $\frac{20}{120}$ of 3,666 = 611.

M.B. Dr Sales 3,500, Cr Freight 240, Port charges 186, Commission 175, Bank 2,899.

4.2 (*a*) Sales 5,900 – Port 720 – Storage 410 – Commission 354 = 4,416.

   (*b*) Debits 720 + 410 + 354, Cash 4,416. Credits, Sales 5,900.

5.1 *Realization* – Dr Buildings 800, Tools 850, Debtors 2,800, Expenses 100: Cr Debtors 2,700, Buildings 400, Tools 950. Discounts 200, Loss on Realisation split Moore 150/Stephens 150.

Capitals: Moore Dr Loss 150, Cash 1,850; Cr Balance b/fwd 2,000, Stephens Dr Loss 150, Cash 1,350, Cr Balance b/fwd 1,500.

Cash: Dr Balance b/fwd 1,800, Debtors 2,700, Buildings 400, Tools 950; Cr Expenses 100, Creditors 2,550, Capitals Moore 1,850/Stephens 1,350.

5.3 (*a*) Realization – Dr Buildings, etc., 8,400, Investments 3,200, Stock 4,000, Debtors/Discounts/Bad debts 200, Costs 150, Profit on realization F three-fifths 4,890, Y two-fifths 3,260.
   Cr M Ltd Purchase consideration 20,000, Investments 2,800, Capitals – F Motor 850, Y Motor 350, Discounts on creditors 100.

   (*b*) *Bank* – Dr M Ltd 11,000, Investments 2,800, Debtors 3,300, Cr Balance b/f (overdraft) 1,596, Creditors 2,400, Costs 150, Capitals F 8,636, Y 4,318.

   (*c*) *Capitals* – Dr Realization – motors F 850, Y 350, Balances c/d F 14,636, Y 7,318, Cr Balances b/f F 7,516, Y 4,408, Loan F 3,080, Profit on realisation F 4,890, Y 3,260. Then after balanced off: Dr M Ltd F (14,000 shares) 6,000, Y (7,000 shares) 3,000, Bank F 8,636, Y 4,318, Cr Balances b/fwd F 14,636, Y 7,318.

5.4 (*a*) Debits 14,000 + 5,000 + 21,000 + 800: Credits 8,000 + 7,000 + 4,000 + 3,000 + 500, Loss X 9,150, Y 6,100, Z 3,050.

   (*b*) X Debits 7,000 + 9,150 + Deficiency 525, Credits 4,000 + Bank 12,675, Y Debits 6,100 + Deficiency 525, Credits 4,000 + Bank 2,625, Z Debit 3,050: Credits 2,000 + shared X 525, Y 525.

6.1 *Branch Stock Account* – Memo Column + Double Entry Column, Memo Column figures shown first – Dr Balance b/f 4,400; 3,300; Goods from Head Office 24,800: 18,600, Gross Profit (no memo) 5,850, Cr Branch Debtors 21,000: 21,000, Cash Sales 2,400: 2,400, Returns to Head Office 1,000: 750, Goods Stolen 600: 450, Profit and Loss Normal Wastage 100: 75, Branch Profit and Loss – Excess Wastage 152: 114, Balance c/f 3,948: 2,961.

Branch Debtors (no memo cols) – Dr Balance b/f 3,946. Branch Stock – Sales 21,000, Cr Bad Debts 148, Discounts Allowed 428, Bank 22,400, Balance c/f 1,970.

6.2 (*a*) Branch Current – Dr Balance b/f 20,160, Goods sent 23,160, Expenses paid 6,000, Net Profit 3,500, Cr Cash 30,000, Goods Returned 400, Balance c/d 22,420.

(*b*) Proof – Branch Assets *less* Branch Liabilities = Branch on Current Account. Indicates: Amount of money invested in Branch.

6.3 Gross Profit H.O. 27,000, Branch 26,400 = 53,400
Net Profit H.O. 8,000, Branch 17,000 = 25,000 – Commission S 1,200 M 2,550 – Interest S 1,100 M 1,100, balance S 9,525, M 9,525.
Balance Sheet: FA 22,000 – 4,400 + Stock 12,200 + Bank 3,000 – Creditors 1,800 = Total 31,000. Capitals, final balances S 14,825: M 16,175 = 31,000.

6.4 (*a*) Trading – Dr Stock Head Office 13,000, Branch 4,400, Purchases Head Office 37,000, Goods from Head Office, Branch 17,200, *less* Stocks Head Office 14,440, Branch 6,570, Gross Profit Head Office 21,440, Branch 10,970. Profit and Loss Dr Salaries Head Office 4,500, Branch 3,200, Administrative Expenses Head Office 1,440, Branch 960, Carriage Head office 2,200, Branch 960. General Expenses Head Office 3,200, Branch 1,800, Provision for Bad Debts Head Office 50, Depreciation Head Office 150, Branch 110, Manager's commission Branch 360, Net Profit Head Office 9,900, Branch 3,600, Cr Gross Profit Head Office 21,440, Branch 10,970, Provision for Bad Debts not required 20. Appropriation Account Dr Packer commission 900, Interest on Capital P 840, S 240, Balance divided P three-quarters 8,640, S quarter 2,880, Cr Net Profits b/d Head Office 9,900, Branch 3,600.

(*b*) *Balance Sheet* – Capital P 14,000, S 4,000, Current Accounts Profits P 8,640, S 2,880, Interest on Capital P 840, S 240, Commission P 900, *less* Drawings P 2,500, S 1,200, = P 7,880, S 1,920, Creditors 6,200, Bank Overdraft 1,350, Manager's commission 120, Balance Sheet totals 35,470. Furniture 2,600 *less* Depreciation 1,110, = 1,490, Stock 21,810, Debtors 10,000 *less* Provision 830, Cash and Bank 3,000.

(*c*) *Branch Current Account* – Dr Balance b/f 6,800, Administrative Expenses 960, Profit 3,600, Cr Goods in Transit c/d 800, Cash in Transit c/d 2,400, Balance c/d 8,160. Balance proved Furniture 1,100 *less* Depreciation 460, Stock 6,570, Debtors *less* Provision 2,820, *less* Creditors 400, Manager's Commission 120, Bank Overdraft 1,350 = 8,160.

6.8

	F1	F1	Rate	£	£
Freehold Buildings	63,000		7	9,000	
Debtors and Creditors	36,000	1,560	8	4,460	195
Sales		432,000	9		48,000
Head Office		504,260	Actual		60,100
Branch cost of sales	360,000		*below	40,400	
Depreciation: Machinery		56,700	7		8,100
Administration costs	18,000		9	2,000	
Stock 30.6.19-8	11,520		8	1,440	
Machinery at cost	126,00		7	18,000	
Remittances	272,000		Actual	29,990	
Balances at bank	79,200		8	9,900	
Selling & Distribution	28,800		9	3,200	
Profit on Exchange		–	–		1,995
	994,520	994,520		118,390	118,390

*Cost of Sales: Branch F1	360,000			
Less Depreciation	F1	12,600 ÷ 7 =	£1,800	
	F1	347,400 ÷ 9 =	£38,600	
			£40,400	

Gross Profit H.O. 80,000, Branch 7,600, Net Profit H.O. 41,200, Branch
2,286 + Balance b/f 2,000 = 45,486. Balance Sheet F.A. 37,400, C.A.
59,890 – C.L. 9,809 = W.C. 50,081. Totals 87,481. Shares 40,000 +
Difference on Exchange 1,995 + Profit & Loss 45,486 = Total 87,481.

(H.O. Books) Branch Account

	£	F1		£	F1
Balance b/d	25,136	189,260	Cash from debtor	36	320
Components	35,000	315,000	Remittances	28,000	256,000
Net Profit	2,286	*24,000	Cash in transit	1,990	16,000
Difference on			Balance c/d	34,391	255,940
Exchange	1,995	–			
	64,417	528,260		64,417	528,260

*This represents the profit per branch profit and loss account if it had
been drawn up using florins.

7.1 *Sinking Fund* – Cr 19-6 Profit and Loss 542.925, 19-7 Profit and Loss
542.925, Interest 27.145, 19-8 Profit and Loss 542.925, Interest 55.649,
19-9 Profit and Loss 542.925, Interest 85.578, 19-0 Profit and Loss
542.925, Interest 117.003. Dr Old Lease written off 3,000.
Investment Account – Dr 19-6 Cash 542.925, 19-7 Cash 570.070, 19-8
Cash 598.574, 19-9 Cash 628.503. Cr Sale of Investment 2,340.072.

7.2 *Loose Tools Account* – 19-4 Dr Balance b/f 1,250, Cash 2,000, Wages
275, Materials 169, Cr Manufacturing Account 994, Balance c/d 2,700.
19-5 Dr Balance b/d 2,700, Cash 1,450, Wages 495, Materials 390, Cr
Manufacturing account 1,695, Balance c/d 3,340. 19-6 Dr Balance b/d
3,340, Cash 1,890, Wages 145, Materials 290, Cr Manufacturing
Account, 1,897, Supplier 88, Balance c/d 3,680.

7.5 19-0: 55,736 + 15,871 + 4,067 = 75,674 − 60,256 − 6,025 = 9,393
19-1: 59,408 + 15,871 + 4,067 = 79,346 − 45,192 − 5,272 = 28,882
19-2: 60,011 + 15,871 + 4,067 = 79,949 − 33,894 − 4,613 = 41,442.

8.1 *Cases Stock Account* − Dr Stocks b/d Factory (600) 900, at Customers (4,000) 6,000, Cash Purchases (5,000) 10,000, Profit on cases service to Profit and Loss 34,525, Cr Sales (450) 100, Cases kept by Customers (800) 4,800, Profit on cases hire 34,000, Stocks c/d Factory (2,150) 3,225, at Customers (6,200) 9,300.
Cases Suspense Account − Dr Customers cases returned (14,000) 84,000, Cases kept (800) 4,800, Profit on cases hire 34,000, Balance c/d (6,200) 37,200, Cr Balance b/d (4,000) 24,000, Customers − Cases sent (17,000) 136,000.

8.2 *Cases Stock Account* − Dr Stock b/d at Warehouse (9,600) 19,200, At Customers (6,100) 12,200, Purchases (18,000) 54,000, Profit to Profit and Loss 37,025, Cr Returned to Supplier (4,000) 11,610, Cash scrapped (3,500) 55, Deficit (420) no money, kept by Customers (5,800) 23,200, Profit on cases hire 47,600, Stocks c/d (4,800) 9,600, Warehouse (15,180) 30,360.
Cases Suspense Account − Dr Returned (43,100) 172,400, kept by Customers (5,800) 23,200, Profit on cases hire 47,600, Balance c/d (4,800) 19,200, Cr Balance b/d (6,100) 24,400, sent to Customers (47,600) 238,000.

9.1 Royalties − Debits 19-1 600, 19-2 800, 19-3 1,200, 19-4 1,400, Credits − transferred to Trading Account 19-1 600, 19-2 800, 19-3 1,200, 19-4 1,400.
Smokers − 19-1 Cr Royalties 600, Short Workings 400, 19-2 Dr Cash 1,000, Cr Royalties 800, Short Workings 200, 19-3 Dr Cash 1,000, Short Workings 200, Cr Royalties 1,200, 19-4 Dr Cash 1,000, Short Workings 200, Cr Royalties 1,400, 19-5 Dr Cash 1,200.
Short Workings 19-1 Dr 400, 19-2 Dr 200, 19-3 Cr 200, written off to Profit and Loss 200, 19-4 Cr 200.

9.2 T.T. 19-3 Dr Cash 500, Cr Royalties 430, Short Workings 70, 19-4 Dr Cash 500, Cr Royalties 490, Short Workings 10, 19-5 Dr Short Workings 45, Cash 500, Cr Royalties 545, 19-6 Cash 525, Cr Royalties 525.
Royalties − 19-3 Dr 430, Cr Man 430, 19-4 Dr 490, Cr Man 490, 19-5 Dr 545, Cr Man 545, 19-6 Dr 525, Cr Man 525.
Short Workings 19-3 Dr TT 70, 19-4 Dr TT 10, 19-5 Cr TT 45, Written off to Profit and Loss 35.

10.1 *Machinery Account* − Dr Vendor 6,000.
Vendor Account − Dr 19-3 J Cash 846, D 2,000, Balance c/d 3,566, Cr 6,000, D H.P. Interest 412. 19-4 Dr December Cash 2,000, Balance c/d 1,851, Cr January Balance b/d 3,566, December H.P. Interest 285, 19-5 Dr December Cash 2,000, Cr January Balance b/d 1,851, December H.P. Interest 149.
Depreciation Account − Cr 19-3, 600, 19-4, 540, 19-5, 486.
Balance Sheet 31 December 19-3 − Machinery 6,000, *less* Depreciation 600, Owing on H.P. 3,566.

10.2 (*a*) Machinery – Dr 2,092, Provn. for Depreciation Cr 19-3 210, 19-4 188, 19-5 170, CD & Co 19-3 Dr January Bank 600, December 600, Balance c/d 1,042; Cr Machinery 2,092, HP Interest (10% × 1,492) 149; 19-4 Dr Bank 600, Balance c/d 545, Cr Balance b/d 1,041, HP Interest 104: 19-5 Dr Bank 600, Cr Balance b/d 545, HP Interest 55.

    (*b*) Balance Sheet: Machinery 2,092, – Depreciation 209: Owing on HP 1,041.

10.5 V & F Co: 19-7 Dr Cash 1,000, Balance c/d 2,081, Cr Lorry 3,081, 19-8 Dr Cash 1,199, Balance c/d 1,090, Cr Balance b/f 2,081, Interest 208, 19-9 Dr Cash 1,199, Cr Balance b/d 1,090. Interest 109.

M. Lorry A/c Dr 3,081. Depreciation 770 + 578 + 433. H.P. Interest 19-8 Dr V & F 208, Cr P/L 208: 19-9 Dr V & F 109, Cr P/L 109. Balance Sheet 19-8 (not 19-9) 3,081 – Dep 1,348. Owing on H.P. 1,090.

10.6 HP Trading. Dr Purchases 120,000, *less* Stock (100 × 60) 6,000 = 114,000, Provision unrealised profit and interest 42,560 (106,400/190,000 × 76,000), Gross Profit 33,440, Cr Sales at H.P. Prices 190,000. Profit and Loss Dr Rent 4,500, Wages 8,600, General Expenses 10,270, Net Profit 10,070.

Balance Sheet – Fixed Assets 10,000, Current Assets Stock 6,000, H.P. Debtors 106,400 *less* Provision Unrealized Profit and Interest 42,560 = 63,840, Bank 10,630 – Creditors 8,400. Capital – Balance 76,000 + Net Profit 10,070, *less* Drawings 4,000 = 82,070.

12.1 *Bank Account* – Dr Application 20,000, Allotment (30,000 *less* excess applications 5,000) 25,000, First Call (119,200 × 0.25) 29,800, Second Call (119,200 × 0.375) 44,700, D. Reagan (800 × 0.9) 720.

D. Reagan Account – Dr Ordinary Share Capital 800, Cr Bank 720, Forfeited Shares 80.

Application and Allotment Account – Dr Ordinary Share Capital 45,000, Cr Bank 20,000 and 25,000.

Ordinary Share Capital Account – Dr Forfeited Shares 800, Balance c/d 120,000, Cr Application and Allotment 45,000, First Call 30,000, Second Call 45,000, D Reagan Shares Issued 800.

First Call Account – Dr Ordinary Share Capital 30,000, Cr bank 29,800, Forfeited Shares 200.

Second Call Account – Dr Ordinary Share Capital 45,000, Cr Bank 44,700, Forfeited Shares 300.

Forfeited Shares Account – Dr First Call 200, Second Call 300, D. Reagan 80, Transfer to Share Premium 220, Cr Ordinary Share Capital 800.

12.2 *Bank Account* – Dr Application (32,600 × 0.5) 16,300, Allotment (20,000 × 1.5 *less* Excess Application Monies 5,000) 25,000, First Call (19,900 × 2) 39,800, Second Call (19,880 × 1) 19,880, B. Mills (120 × 4) 480. Cr Refunds 1,300, Balance c/d 101,460.

Application and Allotment Account – Dr Bank Refunds 1,300, Ordinary Share Capital 40,000, Cr Bank 16,300, Bank 25,000.

First Call Account – Dr Ordinary Share Capital 40,000, Cr Bank 39,800, Forfeited Shares 200.

Second Call Account – Dr Ordinary Share Capital 20,000, Cr Bank 19,880, Forfeited Shares 120.

Ordinary Share Capital Account – Dr Forfeited Share 600, Balance c/d 100,000: Cr Application and Allotment 40,000, First Call 40,000, Second Call 20,000, B. Mills (reissue) 600.

Forfeited Shares – Dr First Call 200, Second Call 120, B. Mills 120, Transfer to Share Premium 160: Cr Ordinary Share Capital 600. B. Mills – Dr Ordinary Share Capital 600: Cr Bank 480, Forfeited Shares 120.

13.1 (Journals entries omitted) Final balance sheets are given

   (i) Net Assets 20,000 + Bank 13,000 = Total 33,000. O. Share Capital 20,000 + Share Premium 2,000 + P/Loss 11,000 = Total 33,000.

   (ii) Net Assets 20,000 + Bank 8,000 = Total 28,000. O. Share Capital 15,000 + Cap. Red. Reserve 5,000 + Share Premium 2,000 + P/Loss 6,000 = Total 28,000.

   (iii) Net Assets 20,000 + Bank 9,500 = Total 29,500. O. Share Capital 16,500 + Cap. Red. Reserve 3,500 + Share Premium 2,000 + P/Loss 7,500 = Total 29,500.

   (iv) Net Assets 20,000 + Bank 6,750 = Total 26,750. O. Share Capital 15,000 + Cap. Red. Reserve 5,000 + Share Premium 2,000 + P/Loss 4,750 = Total 26,750.

   (v) Net Assets 20,000 + Bank 13,000 = Total 33,000. O. Share Capital 22,000 + Share Premium 500 + P/Loss 10,500 = Total 33,000.

13.3 (Journal entries omitted) Final balance sheets given.

   (i) Net Assets 12,500 + Bank 7,000 = Totals 19,500. Pref. Shares 5,000 + Ord. Shares 4,000 + Non-Distributable Reserves 6,000 + Cap. Red. Reserve 4,500 = Totals 19,500.

   (ii) Net Assets 12,500 + Bank 1,000 = Totals 13,500. Pref. Shares 5,000 + Ord. Shares 4,000 + Non-Distributable Reserves 4,500 = Totals 13,500.

14.1 (a) B = pre-incorporation, A = after incorporation. Salaries of vendors B 1,695, Wages B 2,160, A 6,480, Rent B 215, A 645, Distribution B 480, A 1,200, Commission B 200, A 500, Bad Debts B 104, A 210, Interest B 990, A 660, Directors' Remuneration A 4,000, Directors' Expenses A 515, Depreciation – Motors B 400, A 1,500, Machinery B 125, A 450, Bank Interest A 168, Net Profit B 1,631, A 3,672, Cr Gross Profit B 8,000 A 20,000.

Workings – Distribution and Commission split on basis of sales. Depreciation – Motors To 31 March 19-5, 20% × 3 mos × 7,000 + 20% × 1 month × 3,000 = 400.

After 20% × 9 mos × 7,000 + 20% × 9 mos × 3,000 = 1,500.

Machinery – To 31 March 19-5. 10% × 5,000 × 3 mos = 125. After 10% × 5,000 × 9 mos + 10% × 3,000 × 3 mos = 450.

   (b) Transfer to a Capital Reserve.

   (c) Charge to a Goodwill Account.

14.2 Adjusted Profit 19-4 − Profit 16,400 + Motor Expenses saved 620, + Depreciation Overcharged 1,500, + Wrapping Expenses saved 420, + Bank Interest 180 = 19,120 *less* Extra Management Remuneration 1,500, Invest Income 290, Rents Received 940 = 16,390.

Adjusted Profit 19-5 − Profits 23,920 + Motor Expenses 660, Depreciation Overcharged 700, + Wrapping Expenses saved 480 + Bank Overdraft interest 590 + Preliminary Expenses 690 = 27,400 *less* Undervaluation Opening Stock 1,900, Extra Man Remuneration 1,500, Invest Income 340, Rents Received 420, Profit on Property 4,800 = 18,080.

Adjusted Profits 19-6 -- Profit 19,650 + Motor Expenses saving 700 + Depreciation Overcharged 60 + Wrapping Expenses 510 + Bank Overdraft Interest 740 = 21,660 *less* Extra Man Remuneration 1,500, Invest Income 480 = 19,680.

Average Profit 16,390 + 18,080 + 19,680 = 54,150 ÷ 3 = 18,050.

Purchase Price 4 × 18,050 = 72,200.

16.1 (Summarised) CK: Realisation shows profit 8,350: RP Ltd Realisation shows profit 1,500, Balance Sheet C.J.K. Ltd. Fixed Assets, Premises 15,500 + Plant 5,500 + Goodwill 7,500 + Current Assets, Stock 3,600 + Debtors 8,400 − 300 + Bank 3,140 − Current Liabilities 4,700 − 150 = Working Capital 10,290. Totals 38,790. Issed Capital 29,150 + Share Premium 1,640 (Formation Expenses 1,200 + Discount on Debentures 160 have been written off here) + Debentures 8,000 = Totals 38,790.

15.1 Trading Profit 50,000 + Income from related companies 3,000 + Other Interest 1,100 − Interest payable 3,600 − Tax 24,000 + Undistributed profits last year 9,870 − Reserves 5,000 − Dividends 21,000 = Undistributed Profit c/fwd 10,370.

17.1 (*a*) Preference Share Capital Dr 37,500, Ordinary Share Capital Dr 175,000, Capital Reduction Cr 212,500; Capital Reduction Dr 3,375, Ordinary Share Capital Cr 3,375: Share Premium Dr 40,000, Capital Reduction Cr 40,000; Provision for Depreciation 62,500 Dr, Capital Reduction Dr 72,500, Plant and Machinery Cr 135,000: Capital Reduction Dr 176,625, Profit and Loss Cr 114,375, Preliminary Expenses Cr 7,250, Goodwill Cr 55,000: Application and Allotment Dr 62,500, Ordinary Share Capital Cr 62,500: Cash Dr 62,500, Application and Allotment Cr 62,500.

(*b*) *Balance Sheet* − Property 80,000 *less* Depreciation 30,000, Plant 75,000, Stock 79,175, Debtors 31,200, Bank 11,500 *less* creditors 43,500, Balance Sheet totals 203,375. Issued Capital Preference 112,500, Ordinary 90,875, = Totals 203,375.

17.2 (*a*) Realization – Dr Goodwill 20,000. Fixed Assets 100,000, Stock 22,000, Work in Progress 5,500, Debtors 34,000, Bank 17,500, Formation Expenses 1,000, Cr Budgets Ltd 143,150, Loss on Realization 56,850.

Sundry Shareholders – Dr Profit and Loss 40,000, Loss on Realization 56,850, Budget Shares 73,150, Cr Ordinary Share Capital 120,000, Preference Share Capital 50,000.

(*b*) (i) To Debenture Holders – Cash 20,000 + 6 per cent Debentures 30,000, To Creditors – Cash 14,000, Shares 6,000, To Preference Shareholders – Arrears Shares 5,400, For Shares 7 for every 8: 43,750, To Ordinary Shareholders 24,000 shares 1 for 5 = 24,000. Total 143,150 Purchase Consideration.

(ii) Agreed Value Fixed Assets Stock 20,000, Work in Progress 5,500 Debtors 34,000, Bank 17,500, Fixed Assets (balance) 66,150 = Total 143,150.

(*c*) *Balance Sheet* – Fixed Assets 66,150, Stock 20,000, Work in Progress 5,500, Debtors 34,000, Bank (details follow) 104,350, Balance Sheet totals 230,000. Issued Share Capital 200,000, Debentures 30,000.

Workings – Bank 17,500 + Shares Issued (200,000 *less* 79,150) 120,850 *less* paid to Debenture Holders 20,000 and Creditors 14,000 = 104,350.

17.3 (i) Preference Share Capital Dr 37,500, Capital Reduction Cr 37,500.

(ii) Ordinary Share Capital Dr 360,000, Capital Reduction Cr 360,000.

(iii) Capital Reserve Dr 48,000, Capital Reduction Cr 48,000.

(iv) Preference Share Capital Dr 112,500, Ordinary Share Capital Dr 240,000, New Ordinary Share Capital Cr 352,500.

(v) Debenture Holders Dr 150,000, Debentures Cr 150,000, Cash Dr 150,000, Debenture Holders Cr 150,000.

(vi) Capital Reduction Dr 445,500, Goodwill etc. Cr 210,000, Plant Cr 45,000, Furniture Cr 6,600, Profit & Loss Cr 183,900.

Balance Sheet Goodwill 15,000, Plant 169,800, Furniture 6,000, Stock 170,850, Debtors 65,100, Bank 107,400, Cash 150 – Creditors 31,800 = Totals 502,500. Ordinary Shares 352,500, Debentures 150,000 = Totals 502,500.

18.1 Key figures (i) and (ii) Gross Profit 119,700, Profit on Ordinary activities before Taxation 73,690, Undistributed profits carried forward to next year 20,290.

18.2 Key figures (i) and (ii) Gross Profit 336,450, Profit on Ordinary Activities before Taxation 178,820, Undistributed profits carried forward to next year 72,290.

19.1 (Using totals in parts) Called-up Share Capital 150 + Fixed Asset total 98,920 + Current Asset total 43,710 – Creditors within 1 year 24,380 = Net Current Assets 19,330 = Total Assets *less* Current Liabilities 118,400 – Creditors after 1 year 6,000 = Totals 112,400. Capital 75,000 + Share Premium 20,000 + Cap. Red. Reserve 5,000 + General Reserve 4,000 + Profit & Loss 8,400 = Totals 112,400.

19.2 (totals in parts) Fixed Assets 110,900, Current Assets 46,065 − Creditors within 1 year 39,908 = Net Current Assets 6,157 = Total Assets *less* Current Liabilities 117,057 − Creditors after 1 year 13,260 − Provisions 2,500 = Totals 101,297. Share Capital 70,000 + Share Premium 5,000 + Revaluation Reserve 10,500 + General Reserve 6,000 + Foreign Exchange Reserve 3,500 + Profit & Loss 6,297 = Totals 101,297.

19.3 Key figures Gross Profit 241,835, Profit on Ordinary Activities before Taxation 83,520, Undistributed Profit carried to next year 31,720. Balance Sheet: Fixed Assets 72,800 + Current Assets 240,910 − Creditors 113,990 = Total Assets *less* Current Liabilities 199,720. Capital 150,000 + Share Premium 10,000 + General Reserve 8,000 + Profit & Loss 31,720 = Total 199,720.

20.1 *Trust Ltd Consolidated Loan Account* (N stands for Nominal column, I for Income, C for Capital) – Dr Bank (N) 12,000, (I) 200, (C) 7,060, Dr Adjustment for 1 month's interest on sale of 3,000 *ex div* (I) 10, Investment Income Account (I) 420, Profit and Loss: Profit on Sale (C) 75, Cr Bank ½ yrs interest on 12,000 (I) 240, Bank sale at 61 *ex div* (N) 3,000 (C) 1,830, Adjustment per contra (C). 10, Bank ½ yrs interest on 12,000 (I) 240, Balances c/f (N) 9,000, (I) 150, (C) 5,295 *Abee Ltd Ordinary Shares Account* – Dr Bank Purchase (N) 2,000, (C) 4,000, Bonus Issue (N) 3,000, (C) –, Investment Income (I) 225, Profit on Sale to Profit and Loss (C) 500, Cr Bank Sale at £1 each (N) 2,500, (C) 2,500, Bank Dividend (I) 225, Balances c/f (N) 2,500, (C) 2,000.
Ceedee Ltd Ordinary Shares Account – Dr Bank (N) 5,000, (C) 3,875, Rights Issue (N) 2,500, (C) –, Investment Income (I) 625: Cr Bank Sale of Rights (N) 2,500, (C) 625, Bank Dividend (I) 625, Balance c/f (N) 5,000, (C) 3,250.
Note: as no details are given of periods covered by ordinary dividends they have therefore not been apportioned.

20.2 *Investment Account* – Dr Balance b/f (N) 6,000, (C) 7,200, Bonus Issue (N) 3,000, (C) –, Cash (N) 1,800, (C) 1,890, Profit and Loss (C) 765, Investment Income Account (I) 1,490, Cr Cash Sale of Shares (N) 1,000, (C) 1,965, Cash Sale of Rights (C) 210, Cash Dividend (I) 1,000, Cash Dividend (I) 490, Balance c/f at cost (N) 9,800, (C) 7,680.

21.1 *Contract* – Year 1. Dr Plant 16,250, Materials 25,490, Wages 28,384, Direct Expenses 2,126, Gross Profit to Profit and Loss 8,200 Cr Work Certified 58,000, Plant c/d 10,250, Stock and Work in Progress c/d 12,200.
Contract – Year 2. Dr Stock and Work in Progress b/d 12,200, Plant b/d 10,250, Materials 33,226, Wages 45,432, Direct Expenses 2,902, Penalty 700, Gross Profit to Profit and Loss 15,390, Cr Work Certified 116,000, Sale of Plant 4,100.
Workings – Computation Gross Profit Year 1. Contract Price 174,000 *less* Actual Expenditure Year 1 25,490 + 28,284 + 2,126, + Estimated Cost of Plant (16,250 − 4,250) 12,000, Estimated Expenses Year 2: 81,400 = Profit for year 24,600.

Using Formula given by question $\dfrac{52,200 + 5,800}{174,000} \times 24,600 = 8,200.$

21.3 (*a*) *Contract* – Dr Materials Issued 9,411, Materials Purchased 28,070, Direct Expenses 6,149, Wages 18,493, Charge for Administration Expenses 2,146, Plant Purchased 12,180, Accrued Expenses c/d Wages 366, Direct Expenses 49 = 76,864, Profit and Loss Account – Profit 4,050, Cr Balances c/f – Work in Progress 68,600, Stock of Materials 2,164, Plant at cost *less* Depreciation 10,150.

(*b*) *Calculation of Profit* – Work Certified (net after retentions) 64,170 *add* 10 per cent Retention Money (one-ninth of 64,170) 7,310 = 71,300, *less* Cost of Work Certified: Expenditure to date 76,864 *less* w.d.v. of Plant 10,150, Stock 2,164 = 64,550, making Profit on Work Certified 6,750. Two-thirds Profit on Work Certified 4,500 *less* represented by retention money 450 = Profit to be taken to Profit and Loss Account 4,050. Working. Depreciation. Plant cost 12,180. Annual Depreciation Charge one-fifth of 12,180 = 2,436 per annum. Depreciation Charge for 10 months = $\frac{10}{12} \times 2,436 = 2,030$. w.d.v. 10,150.

23.1 Profit 2,408 + Depreciation 1,015 = Total generated 3,423 – Application: Fixed Assets 2,520, Dividend paid 500, Taxation paid 856 = Decrease in working capital 453. (Decrease in stock (116), Increase in debtors 105, Decrease in creditors 218, Decrease in bank (660) = 453).

24.1 Net Present Values – Firm A 3,732.55, Firm B 3,615.41, Firm C 3,519.39. Therefore offer by Firm C chosen.

24.2 (*a*) (i) *Payback:*

Should be calculated on the incremental cash flows, i.e. after adding back depreciation to profits after tax:

A	B	C
$1\frac{5}{7}$ years	2 years	$1\frac{3}{7}$ years

(ii) *Rate of Return:*

$$\frac{\text{Average Profit Net of Depreciation}}{\text{Average Capital}}$$

A $\frac{75}{150} \times 100 = 50\%$

B $\frac{75}{150} \times 100 = 50\%$

C $\frac{75}{150} \times 100 = 50\%$

(iii) *Net Present Value:*

Should be calculated on cash flows, i.e. after adding back depreciation to profits:

A $\dfrac{175}{(1.10)} + \dfrac{175}{(1.10)^2} + \dfrac{175}{(1.10)^3} = 435$

B $\dfrac{125}{(1.10)} + \dfrac{175}{(1.10)^2} + \dfrac{225}{(1.10)^3} = 427$

C $\dfrac{225}{(1.10)} + \dfrac{175}{(1.10)^2} + \dfrac{125}{(1.10)^3} = 443$

(*b*) Choice should be that indicated by N.P.V. method, i.e. project C.

A full answer should back up this choice by enumerating the advantages of the discounting method and the shortcomings of 'payback' and 'rate of return'.

24.3 Cost 26,485 *less* 20 per cent 5,297 = 21,188 by present value of annuity factor 10.594 = 2,000 per annum.

24.4 £52,760 × P.V. factor for annuity of £1 = £200,000

P.V. factor = $\dfrac{200,000}{52,760}$ = 3.79

Referring to 5 period row shows factor of 3.79 under 10% column
∴ interest rate = 10%.

24.5 Rental × P.V. factor of 16% for 5 years = £60,000

Rental × 3.274 = £60,000

Rental = $\dfrac{60,000}{3.274}$ = £18,326.2 per annum

24.6

	Capital amount outstanding at start	Interest at 16%	Capital Repayment	Capital account outstanding at at end
Year 1	60,000	9,600	8,726	51,274
2	51,274	8,204	10,122	41,152
3	41,152	6,584	11,742	29,410
4	29,410	4,706	13,620	15,790
5	15,790	2,526	15,800	–
		31,620		

Note: The difference between 15,790 and 15,800 at the end is due to rounding off the calculations.

Rule of 78

Year	Proportion	Proportion × Finance Charge £31,630
1	$\frac{5}{15}$	10,543
2	$\frac{4}{15}$	8,435
3	$\frac{3}{15}$	6,326
4	$\frac{2}{15}$	4,217
5	$\frac{1}{15}$	2,109
	15	31,630

26.1

	Jan.	Feb.	Mar.	Apl.	May	Jun.
Opening Stock	740	690	780	1,100	1,400	1,160
Add production	750	1,010	1,410	1,620	1,240	800
	1,490	1,700	2,190	2,720	2,640	1,960
Less sales	800	920	1,090	1,320	1,480	1,020
Closing stock	690	780	1,100	1,400	1,160	940

26.2 (*a*) Opening Stock 140, Add Production (figure to be deduced) less Sales of 1,550 = Closing Stock 150. By deduction, given the figures already known the only figure which could be inserted for production so that the equation worked out is 1,560. An even production flow of 1,560 ÷ 12 = 130 units. This has been tested to ensure that stock never becomes a negative figure.

(*b*) Starting with above figures the closing stock at the end of each month would be Jan 160, F 110, M 70, Apr 50, May 60, Jn 90, Jy 150, Aug 250, S 210, Oct 230, N 210, D 150. Lowest closing figure for stock is April 50, if stock is not to fall below 80 units an extra 30 units (80 − 50) will have to be produced in January making production for that month of 160 units.

26.3 Opening stock? (to be deduced) add Production 1,500, less Sales 1,230 = Closing stock 430. By arithmetical deduction the only figure that could be inserted to make the equation agree is 160 units.

26.7 Jan Capital 1,000 + Debtors 3,900 = 4,900 less Payments 5,800 = Overdraft c/f 900, Feb b/f − 900 Add Debtors 5,900, less Payments 7,500 = Overdraft c/f 2,500, March B/f − 2,500, Add Debtors 6,000, Loan 700, Less Payments 10,000, Overdraft c/f 5,800, April B/f − 5,800, Add Debtors 7,100, less Payments 10,800, Overdraft c/f 9,500, May B/f − 9,500, Add Debtors 8,400, Less Payments 9,900, Overdraft c/f 11,000, June B/f − 11,000, Debtors 9,500, Less Payments 8,000, Overdraft c/f 9,500. As permission for overdraft only 10,000 some action will have to be taken to keep overdraft below 11,000 in May.

26.8 Payments Schedules: July, Materials (320 × £4 + 300 × £1) 1,580, D Labour 320 × £8 + 2,560, Variable (300 × £1 + 320 × £1) 620, Fixed Expenses 400, Drawings 300, total 5,460. August, Materials (350 × £4 + 320 × £1) 1,720, D Labour 350 × £8 = 2,800, Variable (320 × £1 + 350 × £1) 670, Fixed 400, Drawings 300, total 5,890. September: Materials (370 × £4 + 350 × £1) £1,830, D Labour 370 × £8 = 2,960, Variable (350 × £1 + 370 × £1) 720, Fixed 400, Drawings 300, Total 6,210. October, Materials (380 × £4 + 370 × £1) 1,890, D Labour 380 × £8 = 3,040, Variable (370 × £1 + 380 × £1) 750, Fixed 400, Machinery 2,000, Drawings 300, Total,8,380. November, Materials (340 × £4 + 380 × £1) £1,740, Labour 340 × £8 = 2,720, Variable (380 × £1 + 340 × £1) 720, Fixed 400, Drawings 300, Total 5,880. December, Materials (310 × £4 + 340 × £1) 1,580, Labour 310 × £8 = 2,480, Variable (340 × £1 + 310 × £1) 690, Fixed 400, Drawings 300, Total 5,410.

Cash Budget Jul, Bal b/f 1,200 + Debtors 4,000, less Payments 5,460, O/d c/f 260, Aug O/d b/f 260, Debtors 6,400, less Payments 5,890, Bal c/f 250, Sept Bal b/f 250, Debtors 5,800, less Payments 6,210, O/d c/f 160, Oct O/d b/f 160, Debtors 8,000, less Payments 8,380, O/d c/f 540, Nov O/d b/f 540, Debtors 6,000, less Payments 5,880, O/d c/f 420, Dec O/d b/f 420, debtors 7,000, Legacy 2,500, less Payments 5,410, Bal c/f 3,670.

26.12 Payments: Totals: Jan 24,510, Feb 1,860, Mar 1,980, Apl 2,340, May 2,760, June 3,460. Receipts: Totals: Jan 400, Feb 600, Mar 1,750, Apl 2,200, May 2,900. June 3,550: Balance end each month: Jan + 890, Feb − 370, Mar − 600, Apl − 740, May − 600, June − 510. Trading P/L: Sales 16,500, Purchases 11,410 − Closing Stock 910 = Gross Profit 6,000 + Rent 300 − Salaries 1,560, Other Expenses 900, Depreciation Fixtures 150 & Motor Van 100 = Net Profit 3,590.
Balance Sheet Premises 20,000, Fixtures 3,000 − 150, Motor Van 1,000 − 100, Stock 910, Debtors, 5,400, − Creditors 2,310, Other 150, Bank Overdraft 510 = Totals 27,090. Capital 25,000 + Net Profit 3,590 − Drawings 1,500.

26.13 Payments Schedule: Jan, Wages 800, Directors 1,200, Total 2,000. Feb, Purchases 48,000, Wages 800, Directors 1,200, Premises 30,000, Other 600, Total 80,600. March, Purchases 16,000, Wages 800, Directors 1,200, Equipment 6,000, Other 600, Total, 24,600. April, Purchases 18,000, Wages 800, Directors 1,200, Other 600, Total 20,600. May, Purchases 20,000, Wages 800, Directors 1,200, Other 600, Total 22,600. June, Purchases 14,000, Wages 800, Directors 1,200, Equipment 6,000, Other 600, Total 22,600. Receipts Schedule: Jan, Capital 60,000, Sales: April 12,000, May 16,000, June 28,000 + and − Balances end of each month: Jan + 58,000, Feb − 22,600, March − 47,200, April − 55,800, May − 62,400, June − 57,000.

Trading A/c: Dr Purchases 126,000, less Closing stock 21,800, Gross Profit 23,800, Totals 128,000. Cr Sales 128,000. Profit & Loss: Dr Salaries 4,800, Other 3,840, Debenture Interest 280, Depreciation 1,200, Directors 7,200, Net Profit 6,480, Totals 23,800. Cr Gross Profit b/d 23,800. Balance Sheets, Fixed Assets, Premises 30,000. Equipment 12,000 less depreciation 1,200 = 10,800, Current Assets, Stock 21,800, Debtors 72,000, Current Liabilities, Bank Overdraft 57,000, Creditors 10,000, Other Expenses 840, Debenture Interest owing 280. Ordinary Shares Capital 52,000, Profit & Loss 6,480, Debenture 8,000.

26.14 Trading Account: Dr Opening Stock 11,000, Add Purchases (this figure is found by inserting all the other figures in the Trading Account, leaving this as the missing figure to make it balance) 99,000, less Closing Stock 20,000, Gross profit 18,000 (this is 16⅔% of sales), Totals 108,000. Cr Sales 108,000. Profit & Loss, Dr Wages 6,600, Administration 4,320, Depreciation 450, Net Profit 6,630, Totals 18,000. Cr Gross Profit b/d 18,000. Balance Sheet, Fixed Assets 9,000 less Depreciation 450, Current Assets: Stock 20,000, Debtors 36,000. Current Liabilities: Creditors 16,500, Bank Overdraft 9,380, Administration Expenses owing 720, Ordinary Shares 15,000. Share Premium 1,250, Profit & Loss 21,700, Bank: June, Bal b/f 5,400. Debtors 9,600, less Wages 1,100, Admin 600, Purchases 9,330, Bal c/f 3,970. Jul, Bal b/f 3,970, less Wages 1,100, Admin 720, Purchases 16,500, O/d c/f 14,350. Aug, O/d b/f 14,350, Debtors 18,000, less Wages 1,100, Admin 720, Purchases 16,500, O/d c/f 14,670. Sept, O/d b/f 14,670, Ordinary Shares 6,250, Debtors 18,000, less Wages 1,100, Admin 720, Purchases 16,500, O/d c/f 8,740. Oct, O/d b/f 8,740, Debtors 18,000, less Wages 1,100, Admin 720, Purchases 16,500, O/d c/f 9,060. Nov, O/d b/f 9,060, Debtors 18,000, less Wages 1,100, Admin 720, Purchases 16,500, O/d c/f 9,380.

496

28.1 Goodwill 10, Stock 140, Bank 50. Total 200: Share Capital 200.

28.2 Fixed Assets 3,800, Stock 1,500, Debtors 700, Bank 300. Share Capital 6,000, Capital Reserve 300, Total 6,300.

28.3 Fixed Assets 62,000, Stock 27,000, Debtors 8,000, Bank 3,000. Share Capital 100,000, Total 100,000.

28.6 Goodwill 300, Fixed Assets 2,000, Stock 1,300, Debtors 900, Bank 300. Share Capital 4,000, Minority Interest 800, Totals 4,800.

28.7 Fixed Assets 3,325, Stock 3,000, Debtors 2,000, Bank 200. Share Capital 8,000, Capital Reserve 375, Minority Interest 150, Total 8,525.

28.10 Fixed Assets 12,600, Current Assets 5,900. Share Capital 10,000, Profit and Loss 6,500, Capital Reserve 600 (Goodwill S1 300, Capital Reserve 900 = Net Capital Reserve 600), Total 18,500.

28.11 Goodwill 350 (Goodwill S1 600, Capital Reserve S2 250 = Net Goodwill 350), Fixed Assets 9,450, Current Assets 6,000. Share Capital 10,000, Profit and Loss 2,000, General Reserve 1,400, Minority Interest 2,400. Total 15,800.

29.1 Goodwill 950, Fixed Assets 10,950, Current Assets 3,900. Share Capital 10,000, Profit and Loss H 4,000 + S 1,800, Total 15,800.

29.2 Fixed Assets 47,400, Current Assets 27,100, Total 74,500. Share Capital 50,000, Profit and Loss (H 14,000 − S 400) 13,600, General Reserve 5,000, Capital Reserve 1,790, Minority Interest 4,110, Total 74,500.

29.4 Goodwill 1,390 (S1 Cost 8,150 − 60% of 10,000 + 1,100 + 2,000 = 290, S2 Cost 11,400 − (8,000 + 500 + 1,800 = 1,100)), Fixed Assets 36,900, Current Assets 20,900. Share Capital 40,000, Profit and Loss (H 7,550 + S1 1,020 − S2 300) 8,270, General Reserve 5,000 Minority Interest (60% of 10,000 + 2,800 + 2,000) 5,920, Total 59,190.

30.1 Goodwill 850, Fixed Assets 2,300, Stock (1,200 + 900 − 90) 2,010, Debtors (2,100 + 1,400 − 220) 3,280, Bank 500. Share Capital 2,000, Profit & Loss (H 3,700 − 90 + S 1,150) 4,760, General Reserve 800, Creditors 900 + 700 − 220 = 1,380, Total 8,940.

30.2 Goodwill 1,600, Fixed Assets 14,200, Stock (3,100 + 7,200 − 50) 10,250, Debtors (4,900 − 600 + 3,800) 8,100 + Bank 2,500. Share Capital 20,000, Profit and Loss (H 4,000 − 50 + S 60% of 2,000) 5,150, Minority Interest (40% of 10,000 + 5,500) 6,200, Creditors (3,800 + 2,100 − 600) 5,300. Totals 36,650.

31.1 Shares bought 31/12/19-4. 10,000, Proportion Profit and Loss at 31/12/19-4 (25% of 24,000) 6,000 = 16,000: Shares bought 31/12/19-6. 14,000, Proportion of Profit and Loss at 31/12/19-6. (35% of 30,000) 10,500 = 24,500. Total 40,500. Paid 19-4 23,500 + paid 19-6 31,000 = 54,500. Goodwill therefore 54,500 − 40,500 = 14,000.

31.3 Shares bought 50,000, (Profit and Loss, balance 31/12/19-7, 36,000, Add Proportion 19-8 profits before acquisition $8/12 \times 42,000 = 28,000$. Total 64,000. Of this proportion of pre-acquisition profits $50,000/80,000 \times 64,000 = 40,000$) 40,000, giving total 90,000. Paid for shares 158,000, therefore goodwill is $158,000 - 90,000 = 68,000$.

32.1 Goodwill (Cost $29,000 - 20,000 - 3,000 -$ Dividend 5,000) 1,000, Fixed Assets 57,000, Current Assets 15,000. Share Capital 50,000, Profit and Loss (H $19,000 + $ S 4,000) 23,000, Total 73,000.

32.3 Goodwill (Cost $47,000 - \frac{3}{4}$ of $40,000 + 4,000$) 14,000, Fixed Assets 80,000, Current Assets 33,000. Share Capital 80,000, Profit and Loss (H $23,000 + $ S $\frac{3}{4}$ of $6,000 + \frac{3}{4}$ of 7,000) 32,750. Minority Interest ($\frac{1}{4}$ of $40,000 + 11,000$) 12,750, C/liabilities, Proposed Dividend 1,500, Totals 127,000.

33.1 Goodwill 100,000, Fixed Assets $500,000 - $ Depreciation 138,000, Current Assets 205,000. Share Capital 500,000, Profit and Loss (H $143,000 - 10,000 + $ S $32,000 + 2,000$) 167,000, Totals 667,000.

33.3 Goodwill 19,000, Fixed Assets 185,000 less Depreciation 33,500, Current Assets 68,000. Share Capital 150,000, Profit and Loss (H $77,000 + $ S $14,000 - 2,500$) 88,500. Totals 238,500.

34.1 Share Capital 100,000, Profit and Loss (H $37,000 + $ S1 90% of $16,000 + $ S2 63% of 3,000) 53,290, General Reserve 10,000, Minority Interest (Shares in S1 $1,000 + $ Shares in S2 37% of 5,000: 1,850, Profit and Loss S1 10% of 23,000: 2,300, S2 37% of 4,000: 1,480, Less Cost of shares in S2 for minority interest of S1 10% of 6,000: 600) 6,030. Totals 169,320. Goodwill (Cost of shares to group, in S1 Ltd 23,000, in S2 Ltd 90% of 6,000: 5,400) 28,400, Less shares: In S1 9,000. In S2 63% of $5,000 = 3,150$. Total 12,150, Profit and Loss in S1 90% of 7,000: 6,300. In S2 63% of 1,000: 630) 9,320, Fixed Assets 127,000, Current Assets 33,000.

35.1 Profits for the year before taxation 110,000, Less Tax $49,000 = $ Profits for the year after taxation 61,000 Less Minority Shareholders Interest 4,000, Group Profits for the period 57,000, Less Appropriations: Proposed Dividends 30,000, Unappropriated profits carried forward to next year 27,000.

37.4 1. A, C, E.
2. A, C, E.
3. E.
4. D, F (assuming current assets exceed current liabilities)
5. No Effect.

37.6 $a = \dfrac{.1}{1.5} = 6.7\%$

$b = \dfrac{15,000}{100.000} = $ £.15 per share

$c = \dfrac{1.5}{.15} = 10.0$

37.8 Selection of five from: –

Current Ratio 1.89: 1; Acid Test Ratio .78:1 (Note Only Bank and Debtor Balances included) Gross Profit/Sales 33⅓% Net Profit/Sales (no tax assumed) 13.3%. Net Operating Profit/Capital Employed

$$\frac{20 + \text{Debenture Interest } 3}{200} = 11.5\%$$

Net Profit/Owners Equity $\frac{20}{140} = 14.3\%$ Stock Turnover $\frac{100}{30} = 3.3$ times.

Sales/Fixed Assets $\frac{150}{120} = 1.3$ times. Days Sales in Debtors = 122.

Net Worth/Total Assets $\frac{140}{290} = 48.3\%$ Fixed Assets/Net Worth $\frac{120}{140} =$ 85.7%. Coverage of Fixed Charges $\frac{20+3}{3} = 7.7$ times.

37.10 Current Ratios 1) 2.4:1 2) 2.4:1, Acid Test Ratio 1) 1.2:1 2) 1.2:1 Gross Profit/Sales 1) 21.3 2) 20.3 Net Profit/Sales 1) 5% 2) 4.5% Operating Profit/Capital Employed:

1) $\frac{30,000}{200,000} = 15\%$ 2) $\frac{38,000}{294,000} = 12.9\%$ Net Profit/Owners Equity:

1) $\frac{30,000}{200,000} = 15\%$ 2) $\frac{34,000}{234,000} = 14.5\%$ Stock Turn (using year end

figures 1) $\frac{472}{120} = 3.9$ times 2) $\frac{596}{188} = 3.2$ times. Sales/Fixed Assets 1) $\frac{600}{60}$

= 10 times 2) $\frac{748}{80} = 93$ times. Collection Period for Debtors 1) = 60.8

days 2) = 80 days Net Worth/Total Assets 1) $\frac{200}{300} = .672$ 2) $\frac{234}{446} = .52$

Coverage of fixed charges. 1) n/a 2) $\frac{38,000}{4,000} = 9.5$

APPENDIX NO I

Table 1

Compound Sum of £1

Year	1%	2%	3%	4%	5%	6%	7%	8%	9%	10%
1	1.010	1.020	1.030	1.040	1.050	1.060	1.070	1.080	1.090	1.100
2	1.020	1.040	1.061	1.082	1.102	1.124	1.145	1.166	1.188	1.210
3	1.030	1.061	1.093	1.125	1.158	1.191	1.225	1.260	1.295	1.331
4	1.041	1.082	1.126	1.170	1.216	1.262	1.311	1.360	1.412	1.464
5	1.051	1.104	1.159	1.217	1.276	1.338	1.403	1.469	1.539	1.611
6	1.062	1.126	1.194	1.265	1.340	1.419	1.501	1.587	1.677	1.772
7	1.072	1.149	1.230	1.316	1.407	1.504	1.606	1.714	1.828	1.949
8	1.083	1.172	1.267	1.369	1.477	1.594	1.718	1.851	1.993	2.144
9	1.094	1.195	1.305	1.423	1.551	1.689	1.838	1.999	2.172	2.358
10	1.105	1.219	1.344	1.480	1.629	1.791	1.967	2.159	2.367	2.594
11	1.116	1.243	1.384	1.539	1.710	1.898	2.105	2.332	2.580	2.853
12	1.127	1.268	1.426	1.601	1.796	2.012	2.252	2.518	2.813	3.138
13	1.138	1.294	1.469	1.665	1.886	2.133	2.410	2.720	3.066	3.452
14	1.149	1.319	1.513	1.732	1.980	2.261	2.579	2.937	3.342	3.797
15	1.161	1.346	1.558	1.801	2.079	2.397	2.759	3.172	3.642	4.177

Year	12%	14%	15%	16%	18%	20%	24%	28%	32%
1	1.120	1.140	1.150	1.160	1.180	1.200	1.240	1.280	1.320
2	1.254	1.300	1.322	1.346	1.392	1.440	1.538	1.638	1.742
3	1.405	1.482	1.521	1.561	1.643	1.728	1.907	2.097	2.300
4	1.574	1.689	1.749	1.811	1.939	2.074	2.364	2.684	3.036
5	1.762	1.925	2.011	2.100	2.288	2.488	2.932	3.436	4.007
6	1.974	2.195	2.313	2.436	2.700	2.986	3.635	4.398	5.290
7	2.211	2.502	2.660	2.826	3.185	3.583	4.508	5.629	6.983
8	2.476	2.853	3.059	3.278	3.759	4.300	5.590	7.206	9.217
9	2.773	3.252	3.518	3.803	4.435	5.160	6.931	9.223	12.166
10	3.106	3.707	4.046	4.411	5.234	6.192	8.594	11.806	16.060
11	3.479	4.226	4.652	5.117	6.176	7.430	10.657	15.112	21.199
12	3.896	4.818	5.350	5.936	7.288	8.916	13.215	19.343	27.983
13	4.363	5.492	6.153	6.886	8.599	10.699	16.386	24.759	36.937
14	4.887	6.261	7.076	7.988	10.147	12.839	20.319	31.691	48.757
15	5.474	7.138	8.137	9.266	11.974	15.407	25.196	40.565	64.359

Year	36%	40%	50%	60%	70%	80%	90%
1	1.360	1.400	1.500	1.600	1.700	1.800	1.900
2	1.850	1.960	2.250	2.560	2.890	3.240	3.610
3	2.515	2.744	3.375	4.096	4.913	5.832	6.859
4	3.421	3.842	5.062	6.544	8.352	10.498	13.032
5	4.653	5.378	7.594	10.486	14.199	18.896	24.761
6	6.328	7.530	11.391	16.777	24.138	34.012	47.046
7	8.605	10.541	17.086	26.844	41.034	61.222	89.387
8	11.703	14.758	25.629	42.950	69.758	110.200	169.836
9	15.917	20.661	38.443	68.720	118.588	198.359	322.688
10	21.647	28.925	57.665	109.951	201.599	357.047	613.107
11	29.439	40.496	86.498	175.922	342.719	642.684	1164.902
12	40.037	56.694	129.746	281.475	582.622	1156.831	2213.314
13	54.451	79.372	194.619	450.360	990.457	2082.295	4205.297
14	74.053	111.120	291.929	720.576	1683.777	3748.131	7990.065
15	100.712	155.568	437.894	1152.921	2862.421	6746.636	15181.122

500

Table 2

Present Value of £1

Year	1%	2%	3%	4%	5%	6%	7%	8%	9%	10%	12%	14%	15
1	0.990	0.980	0.971	0.961	0.952	0.943	0.935	0.926	0.917	0.909	0.893	0.877	0.
2	0.980	0.961	0.943	0.925	0.907	0.890	0.873	0.857	0.842	0.826	0.797	0.769	0.
3	0.971	0.942	0.915	0.889	0.864	0.840	0.816	0.794	0.772	0.751	0.712	0.675	0.
4	0.961	0.924	0.889	0.855	0.823	0.792	0.763	0.735	0.708	0.683	0.636	0.592	0.
5	0.951	0.906	0.863	0.822	0.784	0.747	0.713	0.681	0.650	0.621	0.567	0.519	0.
6	0.942	0.888	0.838	0.790	0.746	0.705	0.666	0.630	0.596	0.564	0.507	0.456	0.
7	0.933	0.871	0.813	0.760	0.711	0.665	0.623	0.583	0.547	0.513	0.452	0.400	0.
08	0.923	0.853	0.789	0.731	0.677	0.627	0.582	0.540	0.502	0.467	0.404	0.351	0.
9	0.914	0.837	0.766	0.703	0.645	0.592	0.544	0.500	0.460	0.424	0.361	0.308	0.
10	0.905	0.820	0.744	0.676	0.614	0.558	0.508	0.463	0.422	0.386	0.322	0.270	0.
11	0.896	0.804	0.722	0.650	0.585	0.527	0.475	0.429	0.388	0.350	0.287	0.237	0.
12	0.887	0.788	0.701	0.625	0.557	0.497	0.444	0.397	0.356	0.319	0.257	0.208	0.
13	0.879	0.773	0.681	0.601	0.530	0.469	0.415	0.368	0.326	0.290	0.229	0.182	0.
14	0.870	0.758	0.661	0.577	0.505	0.442	0.388	0.340	0.299	0.263	0.205	0.160	0.
15	0.861	0.743	0.642	0.555	0.481	0.417	0.362	0.315	0.275	0.239	0.183	0.140	0.
16	0.853	0.728	0.623	0.534	0.458	0.394	0.339	0.292	0.252	0.218	0.163	0.123	0.
17	0.844	0.714	0.605	0.513	0.436	0.371	0.317	0.270	0.231	0.198	0.146	0.108	0.
18	0.836	0.700	0.587	0.494	0.416	0.350	0.296	0.250	0.212	0.180	0.130	0.095	0.
19	0.828	0.686	0.570	0.475	0.396	0.331	0.276	0.232	0.194	0.164	0.116	0.083	0.
20	0.820	0.673	0.554	0.456	0.377	0.319	0.258	0.215	0.178	0.149	0.104	0.073	0.
25	0.780	0.610	0.478	0.375	0.295	0.233	0.184	0.146	0.116	0.092	0.059	0.038	0.
30	0.742	0.552	0.412	0.308	0.231	0.174	0.131	0.099	0.075	0.057	0.033	0.020	0.

Year	16%	18%	20%	24%	28%	32%	36%	40%	50%	60%	70%	80%	9
1	0.862	0.847	0.833	0.806	0.781	0.758	0.735	0.714	0.667	0.625	0.588	0.556	0.5
2	0.743	0.718	0.694	0.650	0.610	0.574	0.541	0.510	0.444	0.391	0.346	0.309	0.2
3	0.641	0.609	0.579	0.524	0.477	0.435	0.398	0.364	0.296	0.244	0.204	0.171	0.1
4	0.552	0.516	0.482	0.423	0.373	0.329	0.292	0.260	0.198	0.153	0.120	0.095	0.0
5	0.476	0.437	0.402	0.341	0.291	0.250	0.215	0.186	0.132	0.095	0.070	0.053	0.0
6	0.410	0.370	0.335	0.275	0.227	0.189	0.158	0.133	0.088	0.060	0.041	0.029	0.0
7	0.354	0.314	0.279	0.222	0.178	0.143	0.116	0.095	0.059	0.037	0.024	0.016	0.0
8	0.305	0.266	0.233	0.179	0.139	0.108	0.085	0.068	0.039	0.023	0.014	0.009	0.0
9	0.263	0.226	0.194	0.144	0.108	0.082	0.063	0.048	0.026	0.015	0.008	0.005	0.0
10	0.227	0.191	0.162	0.116	0.085	0.062	0.046	0.035	0.017	0.009	0.005	0.003	0.0
11	0.195	0.162	0.135	0.094	0.066	0.047	0.034	0.025	0.012	0.006	0.003	0.002	0.0
12	0.168	0.137	0.112	0.076	0.052	0.036	0.025	0.018	0.008	0.004	0.002	0.001	0.0
13	0.145	0.116	0.093	0.061	0.040	0.027	0.018	0.013	0.005	0.002	0.001	0.001	0.0
14	0.125	0.099	0.078	0.049	0.032	0.021	0.014	0.009	0.003	0.001	0.001	0.000	0.0
15	0.108	0.084	0.065	0.040	0.025	0.016	0.010	0.006	0.002	0.001	0.000	0.000	
16	0.093	0.071	0.054	0.032	0.019	0.012	0.007	0.005	0.002	0.001	0.000	0.000	
17	0.080	0.060	0.045	0.026	0.015	0.009	0.005	0.003	0.001	0.000	0.000		
18	0.069	0.051	0.038	0.021	0.012	0.007	0.004	0.002	0.001	0.000	0.000		
19	0.060	0.043	0.031	0.017	0.009	0.005	0.003	0.002	0.000	0.000			
20	0.051	0.037	0.026	0.014	0.007	0.004	0.002	0.001	0.000	0.000			
25	0.024	0.016	0.010	0.005	0.002	0.001	0.000	0.000					
30	0.012	0.007	0.004	0.002	0.001	0.000	0.000						

Table 3

Sum of an Annuity of £1 for N Years

Year	1%	2%	3%	4%	5%	6%	7%	8%
1	1.000	1.000	1.000	1.000	1.000	1.000	1.000	1.000
2	2.010	2.020	2.030	2.040	2.050	2.060	2.070	2.080
3	3.030	3.060	3.091	3.122	3.152	3.184	3.215	3.246
4	4.060	4.122	4.184	4.246	4.310	4.375	4.440	4.506
5	5.101	5.204	5.309	5.416	5.526	5.637	5.751	5.867
6	6.152	6.308	6.468	6.633	6.802	6.975	7.153	7.336
7	7.214	7.434	7.662	7.898	8.142	8.394	8.654	8.923
8	8.286	8.583	8.892	9.214	9.549	9.897	10.260	10.637
9	9.369	9.755	10.159	10.583	11.027	11.491	11.978	12.488
10	10.462	10.950	11.464	12.006	12.578	13.181	13.816	14.487
11	11.567	12.169	12.808	13.486	14.207	14.972	15.784	16.645
12	12.683	13.412	14.192	15.026	15.917	16.870	17.888	18.977
13	13.809	14.680	15.618	16.627	17.713	18.882	20.141	21.495
14	14.947	15.974	17.086	18.292	19.599	21.051	22.550	24.215
15	16.097	17.293	18.599	20.024	21.579	23.276	25.129	27.152
16	17.258	18.639	20.157	21.825	23.657	25.673	27.888	30.324
17	18.430	20.012	21.762	23.698	25.840	28.213	30.840	33.750
18	19.615	21.412	23.414	25.645	28.132	30.906	33.999	37.450
19	20.811	22.841	25.117	27.671	30.539	33.760	37.379	41.446
20	22.019	24.297	26.870	29.778	33.066	36.786	40.995	45.762
25	28.243	32.030	36.459	41.646	47.727	54.865	63.249	73.106
30	34.785	40.568	47.575	56.085	66.439	79.058	94.461	113.283

Year	9%	10%	12%	14%	16%	18%	20%	24%
1	1.000	1.000	1.000	1.000	1.000	1.000	1.000	1.000
2	2.090	2.100	2.120	2.140	2.160	2.180	2.200	2.240
3	3.278	3.310	3.374	3.440	3.506	3.572	3.640	3.778
4	4.573	4.641	4.779	4.921	5.066	5.215	5.368	5.684
5	5.985	6.105	6.353	6.610	6.877	7.154	7.442	8.048
6	7.523	7.716	8.115	8.536	8.977	9.442	9.930	10.980
7	9.200	9.487	10.089	10.730	11.414	12.142	12.916	14.615
8	11.028	11.436	12.300	13.233	14.240	15.327	16.499	19.123
9	13.021	13.579	14.776	16.085	17.518	19.086	20.799	24.712
10	15.193	15.937	17.549	19.337	21.321	23.521	25.959	31.643
11	17.560	18.531	20.655	23.044	25.738	28.755	32.150	40.238
12	20.141	21.384	24.133	27.271	30.350	34.931	39.580	50.895
13	22.953	24.523	28.029	32.089	36.766	42.219	48.497	64.110
14	26.019	27.975	32.393	37.581	43.672	50.818	59.196	80.496
15	29.361	31.722	37.280	43.842	51.659	60.965	72.035	100.815

Year	28%	32%	36%	40%	50%	60%	70%	80%
1	1.000	1.000	1.000	1.000	1.000	1.000	1.000	1.000
2	2.280	2.320	2.360	2.400	2.500	2.600	2.700	2.800
3	3.918	4.062	4.210	4.360	4.750	5.160	5.590	6.040
4	6.016	6.326	6.725	7.104	8.125	9.256	10.503	11.872
5	8.700	9.398	10.146	10.846	13.188	15.810	18.855	22.370
6	12.136	13.406	14.799	16.324	20.781	26.295	33.054	41.265
7	16.534	18.696	21.126	23.853	32.172	43.073	57.191	75.278
8	22.163	25.678	29.732	34.395	49.258	69.916	98.225	136.500
9	29.369	34.895	41.435	49.153	74.887	112.866	167.983	246.699
10	38.592	47.062	57.352	69.814	113.330	181.585	286.570	445.058
11	50.399	63.122	78.998	98.739	170.995	291.536	488.170	802.105
12	65.510	84.320	108.437	139.235	257.493	467.458	830.888	1444.788
13	84.853	112.303	148.475	195.929	387.239	748.933	1413.510	2601.619
14	109.612	149.240	202.926	275.300	581.859	1199.293	2403.968	4683.914
15	141.303	197.997	276.979	386.420	873.788	1919.869	4087.745	8432.045

Table 4

Present Value of Annuity of £1

Year	1%	2%	3%	4%	5%	6%	7%	8%	9%	10%
1	0.990	0.980	0.971	0.962	0.952	0.943	0.935	0.926	0.917	0.90
2	1.970	1.942	1.913	1.886	1.859	1.833	1.808	1.783	1.759	1.73
3	2.941	2.884	2.829	2.775	2.723	2.673	2.624	2.577	2.531	2.48
4	3.902	3.808	3.717	3.630	3.546	3.465	3.387	3.312	3.240	3.17
5	4.853	4.713	4.580	4.452	4.329	4.212	4.100	3.993	3.890	3.79
6	5.795	5.601	5.417	5.424	5.076	4.917	4.766	4.623	4.486	4.35
7	6.728	6.472	6.230	6.002	5.786	5.582	5.389	5.206	5.033	4.86
8	7.652	7.325	7.020	6.733	6.463	6.210	6.971	5.747	5.535	5.33
9	8.566	8.162	7.786	7.435	7.108	6.802	6.515	6.247	5.985	5.75
10	9.471	8.983	8.530	8.111	7.722	7.360	7.024	6.710	6.418	6.14
11	10.368	9.787	9.253	8.760	8.306	7.887	7.499	7.139	6.805	6.49
12	11.255	10.575	9.954	9.385	8.863	8.384	7.943	7.536	7.161	6.81
13	12.134	11.348	10.635	9.986	9.394	8.853	8.358	7.904	7.487	7.10
14	13.004	12.106	11.296	10.563	8.899	9.295	8.745	8.244	7.786	7.36
15	13.865	12.849	11.938	11.118	10.380	9.712	9.108	8.559	8.060	7.60
16	14.718	13.578	12.561	11.652	10.838	10.106	9.447	8.851	8.312	7.82
17	15.562	14.292	13.166	12.166	11.274	10.477	9.763	9.122	8.544	8.02
18	16.398	14.992	13.754	12.659	11.690	10.828	10.059	9.372	8.756	8.20
19	17.226	15.678	14.324	13.134	12.085	11.158	10.336	9.604	8.950	8.36
20	18.046	16.351	14.877	13.590	12.462	11.470	10.594	9.818	9.128	8.51
25	22.023	19.523	17.413	15.622	14.094	12.783	11.654	10.675	9.823	9.07
30	25.808	22.397	19.600	17.292	15.373	13.765	12.409	11.258	10.274	9.42

Year	12%	14%	16%	18%	20%	24%	28%	32%	36%
1	0.893	0.877	0.862	0.847	0.833	0.806	0.781	0.758	0.73
2	1.690	1.647	1.605	1.566	1.528	1.457	1.392	1.332	1.27
3	2.402	2.322	2.246	2.174	2.106	1.981	1.868	1.766	1.67
4	3.037	2.914	2.798	2.690	2.589	2.404	2.241	2.096	1.96
5	3.605	3.433	3.274	3.127	2.991	2.745	2.532	2.345	2.18
6	4.111	3.889	3.685	3.498	3.326	3.020	2.759	2.534	2.33
7	4.564	4.288	4.089	3.812	3.605	3.242	2.937	2.678	2.45
8	4.968	4.639	4.344	4.078	3.837	3.421	3.076	2.786	2.54
9	5.328	4.946	4.607	4.303	4.031	3.566	3.184	2.868	2.60
10	5.650	5.216	4.833	4.494	4.193	3.682	3.269	2.930	2.65
11	5.988	5.453	5.029	4.656	4.327	3.776	3.335	2.978	2.68
12	6.194	5.660	5.197	4.793	4.439	3.851	3.387	3.013	2.70
13	6.424	5.842	5.342	4.910	4.533	3.912	3.427	3.040	2.72
14	6.628	6.002	5.468	5.008	4.611	3.962	3.459	3.061	2.74
15	6.811	6.142	5.575	5.092	4.675	4.001	3.483	3.076	2.75
16	6.974	6.265	5.669	5.162	4.730	4.033	3.503	3.088	2.75
17	7.120	5.373	5.749	4.222	4.775	4.059	3.518	3.097	2.76
18	7.250	6.467	5.818	5.273	4.812	4.080	3.529	3.104	2.76
19	7.366	6.550	5.877	5.316	4.844	4.097	3.539	3.109	2.77
20	7.469	6.623	5.929	5.353	4.870	4.110	3.546	3.113	2.77
25	7.843	6.873	6.907	5.467	4.948	4.147	3.564	3.122	2.77
30	8.055	7.003	6.177	5.517	4.979	4.160	3.569	3.124	2.77

Index